Workplace Basics

Anthony P. Carnevale
Leila J. Gainer
Ann S. Meltzer

Workplace Basics

**The Essential Skills
Employers Want**

Jossey-Bass Publishers

San Francisco • Oxford • 1991

WORKPLACE BASICS
The Essential Skills Employers Want
by Anthony P. Carnevale, Leila J. Gainer, and Ann S. Meltzer

Copyright © 1990 by: Jossey-Bass Inc., Publishers
350 Sansome Street
San Francisco, California 94104

Jossey-Bass Limited
Headington Hill Hall
Oxford OX3 0BW

American Society for Training and Development
1630 Duke Street, Box 1443
Alexandria, Virginia 22313

Library of Congress Cataloging-in-Publication Data

Carnevale, Anthony Patrick.
  Workplace basics: the essential skills employers want / Anthony
P. Carnevale, Leila J. Gainer, Ann S. Meltzer. — 1st ed.
    p.   cm. — (The Jossey-Bass management series)
  Includes bibliographical references.
  ISBN 1-55542-202-0
  1. Employees—Training of—United States.   2. Employer supported
  education—United States.
  I. Gainer, Leila J.   II. Meltzer, Ann S.
  III. Title.   IV. Series.
  HF5549.5.T7C2985 1990
  658.3'124—dc20   89-48804
                                                              CIP

Manufactured in the United States of America

The paper in this book meets the guidelines for
permanence and durability of the Committee on
Production Guidelines for Book Longevity of
the Council on Library Resources.

JACKET DESIGN BY WILLI BAUM

FIRST EDITION
    First printing: March 1990
    Second printing: April 1991
Code 9010

The Jossey-Bass Management Series

ASTD Best Practices Series:
Training for a Changing Work Force

The material in this project was prepared under Grant No. 99-6-0705-75-079-02 from the Employment and Training Administration, U.S. Department of Labor, under the authority of Title IV, part D, of the Job Training Partnership Act of 1982. Grantees undertaking such projects under government sponsorship are encouraged to express freely their professional judgment. Therefore, points of view or opinions stated in this document do not necessarily represent the official position or policy of the Department of Labor.

Contents

Preface

Increasingly, employers have been discovering that their work forces need skills that seem to be in short supply, skills over and above the basic academic triumvirate of reading, writing, and computation. The skills that employers are looking for include problem solving, personal management, and interpersonal skills as well as the abilities to conceptualize, organize, and verbalize thoughts; to resolve conflicts; and to work in teams—all of these skills are critical but often lacking.

Basic workplace skills are of interest because rapid technological change, participative management, just-in-time production, and other workplace innovations have created a demand for more flexibility, adaptability, and a higher "base" level of skills from all workers, including those at the nonsupervisory level. While it is recognized that a percentage of America's workers have always done well in the workplace despite skills deficiencies, it is increasingly apparent that such success in the future will be illusory for many workers if they continue to be ill-equipped in a broad spectrum of basic workplace skills.

The American Society for Training and Development (ASTD), a nonprofit professional association representing approximately 50,000 practitioners, managers, administrators, educators, and researchers in the field of human resource development, through a grant underwritten by the U.S. Department of Labor (DOL) decided to explore the ramifications of this problem. ASTD took a look at the sixteen skills that employers say are basic to success in the workplace and developed suggestions on how training programs can be established to provide these skills to workers.

What we uncovered was the fact that these challenges to an effective work force are being compounded by demographic trends that project a shrinking entry-level work force (sixteen- to twenty-four-year-olds), and we realized that an increasing number of entry-level workers will be coming from groups where, historically, human resource investments have been deficient. It became apparent to us that America's new demographic reality is on a collision course with the notion that employees must be able to understand and acquire new and different skills quickly.

Some of the key findings of this part of the project reveal that in addition to reading, writing, and computation, the thirteen other skills that employers have identified as "basic" to success in the workplace range from learning to learn to shared leadership. We have also confirmed that there is an undeniable link between work force basics and the competitive life cycle of any new strategy, technology, product, or service. Deficiencies in basic skills can undermine the cycle and cause delays, defects, and customer rejections.

Our research revealed that the most effective methodology for providing training in workplace basics is the applied approach, which links learning outcomes directly to job performance. Using this approach, American employers can begin to fill in employee skill gaps and help build individual competence in workplace basics.

The information in this volume reflects only some of the findings gathered during a thirty-month research effort that explored training practices in America's employer institutions. Other findings are detailed in two companion books — which deal with the organization and strategic role of training and technical training — and a workplace basics manual, which provides a step-by-step process for establishing training programs in the basic skill areas described in this book (all published by Jossey-Bass). In addition, the project produced several booklets: *Workplace Basics: The Skills Employers Want, The Learning Enterprise, Train America, Training Partnerships: Linking Employers and Providers,* and *The Next Economy* (available from the American Society for Training and Development, 1630 Duke Street, Box 1443, Alexandria, Virginia 22313).

How the Research Was Conducted

The ASTD-DOL research was conducted by a team of ten professionals and a support staff. This team was greatly assisted by ASTD members who volunteered their expertise and provided access to their own corporations. In addition, experts from the fields of economics, adult education, training, public policy, and strategic management contributed analyses that provided a contextual backdrop for our work.

When we began our research in 1986, we first looked at the basic skills that had received the most attention in the press and the business literature: reading, writing, computation, and problem solving. As we talked with more and more employers, however, we discovered that the skills employers want go beyond those "big four." Out of such early discussions, our list of sixteen skills evolved.

In all study areas, including basic skills, we launched our work by surveying the current literature, looking for trends and patterns; this effort helped us to identify the leaders in various disciplines and to draw some preliminary conclusions. We tested our preliminary findings on a cadre of individual experts drawn from ASTD's membership and asked those members to identify other experts and practitioners who might provide feedback and insights. We continued along this path and our list of contacts grew. From them we formed advisory panels that met during 1987 to advise us on our direction and findings. We also built networks of more than 400 experts and practitioners (the basic skills network alone had 175 members) who received periodic updates of findings and were asked for feedback.

Corporations and other private and public employer institutions were tapped extensively to provide actual examples of successful training systems and practices. We conducted onsite studies and much telephone interviewing, using specially constructed interview instruments that assured we would gather uniform information. The resulting employer "snapshots" are used throughout this book to complement and illustrate our findings and to support the theoretical underpinnings of our work.

After developing our first draft reports, we enlisted more

than thirty experts and practitioners to review and comment on them. Their insights are reflected in *Workplace Basics,* which constitutes our final report.

Who Should Read This Book

The findings in this book are designed to provide readers with an understanding of the sixteen skills that employers believe are workplace basics. We discuss why each skill is basic, its theoretical underpinnings, and its strategic relevance for employers. Recognizing that training for many of the skills is usually provided at the first level of supervisory training and succeeding levels, we explore how trainers should teach each skill as a basic. We also include guidance for trainers wishing to develop and establish workplace basics programs.

This book should serve both as a useful reference document and as a tool. When used in concert with our *Workplace Basics Training Manual,* it provides a complete picture of the who, what, where, when, and how of basic workplace skills training. Its intended audience includes executives and managers in all kinds of public and private organizations; human resource development and training practitioners; personnel and human resource management practitioners; business and management consultants; secondary, postsecondary, and adult educators and guidance counselors; and college and university administrators.

Organization and Content

Readers should view this book as an examination of the sixteen workplace basics and suggested solutions for addressing the basic skills challenge facing employers and employees in the future. It is organized into nine parts with nineteen chapters.

Part One lays the groundwork for this book. Discussion centers on the economic importance of the sixteen basic workplace skills and provides the theoretical basis for why these skills are important. Part One consists of Chapters One and Two.

Chapter One considers the economic importance of basic skills and how they contribute fundamentally to the ability of the United States to compete in the global marketplace. Chapter Two explores the skills employers want in the present-day work force, why those skills are strategically important to organizations, and why they should be considered basic.

Parts Two through Nine examine each of the sixteen workplace skills in detail, including the definition of each skill, its theoretical underpinnings, its essential elements, and what constitute competency in and mastery of the skill. Each chapter also contains at least one example of a successful training program that is operating in the workplace today and a sample curriculum outline for each skill.

Part Two discusses the foundation skill—learning to learn—on which all other skills are based and consists of one chapter, Chapter Three.

Part Three, which includes Chapters Five and Six, explores the skills on which technical competence is built: reading, writing, and computation. These are the skills employers consider basic for entry into and career mobility within an organization.

Part Four treats the skills that enable people to communicate effectively on the job: oral communication and listening. Part Four consists of Chapters Seven and Eight.

In Part Five, Chapters Nine and Ten cover the adaptability skills—problem solving and creative thinking—that enable workers to be flexible in the workplace, particularly in areas of multi-skilling.

Part Six discusses the developmental skills—self-esteem, motivation/goal setting, and employability/career development—that enable people to keep and hold jobs and to move up the career ladder. Part Six consists of Chapters Eleven, Twelve, and Thirteen.

Chapters Fourteen, Fifteen, and Sixteen in Part Seven examine the group effectiveness skills—interpersonal skills, teamwork, and negotiation—that enable people to work together productively.

Part Eight considers the influencing skills—organizational effectiveness and leadership—that enable people to navigate in the organization, take charge down the line, and use personal strengths to bring a task to completion. Part Eight consists of Chapters Seventeen and Eighteen.

Part Nine presents the applied approach for presenting employer-sponsored training in the workplace. Chapter Nineteen, the final chapter, provides a model for establishing a workplace basics program. This model is the basis for the step-by-step process called the "blueprint for success" in the companion manual *Workplace Basics Training Manual* on how to implement a workplace basics training program.

Acknowledgments

Special thanks to Shari L. Holland, who served as research assistant on the project; Dawn Temple, Kim Genevro, and Stacey Wagner, who provided administrative assistance; Diane L. Charles, who managed our research symposium and the production of the manuscript; Diane Kirrane, who provided editorial assistance; Gerald Gundersen and Ray Uhalde of the U.S. Department of Labor, who provided insights and guidance along the way; and J. R. Reingold & Associates, Inc., for its help in producing the *Workplace Basics Training Manual*.

The project team also wishes to acknowledge the contributions of the following people who worked closely with us on the four workplace basics publications: Elaine M. Brady, Janet G. Elsea, Greta Kotler, Stephen K. Merman, Jorie W. Phillippi, Virginia Polytechnic Institute (Libby Hall, Charles W. Humes, Linda Kunder, Martha Livingston, Ronald L. McKeen, Harold W. Stubblefield, Albert K. Wiswell), and Dale Yeatts.

Finally, we wish to thank our advisory panel and network participants, who contributed their advice and counsel.

Alexandria, Virginia   Anthony P. Carnevale
February 1990   Leila J. Gainer
                                          Ann S. Meltzer

The Authors

Anthony P. Carnevale was project director and principal investigator for the ASTD-DOL project and is chief economist and vice-president of national affairs for ASTD. Carnevale also currently serves as a board member of the National Center on Education and Employment at Columbia University; the National Center on Education and the Economy, cochaired by Mario Cuomo and John Scully; and the National Commission on the Skills of the American Work Force, comprised of America's leading business executives, union leaders, and education and government officials.

Prior to joining ASTD, Carnevale was the government affairs director for the American Federation of State, County, and Municipal Employees (AFSCME). He also served as a comoderator for the White House Conference on Productivity and as chairman of the Fiscal Policy Task Force for the U.S. Council on Competitiveness. Carnevale has held positions as senior policy analyst for the U.S. Department of Health, Education, and Welfare; senior staff economist for the U.S. House of Representatives Government Operations Committee; and senior staff member for education, employment, training, and social services for the U.S. Senate Committee on the Budget. He also was a high school teacher and social worker in his home state of Maine. Carnevale was coauthor of the principal affidavit in *Rodriguez* v. *San Antonio,* a U.S. Supreme Court action to remedy unequal tax burdens and education benefits.

Carnevale has a Ph.D. degree from the Maxwell School of Public Affairs, Syracuse University. He holds M.A. degrees in social science and in public administration from Syracuse University and a B.A. degree in intellectual and cultural history from Colby College.

Leila J. Gainer managed the daily operations of the ASTD-DOL project and is ASTD's director of national affairs. She serves as a member of the advisory board for the Center for Business and Government Services of the Northern Virginia Community College and as a member of the National Alliance of Business advisory committee on structural work-based learning. In 1989 she also served as an informal adviser to ABC and PBS for the Project Literacy U.S. (PLUS) Campaign.

Before joining ASTD, Gainer directed the Center for Regional Action for the National Association of Regional Councils (NARC), working with state and local government-elected officials around the nation. In her nine years at NARC, Gainer served as director of federal liaison, communications, and research; Washington information coordinator; and editor of the *Washington Report*. While at NARC, Gainer was honored by President Carter for her efforts leading to passage of the Rural Development Act of 1980. Gainer served as a reporter and editor for Commerce Clearing House, Inc.'s (CCH) bi-weekly publications *College and University Report* and *Commodity Futures*. In the early 1970s she was managing editor of CCH's *Labor Law Guide* and on the staff of *Labor Law Report*. Gainer has a B.A. degree from Frostburg State College, Maryland.

Ann Meltzer served as writer and researcher for this book. After completing her work at ASTD, Meltzer took a position as project director for Pelavin Associates, a social science research consulting firm.

Prior to joining the ASTD-DOL project and throughout most of her career, Meltzer has been president of ASM Associates, where she managed a variety of domestic and international training-related projects and authored two manuals and several series of monographs. Meltzer also was a training program specialist for the San Diego Private Industry Council, where she developed an innovative occupation-specific training program for adults. Before joining the Private Industry Council, she was a labor liaison representative for the Rail Services Planning Office of the U.S. Interstate Commerce Commission. Meltzer also served as the vocational training coordinator for the Transportation Communications International Union, where she helped establish a railroad-specific manpower training department.

Meltzer has an M.B.A. degree from the National University in San Diego, California, an M.A. degree from Johns Hopkins School of Advanced International Studies, and a B.A. degree from the University of Massachusetts.

Workplace Basics Advisory Panel

Joseph Cooney
Regional Representative
The National Alliance of Business

Brian Elrod
Skills Enhancement Program
  Associate
UAW-Ford National Education
  Development Center

Mike Fox
Executive Director
Push Literacy Action Now

Karl O. Haigler
Director
Adult Literacy Initiative
U.S. Department of Education

Renee Lerche
Education Consultant
Ford Motor Company
(formerly with General Motors)

Larry Mikulecky
Director
Learning Skills Center
Indiana University–Bloomington

Robert E. Norton
Senior Research Development
  Specialist
National Center for Research in
  Vocational Education

Phillip M. Plott
Manager
Professional Development
Duke Power Company

Thomas G. Sticht
President
Applied Behavioral and Cognitive
  Sciences, Inc.

Linda E. Stoker
Vice President
Cox Educational Services, Inc.
(formerly with Polaroid Corporation)

Workplace Basic Skills Network

Mike Allen
Dana Corporation

Ray Balcer
Datapoint Corporation

Renate Banks
Xerox Corporation

Mary Jo Beans
Center for Applied Linguistics

Sue Berryman
Columbia University

Kathy Blair
AT&T Communications

xxiii

Richard Blue
Dayton Progress Corporation

Francine Boren
Consortium for Worker Literacy
  Program

Susan Bourgeois
Penn Valley Community College

Ron Bradley
Blue Cross/Blue Shield of MA

Franklin Brown
Horizon's Technology, Inc.

Christina Caron
British Embassy

Ivan Charner
National Institute for Work and
  Learning

Mat Chavez
Rockwell International

Susan Chipman
Office of Naval Research

Andrea Couture
United Negro College Fund

Doug Crawford
Athabasca University

Kerry Crist
70001 Training and Employment
  Institute

Susan P. Curnan
Brandeis University

Judy B. Dailey
Ashland Oil Foundation, Inc.

Richard Danakowski
Ford Motor Company

Louis D. Dantiago
Amalgamated Clothing & Textile
  Workers

E. Jewell Dassance
U.S. Basics

Dr. Leland Davies
Victoria Hospital Corporation

Libert V. P. Diaforli
McGraw-Hill, Inc.

Ralph Dosher
Texas Instruments

John Dresher
Merck, Sharp and Dohme

Paula Duggan
Northeast-Midwest Institute

Amy Dyar
Northern Telecom

Michael Emmott
Manpower Services Commission

Michael Erickson
National Job Training Partnership

Carol Ewart
Rhode Island Hospital

Cheryl Feldman
Philadelphia Hospital & Health Care

Robert Fenn
The Travelers

Joseph Fernandez
City Bank

Ernest Fields
National Center for Research in
  Vocational Education

Arlene Fingeret
NCSU Governor's Commission on
  Literacy

David M. Finley
Southland Corporation

Badi G. Foster
Aetna Institute

Charlotte Frank
Twin County Credit Union

Dewey L. Gilbertson-Winburne
The Creative Rapid Learning Center

Irvin Gordon
Independence Bancorp

Bill Grace
Central Kansas Cooperative Education

Susan Greenblatt
D.C. Office of Family Assistance

Norman T. Halls
MA Career Development Institute

Al Halseth
Upjohn Corporation

Mary Ann Haney
Michigan Consolidated Gas Company

William L. Hardy
Florida Department of Transportation

David Harman
Institute for Corporate Education

Robert Harris
Harris Design Group

Carrie A. Haynes
National Association of University
    Women

Sara Hayward
3M Corporation

Curtis Heath
Brown & Williamson Tobacco
    Corporation

Roberta Henrichs
Michigan Consolidated Gas Company

Larry Hirschhorn
Wharton Center for Applied Research

Ross L. Hodgkinson
TACK

Jo Hogin
IBM/Rolm Systems

C. E. Jannetti, Director
Kepner-Tregoe, Inc.

Sue Jones
Planters Peanuts

Norfleet Jones
Aqualon Company

Pauline R. Jordan
General Electric Company

Paul Jurmo
Business Council on Effective Literacy

Barbara Kairson
District Council 37, AFSCME

Jan Kakela
Capital Area Career Center

Dianne Kangisser
The Robert Bowne Foundation

Gary M. Kaplan
Jobs for Youth–Boston, Inc.

Rita Kaplan
Honeywell Inc.

George R. G. Karlsson
Growth Communications, Inc.

Leslie Kelly
Kelly and Associates

George R. Kent
Milwaukee Electric Tool Corporation

Daryl Kinney
Arizona State University

Paula Kirby
UniSys Corporation

Robert Knight
National Association of Private
    Industry Councils

Susan L. Koen
MATRICES Consultants Inc.

Judith Ann Koloski
American Association for Adult and
    Continuing Education

Robert Koppes
Gillette Company

Linda Lampkin
AFSME

Wendy Lawson
Washington Gas and Light Company

Luba B. Lewytzkyj
Control Data Corporation

Harvey S. Long
IBM

Jerry Lord
Higher Education & Adult Learning

John Purnell
Digital Equipment Corporation

Don Robbins
Florida Steel Corporation

Ned Roberts
Citicorp

Bernard Robinson
Washington Hospital Center

Raymond Romero
SER-Jobs for Progress

Veda Ross
St. Vincent Hospital

Trenda Rusher
EAST-WALTEC

Carol Russo
UpState Federal Credit Union

James T. Ryan
District 1199C

Thomas C. Saba
Plymouth, MN Police Department

Mike Sack
Public/Private Ventures

Debra Savage
Honeywell

Robert E. Scarborough
Greater Cincinnati Industrial
  Training Corporation

Betty Scharfman
Valley National Bank

Katherine Schrier
District Council 37, AFSME

Ruth Ann Sieber
Ohio Department of Human Services

Jane Baldus Smith
Manpower, Inc.

Ron Smith
Ford Motor Company

William F. Smith
General Motors

Rena Soifer
Ford Motor Company

Sheryl Soifer
Walgreen Company

Benita Somerfield
U.S. Department of Education

Sister Madeliene Sophie, C.S.C.
St. Joseph's Medical Center

Donna Sosnowski
The Provident

Gail Spangenberg
Business Council for Effective Literacy

Sondra Stein
Commonwealth Literacy Campaign

Mary Louise Strom
Northeast Iowa Technical Institute

Lori Strumpf
Center for Remediation Design

Fred A. Swan
University of Massachusetts–Amherst

Bob Taggart
Remediation Training Institute

James O. Tatro
Aetna Institute

Jackie Taylor
Kelly Springfield Tire Company

Mary L. Tenopyr
AT&T Communications

Sara B. Toye
National SER Policy and Research
  Institute

Sarah Turner
Xerox Corporation

L. L. Vickery
Buick-Oldsmobile-Cadillac
  Headquarters

Dale Wade
Fisher Controls

Workplace Basics

PART 1

Setting Standards for Competency at Work

New technology, participative management, sophisticated statistical quality controls, customer service, just-in-time production — the workplace is changing and so are the skills that employees must have in order to change with it.

Many employees, however, do not have basics essential for acquiring more sophisticated technical skills. While deficiencies in basic workplace skills are not a new problem, they are a growing one. A challenge is emerging from a volatile mix of demographic, economic, and technical forces. Combined, these forces are driving the nation toward a human capital deficit among both new and experienced workers that threatens the competitiveness of economic institutions and acts as a barrier to the individual opportunity of all Americans.

The nation is facing a startling demographic reality that is not likely to go away. The group of sixteen- to twenty-four-year-olds that is the traditional source of new workers is shrinking, and employers will have to reach into the ranks of the less qualified to get their entry-level work force. Thus, an increasing number of entry-level workers will come from groups in which human resource investments have historically been deficient.

If that is news to you, don't feel bad; it is news to most Americans, who are predisposed to the view that there are too many qualified people and not enough good jobs to go around. Our recent history encourages us to believe that people are superfluous, whereas machinery, financial capital, and natural resources are hard to come by. However, things are rarely as they first appear. Closely examined, the apparent excess of American workers proves illusory. In the future, there will likely be too few well-educated and trained American workers looking for their first job.

Ironically, this demographic reality is on a collision course with the notion that employees must be able to understand and acquire new and different skills quickly. As technology becomes more footloose and instantaneously available worldwide, the skills of employees become the employer's competitive edge.

Today's workplace demands not only a good command of the three R's, but more. Employers want a new kind of worker with a broad set of workplace skills — or at least a strong foundation in the basics that will facilitate learning on the job.

For employers, the basic workplace skills challenge has been coming into focus for some time. Reading, writing, and math deficiencies have been the first to appear in the workplace; but increasingly, skills such as problem solving, listening, negotiation, and knowing how to learn, as well as teamwork, self-esteem, leadership and motivation/goal setting, organizational effectiveness, employability/career development, oral and listening skills, and creative thinking are also viewed as essential. Figure 1 illustrates the skills employers want. Deficiencies in many of these basic workplace skills are barriers to entry-level employees, experienced employees, and dislocated workers attempting to adapt to economic and technological change within employer institutions.

Employer interest in improving basic skills is driven by economic concerns. When deficiencies affect the bottom line, employers respond with training or replacement. But the time-honored choice, replacement, is becoming less and less practical because the supply of workers is shrinking. Increasingly, employers are forced to make rather than buy productive employees. As a result, interest in providing training in basic workplace skills is growing.

Employee interest also is growing, primarily because workers are being challenged as never before. For those already employed, deficiencies in basic workplace skills threaten adap-

Figure 1. The Seven Skill Groups.

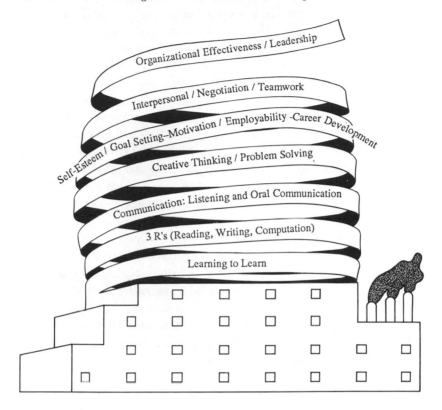

tation and short-circuit successful job transitions and career growth. The ground under them is shifting as the range of skills they need to participate successfully in today's economy expands. They are less supervised but more frequently called upon to identify problems and make crucial decisions.

Perhaps the most devastating impact of basic workplace deficiencies falls upon the disadvantaged who are outside the economic mainstream and struggling to get in. For those attempting to enter the work force and those who have been displaced from their jobs, such deficiencies inhibit entry into productive and well-paying work, pinning those disadvantaged at the bottom of the economic heap.

The *upskilling* of work in America is driven by technical changes, innovation, and a sense of heightened competition.

The picture is further complicated by competitive challenges driving companies toward employing an array of strategies that require adaptive and innovative workers with strong interpersonal skills. Business strategies—such as collaboration (the work team concept), exemplary customer service, and emphasis on quality—demand teamwork, listening skills, the ability to set goals, creativity, and problem-solving skills. Couple this with the movement toward more participative management and employers aggressively driving workers toward decision making at the point of production or point of sale, and it is easy to see that new skills must be applied if employees—and their employers—are to succeed in the marketplace. In fact, one might even say that a new kind of American worker is being ordered up, a worker who will be expected to have a broad set of skills that were previously required only of supervisors and managers.

For example, one job already in transition is that of bank teller. Competitive shifts and new technologies have had a profound effect on the structure, organization, and management of banks. A new customer service philosophy demands that traditional institutional and professional specialties give way to a "one-stop-shopping" approach for financial services.

Traditionally a processor, the bank teller's primary role was to perform a series of repetitive tasks (taking checks in, giving money out, reconciling) very well. Competitive pressures to satisfy customers' "one-stop" desires have expanded the bank teller's role to include advising customers on a wide range of customized financial services. The teller now is privy to an array of information previously in the domain of midlevel managers, is empowered to advise customers, and is charged with making judgment calls "on the line," that is, at the point of customer contact. Moreover, the teller is linked with data via a computer terminal, requiring a new range of skills to operate the equipment and access relevant information speedily. In short, to be effective in the workplace, today's bank teller may not need to have the same degree of skills in a narrow area of expertise but instead must have a good knowledge of a wide *range* of skills.

The Economic Impact of Basic Skills

Basic Skills and Competitiveness

Individuals and employers have viewed basic workplace skills differently. For workers, competency in basic workplace skills has always been important because sound basic skills leverage earnings and opportunities. American employers have seen competency in workplace basics as a prerequisite for hiring and viewed the accumulation of such skills as solely the responsibility of the individual worker. The employer's interest has focused on measuring the skills of prospective employees and screening out those who are most suitable for hiring.

But times are changing. Employers are beginning to see that they must assist their current and future workers to achieve competency in workplace basics if they are to be competitive. This sense of shared responsibility is grounded in economic realities and is compelling employers to invest in workplace basics training programs.

Why this shift in attitudes? The answer lies, in part, in demographics and technology. The demography is clear. The entry-level labor pool is shrinking and will continue to do so through the year 2000. More and more, American employers will no longer enjoy the luxury of selecting from a field of workers with strong basic skills. The demand for labor will create opportunities for those who are less skilled; the disadvantaged will move up the labor queue and be hired in spite of obvious skill

5

deficiencies. American employers will fill in the skill gaps and help build employee competence in the basics.

Technology creates both opportunities and problems for employers. Its very transferability has leveled the worldwide playing field. An employer's competitive edge is increasingly reliant upon how effectively and efficiently workers and machines are integrated and move through the production cycle. Successful integration is dependent upon how quickly veteran workers accumulate new skills. And acquisition of new skills is facilitated when a worker has a solid grounding in the basics.

Basic Skills and the Competitive Cycle

An undeniable linkage exists between work force skills and the competitive cycle. The competitive life cycle of any new strategy, technology, product, or service usually consists of six distinct stages: discovery, design, development and articulation of the management and production systems and processes, production and service delivery, and development of new applications. The time it takes to move through these stages is called cycle time. Reducing that time while maintaining quality can mean competitive advantage.

The company that develops and delivers a product to the marketplace in the least amount of time is able to pass on the savings of the shorter production cycle. This gives a company the edge in (1) offering a less expensive product, (2) capturing initial consumer interest in a product, (3) promoting consumer loyalty, and (4) establishing a niche in the marketplace that gives the product an advantage over similar products that are likely to follow.

Employers have learned that their employees' basic skills will be tested at every stage of the competitive cycle, influencing cycle time. Good basic skills can mean a shorter production cycle, improved products, and high quality. Deficiencies in such skills can undermine the cycle and cause delays, defects, and customer rejections.

In employer institutions, the initial discovery and design stages of a new strategy, technology, product, or service are exploratory and experimental. Often, though the work force may be aware of a change in strategic direction, the institution has not fully integrated the new strategy into its culture. With change come new methods of production or service delivery, which overlap with old methods. Moreover, in these early stages of an innovation, individual job assignments are still unclear. As a result, employees' job responsibilities are broad and ambiguous.

To adapt quickly to new workplace demands, employees must know how to learn. They need problem-solving skills to overcome barriers that arise in new situations. In addition to feeling comfortable with innovation, they must be able to think creatively as they cope with new challenges.

During the discovery and design stages, employee roles are vague. Employees and working teams are left on their own to deal with the unstructured environment characteristic of the early phases of an innovation. Employees must have the capacity to take responsibility for themselves. They need personal and career management skills, a strong, realistic sense of self-worth, and the ability to set and meet goals.

Individual employees also need the basic skills that allow them to interact effectively with other members of the working team. To do this, they must know how to listen and how to communicate their thoughts clearly. Effective interaction involves knowing how to influence others within the organization's culture. Employees must also be capable of recognizing when, where, and how they should assume a leadership role.

Eventually, innovations will be integrated into the production or service delivery system in an employer institution. At this point the basic skills of the entire employee population — including nonsupervisory personnel — will determine the institution's ability to produce products or deliver services while maintaining efficiency and quality. The basic skills of production and service delivery employees will also determine the employer's ability to customize products and services for a wide array of customers.

The development of new efficiencies, quality improvements, and new applications for the original innovation is the last phase in the cycle, one that is key to an expanded market-place and long-term profitability. In this stage, creative thinking and problem solving are essential. As employees apply their learning, the employer's store of new knowledge is enriched. New knowledge eventually translates into efficient production, improvements in quality, and new applications for products or services. Sometimes changes and new information yield major advances in strategy and technology or new products and services, and this triggers yet another competitive cycle.

Workplace basics are important throughout the life cycle of a product and the process of service delivery. With good solid basics, the work force can meet the challenge of change because employees continue to build on the knowledge and skills they need to adapt to innovations. Solid basic skills are critical for all employees, not just white-collar and technical elites, such as engineers. Production and service delivery personnel with high levels of basic skills allow employers to decentralize production and service delivery. Such decentralization improves the institution's ability to customize its product or service and respond more effectively to customers. Decentralization also allows employers to avail themselves of the skills of all employees in finding new cost-effective methods for providing production or service delivery, generating quality improvements, and finding new applications for existing products and services.

Basic Skills and Technical Change

New technologies are redefining basic skill requirements. By decentralizing the production of products and services, information-based technologies are increasing the autonomy and value of employees at the point of production and service delivery. At all organizational levels the roles of employees have expanded, and they are now responsible for a wider range of products and for the customization of an array of products for individual customers. With those broader roles comes greater opportunity to have a positive or negative effect on efficiency, quality, and innovation.

Technical changes on the job tend to change basic skill requirements incrementally. Sometimes these changes accumulate to the point of creating new occupations. In manufacturing, craft occupations such as machinist and tool and die maker are evolving quickly into technician and technologist jobs. The same has happened with the skill jobs of the assembler, repair person, and materials handler. In services, the secretary is evolving into the information manager and the bank teller is becoming the financial services portfolio consultant for individual customers.

While technologies are eliminating jobs, they are also increasing the range of skills needed to perform jobs that remain. Over the past decade the most prominent example of this has taken place on the factory floor. The machinist, once the status leader and central figure on the working team, applied various technologies to shape individual parts of a final product. Career advancement depended on sharpening the essential job skill of hand-to-eye coordination. Eventually, when the machinist's hand-to-eye coordination skills were good enough, he or she became a tool and die maker. Enter the robot with more consistent hand-to-eye coordination than the machinist. A better performer of the basic job task, the robot took the machinist's place.

At the same time, the technology of advanced automated manufacturing began doing the jobs of other members of the shop floor team, including the laborer, the materials handler, the operator/assembler, and the maintenance person. Ultimately, all these jobs have become one job that combines a greater use of technology with a single employee—the new technician responsible for all the functions performed by the displaced workers. Moreover, although the new job may not require the same depth of skill in each of the narrower jobs it absorbs, it does require a wider variety of basic skills than any one of the other jobs.

The expanding range of job tasks and responsibilities in the manufacturing technician job demands higher basic levels of reading, writing, and computation. The job of technician requires an understanding of each task associated with the responsibilities included in the technician position. Generally more autonomous than the machinist, the technician must have higher-level personal management skills. Also responsible for troubleshooting, maintaining, updating, and exercising quality control over highly complex mathematically based machinery, the technician must have better computational skills and be able to read and to comprehend technical manuals. Besides demanding higher competencies in math and reading, these new tasks require the skills to adapt successfully to the job—learning to learn, creative thinking, and problem solving.

Other effects of technological change will also increase basic skill requirements. Technology is the means to product diversification. This creates a greater need for job-specific product knowledge and basic learning skills, strengths that help employees keep pace with development, design, production, and the sale of changed and new products. To perform successfully in this situation, an employee must know how to learn. Examples of industries in which recent diversification has expanded workplace skill requirements include the communication and banking industries. In the communication industry a basic line of voice instruments has expanded into a myriad of delivery systems for communicating data and imagery. In the banking industry a basic line of checking and savings products has grown into an array of financial services.

New information technologies also make it possible to customize products. Over the past decade, both batch production in manufacturing and the customization of service products have advanced markedly. The ability to tailor products and services requires the learning and problem-solving skills that make employees adaptable. And with customization comes the need for customer relations. Employees at the point of production and service delivery must know how to listen and to articulate their thoughts clearly—to understand *and be understood.* To interact successfully with customers, employees need strong communication skills. They also need interpersonal and negotiation skills to deal with customer grievances and complaints.

Changing economic and technical realities alter the institutional structures themselves. These new structures, in turn, change basic skill requirements. Because of technological change, more and more institutions are becoming highly decentralized — with profound implications for basic skills. Among American employers, the new effective institution recognizes the autonomy of individual employees and teams in production, sales, or service. The decentralized, flexible institution will meet the challenge of product diversification and intensive competition.

With the new decentralized institutional model, resources and authority become available to employees at the lower level of the structure. This decentralized model eliminates the middle layers of management and flattens the institutional hierarchy; this narrows the gap between those in control of institutional leadership, product development, and strategic decision making and those responsible for the production and delivery of the product or service. Instead of managing production and delivery processes, the new institution establishes accountability by monitoring outcomes. Managers guide individual employees or working teams and intervene only when the work is unsatisfactory.

Employees of the new institution need significantly higher basic skills. The new autonomous workers must have personal management skills to maintain self-esteem, set goals, and be motivated. As full members of an autonomous working team, these employees need higher levels of interpersonal, teamwork, negotiation, and organizational skills, skills that enhance group effectiveness. At various points in the production or service delivery process, each individual member of the working team needs leadership skills. To be effective in their organization, employees must understand how their own personal goals and objectives fit into the organization's culture and strategic goals. With this understanding, employees can influence the organization to use and develop their skills in a mutually productive way.

To advance in a single evolving institution, industry, or occupation, employees must be capable of taking charge of their own working lives. As economic and technological changes occur, the new, more flexible institution will continue to modify and rebuild itself. In turn, employees will have to adapt skills for new roles within the changing institution. But as the institution constantly changes form, appearing and disappearing with economic circumstances, the commitment between individuals and any specific institution declines. With this new, more temporary institutional "format," employees must be more responsible for their own career development and job security. More dependent on skill development than any one employer for job security and career development, employees need personal management and career development skills.

Basic Skills and Individual Opportunity

A work force with sound basic skills will strengthen its employer's ability to compete. For the individual worker, basic skills are also the keys to greater opportunity and a better quality of life. Workers with good basic skills find it easier to acquire more sophisticated skills that leverage better jobs and higher pay.

Research shows that in the United States roughly half the differences in earnings can be attributed to learning in school and on the job. Accidents of geography, career choices, and the selection of an employer account for the other half. Earnings are a function of the skills people have and the choices they make regarding how and where they use those skills. Poor basic skills limit individuals' choices and their potential for earning.

The processes of developing basic skills in school and applying them on the job complement each other. Basic academic skills expand and grow when used on the job. People use what they learned on one job to move up to a better job. Compared with all other variables that affect earnings, learning on the job has the most powerful effect. Available data tend to support the fact that on-the-job learning — especially formal learning — can increase one's earnings by as much as 30 percent.

In most studies, between 10 and 13 percent of lifetime earnings among Americans can be attributed to the initial learning that takes place in school. But these studies do not address the fact that academic preparation leverages learning on the job. For instance, those with only a high school diploma are not likely to get on-the-job training, whereas those with a diploma *plus* two years of formal education have a 20 percent greater chance of securing such training. Those who have had some college education have a 50 percent greater chance. The increasing probability of getting training on the job peaks at sixteen years of schooling for all but the high-tech industries. There the connection between education and on-the-job training continues to increase for those with postgraduate degrees.

The relationship between basic skills and opportunity seems to be strengthening over time. According to Gordon Berlin and Andrew Sum (1988), while inflation and declining productivity reduced the earnings of all Americans, the earnings of the least educated declined most. During the last recessionary period, high school dropouts experienced a staggering 40 percent decline in earnings, whereas the earnings of those with a high school degree, some college, or a college degree declined by 30 percent, 26 percent, and 11 percent, respectively. Between 1960 and 1984, the earning difference between high school dropouts and graduates increased from 30 percent to 60 percent.

Many have argued that during the late 1960s and throughout the 1970s employers established increasing educational requirements for jobs to sort through the volume of baby boomers. And, say Berlin and Sum, many employers continue to do so despite the growing scarcity of entry-level job seekers.

Studies by John Bishop have demonstrated that employees with strong basic skills are more productive than those with weaker skills. However, Bishop (1987) also points out that employers do not fully reward the contributions of more skilled and productive employees because reward systems are tied to such factors as academic credentials, seniority, and job classifications.

Available evidence also shows that although employers do not fully reward employees for their basic skills, there is some correlation between abilities and rewards. When Berlin and Sum (1988) analyzed the earnings of young workers who had taken the Armed Forces Qualifying Test, they discovered major differences in earnings among people with the same number of years in school but different basic skill levels. The analysis revealed that dropouts who scored a "low high" on the Armed Forces Qualifying Test earn only half as much as dropouts with higher scores. Among high school graduates, males with the better basic skills earn two-thirds more and females three times as much. Deficiency in basic skills stands as the final barrier to employment of the poor and disadvantaged. Though the current scarcity of entry-level labor offers a steady supply of work to those prepared for jobs, lack of preparation is an obstacle to reducing unemployment rates among the poor. Such skill deficiencies are also among the principal causes of the social pathology that torments the poor.

In a survey of disadvantaged nineteen- to twenty-three-year-olds, Berlin and Sum found that low basic skills were distinguishing characteristics of the group: 68 percent were arrested, 85 percent were unwed mothers, 79 percent were welfare dependants, 85 percent were dropouts, and 72 percent were unemployed.

The American Challenge

How a country responds to economic and technical change — whether its response will be strong or weak — depends on how the country integrates learning within its employer institutions. That integration also determines how such institutions will be structured.

The American and French economies invest heavily in the formal education and workplace learning of white-collar and higher-level technical elites but less in the formal training of non-college skill employees and craft workers. The result is that in French and U.S. institutional structures, managers, senior-level technical personnel, and other white-collar employees have vested control over the production processes. Institutions in the United States and France focus on educating technical elites, creating a highly structured managerial hierarchy that controls mass production. Such institutions combine large doses of technology *developed by technical elites* with the relatively unskilled labor in production.

In contrast, Germany relies more on the formal training of craft and skill employees for technical direction, and its employer structures have fewer layers of managerial and white-collar personnel than those of either France or the United States.

Most countries specialize in the goods and services that give them comparative advantage in the production and organizational uses of human resources. The United States enjoys this advantage through its development and use of higher-skilled white-collar and technical personnel. As a result, we do well in the early stages of a new technology or product line when higher-level skills are critical. In later phases of the development of new technologies or new products, Americans extend market penetration by combining mass production technologies with intensively managed organizational innovations.

Americans rely on highly skilled scientists and engineers for mass production technology. They rely on managerial, supervisory, and other white-collar and professional personnel to develop institutional alternatives to achieve low production costs and wide dissemination of products. Uses of white-collar and managerial talent, such as decentralized management, diversified firms, and the multinational corporation, have made the United States successful in expanding the dissemination of new products and exploiting new technologies.

However, while these links between our human resource development system and the employer economy have given the United States a competitive advantage during early stages of new products and technologies, the nation is less competitive in later phases of mass production and technological dissemination. In the production phase of the competitive cycle the United States does not compete well. It does not satisfactorily develop efficiency or quality during that phase. It needs improvements in developing applications of new strategies, technologies, and products and services.

America's inability to sustain competitive advantage argues for better basic skills among nonsupervisory skill and craft employees. With better skills, this group can participate more effectively in the phases that need improvement. Upskilling is becoming more crucial as technical and economic changes increase companies' reliance on individuals and working teams who are directly responsible for the production and the sale of competitive products and services.

In a comparison among countries, the more educated and trained half of the American work force competes well wth the white-collar and technical elites of its economic rivals. The other half of the work force is not as well prepared, however, and this is where the United States is losing the competitive race. This fact presents a major challenge for American educators and employers. Academic and employer institutions must stop catering to the development and use of white-collar and technical elites. Instead, they must choose a more broadly based mission that is attentive to the noncollege-bound and the nonsupervisory employee.

CHAPTER 2

The Skills Employers Want

The Foundation Skill: Learning to Learn

Most adults in today's fast-changing work world are scrambling to catch up. Even routine jobs are evolving as the demands of the workplace expand. Competitive pressures compel employers to shift employees between jobs and responsibilities, putting a premium on the ability to absorb and process new information quickly and effectively. Moreover, the complexity, amount, and availability of information compound the pressure to learn and apply.

In today's workplace, learning is an integral part of everyday life. The skill of knowing how to learn, or learning to learn, is a must for every worker. The skill of learning to learn is the key to acquiring new skills and sharpening the ability to think through problems and to surmount challenges in the office, ship, laboratory, or sales area. It opens the door to all other learning and facilitates the acquisition of other skills from literacy to leadership.

From the employer's perspective, the skill of knowing how to learn is cost-effective because it can mitigate the cost of retraining efforts. When workers use efficient learning strategies, they absorb and apply training more quickly, saving their employers money and time. When properly prepared, employees can use learning-to-learn techniques to distinguish between essential and nonessential information, discern patterns in information, and pinpoint the actions necessary to improve job performance.

Many employers — particularly those dealing with rapid technological change — have come to see the learning-to-learn skill as an urgent necessity for their workers. If, indeed, learning-to-learn is at the heart of the concept of lifelong learning, then such employer recognition represents something of a "coming of age" for the concept.

Reports concerning the use of learning-to-learn techniques confirm that they are largely successful. For example, one company in Great Britain chose to use innovative learning skills techniques as the backbone of a retraining effort rather than lay off technologically obsolescent workers. The existing work force learned totally new working methods and groupings from those previously used at the company and successfully took over operations of their new computer-based factory. Cost savings resulted from not having to find and hire new qualified workers who would need training in company-specific standards. In addition, the retraining effort for existing employees boosted morale and contributed to increased productivity and worker flexibility.

Productivity, innovation, and competitiveness all depend on developing the learning capability of the work force. Machinery and processes are transferable from company to company and country to country, but it is the application of human resources to technology and systems that provides the competitive edge.

Competence: Reading, Writing, and Computation

The inability of large numbers of new work force entrants to meet the reading, writing, or computational standards required by many segments of American business is fast becoming an economic and competitive issue for U.S. companies challenged by foreign enterprises. (*Note:* The term *computation* is used interchangeably with the term *mathematics* throughout this book.) This is forcing employers to spend more of their training dollars on these critical competence skills.

The United States is fortunate in that a majority of its workers are literate and numerate. Frequently, however, employees cannot use these skills effectively in the workplace. Sometimes it is because the workers are "rusty" and are called upon to use mathematical principles they have not used for twenty or more years. Sometimes it is because the workers must use skills in a context different from the one in which they originally learned them. In still other situations, the base knowledge is there, but the workers have no understanding of how to expand and apply it. All of these problems create the need for employer-provided training in reading, writing, and computation.

Reading has historically been considered *the* fundamental vocational skill. A person must be able to read to find out about available jobs, to get a job, to keep a job, to get ahead in a job, and to change jobs. National concern over the rapidly shrinking pool of qualified applicants for entry-level jobs has brought intensified attention to the need for reading training in the workplace. Demographic experts paint a portrait of a work force with an increasing proportion of unskilled workers and workers at skill levels too low to compete for entry- or reentry-level positions (Brock, 1987; Montague, 1987; Semerad, 1987). Meanwhile, employment experts see a clear trend toward the elimination of many unskilled jobs, with a corresponding rise in skill-level requirements for remaining positions because of technological advances and industrial restructuring. One educational assessment (Kirsch and Jungeblut, 1986) indicates that there is a large nationwide population of "intermediate literates" who only have fourth to eighth grade literacy equivalency (although some are high school graduates) and who have not obtained a functional or employable literacy level. This group will make up as much as 65 percent of the entry-level work force over the next fifteen years (Semerad, 1987).

The 1983 report *Basic Skills in the U.S. Work Force,* published by the Center for Public Resources (CPR), asserts that the data clearly show "a consistently perceived reading deficiency in many job categories on the part of 40 percent of the respondees [businesses and unions]" (p. 19). CPR cites some examples of the operational impact of reading deficiencies. These include increased problems with worker safety and lost time as a result of having to verbalize instructions because workers cannot read well enough to understand them. Other examples include employee failure to understand incoming correspondence and orders for goods and employee inability to enroll in skill-upgrading courses because workers cannot follow directions on how to fill out the application, cannot read the training material, and cannot perform many other tasks (p. 18). Every problem has an incremental negative impact on a company's capacity to improve its bottom line.

It should be noted, however, that of the "three R's," employers generally found the fewest deficiencies in reading relative to the other skills. Only in secretarial/clerical and technical positions did a significant portion of the respondents find deficiencies. Contrary to the assumption that personal computers with "spellcheck" capabilities will alleviate this problem, Paul Delker, president of Strategic Educational Systems, flatly states that "automatic spelling typewriters require highly literate operators who need to know syntax and spelling more than ever . . . [although the machine] will beep if the typist enters a word that doesn't exist, like *thier* instead of *their,* it won't tell the typist whether *their* or *there* is correct in the context of the sentence" (Business Council for Effective Literacy, 1988b, p. 5).

The CPR survey dealt with already employed workers and did not reflect the cost employers must bear for extensive testing of applicants in order to find qualified workers. The Business Council for Effective Literacy (BCEL) in its April 1988 issue stated, "Last year New York Telephone had to process 57,000 applications to find 2,000 qualified entry-level workers" (p. 4). A significant portion of the applicants had deficiencies in reading level sufficient to deny them employment with New York Telephone. This is not an issue that affects only major employers in large urban areas where the educational preparation system is besieged by tangential problems such as drugs and violence that have made it very difficult to maintain a quality educational environment. Although some parts of the country may not yet have a significant competency skill problem because their education systems have an easier time focusing resources, they are not insulated from the demands of technology and the information explosion. In short, this is a concern for all the nation's employers — either now or in the future.

Just as reading is important, so too is its companion skill, writing. The historical importance of writing in American society was evident as early as the time of the Massachusetts Bay Colony, which in 1647 passed the "Old Deluder Satan" law, one of the first recorded compulsory school maintenance laws in American history. That law represents the beginning of this country's ongoing concern that citizens achieve a level of literacy that enables them to participate fully in society. For the American colonists, that meant providing education and training to ensure continuation of the cultural, economic, and religious values on which their communities were founded and maintained. The 1647 Massachusetts law updated an earlier version, which was based on the belief that everyone should be able to read and understand "the capital laws of the country" so that they would not unwittingly commit crimes punishable by the death penalty (Frost and Bailey, 1973). One of the major revisions in the 1647 version added writing to reading, as a necessary skill for functioning on all social class levels and as a prerequisite for additional schooling and social and economic advancement. These colonial laws laid the foundation for the establishment of the "reading schools" and "writing schools" of the late eighteenth century, which in turn evolved into today's U.S. public education system.

Writing skills today are important in almost every occupational field. Employers first judge a would-be employee's writing ability by the quality of an application, cover letter, or résumé. In large organizations, an employee's retention and promotion often depend on decisions by managers or executives the employee has never met. The quality of letters, memoranda, progress reports, work orders, requisitions, recommendations, and instructions is regarded as an indicator of the overall quality of an employee's work. The higher an employee's professional goals, the better the writing skills he or she will need (Lannon, 1982).

Certainly, top business administrators consistently rank writing competency among their highest priorities for job applicants and employees. The following employer comments are typical: "Certainly it is not necessary that every[one] we hire be a finished . . . writer, but it is necessary that [he or she] be able to communicate. . . . Some of the reports that I have had occasion to read over the years would curl your hair — many of them can charitably be called atrocious" and "An applicant or employee who lacks writing skills is a lost cause" (Orange, 1973, pp. 4–5).

The CPR report (1983) states that more than 50 percent of the businesses responding to its survey identified writing skill deficiencies in secretarial, "skilled," managerial, supervisory, and bookkeeping personnel. In jobs requiring medium to high levels of writing ability, an average of 45 percent of personnel were reported to be functioning at only low to medium levels; in jobs requiring high levels of writing skill, an additional 17 percent were reported to be performing at only low levels. The most frequently cited symptoms were poor grammar, spelling, and punctuation.

The same report also points out the costs businesses incur because inadequate employee writing skills have a negative effect on productivity and product quality. By way of example, it cites a company in which 70 percent of outgoing correspondence had to be corrected and retyped at least once because of employee errors. Further, responding businesses expressed concern about the impact such skill deficiencies have on employee retention and promotability, which has a direct impact on turnover costs. Of the companies surveyed by CPR, 65 percent reported limited job advancement for skill-deficient employees with high school diplomas; 73 percent reported little or no advancement for skill-deficient employees without high school diplomas.

The third competence skill — computation — is no less important than the first two. There is no question that employers today are focusing more and more on an employee's ability to compute at increasing levels of sophistication. The reason for this is simple — technology requires it. Moreover, the introduction of sophisticated management and quality control approaches such as statistical process control (SPC) demand higher mathematical skills. Ironically, as occupational skill-level requirements climb, higher educational dropout rates and worsening worker deficiencies in computational skills are appearing (Brock, 1987;

Kirsch and Jungeblut, 1986; Semerad, 1987). Employers already are complaining of their workers' computational skill deficiencies, particularly those evidenced by miscalculations of decimals and fractions, resulting in expensive production errors (Henry and Raymond, 1983).

The Educational Testing Service (ETS) in its June 1988 publication *The Mathematics Report Card, Are We Measuring Up?* notes that "The most recent international mathematics study reported that average Japanese students exhibited higher levels of achievement than the top 5 percent of American students enrolled in college preparatory mathematics courses" (Dossey, Mullis, Lindquist, and Chambers, 1988, p. 8). ETS states that "too many [American] students leave high school without the mathematical understanding that will allow them to participate fully as workers and citizens in contemporary society" (p. 9).

Similarly, in 1988 Motorola conducted a study that showed that a Japanese student can be moved into the workplace at an employer cost of $0.47, while an American student's transition costs the employer $226. This is primarily due, says Motorola, to the emphasis on statistics and applied diagnostics in Japanese schools.

The executives surveyed by CPR reported that "medium-to-high levels of mathematics skills are required across job categories, with consistently high levels required in the manufacturing, utilities, and finance industries" (Center for Public Resources, 1983, p. 13). Employees must calculate correctly to conduct inventories, complete accurate reports of production levels, measure machine parts or specifications, and so on.

The CPR respondents described the business effects of employees' skill deficiencies in computation in terms of production mistakes that translate into costly bottom line losses. Respondents indicated that deficiencies in mathematical skills were identified in an average of 43 percent of their employees across many job categories and at all required performance levels, including skilled, semiskilled, technical, clerical, and supervisory. This 43 percent reflects only mathematics skill deficiencies among the workers that were hired. It excludes the 49 percent of out-of-school job applicants with more severe computational deficiencies who were *not* hired for entry-level positions in respondents' companies.

Employees in the "new" workplace will be expected to have the basic computational skills required to organize and track large-scale shipments of merchandise, and more and more they will be expected to have the expertise to assist in making new technological discoveries. Whatever the specifics of this challenge, mathematics is critical to the economic success of the individual worker, the employer, and in the larger context to the nation's continuing competitive success.

Most employers today cannot compete successfully without a work force that has sound competence skills. Deficiencies in such basics create barriers that impair an employer's ability to meet its strategic goals and to be competitive at home and in foreign markets. Such deficiencies surface in the form of increased accident rates, costly production errors, and the inability to implement critical job-training programs that state-of-the-art management requires.

Communication Skills:
Oral Communication and Listening

Reading and writing are essential tools, but it is through listening and speaking that we interact most frequently. Among the skills most basic to individual and organizational success, the skills of communicating orally and listening intelligently stand out.

For most people, formal education in communication has been directed at those skills that are used least in the workplace: reading and writing (Burley-Allen, 1982). Surveys show that, in theory at least, most Americans have had approximately twelve years of formal training in writing and six to eight years in reading; but they have had only one or two years in speech-related courses such as public speaking, interpersonal communication, drama, debate, and oral interpretation of literature and virtually no formal training in listening (Werner, 1975, in Wolvin and Coakley, 1982).

In the mid 1970s federal legislation recognized that speaking and listening skills — along with reading, writing, and computation — should be considered basic competencies and measures of functional literacy. People who lack proficiency in the skills of oral communication are handicapped not only in communicating with others but also in learning for personal and professional development.

Workers who can express their ideas orally and who understand verbal instructions make fewer mistakes, adjust more easily to change, and more readily absorb new ideas than those who do not ("The Productivity Paradox," 1988). Thus career development is enhanced by training in oral communication and listening because these skills contribute to an employee's success in all of the following areas:

- Interviewing
- Making presentations at or conducting meetings
- Negotiating and resolving conflict
- Selling
- Leading
- Being assertive
- Teaching or coaching others
- Working in a team
- Giving supervisors feedback about conversations with customers
- Retraining

The strategic importance of oral communication skills in today's workplace has been amply documented and cannot be overstressed. Employees are already spending most of the workday communicating, and the time they spend in interpersonal communication will increase as robots, computers, and other machines take over more and more mundane, repetitive jobs. Moreover, according to the Forum Group — a major provider of corporate training — "a manager's overall performance was influenced as much, or more, by his or her ability to network through the organization as by the way he or she managed subordinates" (Burlingham, 1987, p. 52).

Skill in oral communication is a key element of good customer service. In general, U.S. customers are reasonably satisfied with the merchandise they buy, but they are disgruntled about the quality of service they receive (Albrecht and Zemke, 1985). More than 76 million workers — a majority of the U.S. labor force — are in the service sector, and companies that provide excellent service tend to stay far ahead of their competitors.

A recent government-sponsored study reported the following:

- For each complaint a company receives, it actually has, on average, twenty-six customers with problems, six of whom have "serious" problems.
- Of customers who register complaints, between 54 and 70 percent will do business with the organization again if their complaints are resolved. This figure rises to 95 percent for customers who believe their complaints were resolved quickly.
- Customers who have complained to an organization and had their complaints satisfactorily resolved tell an average of five people about the treatment they received (Albrecht and Zemke, 1988; Gorman, 1988; Kotkin, 1988).

To provide good service, employees must be trained in more than the technical aspects of their jobs; they must learn how to talk to customers, listen to them, handle their complaints courteously, deal with them even if they are difficult or unclear in their demands, and solve their problems.

Good oral communication is the core of persuasion, selling, and marketing. Getting and keeping customers means that people from all areas of a company, not just its designated sales and marketing department, must communicate effectively. Keeping today's customer means selling a continuing relationship.

Equally important is the skill of listening. Few American companies have addressed employees' lack of functional listening skills by providing training in this arena. However, the need for listening instruction was recognized by a committee of the Association for Business Communication when it surveyed business executives and found an urgent cry for listening instruction to be increased. Moreover, in a survey by a professional organization of educators who teach business communication, those educators agreed that listening is a critical skill and should be taught (Glassman and Farley, 1979). Some movement is occurring in this arena; since the International Listening Association was founded in 1979, there has been an increase in listening improvement courses for students from kindergarten through college.

Workers spend 54.93 percent of their time listening, yet the listening skills of modern Americans are appalling:

- We use only 25 percent of our listening capacity.
- We use only 10 percent of our memory potential.
- We forget half of what we have heard within eight hours.
- Eventually, we forget 95 percent of what we have heard unless cued by something later on.
- We distort what little we do remember (Nichols and Stevens, 1957; Barker, 1971).

If we translate all that into an eight-hour workday, it breaks down as follows:

- We spend about four hours in listening activity.
- We hear for about two hours.
- We actually listen for an hour.
- We understand thirty minutes of that hour.
- We believe only fifteen minutes' worth of what we listen to.
- We remember just under eight minutes' worth (Elsea, 1986).

Unfortunately, despite the importance of listening skills and despite evidence that where listening programs are offered, they are among the most popular training programs (Gordon and Zemke, 1986), only 33 percent of organizations with fifty or more employees provide listening skill training.

Author and businessman Tom Peters believes the listening habits of American workers to be so poor he states that the bottom line of American businesses will not improve unless listening skills are enhanced. Peters is only one in a long list

of corroborative voices that rate communication skills as second
in importance only to job knowledge in an employee's career
success (Mundale, 1985).

Importantly, the percentage of time workers engage in
listening increases the higher they go up the corporate ladder,
with top managers spending as much as 65 percent of their workday listening (Keefe, 1971). Because most people have had no
training in this critical skill, Americans' poor listening habits
cost hundreds of millions of dollars each year in productivity
lost through misunderstandings and mistakes. And there is no
dollar value to assess the cost of physical and emotional stress
that results from countless breakdowns in human relationships
(Steill, 1980).

One example of how measurable poor listening costs can
mount comes from the case of the typical business letter, which
when all goes well costs $12 to $15 in employee time and effort
to create and mail. If a person does not listen carefully and consequently addresses a letter incorrectly, the cost of preparing
and sending the letter is wasted if it cannot be delivered. Even
if experienced postal workers manage to figure out the letter's
correct address and deliver it, the delay may mean its contents
are outdated or that the person receiving the letter will be less
receptive to its message. Perhaps an order worth much more
than the cost of the letter itself will be lost. Not every employee
addresses (or misaddresses) letters, but nearly every employee
makes comparable costly listening mistakes. At the rate of just
one such $15 mistake per U.S. employee per year, the annual
cost of poor listening would equal more than a billion dollars.

Oral and listening communication skills, therefore, are
central to the smooth operation of a competitive venture. They
are at the heart of getting and keeping customers. Pitching innovation, contributing to quality circles, resolving conflict, and
providing meaningful feedback all hinge on the capacity to speak
and listen well.

Adaptability: Creative Thinking and Problem Solving

An organization's ability to achieve its strategic objectives
also often depends on how quickly it can bring into play the

skills of problem solving and creative thinking. Problem-solving skills include the ability to recognize and define problems, invent and implement solutions, and track and evaluate results. Creative thinking requires the ability to understand problem-solving techniques but also to transcend logical and sequential thinking and make the leap to innovation.

New approaches to problem solving, organizational design, and product development all spring from the individual capacity for creative thinking. In the workplace, creative thinking is generally expressed through the process of creative problem solving. Increasingly, companies are identifying creative problem solving as critical to their success and are instituting structured approaches to problem identification, analysis, and resolution.

Unresolved problems create dysfunctional relationships in the workplace. Ultimately, they become impediments to flexibility and to dealing with strategic change in an open-ended and creative way. Creative solutions help the organization to move forward toward its strategic goals.

William C. Miller, author of *The Creative Edge* (1987), goes so far as to describe organizational strategy itself as an example of creative thinking. He says that "At the heart of the creative strategy-development process is an innovative search that encourages the creative freedom to generate options that are unique and relevant" (p. 167).

In less theoretical terms, employers want to improve the creative problem-solving capabilities of their employees to enhance the productivity of work teams. A primary task of the work team is plugging the "error leak" through early identification and resolution of problems that affect productivity, image, or sales. For example, Milwaukee Amstar, a producer of heavy-duty electric tools, has institutionalized a "productivity team concept" that focuses on problem solving. SWAT (*s*olutions *w*e *a*chieve *t*ogether) teams provide an opportunity for employees to become as involved in the creative problem-solving effort as they choose to be. Team objectives include the following:

- Fostering employee involvement
- Developing and displaying decision-making and implementation ability

- Increasing quality and cost awareness
- Learning to work together and helping others grow
- Using worker creativity to solve problems

Personal Management: Self-Esteem, Motivation/Goal Setting, Employability/Career Development

Another key to individual effectiveness in the workplace is good personal management. Self-esteem, motivation/goal setting, and employability/career development skills are critical to the workplace because they impact heavily on individual morale, which in turn plays a significant role in an institution's ability to achieve bottom line results.

Employers have been feeling the pressure to make their own provisions for addressing perceived deficiencies in these skill areas because they realize that a work force without such skills is less productive. Conversely, solid personal management skills are often manifested by efficient integration of new technology or processes, creative thinking, high productivity, and a pursuit of skill enhancement through training or education. Unfortunately, problems in the workplace related to these skill areas have increased primarily because entry-level applicants are arriving at the "hiring hall" deficient in personal management skills. Moreover, many potential employees never get hired because they do not possess even the most rudimentary skills for finding employment; although they may be qualified to hold a job, they don't respond to job advertisements or show up at employment interviews.

Once on the job, an employee's lack of competence in personal management skills affects the following areas.

Hiring and training costs: Workers may fail in the initial tasks set for them by management, driving the employer to continually hire and fire. This leads to excessive spending on the orientation and training of new employees as well as the cost of processing outgoing workers from the organization.

Productivity: New and inexperienced replacements face a significant learning curve that affects overall activity by slowing down the production process; experienced workers lacking adequate personal management skills may not work up to their full potential.

Quality control: Product defect rates may be very high among workers who have low confidence in their own ability to do the job.

Creativity: People who lack confidence in their ability to devise new or corrective solutions or to set work goals will reject their own ideas rather than bring them to the attention of a supervisor.

Ability to develop worker skills to meet changing needs: People with impaired self-esteem, poor self-motivation, and unfocused career plans may see themselves as trapped at entry-level positions, unable to cope with change, or doomed to failure and firing. These negative feelings are frequently reflected in poor job performance.

Cumulatively, employees' personal management problems present a series of roadblocks that slow or halt an organization's progress. An organization with such difficulties cannot plan accurately for its future in terms of integrating new technology, establishing new work structures such as work teams, or implementing new work processes.

Group Effectiveness: Interpersonal Skills, Negotiation, and Teamwork

Organizations are composed of individuals with differing opinions and operating styles. Whenever people work together, successful interaction depends upon effective interpersonal skills, focused negotiation, and a sense of group purpose (teamwork). Of course, diversity inevitably results in conflict from time to time. In today's workplace, the move toward participative decision making and problem solving inevitably increases the potential for disagreement, particularly when the primary work unit is a peer team with no single person taking on the role of decision maker (that is, supervisor or manager). All this puts a premium on developing employees' group effectiveness skills.

Interpersonal skills training can help many employees recognize and improve their ability to determine appropriate self-behavior, cope with undesirable behavior in others, absorb stress, deal with ambiguity, structure social interaction, share responsibility, and in general interact more easily with others. This is particularly relevant to working teams. Teamwork skills are critical for improving individual task accomplishment at work because practical innovations and solutions are reached sooner through cooperative behavior. Furthermore, a person's human needs and individual job responsibilities are addressed more directly in a team environment. Developing cooperative skills is a requirement if employees' talents are to be used effectively to influence organizational change strategies.

Negotiation skills are critical for the effective functioning of good teams as well as for individual acceptance in an organization. The increasing interdependency of people from the shop floor to the CEO's office creates a need for skills in constructive face-to-face relations that maintain harmony and build intergroup trust. Besides being important for building constructive interpersonal relationships, skills in negotiating are basic and crucial to the problem-solving process at all levels of an organization (Mastenbroek, 1983). Moreover, good interpersonal skills provide the foundation for organizational effectiveness and success as a leader.

In the past two decades, there has been a tremendous increase in the use of teams in the workplace. The team approach has been linked conclusively to higher productivity and product quality, as well as to increased quality of work life. Change strategies are usually dependent upon the ability of employees to pull together and refocus on the new common goal.

Anthony P. Carnevale, chief economist for the American Society for Training and Development, writes in *Human Capital: A High Yield Corporate Investment* (1983) that there are two ways to increase productivity. "The first is by increasing the intensity with which we utilize [human] resources (working harder), and the second is by increasing the efficiency with which we mix and use available resources (working smarter). Analysis of data as far back as 1929 demonstrates that 'working smarter'—the ability of working teams to learn together—is the most significant among human factors in producing income and productivity growth" (p. 15).

Organizations establish teams for many reasons, both positive and negative:

- Loss of production or unit output
- Increase in staff grievances and complaints
- Evidence of staff conflict and hostility
- Confusion about assignments, missed signals, and other evidence of unclear relationships
- Decisions misunderstood or not carried through properly
- Apathy—general lack of interest or involvement by staff
- Apparent lack of staff initiative, imagination, and innovation
- Ineffective staff meetings, low participation, minimally effective decisions
- Formation of a new group that needs to develop quickly into a working team
- High dependency on or negative reactions to the manager
- Complaints from customers and users about the quality of services
- Continued, unaccounted-for increases in costs (Dyer, 1987, p. 39)

At Texas Instruments (TI) the written goal of its Effectiveness Teams program is "to improve the quality of our products, increase company profits, and make working at Texas Instruments more fun" (Texas Instruments, 1984, p. ii). So like most companies using teams, TI expects teamwork to improve company productivity and competitive position.

Whenever people work together, successful interaction depends upon effective interpersonal skills, focused negotiation, and a sense of group purpose. The quality of these three factors defines and controls working relationships. The strategic relevance of interpersonal, negotiation, and teamwork skills is evident. They are basic tools for achieving the flexibility and adaptability that America's work force must have in order to remain competitive.

Influence: Organizational
Effectiveness and Leadership

To be effective in an organization, employees need to have a sense of how the organization works and how the actions of each individual affect organizational and strategic objectives. Skill in determining the forces and factors that interfere with the organization's ability to accomplish its tasks can help the worker become a master problem solver, an innovator, and a team builder.

Organizations are a tapestry of explicit and implicit power structures. In the explicit structure, leadership is conferred and represented by title and authority. In the implicit structure, leadership is a delicately woven image achieved by cultivating the respect of peers and projecting a sense of reliability, goal orientation, and vision. Both organizational effectiveness and leadership skills are basics for success in tomorrow's workplace. People who have these skills can help employers create the conditions for achieving success in the marketplace.

Basic training in organizational effectiveness is geared toward providing the trainee with an understanding of what organizations are, why they exist, and how one can navigate the complex social waters of varying types of organizations. Once armed with this basic framework, the trainee is exposed to the organizational culture of his or her employer, its goals, values, culture, and traditional modes of operation. Finally, training in skills that make the employee a fully functioning member of the organization—interpersonal, communication, and group dynamic skills—completes the picture.

Some employers, such as Honda (at its Ohio plant), are in the enviable position of having a large enough employment pool to screen out unsuitable applicants through cultural pre-job assessment. This ensures that employees who are hired will fit into the existing institutional environment (Tichy and De-vanna, 1986). An applicant who wants a job at the Honda plant is required to write an essay about his or her life goals and how employment with Honda will fit in with those goals. The requirement eliminates the 90 percent of applicants who cannot identify a place for Honda in their lives. Honda then focuses on the remaining 10 percent for hiring. New employees go through initial training for three weeks (three to eight hours is typical of American automobile manufacturers). At Honda, it is the best workers who train new employees so that newcomers learn the ins and outs of the organizational structure and the preferred way of working. Although many people look with amusement at this kind of cultural indoctrination, it is the same kind of indoctrination that makes the United States Marine Corps such a unique fighting force. The result in both cases is people who become excellent workers and who make a maximum effort to return to the organization what the organization took so much time to give to them (Tichy and Devanna, 1986, pp. 242–243).

Organizational effectiveness skills are the building blocks for leadership. Without them, leadership efforts can be misplaced and even counterproductive. A proactive approach toward increasing organizational effectiveness skills through training is a reflection of a commitment to shared leadership concepts operating throughout the organization. Implementing shared leadership values has been shown to have a positive impact on productivity. When leadership functions are dispersed throughout an organization, those who perform in leadership roles willingly take on the responsibility for creating and communicating the vision of the organization and what its work groups should accomplish. By their proximity, they are also better able to create and communicate the quality of the work environment necessary to realize that vision. One discussion of the importance of encouraging visionary leadership practices throughout an organization involves the concept of the superteam (Hastings, Bixby, and Chaudhry-Lawton, 1986). A superteam is defined as "a high performing team which produces quite outstanding achievements" (p. 8). Leaders of superteams are described as "good at creating visions. . . . The leaders of superteams spend as much time anticipating the future as they do managing the present . . . they devote their time to thinking forward to, and talking to others about, their goal, for it is this that provides the team with its purpose and direction" (p. 81). Every team can be a superteam if it has good shared leadership practices and an understanding of how the organization functions and what its goals are.

One reason for encouraging the deployment of visionary leaders throughout the organization is to improve institutional response time to changing and increasingly complex external environment factors that affect the organization's ability to operate effectively.

At its most elementary level, leadership means that one person influences others. An organization that supports the concepts of shared leadership encourages employees at all levels to assume this role where it is appropriate. The functions of leadership include stating basic values, announcing goals, organizing resources, reducing tensions between individuals, creating coalitions, coalescing the work force, and encouraging better performance. There is a direct correlation between the implementation of shared leadership practices and product improvement, higher morale, and innovative problem solving, which leads to a more hospitable environment for instituting change.

Leaders at the top cannot make an organizational system work without the willingness of employees throughout the corporate structure to take on shared leadership roles. A great many people throughout the system must be in "a state of psychological readiness" (Gardner, 1987, p. 10) to take leaderlike action to improve the functioning at their levels. Historically, the roots of business failure can often be traced to inadequate training in and attention to the importance of leadership as a basic workplace skill. Too frequently, companies designate people as leaders without providing proper evaluation and training to ensure that they are sufficiently qualified to assume leadership roles.

PART 2

The Foundation:
Learning How to Learn

The accumulation of knowledge is respected and encouraged in our society. But rarely do we, in our childhood years, learn the principles that prepare us to absorb and apply information effectively.

Knowing how to learn is the most basic of all skills because it is the key that unlocks future success. Individuals who know how to learn can more easily acquire other skills. Without this essential skill, however, one's learning is not as rapid or as comprehensive and long lasting.

Individuals begin to develop informal learning-to-learn strategies in infancy and may subconsciously continue to make marginal improvement in this skill throughout their lives. It is probable, however, that in the absence of explicit training in this fundamental skill, many will reach a learning process plateau. That is, while they may continue to accumulate knowledge, they will not learn as effectively as they could if they used explicit learning-to-learn strategies. Clearly, for some people, the failure to acquire adequate learning-to-learn skills will result in unrealized personal and economic potential.

A modern worker—whether an unlettered laborer attempting to break the code of written language, a technically skilled factory employee joining a new work team, or a highly educated manager negotiating a pivotal deal—needs to be aware of the techniques, attitudes, and knowledge that facilitate the processing of information. A worker needs to know how to work effectively and efficiently.

Each adult brings a different personal data base of experience and learning to the workplace. This base cannot remain static because our lives are a caldron of experiments responding to the need to adapt to changing circumstances. How we process incoming information is governed by our ability to learn, and this ability is made more valuable by our becoming aware of how we process and develop strategies for applying information.

According to engineer-architect R. Buckminster Fuller, "Every time you make an experiment, you learn more; quite literally, you cannot learn less" (Kehl, 1983, p. 35). But like scientists whose experiments yield an unexpected result, we need strategies for understanding and utilizing the information that confronts us.

CHAPTER 3

Learning to Learn:
Strategies for Acquiring Skills

The only man who is educated is the man who has learned
how to learn . . . how to adapt and change.

Carl Rogers
Freedom to Learn, 1969

What Is Learning to Learn?

According to Robert M. Smith, professor of adult education at Northern Illinois University, "Learning how to learn involves possessing, or acquiring, the knowledge and skill to learn
effectively in whatever learning situation one encounters" (1987,
pp. 137–138). The process by which one acquires learning-to-
learn skills is based on three factors:

1. *Learner needs:* what a person needs to know and to be able
   to do for success in learning
2. *Learning style:* a person's highly individualized preferences
   and tendencies that influence learning
3. *Training:* organized activity or instruction to increase a person's competence in learning

Among the many approaches to learning that one can use
to develop learning-to-learn skills are the following (Rae, 1985):

- Reading
- Attending lectures

39

- Direct on-the-job training
- Action/hands-on learning
- Coaching by a supervisor or other expert
- Self-development
- Training courses outside of work

No one of these activities is *the* right or wrong approach to learning to learn. Rather, each learning situation dictates the approach or combination of approaches that will best meet a particular person's needs.

Early in this century, it was possible for an organization to expect its workers to take direction and carry out simple tasks without the work force or its managers worrying much about the mechanics of how tasks were to be done, how to learn to do them better, or how to learn many new tasks quickly several times in a career. What has evolved, however, is a workplace that requires employees who understand what they are doing, can be analytical, see how their tasks fit into a greater organizational whole, can innovate to improve a product line, and can change to keep pace with advances in theory and technology. A prerequisite for becoming that kind of employee is the acquisition of learning-to-learn skills that are transferable from one subject-specific area to another.

Lauren Resnick of the Learning Research and Development Center of the University of Pittsburgh has provided advice that, although aimed at educators, is equally relevant to trainers charged with improving workers' learning-to-learn skills. "School," Resnick says, "should focus its efforts on preparing people to be good *adaptive* learners, so they can perform effectively when situations are unpredictable and task demands change" (Raspberry, 1988).

Whether one is in school or on the job, learning to learn is a process, not a product, and its basic tenets are communicated effectively only when they are contextually grounded. Good learning-to-learn skills are self-perpetuating, self-generating, and self-rewarding in that "better ways to learn may lead to better ways to *'learn to learn,'* which could make the crucial difference between what we call normal thought and creative thought" (Minsky, 1985, p. 80).

Expressed in terms meaningful to employers, learning-to-learn training provides techniques for ensuring that employees in all occupations and at all skill levels can learn and think faster and more thoroughly and efficiently. Learning to learn involves a set of learnable (therefore trainable) skills that enable employees to understand and manipulate new information quickly and confidently.

What Theories Support Current Training in Learning to Learn?

Historically, learning to learn reaches back to ancient Greece as embodied in the *Socratic method*. In this approach, a learner asks questions and seeks definitions and models, with the questioning process giving rise to new ideas by drawing on prior knowledge. Seeking means for assessing the validity of ideas, the Greek philosophers also laid the foundation on which contemporary views of logic and scientific inquiry are built.

In the United States, the importance of learning to learn has been reinforced by such prominent and colorful historic figures as Benjamin Franklin. He found his contemporaries so deficient in this skill that he was inspired to train members of the Junto, a discussion club that he founded in 1727. Franklin insisted on club rules that "forestalled dogmatism, minimized conflict, and fostered productive inquiry; rule breakers were assessed fines" (Grattan, 1959).

In this century, Arnold Toynbee, the distinguished British historian, noted that learners need to learn how to transform themselves into "self-teachers" (Tough, 1979). Educational philosopher John Dewey (1966) suggested that we evaluate schooling according to its success in creating in students a desire for "continual growth" and in providing them with the means for making that desire "effective" in fact.

Ever-increasing interest in spreading the gospel of learning to learn can be attributed to a number of factors:

- Acceptance by mainstream educators of the idea that education is a lifelong process
- A shift in emphasis from teaching to learning as more in-

depth studies have yielded more practical information about
how adults learn

- A proliferation of approaches and techniques for providing
  adult education
- Research and experimentation with useful results on individual learning styles and how they affect a person's ability to perceive and process information

More than 100 training programs concerning learning to
learn are currently operating in the United States. Although
some of them actually provide training in techniques for improving learning skills, many are simply attempts to achieve
one particular result, for example, higher scores on standardized
intelligence tests. Although learning-to-learn programs are usually, albeit sometimes unwittingly, based on one or another
learning theory, most are not rigorous enough to have a clear
connection between a specific learning theory or theories and
the learning-to-learn strategies they promote. Yet experience
and research demonstrate that when learning theory is embedded
in subject-specific practical exercises and when skills to enhance
learning-to-learn capabilities or techniques in critical thinking
are *explicitly* identified and taught, learners' test scores improve.
Further, their learning gains are retained over time and transfer
across subject areas (Resnick, 1987c; Heiman and Slomianko,
1987).

Table 1 provides a paradigm for illustrating how learning theories can be correlated with training techniques based
on assumptions about how people learn how to learn (Brostrom,
1979) and tailored to the learning needs of each participant.

Using this paradigm, a trainer can select and translate
learning theory into practical training exercises based on the
range of the learner's learning needs. In this way, learners use
and develop generic learning-to-learn strategies that increase
knowledge and retention regardless of the subject under study.
A thorough trainer will consider presenting learning content,
to a greater or lesser degree, through the use of the appropriate
learning theory (Brostrom, telephone interviews, March and
April 1988). This is because each theory has some degree of

applicability to all content and to the individual ways in which learners learn. If, for example, a trainer designs a course on aspects of automation, the trainer might select a behaviorist approach such as computer-aided programmed instruction as the main means of delivering content. However, to offer more variety and improve the likelihood of meeting the learning-to-learn needs of individual training participants, the trainer could supplement the computer-based instruction with a structuralist approach (a walk-through of an automated facility), a functionalist approach (a brief research and writing assignment), and a humanist approach (a support group exercise).

Broadening training techniques to increase the probability that learners will be provided with transferable learning-to-learn skills is only a starting point. Experience shows that learners may favor specific training/learning methods for acquiring new information. For example, to learn how to operate a complex machine that learners have never seen before, for some, the best approach will be hands-on exploration of the equipment, followed by an opportunity to read written operating instructions. For others, the best approach will be to read the instructions first. Nevertheless, training content and learning task objectives also require consideration. For example, some learners may, as a rule, learn best by listening. If they are trying to learn how to be good public speakers, however, listening to even the best-presented lecture will not have as significant an outcome as their standing up, delivering a speech, and receiving feedback on their performance.

The method by which an individual prefers to learn is not necessarily static; it may change at different stages of a person's life and career (Rae, 1985). Early in their employment, many learners prefer settings and methods similar to those in the academic environment they have recently left. This preference is partly a conditioned response, the association of learning with familiar aspects of a classroom environment. As midcareer approaches, learners' preferences may switch to more experiential (on-the-job or job simulation) learning environments and methods (small group activities, case studies, decision-making discussions, and so on). Beyond this point and taking into account

Table 1. Learning-to-Learn Theories and Techniques.

	Behaviorist	Structuralist	Functionalist	Humanist
Orientation to learning	New behavior can be caused and "shaped" with well-designed structures around the learner	The mind is like a computer; the teacher is the programmer	People learn best by doing, and they will do best what *they* want to do. People will learn what is practical.	Learning is self-directed discovery. People are natural and unfold (like a flower) if others do not inhibit the process.
Assumptions about learning to learn	Training designers select the desired end behaviors and proceed to engineer a reinforcement schedule that systematically encourages learners' progress toward those goals. Imaginative new machinery has made learning fun and thinking unnecessary. Learners often control the speed.	Content properly organized and fed bit-by-bit to learners will be retained in memory. Criterion tests will verify the effectiveness of teaching. The teacher "keeps people awake" while simultaneously entering data—a much-envied skill.	The learner must be willing (or motivated) by the process or the product. Otherwise it is useless to try teaching. Performance "on-the-job" is the true test. Opportunity, self-direction, thinking, achieving results, and recognition are important.	"Anything that can be taught to another is relatively inconsequential" (Rogers). Significant learning leads to insight and understanding of self and others. Being a better human being is considered a valid learning goal. Can be a very inefficient, time-consuming process.
Teaching/training	*Supportive*: emphasis on controlling and predicting the learner and learning outcomes—cooperative, stimulus-response mentalities are valued. Process is product centered.	*Directive*: planning, organization, presentation, and evaluation are featured. Process is teacher centered.	*Assertive*: a problem-focused, conditional, confrontational climate—striving, stretching, achieving. Process is task oriented and learner centered.	*Reflective*: authenticity, equality, and acceptance mark relationship. Process is relationship centered.

	"The Doctor" / "The Manipulator"	"The Expert" / "The Elitist"	"The Coach" / "Sink or Swim"	"The Counselor" / "The Fuzzy Thinker"
Strengths	"The Doctor": clear, precise, and deliberate; low risk; careful preparation; emotionally attentive; complete security for learners; a trust builder; everything "arranged"; protective; patient, in control.	"The Expert": Informative; thorough; certain; systematic; stimulating; good audiovisual techniques; well rehearsed; powerful; strong leader; expressive; dramatic; entertaining	"The Coach": emphasizes purpose; challenges learners; realistic; lets people perform and make mistakes; takes risks; gives feedback; builds confidence; is persuasive; gives opportunity and recognition	"The Counselor": sensitive; empathic; open; spontaneous; creative; a "mirror"; nonevaluative; accepting; responsive to learners; facilitative; interactive; helpful
Limitations	"The Manipulator": fosters dependence; overprotective; controlling; manipulative; "for their own good"; sugarcoating; hypocritical agreeing; deceptive assurances; withholds data.	"The Elitist": preoccupied with means, image, or structure rather than results; ignores affective variables; inflexible (must follow lesson plan); dichotomous (black or white) thinking; superior.	"Sink or Swim": ends justify means; loses patience with slow learners; intimidating; insensitive; competitive; overly task oriented; opportunistic; return-on-investment mentality.	"The Fuzzy Thinker": vague directions; abstract, esoteric, or personal content; lacks performance criteria; unconcerned with clock time; poor control of group; resists "teaching"; appears unprepared.
Major theorist	B. F. Skinner	Robert Mager	David McClelland	C. R. Rogers
Key words and processes	• stimulus-response • practice • shaping • prompting • behavior modification • pinpointing • habit formation • reward and punishment • teaching machines • environmental design • successive approximation • sensitizing • training • extinction	• task analysis • lesson planning • information mapping • chaining • sequencing • memory • audiovisual media • presentation techniques • standards • association • evaluations • measuring instruments • objectives • recitation	• problem solving • simulation • "hands-on" • reasoning • learner involvement • reality based consequences • achievement • failure • confidence • thinking • motivation • competence • discipline • recognitions • feedback • working	• freedom • individuality • ambiguity • uncertainty • awareness • spontaneity • mutuality • equality • openness • interaction • experiential learning • congruence • authenticity • listening • cooperation • feelings

Source: Adapted from Brostrom, 1979.

an employee's position, the training format that learners prefer usually depends on the training culture of the company — experiential (self-directed) or prescriptive (trainer-directed).

Another important factor influencing a person's learning facility is perceptual style preference for learning. For example, if you ask a group of people how to spell a difficult word, you may observe that some people close their eyes and whisper to themselves; some appear to be writing with an invisible pen; some hunt for paper and a real pen or pencil so they can write the word. In trying to retrieve the word's spelling from their memories, they reveal something about the *sensory intake* or *perceptual style* with which they originally learned the word's spelling. In this case, some people hear the spelling; some feel it; some see it (American Society for Training and Development, 1988).

According to studies by James and Galbraith (1985), there are seven primary perceptual preferences:

1. *Print:* the preference of the reader/writer, who learns well from traditional texts and pencil-and-paper exercises
2. *Visual:* the preference of the observer, who likes to look at slides, films, videotapes, exhibits, demonstrations, photographs, charts, and graphs
3. *Aural:* the preference of the listener, who enjoys most lectures and also learns well from audiotapes and records
4. *Interactive:* the preference of the talker, who learns best from discussions and question-and-answer sessions
5. *Tactile/manipulative:* the preference of the toucher/handler, who wants hands-on activities and also learns well from model building or sketching
6. *Kinesthetic/psychomotor:* the preference of the mover, who likes role plays and physical games and activities
7. *Olfactory:* the preference of the smeller/taster, who associates learning with smells and tastes. This style is not often used in the classroom, but has much interest for industries such as candy making, wine producing, and pharmaceuticals, where employees must learn the significance of subtle differences in odors, aromas, tastes, or flavors.

Sensory perceptions affect other learning capabilities too. For example, some people are basically *field-dependent,* whereas others are *field-independent.* Field-dependent people are inclined to view the big picture (the forest) but find it hard to focus on details. Field-independent people can easily distinguish details (the trees) but find it difficult to see the whole. Although a few people are at each extreme for this kind of perception, most people show only a slight preference for one or the other. In fact, either extreme is associated with learning disability.

Research (James and Galbraith, 1985) indicates that more adults are in the visual learner group than in any one of the other six groups. Still, whatever our primary learning preference, we also learn—although with varying degrees of efficiency—through all our senses. Good learning-to-learn training reflects the need to use all available learning tools, even if they are not the most personally suitable.

From the perspective of having to create learning-to-learn materials, information about individual learning styles enables curriculum designers and developers to modify and balance training techniques to satisfy the needs of each training group member. If a training group has a full mix of learning styles, this replicates the situation in the workplace, providing a natural training ground for demonstrating to employees how they can use and improve learning-to-learn skills on the job.

Adult education experts have also recognized and regularly stressed the importance of learning how to learn. From Joseph K. Hart, a leader in the adult education movement of the 1920s, to contemporary adult education expert Malcolm Knowles, a major objective has been the development and refinement of a process for improving the learning-process skills of adults. That process is known today as *andragogy.*

Basically, these are the principles of the andragogical style of instruction:

- Set the climate; make it physically and psychologically receptive to learning.
- Involve learners in mutual planning, and make people feel

committed to their decisions by providing them a role in making them.

- Involve participants in diagnosing their learning needs, and use a model of competencies that reflects both individual and organizational needs that allows people to see the gap between the skills they possess and the skills they need.
- Involve learners in formulating their learning objectives and using a learning contract.
- Involve learners in designing learning plans, again through a learning contract.
- Involve learners in evaluating learning.

Recently, some people have questioned whether there really is a difference between the way children learn and the way adults learn. This has resulted in Knowles himself commenting that what is important is the individual learner in the context of a given situation, regardless of whether we are talking about adults or children; "certain cases call for an andragogical approach, while others demand pedagogical methods" (Feuer and Geber, 1988, p. 36). Pedagogical methods would probably be indicated in a situation where there is an established "best way" to perform a task. In this instance it probably does not make much sense to encourage the individual to explore options or actively filter the new information through his or her own experiences.

Leonard Nadler, professor of human resource development (retired) in the School of Education and Human Development at George Washington University, argues that the concept of self-directedness (the heart of adult learning theory) applies differently in the workplace than in adult education schools (see Feuer and Geber, 1988). In the latter, students are in class because they are self-motivated to be there; in the workplace, workers attend training primarily because management has decided it is necessary, which tends to strip the learner of self-directedness and, frequently, the enthusiasm to learn. One way around this is to help the learner discover his or her developmental needs. For example, provide a worker with a job exercise that requires more computational knowledge than previously, and he or she will soon discover what additional learning is necessary to do the job right.

The jury is out on just what andragogy is, but "whether you call it a theory, a philosophy, or merely a set of assumptions, whether it speaks about adults or people of all ages, andragogy is an honest attempt to focus on the learner. In this sense it does provide an alternative to the methodology-centered instructional design perspective" (Feuer and Geber, 1988, p. 39).

What Are the Essential Elements of Training in Learning to Learn?

Regardless of which learning-to-learn training design and activities one uses, all of them share certain basic components. These components are characterized below.

Knowledge of Domains of Mental Activity. A category germane to both a trainer's and a learner's tasks is knowledge of spheres (domains) of mental activity. Such knowledge helps a trainer create learning experiences that take advantage of an individual's learning preferences. By developing more efficient modes of instruction, a trainer helps learners achieve desired performance outcomes. For learners themselves, an understanding of spheres of learning helps to illustrate the variety of activities that constitute learning.

Bloom's taxonomy (1956, 1964) usefully categorizes the variety of activities that constitute how people learn in the various domains of mental activity.

The *cognitive (thinking/knowing) domain* involves understanding that responses may vary from simple recall of material to original and creative ways of combining and synthesizing new ideas. Simplified, this domain involves the skills people use to know, understand, or comprehend information. The cognitive domain includes such skills as knowledge, comprehension, application, analysis, synthesis, and evaluation.

The *psychomotor (physical) domain* emphasizes muscular or motor skills that people use to learn how material and objects can be manipulated or how to perform tasks that involve neuromuscular coordination. This domain involves the skills people use to control their bodies.

The *affective (behavioral/attitudinal) domain* involves the skills and processes that people use to deal with their feelings, emotions, or degree of acceptance or rejection. The affective domain (Bloom, 1964) includes such skills as receiving, responding, valuing, organizing, and characterizing.

The categories of learning within the domains of cognitive (knowledge) and affective (attitudes) learning form a hierarchy because the categories are viewed as increasingly more difficult to achieve. This hierarchy is useful to both learner and trainer. It helps the former understand the characteristics of a learning need; for the latter, it is a tool for designing a building-block, step-by-step training format to help one grasp learning-to-learn strategies.

Understanding Formal Learning Strategies. Once a trainer understands the different ways in which individuals absorb information, he or she needs to develop instructional strategies for helping training participants actually acquire knowledge. Formal learning activities constitute an increasingly important aspect of all levels of organizational life. This has led to heightened sophistication and academic attention to instructional strategies, especially those concerned with adult learners. Instructional strategies refer to the modes of training organization and delivery used to increase the effectiveness of learning.

Equal attention has been given to learning strategies, that is, the techniques a learner employs to increase learning ability (learning-to-learn skill). The appropriate choice of strategies depends on learning content and learner characteristics (perceptual preference and learning style). These strategic techniques have been grouped into eight categories (Weinstein and Mayer, 1986).

1. *Basic rehearsal strategies* are used for learning information such as items in a list. For example, repeating items orally or mentally is a strategy that most people develop by adulthood. This strategy can be enhanced if it takes place in an environment free from distraction and is supplemented by visual imagery to facilitate learning.

2. *Complex rehearsal strategies* are used for learning material from written passages and are enhanced by taking notes or copying important information.

3. *Basic elaboration strategies* focus on making internal connections among items that do not have those connections externally, such as learning foreign words. These strategies include mental imagery of the connections and the generation of a sentence that connects the items. Learner-generated images are more effective in adults than images imposed by others. In learning the meaning of foreign words, there is often not a root that connects the meaning of the words, so the learning is of a *paired-associate* structure. Two unrelated words must be connected mentally to a common meaning. A well-known strategy for enhancing this learning is referred to as the keyword method. Learning an association such as the meaning of a foreign word by key word involves two stages: the acoustic link by which the sound of a foreign word is associated with the sound of a word familiar to the learner that easily evokes an image, which becomes the *key word;* and the imagery link that connects the key word through imagery to the native word of the learner that corresponds to the foreign word, thereby establishing the association. An example is the Spanish word *trigo,* which means "wheat." An acoustic link is created by linking "tree" to trigo. Then the imagery link is formed with "wheat" by picturing a tree that grows wheat stalks instead of leaves (Weinstein and Mayer, 1986, p. 319).

4. *Complex elaboration strategies* are used for integrating new information with prior knowledge. These strategies include paraphrasing, summarizing, creating analogies, generative note taking, and question answering. Generative note taking is a technique in which people create new analogies or relationships for what they already know and then draw implications from the new knowledge and state those implications in their own words.

5. *Basic organizational strategies* are used for clustering items into groups that share some characteristics that can facilitate recall. The most effective basis for clustering is meaning rather than, for instance, visual shape.

6. *Complex organizational strategies* are used for building internal connection to new material. This involves outlining through

a traditional topical outline or a graphic diagram such as a *mind map* that associates key ideas. A strategy called *networking* (Dansereau, 1978) specifies six links to look for among ideas: part, type, leads to, analogy, characteristic, and evidence.

7. *Comprehension monitoring strategies* are used in a process whereby people become aware of their learning progress and are able to control their cognitive processes and to modify them if necessary. Skills for doing this include self-questioning about the nature of the task, consciously focusing attention on a task, giving positive self-reinforcement during the process, and realistically coping with error and correction.

8. *Affective and motivational strategies* are used in a process for dealing with anxiety about and generating and sustaining motivation for learning. This can be done through positive self-talk, rationalizing negative evaluations, and turning the focus away from self-deprecating thoughts.

Awareness of Informal Learning Strategies. People usually consider learning and learning to learn in the workplace as being related to the organized, formal learning experiences described above. Furthermore, most people would acknowledge that learning and learning how to learn also occur naturally and informally outside that context. The problem with informal learning-to-learn activities is the difficulty in assessing outcomes because the person or people involved may not be aware that they are acquiring a useful, transferable learning process. Learners who are unaware of informal learning strategies cannot consciously select them for application in other relevant situations. Training that enhances learners' awareness of unstructured learning-to-learn strategies unquestionably enhances the learners' functioning in the workplace.

Learners need to be aware of and employ informal learning-to-learn strategies such as the following:

• *Identify the assumptions underlying interpretations.* Faulty assumptions can lead to faulty conclusions. When we enter a situation with unidentified assumptions, if they are incorrect or not pertinent to the situation, the likelihood of our discovering error is low. The importance of identifying and validating our assumptions increases in proportion to the negative consequences of making errors.

- *Test assumptions for validity.* Once identified, assumptions can be tested by various means. These range from low-power tests such as looking for a single piece of confirming evidence to relatively high-power tests such as seeking disproving evidence or conferring with other people to get their views.
- *Generate and test alternative interpretations.* This allows consideration of alternatives that may have different consequences and implications and may result in more valid interpretations of possibilities and experiences.
- *Develop an orientation that decreases the likelihood of error.* This involves testing assumptions and proposing and testing positions to discover which seem to be more functional in a situation for which information is incomplete or ambiguous. It is important to take a testability stance. This means that interpretations of experience are recognized for what they are, not misconstrued as conclusions or facts unless testing confirms them as such. With this orientation, a person views mistakes or errors as learning opportunities, not as unfortunate incidents best covered up and forgotten.

The foregoing strategies improve a person's quality of learning by decreasing incorrect learning. Strategies also may be developed for exploiting opportunities for learning in informal situations. There are two basic, beneficial approaches for accomplishing this. The first involves building an awareness of informal learning as a technique for enhancing the learning process. Simply by becoming sensitive to the fact that much learning can occur outside structured learning experiences, people can enhance their subject-specific learning—because they become more alert to opportunities for informal learning. The second approach is actively to seek opportunities for informal learning experiences. A proactive approach to uncovering informal learning-to-learn experiences can improve people's skill in learning from these situations.

Knowledge of Learning Styles. In his book *Learning How to Learn,* Robert M. Smith (1982) lists seventeen learning style inventory instruments. Smith states that a person may score differently on different inventories — or differently on the same inventory at different times. These differences are partly explained by the subjective nature of the instruments; the person's preferences may fluctuate, or his or her self-awareness may be heightened by having worked through one inventory that then influences the results of the next. When administered and interpreted by a trained expert, these instruments can yield useful learner profiles. Proper interpretation leaves no one mistakenly thinking that any learning style is generically better than another. Rather, the purpose of learning style inventories is to improve learners' self-awareness and, potentially, to improve their communication.

Currently popular instruments that exemplify what these tools can reveal are the Myers-Briggs Type Indicator (MBTI), a personality assessment instrument, and psychologist David Kolb's Learning Styles Inventory (LSI). The MBTI is based on the work of Swiss psychologist Carl Jung (see Table 2).

The MBTI depends on self-analysis and reporting. Therefore, what is being assessed is whether a person who completes the instrument agrees with predictions of similarity between Jung's concepts and those of experiential learning theory; what is *not* being assessed, except by inference, is the person's actual behavior.

Kolb developed the Learning Style Inventory as part of his work in experiential learning, which he describes as an "integrative perspective . . . that combines experience, perception, cognition and behavior" (American Society for Training and Development, 1988, p. 9). Despite having a few detractors, Kolb's influence is seen in most models and descriptions of learning styles. He has developed an impressive body of research that relates learning style to Jung's personality types (and those more recently defined by MBTI), educational specialization, careers/jobs, and adaptive competencies (of decision making, valuing, thinking, and acting). Kolb categorizes learners as *convergers,* those who do best with "one right answer" tests and situations;

Table 2. Jung's Psychological Types.

Mode of relation to the world	*E* EXTROVERT TYPE Oriented toward external world of other people and things	*I* INTROVERT TYPE Oriented toward inner world of ideas and feelings
Mode of decision making	*J* JUDGING TYPE Emphasis on order through reaching decision and resolving issues	*P* PERCEIVING TYPE Emphasis on gathering information and obtaining as much data as possible
Mode of perceiving	*S* SENSING TYPE Emphasis on sense perception, on facts, details, and concrete events	*N* INTUITION TYPE Emphasis on possibilities, imagination, meaning, and seeing things as a whole
Mode of judging	*T* THINKING TYPE Emphasis on analysis, using logic and rationality	*F* FEELING TYPE Emphasis on human values, establishing personal friendships, decisions made mainly on beliefs and likes

Source: D. Kolb, *Experiential Learning: Experience as a Source of Learning Development,* p. 80, © 1984. Reprinted with permission of author.

divergers, those who are imaginative and sensitive to meanings, values, and feelings; *assimilators,* those who are good at creating abstract models; or *accommodators,* those who take risks, adapt to circumstances, and take action. Most people rely predominately on one of these four learning-to-learn styles in their approaches to learning tasks. The key to learning how to learn effectively, however, is to become competent in skills related to all four styles.

Kolb's categories of learners are particularly relevant to problem-solving skills (see Chapter Nine). He believes that a group's ability to solve problems is directly related to whether or not the strengths of the four major learning-style categories are adequately represented among individual group members. He states that an accommodator's problem-solving strengths lie in initiating problem finding on the basis of a goal or model of how things should be and in executing solutions. The diverger's problem-solving strengths lie in identifying the multitude of possible problems and opportunities that exist in reality (by comparing model with reality and identifying differences). The assimilator excels in the abstract model building that is necessary to determine which problems are priorities and to create alternative solutions. The converger's strengths lie in the evaluation of solutions' likely consequences and therefore in solution selection (Kolb, 1984).

A person's awareness of his or her dominant learning style, used knowledgeably, can greatly accelerate the speed with which he or she acquires learning-to-learn skills and, as a correlative, the ease with which he or she accomplishes domain-specific learning.

Sylvia Downs (1987, pp. 7–17) of the University of Wales Institute of Science and Technology developed a program designed to help both young people and adults improve their learning skills. Later, the program was adapted for use in the workplace.

During the program's initial research project, a simple taxonomy was developed to separate things to be learned according to the methods that would be used to learn them. This resulted in a training tool with the acronym of *MUD*, which stands for learning in which a person has to *m*emorize (facts), needs to *u*nderstand (concepts), or needs to learn by *d*oing (physical skills). These categories quite neatly match two of the three categories of Bloom's taxonomy: cognitive and psychomotor.

During Downs's experiment, training groups were set up to explore which of the three ways of learning should be employed for a variety of tasks. The groups were provided with a number of techniques that they could use to learn different things (learning tasks) under each MUD category. This research revealed two factors important for improving how people learn how to learn: Trainers need to tell learners the learning skills/ methodologies they are expected to use, and to work well, learning skills must be practiced. (See Table 3 for a comparison of conventional training and training that develops participants' learning skills.)

The success of the original MUD research project, as demonstrated through examinations taken by people exposed to MUD learning techniques, led directly to a second research

Table 3. How Conventional and
Learning-to-Learn Training Approaches Diverge.

Conventional	*Developing Learning Skills*
Skills of learning are covert.	Skills of learning are made overt and discussed.
Concepts are explained by the trainer.	Concepts are developed by the learners.
Information is controlled by the trainer, with emphasis on convergent thinking.	Learning content is explored by both, with emphasis on divergent thinking.
The learner is receptive of information (passive).	Learner seeks information (active).
Mistakes are mostly avoided.	Mistakes in concepts are viewed as useful learning opportunities.
The trainer often poses questions and gives solutions.	The trainer poses problems and discusses the learner's solutions.
Measures and standards are primarily concerned with product.	Measures and standards are concerned with product and process.
The trainer checks and marks.	The learner can check and mark.
The concern is with what is learned, so product is all important.	The concern is with how and what is learned, so that product and process are both seen as important.
Individual differences are only seen in terms of success or failure.	Individual differences in learners are allowed for and explained through the teaching material.

Source: S. Downs, "Developing Learning Styles," in M. E. Cheren (ed.), *Learning Management: Emerging Directions for Learning to Learn in the Workplace.* (Columbus, Ohio: National Center for Research in Vocational Education, The Ohio State University, 1987.) Reprinted with permission.

project. This project addressed adults who were employed but needed training or retraining because of technological or organizational change, unemployed adults who needed training to enter new employment, and long-term unemployed adults who were to be given training that was not job-specific. In this project, a major result of MUD training was that group members began thinking in terms of the process of learning rather than just the product. In other words, the MUD approach gave them means for analyzing what they were to learn in terms of how they should go about learning it, and that provided a framework for the course.

Another outgrowth of this project was the Job Learning Analysis (JLA) for sytematically analyzing jobs' contents and associated learning needs. A British company that used the JLA found that the jobs it analyzed consisted primarily of exercising discretionary understanding but that training for the jobs consisted, to a large extent, of memorizing material. As a result of these findings, the company reorganized its training and introduced new training methods.

After the MUD research projects' findings were translated into training, they were pilot tested in two of the United Kingdom's top ten companies. One company used MUD techniques for successful retraining of its existing work force to operate a new computer-based factory that required totally different working methods and groupings. The other company embedded MUD techniques in its own subject-specific training, and eventually the ideas permeated the company and even spread to other organizations that came in contact with the learning techniques. Both companies "saw for themselves that developing learning skills changed the way people from the shop floor upwards behaved, how they went about learning new things, and how effective they were at it. The trainers saw both a new role and excitement in helping people to learn and in the energy that seemed to be released by the changes" (Downs, 1987, pp. 7–15).

The main point about this and most successful learning-to-learn training programs is that "if we give advice in a *generalized way,* without regard to the individual student, or the particular course he [she] is taking (or the demands of its assessment system), then it [is unlikely to] have a positive effect" (Gibbs, 1981, pp. 160–161).

What Constitutes Competency in Learning to Learn? What Constitutes Mastery?

Learning is usually differentiated from performance in that a person may acquire a particular knowledge, skill, or attitude, but the learning-to-learn skills that he or she uses may not be reflected in observable behavior. This is a problem in the measurement and evaluation of training programs. Frequently, training program plans for determining whether learning processes have been transferred are absent or inadequate. This transfer of learning-to-learn skills, along with the ability to learn in a meaningful, useful way, should be measured and considered as one of the major evaluative criteria when determining competency and mastery in all skill areas.

Research and development studies about learning how to learn have included efforts to identify the essential general proficiencies of a skilled learner. At a recent international conference, fifteen learning-to-learn experts identified competencies for learning that fell into three categories: cognitive, personal and understanding, and interpersonal (Smith, 1988).

According to Smith (1987, p. 45):

There seems to be a growing agreement that the keys to learning to learn more effectively are (1) increased understanding of self as learner; (2) increased capacity for reflection and self-monitoring of the process as one goes about the tasks and activities directed toward learning (such as when note taking, meeting with a mentor, studying, locating community resources); and (3) more realistic understanding of the nature of knowledge (such as its structure, assumptions, limitations, validation processes). A variety of methods can be employed to foster these competencies . . . by diagnosing learning style and feeding back the results to the individual; having people keep logs and journals as they learn; assigning retrospective reports after learning episodes have taken place; providing exercises to help people reflect on the purpose of the strategies they employ; conducting critiques to analyze the process dimension of such an activity group discussion; and making relevant theory inputs through lecture, assigned reading, and so forth.

Mastery of learning-to-learn skills should be measured according to a person's demonstration of increased ability to accrue additional responsibility and to advance to more responsible job areas through the learning of complex subject-specific material. On a continuum from competency to mastery, the move toward and designation of mastery should require proof of a person's knowledge about how individuals learn, demonstrated skills in particular strategies for learning, and ability to operate on a level of complex, interpersonal learning.

What Is an Example of a Successful Workplace Training Program in Learning to Learn?

Planters LifeSavers Company (PLC) is a division of RJR-Nabisco Corporation, a Fortune 500 company. It produces snack foods, including candies. PLC has six plants, although only the 800-employee Franklin Park, Illinois, plant currently offers the learning-to-learn program described below. The Franklin Park plant manufactures confections and is used regularly as a research and development facility.

PLC calls its learning-to-learn program Learning Management. The idea for the program arose several years ago when new equipment was being introduced in the Franklin Park plant. Formal employee training on how to use the equipment was impossible because the manufacturing systems were in the process of being designed. A job analysis could not be done since it was not yet known what job tasks would be necessary to operate the system. Because PLC could not use the traditional methods of teaching employees how to operate equipment, the company felt the need to teach generic learning-to-learn skills applicable across job areas in a constantly changing work environment. PLC believes that the future will hold more and more technological changes and that employees must be provided with learning tools for anticipating and successfully adapting to those changes.

In 1985, in order to see what effects the learning-to-learn concepts would have on employees, PLC began to include portions of the program in other training courses for hourly wage workers and supervisors. In late 1988, Learning Mangement was implemented as a separate course.

Employees attend the week-long course as part of their normal workday. The plant budget pays for the course (as it does for all training that takes place in the plant). The course is offered to targeted employees — those most directly involved with the new equipment. On average, ten to twelve people attend the course at a time. The highly interactive course includes both group and individual work and is offered approximately every three months or as needed. Eventually, the course may be offered at other PLC or RJR-Nabisco locations.

The strategic goal that the course addresses is for employees to be able to perform more different tasks across job areas as manual labor is eliminated and computerized equipment is put into place. Course evaluation includes interviews conducted with participants immediately after the workshop has ended and during a three-month period following completion. Production figures are reviewed to see whether any changes occur after employees have participated in the training. The most visible change that PLC has identified has been a reduction in downtime; it is too soon to tell what other changes may have taken place.

Several components of PLC's Learning Management course collectively serve to make participants aware of how they can get the most out of each new learning situation. The first step in the course is to determine and explore each participant's learning style so that he or she becomes aware of how he or she learns best and also learns to tolerate, even appreciate, the ways in which others learn. Also explored is how individuals learn through the experiential learning process. Kolb's four-step learning cycle model is presented, and participants learn how they use the four steps and discover that nearly everyone uses the four steps, although people may use them in different ways, starting at or emphasizing different ones.

Course participants are given the opportunity to reflect on events to analyze what happened (or is happening) and why. This activity is practiced in small groups that use various questions and techniques to analyze a situation or event. Employees then practice planning for learning — to plan how to learn something. To practice this, participants may take nonwork examples of learning tasks (such as learning to play golf well) and list the different ways they could learn to do each (such as read a book or watch a videotape by a nationally known professional golfer, get advice or lessons from a local pro, practice on their own, and so on) and list the strengths and limitations of each approach. The different approaches are then related to the work environment to determine each one's strengths and limitations in the workplace.

Employees then work in small groups to explore the strengths and limitations of collaborative learning. This activity is based on a teamwork concept, but the course goes beyond how groups learn to look at the way individuals learn. An activity that has been used for this part of the course is a desert survival activity. Participants may also practice group and individual problem-solving skills through activities such as the "stuck truck" exercise, in which team members must work together to resolve a problem on the basis of learning style insights. After all the groups have worked on a problem, participants contribute examples of on-the-job problems, and each group works to develop an action plan for solving one of them.

Next, participants are presented with practical strategies for learning from various media, including books, plays, lectures, videotapes, demonstrations, and experiments. Participants then practice work-related strategies such as note taking and interviewing.

Throughout the course, participants gain experience in the importance of the climate and environment for learning (for example, the room where learning is to take place should have adequate lighting and a comfortable place to sit or recline) and of preparedness to learn (for example, getting enough sleep and having the necessary materials at hand).

During the course, each participant receives individual attention to identify his or her specific developmental needs. This puts the learning-to-learn course into a functional context by addressing the professional and skill development needs of each participant. A personal needs assessment is conducted to determine the extent to which participants have moved toward the goals they set out to accomplish, and periodic individual performance checks are included as an essential part of evaluation (David Matuszak, telephone interview, Sept. 1988).

What Should Be Included in a Generic Workplace Learning-to-Learn Curriculum?

Several different approaches to providing workplace training in learning-to-learn skills are described below.

Training for Self-Directed Learning. The objectives of training for self-directed learning are to encourage trainee awareness of the self as a learner; to establish that the identification and analysis of learning processes can be interesting and productive; to introduce the learning-style concept and assist participants in gaining a perspective on their own learning styles; to prepare participants to carry out and analyze a personal learning project; to provide information useful to participants in conducting their personal learning projects and in meaningfully analyzing them; to increase skill in using resource people on a one-to-one basis; to extract relevant process learning from the project that each person has conducted; and to synthesize what has been learned about self-directed learning and encourage postworkshop application of training (Smith, 1982, pp. 145–149).

Training for Collaborative Learning. The goals of training for collaborative learning are improved membership skills and teamwork development. Training involves helping people to understand the conditions under which adults learn best in face-to-face groups, helping people learn how to learn with and from one another while using other resources as needed, and fostering the development of diagnostic skills and the ability to distinguish content from process (Smith, 1982, p. 152).

Training Through Educational Institutions. Helping participants get the most from programs and resources found outside the employer institution is the goal of training through educational institutions. Relevant courses help participants gain an understanding of thinking processes, an understanding and appreciation of nonlinear and intuitive thinking and problem solving, and the ability to assume more authority for their own learning. Experience and research show that six types of training exercises provide excellent training for improving learning-to-learn skills: learning, reading, taking notes, writing, taking exams, and organizing oneself (Smith, 1982, pp. 160–161).

Exhibit 1 provides a content guideline for skills that need to be at the heart of a learning-to-learn curriculum and is adapted from Smith, 1988, pp. 82–83. The subject-specific areas, formal and informal learning strategies, and learning styles would be integrated throughout the training process and overtly identified for the training participant where the trainer believes it is appropriate.

Exhibit 1. Learning-to-Learn Proficiencies:
What You Should Know in Order to Learn.

What are the objectives of this training?
–To understand the nature of knowledge
–To be able to organize learning activities
–To develop the critical skills of evaluation
–To understand how to apply appropriate thinking (convergent, divergent, critical, and intuitive)
–To understand the importance of and be able to do self-assessment and needs assessment

What are cognitive learning-to-learn skills?
–Understanding the nature of knowledge
–Organizing learning activities
–Learning critical evaluation skills
–Thinking convergently, divergently, critically, and intuitively
–Relating and recalling information
–Relating and organizing information
–Developing basic skills (reading, writing, computing)
–Problem solving
–Understanding the feasibility and usefulness of learning to learn or learning-process consciousness
–Transferring learning strategies
–Communicating, including active listening and viewing
–Developing knowledge about resource availability and assessment
–Organizing learning/development activities
–Understanding cognitively the difference between learning and being taught

What are personal understanding learning-to-learn skills?
–Understanding the self as learner in terms of
   –preferred styles and adaptations
   –personal resources inventory (assessment)
   –personal awareness and monitoring

**Exhibit 1. Learning-to-Learn Proficiencies:
What You Should Know in Order to Learn, Cont'd.**

–Conducting self-assessment and needs assessment in terms of
  –sense of direction
  –sense of purpose
  –life planning
  –ability to create/generate resources
–Building confidence, persistence, openness, and flexibility

What are interpersonal learning-to-learn skills?
–Accessing and evaluating resources
–Giving and receiving feedback by
  –seeking information nondefensively
  –seeking important feedback
  –analyzing feedback
  –giving feedback when needed
–Developing strategies for performing contextual analysis
–Developing strategies for using collaborative inquiry
–Understanding how to find and use resources, including expert sources,
  peer support, and media

Source: Adapted from Smith, 1988.

PART 3

Basic Competency Skills: Reading, Writing, and Computation

An old song reminisces about learning the three R's in youthful school days. But although some people gain adequate reading, writing, and computation skills through schooling, an alarming number of people do not.

As Gorman (1988) reports in *Time* magazine, "one . . . of . . . four teenagers drops out of high school, and of those who graduate, one . . . of . . . four has the equivalent of an eighth-grade education" (pp. 49–55). In addition, the United States has a new wave of immigrants, some of whom have little or no schooling and some of whom are educated but not proficient in English. Moreover, a spreading labor shortage means that employers can no longer pick and choose to avoid hiring people lacking academic preparation in the competence skills of reading, writing, and computation.

Even when a person has met America's high school or college-level standards of literacy and numeracy, the work environment often calls for higher, more complex and integrated application of these related skills. For example, in the academic world, students nearly always read well-written prose and poetry (although, admittedly, much literature is dated in style). However, on-the-job reading often requires workers to decipher "explanatory" writing that is *not* clear, to discriminate between important and trivial messages, to respond rapidly to messages, and to learn and develop specialized vocabularies. In schools, some teachers still require students to write compositions with

67

a minimum word count but fail to explain that tedious verbiage is not the goal. At work, Benjamin Franklin's dictum "time is money" holds sway. Thus, in proportion to the message that must be conveyed, conciseness is valued almost as much as clarity.

In traditional computation classes, the emphasis is on students' ability to find the answers to individual problems or formulas. Closer to the challenges of the working world are the much-maligned computational word problems that require students to read words and numbers, determine what parts of the information presented are pertinent (perhaps, by taking notes and rearranging data), and what formula(s) applies to the situation described *before* they perform any mathematical operations.

Reading, writing, and computation skills have long been viewed as academic basics, but only recently have they been seen as employment essentials. Advancing technology demands that modern workers have these skills—and at higher levels. Machines are increasingly taking on the tasks once accomplished by human muscle power and manual dexterity, and they are also performing the tasks that demand lower-level application of reading, writing, and computation skills. For example, in department stores, factories, and warehouses, machines "read" bar codes of inventory descriptions and prices, then "write" reports showing various computations (such as sales totals, variance between projected and actual sales, and remaining inventory). Technology's influence is pervasive. Where facsimile machines are used, for example, the cost of preparing, transmitting, and receiving facsimile messages means that concise writing is more important than ever. In some fast-food restaurants, where workers until recently needed little reading skill (thanks to "smart" cash registers with keys that depict menu selections), fascimile machines are being installed to receive written carry-out orders for office groups.

Throughout the workplace, people at all levels are being required to develop their command of the interrelated competence skills of reading, writing, and computation.

CHAPTER 4

Reading for the New Workplace

We must recognize that reading involves as wide a range
of different types of texts as there are types of food. And to
imply . . . that reading is a single skill suited to all types of
texts does not do justice to the range of reading types.

Beach and Appleman
Becoming Readers in a Complex Society

What Is Reading?

Although applications of reading skills vary, in the act
of reading, a person acquires information from printed or written
symbols. Reading comprehension — understanding — primarily
depends on a reader's ability to make sense of printed or written material by fitting its information into the context of what
he or she already knows. Without interaction between the knowledge stored in a reader's memory and the new information presented by a printed page, computer screen, or sign, words will
not impart meaning.

Reading is a highly complex process comprising an integrated group of physical and mental activities. As defined in
How to Teach Reading (Harris and Sipay, 1979, p. 27), "Reading
is the attaining of meaning as a result of interplay between
perceptions of graphic symbols that represent language, and
the memory traces of the reader's past verbal and nonverbal
experiences."

For a sighted person, the reading process begins when the eyes focus on printed symbols (such as letters), which represent language sounds, and on the background space around them. The symbol patterns are reflected onto the retinas, creating chemical changes that trigger electrochemical impulses in the fibers of the optic nerves. When these impulses reach the brain, they are compared with memory traces of similar patterns. If the person recognizes the perceived symbol patterns, he or she assigns meaning to them. The reading process involves a rapid series of perceptions as the eyes move in quick, sideways sweeps alternating with pauses. Patterns, in the form of letters, are reflected onto the retinas only during the pauses, when the eyes are motionless. Normally, during each pause, a reader's span of vision encompasses a combination of fifteen letters and spaces — approximately three words; on average, four pauses occur as the eyes move across a line of print on a page (Spache, 1963; Massaro, 1984). A person who is blind may perceive language's symbolic patterns (such as the raised dot patterns of braille) through touch.

Reading comprehension takes place when, from a series of sequential pattern perceptions, a reader is able to recreate a writer's ideas. Nonetheless, reading is a constructive process in which a reader builds personal meaning through interpretation of what a writer meant to communicate. Only by retrieving previously acquired knowledge of language — spelling patterns, significance of word order, word meanings, and so on — as well as knowledge related to the topic written about, can a competent reader understand and interact with the ideas presented.

What Theories Support Current Training in Reading?

Literacy — the ability to read — changes significantly depending on its situational context. In schools where reading skills are being taught formally, literacy standards are tied closely to grade levels. For example, students in junior and senior high school grades are considered literate if they are proficient in the basic reading skills taught in lower grades. Outside the academic environment, literacy is more difficult to define because besides being dependent on context, literacy requirements change over time. Two hundred years ago people were deemed literate if they could sign their names, but societal demand for documented knowledge increased. Consequently, the quantity of printed and written material increased, and standards for measuring literacy were raised (Venezky, 1987).

Performance levels and task criteria required for useful functioning in one area of society may not be appropriate when applied to other areas. For example, the functional reading knowledge and skills that a lawyer needs to discern the implications of legal statutes are different from those required of an engineer charged with assessing the validity of technical reports replete with diagrams. Although the lawyer and engineer may use the same problem-solving strategies for finding main ideas, they will need to call on different vocabularies of words and symbols.

In contrast, a worker in a partially automated factory may spend much less of the workday reading but may need to read and respond quickly and properly to succinct computer-generated directions and safety warnings. The factory worker, then, needs yet a different vocabulary and must be prepared for rapid comprehension of work-related messages.

Contemporary concern with setting literacy standards traces back to World War II when the U.S. military's immediate need for recruits led to the use of the selective service, or draft. Many recruits proved educationally underqualified for performing the training and defense tasks required of them. To identify which recruits would need additional literacy training to become functional in military-specific tasks, the military estimated the average readability (by grade level) of job manuals and materials, and compared the results with incoming recruits' reading test scores. The military coined the term *functionally illiterate* to describe recruits who were unable to read at a fifth grade entry level (5.0 grade equivalency). Such recruits were enrolled in an intensive remedial training program geared to helping them function at the minimum reading level considered necessary for satisfactory performance of their military job tasks.

From this first attempt to define functional literacy or

illiteracy by set standards, an entire vocabulary of comparative, associated terms has grown. These terms address readers'
ability or inability to achieve standards that measure reading
performance. The following are among the most frequently
used terms:

- *Nonliterate:* unable to read a word
- *Marginally literate:* able to decode, but with only minimal
  comprehension skills
- *Intermediate literate:* able to read at a sixth to eighth grade level,
  with some effort
- *Aliterate:* able to read, but regularly choosing not to read
- *Survival literacy:* ability to read labels, menus, bus schedules,
  and the like
- *Cultural literacy:* ability to identify the literary ideas that have
  passed down from generation to generation, shaping our
  culture
- *Civic literacy:* ability to take an active, knowledgeable role
  as a citizen
- *Job/occupational literacy:* ability to perform the job-related reading and writing tasks demanded in the workplace

Since World War II, government agencies and researchers
have continued to try to link definitions of literacy to grade level
performance, with standards ranging from the fourth to twelfth
grade levels (Harmon, 1987a). The problem with this approach
is that it does not account for the wide range of individual differences in skill achievement within any actual grade level (Kirsch
and Guthrie, 1977–1978). For example, tenth grade students
may have reading ability test scores of grade level equivalents
of from 3.2 to 12.9 or anything in between.

In the mid-1970s, a study that received much media attention redefined adult literacy standards in terms of performance
on a series of tasks called *adult performance levels* (Northcutt, 1975).
Although this study's finding of serious, widespread illiteracy
remains highly controversial, its underlying theory of using task-
performance criteria for determining literacy has proved valid.
In the early 1980s, using this concept and a refined list of performance tasks, the National Assessment of Education completed

two studies that estimated levels of literacy for young adults aged seventeen to twenty-five (Applebee, Langer, and Mullis, 1985; Kirsch and Jungeblut, 1986). Simulated job tasks were assembled and ranked from easy to difficult for three aspects of literacy: *prose literacy,* the ability to understand and use information from texts; *document literacy,* the ability to locate information in forms, maps, tables, charts, indexes, and so on; and *quantitative literacy,* the ability to apply arithmetical operations to problems embedded in printed materials.

From the results of this study, researchers categorized literacy achievement by ranking performance tasks according to five levels: rudimentary, basic, intermediate, adept, and advanced. Although these categorical levels may be compared to ranges of grade level attainment for populations with similar abilities, the levels are not actual measures of grade level equivalency. Rather, these categories and scaled performance tasks bring a more precise tool to the establishment of literacy standards because they are based on the complex information-processing skills and strategies people must use to perform literacy tasks successfully in functional contexts. The results of these efforts further support the concept that "literacy depends on the context of the situation, not on [a] specific achievement level" (Guthrie, 1983).

How Is Reading Taught in the Schools?

The reading skills that workers learn in schools often do not meet the needs of routine on-the-job reading requirements. Even so, academically acquired skills are fundamental and useful. Workplace literacy training needs to build on whatever skills workers have been able to master during their school careers. For that reason, it is important to understand how reading is taught in elementary and secondary schools.

Formal reading instruction in schools may be divided into two categories. The first, *learning to read,* deals with developmental reading skills and usually begins when a child first enters school and continues through the end of third grade. The second, *reading to learn,* emphasizes functional reading skills to enhance comprehension and, as a rule, is offered from fourth grade through the end of junior high school.

Instruction in learning to read focuses on the mastery of translating printed symbols into the speech sounds they represent. Students are taught an awareness of symbol-sound correlations and how the sound representations of letters are blended together to form units that convey meaning—words. Repeated exposure to frequently encountered letter combinations helps students establish them in long-term memory for quick recall. In this phase of learning to read, which is called *decoding,* students consciously process printed symbols through the medium of speech; the pronunciation of words gives access to their meanings. Beginning readers speak words aloud as they read because their attention, out of necessity, is focused on the translating/decoding process rather than on the content of a writer's ideas. At this stage, the act of reading is slow and laborious, with students often able to progress through material only one word at a time.

Students in this stage of learning need to be instructed individually or in small groups and need to receive immediate feedback on their efforts. Over several school years, teachers and instructional materials methodically present increasingly complex letter patterns and additional vocabulary words appearing in otherwise familiar content. Through frequent, repeated exposure to commonplace patterns and words, students may enter them into long-term memory. With sufficient practice, beginning readers usually are able to recognize printed symbol patterns more quickly and thus decrease the time they require to decode. Once the techniques for blending sounds and for recognizing familiar letter patterns and word meanings have been presented, speeding up the decoding process to a rate at which its use is automatic becomes the instructional goal of learning to read (Anderson, Hiebert, Scott, and Wilkinson, 1985).

To accommodate learners' various learning styles, educators have developed many methods for teaching learning to read. Some school programs stress recognition of the symbol-sound relationship (phonics, linquistics, special alphabets). Others highlight the recognition of meaningful units (language experience, sight-word approaches). Still others place primary importance on the sequence in which decoding skills are presented (diagnostic-prescriptive basal series). No one method appears to be effective for all students. Any single approach or any combination of approaches may be used in a given elementary school. Most schools adopt basal reading programs as the core of their reading curriculum. These programs are based on a selected series of reading books containing short stories and on companion workbooks, all written at graduated levels of difficulty. Basal series are used in 75 to 90 percent of U.S. elementary classrooms because they present detailed, easy-to-follow scripts for teachers—eliminating the need for extensive teacher training while promoting somewhat uniform delivery of instruction throughout a school system—and because most basal series are reasonably comprehensive in skill coverage (Anderson, Hiebert, Scott, and Wilkinson, 1985). Sometimes computer-assisted instruction supplements the primary instructional program by giving students more individual instruction and practice time for particular skills.

Only a small percentage of today's young adults have not mastered learning-to-read skills. In *The Reading Report Card* (Applebee, Langer, and Mullis, 1985), the National Assessment of Educational Progress (NAEP) published findings that indicated that only 6 percent of the seventeen-year-olds studied read below the fourth grade level, and only 1 to 2 percent of those could be categorized as barely able to decode a single word.

When decoding skills become automatic for students and their reading speed increases, they pay closer attention to reading content. At this stage, the instructional focus shifts from learning to read to reading to learn. For most students, this transition occurs around the beginning of the fourth grade and, in American school systems, coincides with the introduction of subject-specific textbooks and class periods into the curriculum.

From that point onward, students become increasingly responsible for acquiring new knowledge from direct classroom instruction and from what they read, just as they will later be responsible in the context of work-related situations. To facilitate students' gathering of facts from print, teachers present specific reading strategies for identifying details, finding the main idea, drawing conclusions, recognizing cause and effect, determining the meanings of unknown words in context, and so on. Direct instruction in these reading-to-learn skills for improved comprehension usually continues through the middle school years. Typically, when students reach junior and senior high school, reading improvement strategies are taught infrequently and incidentally within the context of content-specific assignments for classes in literature, science, history, and so on. Higher-level thinking processes (such as predicting outcomes, comparing and contrasting, problem solving, and monitoring thinking strategies) have only recently been introduced into regular reading-to-learn curricula (Baker and Brown, 1984; Jones, 1986). Historically, these skills have been reserved as final steps in reading instruction to be taught only to high-achieving students thought to be capable of using, or needing to use, them.

Traditionally, students' progress in mastering learning-to-read and reading-to-learn skills is assessed by both periodic classroom tests and standardized tests. Standardized tests are assessment instruments for which performance standards have been established on the basis of the performance of representative sample populations. To make students' standardized test scores easier to understand, results usually are converted from raw scores into grade equivalents. Grade equivalents derive from median scores of the sample populations for several school grades. A student may be designated as reading "above grade level," "below grade level," or "on grade level." If a student's reading skill rates one or more years below grade level, he or she may be taken out of the "regular" classroom and sent to special reading classes for part or all of the school day.

Normally, when adults enroll in basic education reading programs, they are tested to determine the grade level of their reading proficiency. People who perform at the fourth grade level or below are assigned exercises to improve their learning-to-read (decoding) skills, schoolroom fashion. People who demonstrate reading abilities at the fifth grade level or above usually work on general vocabulary and discrete reading-to-learn (comprehension) skills, such as finding the main idea or recognizing an author's point of view. In most programs, these skills are taught in isolation, without contextual application.

How Should Reading Be Taught in the Workplace?

Adult learners who participate in workplace literacy programs have not achieved job-reading success despite their years of exposure to traditional reading instruction for general skills development. Clearly, a different approach is needed.

Developing a job-literacy training program that is contextually functional ensures that instruction will be meaningful to employees in terms of their prior knowledge. When instruction encourages adult learners to attach new information to "mental hooks" derived from their work environment and experience, it helps them incorporate new knowledge into old (Shoemaker, 1967; Fingeret, 1984; Farr, Carey, and Tone, 1985; Valentine, 1985). In the workplace, then, literacy should be taught through an interactive approach to learning, stressing a top-down model of instruction that uses the learner's job knowledge to construct meaning, while also allowing for bottom-up development of specific skills as needed.

The primary goal of a workplace reading program should be to increase workers' ability to perform job-reading tasks, thereby improving their job performance and enhancing their employment qualification skills, potential for retention and promotion, and self-esteem. Before employees enroll in a program, it is important to inform them of its goals, who its participants will be, what content it will cover, and what a typical instructional session will be like. This preview helps prevent discrepancy between students' expectations and actual experiences, which is a major cause of program dropout for adult learners (Darkenwald and Gavin, 1987). It is also important that employees view the program goals as relevant to their jobs, in keeping with employer priorities, and attainable within a reasonably brief period of instructional time. If these considerations are dealt with, the main barriers to program participation are eliminated (Darkenwald and Valentine, 1985).

Teaching job-specific reading competencies with actual job-reading materials helps workers see that the purpose of instruction is their achievement of job proficiency. They may even experience a direct transfer of the reading skills they learn to their job performance (Sticht, 1975b). And where workers have used job-specific materials to improve reading skills, the effects of instruction proved less susceptible to attrition over time (Sticht, 1982).

The first step in developing such a reading program is to perform a modified task analysis of on-the-job reading to provide the basis for curriculum design. An analyst should examine job-reading tasks and materials to identify the reading processes necessary for successful workplace performance. Analysis of on-the-job reading is done at the task level because, by definition, a task is the lowest level of job behavior that describes the performance of a meaningful function. After job tasks have been prioritized according to level of difficulty, the analyst should identify the cognitive reading processes each employs and the concepts workers need to know to perform each process (Davies, 1973; Gagne and Briggs, 1979). A helpful strategy for identifying required job-reading processes is self-questioning. The analyst should ask, "What do I think about and do to get the necessary information as I read these job materials?" The answers will lead to awareness of the mental processes involved in successful performance of job-reading tasks. Therefore, the answers will guide development of instructional strategies to show employees how to identify and implement the processes in their job-related reading (Philippi, 1988).

Good curriculum design for teaching reading is competency based or performance based. This means that the design includes clearly defined learning objectives for each reading process to be taught and corresponding instructional activities leading to measurable mastery of those objectives. Mastery of objectives should be measured by a postinstruction test of performance.

In job-literacy programs, the main audience should be that majority of workers who are intermediate literates with fourth to eighth grade literacy equivalency. But curriculum materials should also make instructional provisions for helping severely disabled readers who have yet to master fundamental decoding skills. Overall, curriculum materials should concentrate on teaching reading-to-do and reading-to-learn processes.

(For a list of job-reading processes and competencies, see "What Should Be Included in a Generic Workplace Reading Curriculum?" later in this chapter.)

Printed job-reading materials should be gathered and matched with the crucial reading processes the analyst has identified. Sample passages from the materials may be used intact, modified, or simulated (for instance, by printing a message that might appear on a computer screen or by drafting a teaching document that incorporates key phrases from several actual work documents). If a job task requires a combination of reading processes, only one reading process should be targeted for instruction with any given passage.

Vocabulary instruction may be treated as an integral part of instruction for each reading process or as a separate instructional component. Research supports both approaches (Eysenck, 1977; Gipe, 1978; Smith, 1980; Carnine, Kameenui, and Coyle, 1984; Nagy, Herman, and Anderson, 1985). The crucial point is that vocabulary selected for instruction should be functional—should be words that often appear in job materials—because the sole purpose for vocabulary instruction in a job-literacy program is to facilitate trainees' understanding of job-reading materials.

Reading instruction may be delivered by a current in-house training staff, by outside educational providers (such as consultants, community colleges, or adult basic education programs), or by specially hired teachers who have had pretraining in job materials. Staff training professionals have the advantage of familiarity with job-reading tasks and materials but may not have the necessary educational background to teach reading. Professional educators from outside the organization should be capable of presenting well-designed instruction effectively, but they may lack depth of knowledge about job-reading tasks and materials. Therefore, whatever choice of instructors an organization makes, the instructors must have some degree of pretraining and preparation if they are to provide competent, effective curriculum delivery. Moreover, if program design includes peer tutoring or computer-assisted instruction (CAI), caution should be exercised to ensure that these program components are not used exclusively and do not supplant direct instruction and modeling of thinking procedures by qualified instructors using contextual job-reading materials.

What Are the Essential Elements of Training in Reading?

Traditionally, remedial reading instruction for adult learners has addressed the nonreader or marginal literate, and has been related to a job only to the extent that it thematically explores occupational career possibilities. The theory has been that by raising the reading grade levels of adult learners, they would improve their job skills performance, thereby gaining opportunities for employment and promotion. For many years, teachers of basic skills have provided general reading instruction for low-achieving employees, many of whom were enrolled in community adult education programs or vocational/industrial training. Instruction in these institutional settings aims to improve students' academic reading performance, as measured by standardized tests, and to help students in their preparation for the General Education Development Test (GED), popularly referred to as a test of high school equivalency. In fact, improving adult students' general reading ability builds their self-confidence and enables them to function better in a literate society—but it does not necessarily improve their performance of on-the-job reading tasks. General improvement in reading skills does not transfer automatically to reading in the workplace, where among other considerations, reading material usually is more specialized and less structured than in traditional texts.

Traditional classroom reading instruction is designed to teach discrete reading skills in isolation for the purposes of increasing students' ability to follow directions, to internalize content for future recall (Diehl and Mikulecky, 1980; Mikulecky, 1982b; Mikulecky and Ehlinger, 1986; Sticht, Fox, Hauke, and Zapf, 1977), and to respond correctly to general vocabulary and comprehension questions on standardized tests.

Workplace basic skills training should be based on accomplishment of real-world performance standards, however.

Achievement of job literacy should be measured in terms of workers' ability to perform actual or simulated job-specific, contextually functional reading tasks, not in terms of their ability to meet a grade level equivalency standard as measured on generic materials or standardized tests. Studies of occupational literacy, with both civilian and military populations, have demonstrated that job-reading tasks differ significantly from academic-reading tasks. For this reason, even students who master basic reading skills in an academic setting are seldom prepared for the ways in which they will need to use those skills in the workplace. On the job, workers spend an average of one and a half to two hours per workday reading forms, graphs, charts, schematics, manuals, and computer terminals (Diehl, 1980; Mikulecky, Shanklin, and Caverly, 1979; Philippi, 1986–1987; Rush, Moe, and Storlie, 1986; Sharon, 1973–1974; Sticht, 1975b). On-the-job reading emphasizes locating information for immediate use and using inferential processes for problem solving. Job-reading tasks regularly require workers to be proficient in setting purposes, self-questioning, summarizing information, and monitoring comprehension as they read. Researchers have found that the ability to use these higher-level reading processes correlates with superior job performance (Mikulecky and Ehlinger, 1986; Mikulecky and Winchester, 1983).

Because job-reading tasks are so different from academic-reading tasks, specific, specially designed instructional programs are needed to improve adult learners' job-related reading performance. Curriculum materials developed for these programs should center on teaching and providing practice in reading processes that fall into two functional categories commonly referred to as *reading to do* and *reading to learn.* Job-reading processes classified as reading to do involve strategies for locating information for immediate use from printed materials readily available for reference on the job. Reading-to-do processes require only the use of short-term memory and limited information processing. On the other hand, reading-to-learn processes involve using job-reading information to make job decisions, problem solve, or troubleshoot. Thus reading to learn requires input to and retrieval of job information in long-term memory and more complex knowledge processing (Diehl and Mikulecky, 1980; Sticht, 1975b).

Job-literacy training that is contextually functional helps ensure that instruction is meaningful to employees striving to achieve job proficiency. This motivates them for successful learning (Shoemaker, 1967; Sticht and Hooke, 1982) and also, according to fifteen years' research of effective adult education programs, seems to play a significant role in lowering attrition rates of basic skills training programs (Darkenwald, 1975, 1981, 1986; Darkenwald and Anderson, 1979; Darkenwald and Gavin, 1987; Darkenwald and Merriam, 1982; Darkenwald and Valentine, 1985). These benefits occur because workers see the relevance of the material to their present job tasks; as they learn, they recognize that these are reading tasks they actually will be — indeed, may already have been — asked to perform.

In addition to using contextual learning as a theoretical base for job-related literacy training, the curriculum's instructional design should be built on the theory of information processing. In practice, this means that for each job-reading process in the program, instruction should concentrate on showing workers how they can perform the process — on their learning how to learn (Laster, 1985). Lessons should be structured so that the instructor models each process, using direct instruction to introduce a lesson. Modeling begins with a demonstration in which the instructor "thinks aloud" through each step of a process. Then, as trainees master individual steps, they incrementally assume responsibility for performing the entire process. By dividing each process into procedural steps and by providing direct, explicit instruction in thinking strategies, instructors encourage trainees to develop self-questioning and mental-activity monitoring patterns that help them become independent learners who are able to recognize and correct their own processing errors.

What Constitutes Competency in Reading?
What Constitutes Mastery?

As adult learners progress in a job-reading program, their mastery should be measured in terms of competency achieved in job-reading processes. Competency-based evaluation may take the form of instructor evaluation or paper-and-pencil exercises. In performance-oriented, competency-based instructional programs, learners are commonly regarded as having achieved mastery if they can demonstrate correct performance of a particular skill or process 75 to 80 percent of the time. The absence of grade level designations and the direct measurement of achievement on actual job-reading tasks helps preserve adult learners' self-esteem and motivates them for continued progress (Philippi, 1988).

What Are Examples of Successful Workplace Training Programs in Reading?

Surveys conducted by the National Center for Research in Vocational Education (NCRVE) (Hull, Fields, and Sechler, 1986) and by the Business Council for Effective Literacy (BCEL) (1987) reveal the existence of a growing number of ongoing basic-skills training programs designed to improve workers' reading skills. These programs vary in size, goals, content, cost, implementation practices, and funding structures, depending on who sponsors them. Because the purposes for establishing reading improvement programs are so diverse, it is virtually impossible to cite general examples of best practices. Many programs exhibit exemplary instructional strategies developed to achieve their specific desired outcomes; but because of that specificity, no single program can serve as a prototype for other organizations wishing to develop job-reading programs.

Nevertheless, there are certain trends in skills training and program similarities worth noting. The NCRVE study describes four types of industry-based programs:

1. *Indirect/individual:* in which a company offers tuition reimbursement incentives to employees who participate in general education improvement programs on an individual basis.
2. *Indirect/group:* in which a company sponsors general educational development programs for groups of employees who request them.
3. *Direct/individual:* in which a company provides individual employees with the skills training needed to perform current

jobs or to retain or advance to higher positions for which
the employees are otherwise qualified (by seniority, for
instance).

4. *Direct/group:* in which a company offers prerequisite skill
    development for targeted employee groups to prepare them
    for more advanced courses related to upcoming job changes
    demanded by technological advances.

Throughout business and industry, there is a dramatic
increase in the provision of the fourth category of training because it directly affects the long-term economic survival of both
employers and employees. The NCRVE study also found that
in order for workers to keep abreast of spreading and changing
on-the-job technology, employer-based basic skills training must
provide workers with the means for developing more and higher-
level cognitive (thinking/reasoning) and information-processing
skills. These findings point to mounting pressure on employer-
based trainers to design effective job-reading programs or to
locate competent educational providers of contextually structured basic skills instruction.

The BCEL report highlights businesses — large and small,
independently and in collaboration with unions — that have already created exemplary basic-skills training programs for their
employees.

Control Data. Control Data is a Minnesota-based computer services and manufacturing company. Its training program began with the creation of a planning team that included
representatives from the company's personnel management and
training and development departments, as well as outside consultants who were literacy specialists. The team oversaw the
design and implementation of a formal needs assessment by
means of surveys, questionnaires, and employee interviews. The
planning team developed program goals on the basis of the needs
assessment's findings and formulated general plans for a pilot
program. Then basic-skills training providers were recruited to
staff a pilot program and develop its curriculum. These providers designed instruction to remediate employees in the basic

skills that the needs assessment found necessary for on-the-job functioning. Employees targeted for program participation were recruited through personal encouragement from their managers; management support at all levels was a key factor in the successful program implementation. To offer participants additional support, an employee advocate/counselor was added to the program staff. Eventually, program evaluation and cost analysis demonstrated that participants' skills improvement and the subsequent positive impact on their job performance had been accomplished at less cost than that for a typical in-house course. The original program design was fine-tuned using information gathered through experience with the pilot program and its evaluation. Using the refined design, Control Data established a comprehensive, long-term job-literacy program for employees.

Companies Described in a Report to the Indiana State Board of Vocational and Technical Education. A report sponsored by the Indiana State Board of Vocational and Technical Education describes several public- and private-sector training programs (Mikulecky and Drew, 1987–1988). For example, one program trained new word processors, and another retrained wastewater plant employees. Both programs used contextually job-specific materials for providing successful basic skills training. Job simulation was the main training device for the word processors, who worked toward performance standards matching those found on the job. The retraining of wastewater plant workers superimposed basic educational strategies onto existing job materials by breaking learning into manageable tasks that helped trainees master new job-related technical vocabulary and concepts. Both programs were collaborative efforts between industrial and educational specialists. The successful transfer of basic skills training to the job environment is attributed, in both instances, to the increased time spent on task, which was provided by using the job context as a vehicle for basic skills training.

The U.S. Military. As mentioned earlier, the U.S. military pioneered in broad-scale literacy testing and in the setting of job-literacy standards. The military services have long incorporated literacy programs in their job training. Over the past fifty years, numerous exemplary job-related literacy training programs have come from a host of military-sponsored, extensively funded research and development projects. In 1971, the U.S. Army sponsored research that led to the development of the landmark Functional Literacy (FLIT) program (Sticht, 1975b). Based on a psycholinguistic, information-processing model, the curriculum was designed to enable soldiers to use their job-reading materials effectively. In this context, the term *psycholinguistic* (Goodman, 1968) relates to fundamental psychological processes (perception and cognition) as well as to language processes (phonology, grammar, and semantics).

Seven military occupations were analyzed to determine their types of job-reading tasks and the readability (grade) levels of their job materials. Then instructional materials were created for each occupation. Exercises based on actual job-reading materials trained participants in reading-to-do skills for carrying out the tasks of locating information in manuals, following directions, and completing job forms. Reading-to-learn skills development helped trainees master and remember the information (knowledge base) they would need on the job. Program evaluation showed that soldiers' job reading scores increased an average of two and a half grade levels after 120 hours of instruction, with 80 percent of the gain retained for longer than three and a half months (Sticht, 1975a).

In the following decade, the U.S. Navy researched and developed a series of programs derived from the FLIT prototype (Sticht and others, 1986). The latest of these to date, the Experimental Functional Skills Program in Reading (XFSP/Read) focuses on teaching reading-to-learn processes that facilitate input and retrieval of job knowledge from long-term memory, but also provides instruction in reading-to-do activities. Both categories are taught with a specially constructed navy job knowledge base, as well as actual job materials. Materials in the knowledge base contain information about naval history, conduct, shipboard organization, safety, and so forth. Research done prior to curriculum development indicated that having this knowledge enhances trainees' performance of job-reading tasks and increases their scores on promotion tests (Sticht, Fox, Hauke, and Zapf,

1976). Job-literacy training becomes more efficient when job knowledge and job-reading tasks are taught simultaneously. Sailors participating in XFSP/Read can improve their job performance and promotion potential quickly because contextual (background) knowledge needed for comprehension of on-the-job reading has been entered into their long-term memories (Craik and Lockhart, 1972; Anderson, Pichert, and Shirey, 1979; Mayer, 1984). Program evaluation shows sailors' average gains of 20 percent on separate posttests of job knowledge and job-reading tasks, and an average gain of one grade level on the Gates MacGintie General Reading Test after thirty to forty hours of instruction with XFSP/Read materials (Sticht and others, 1986).

Another successful job-literacy effort that evolved from the FLIT program is the army's Basic Skills Education Program in Reading (BSEP), currently in use throughout Europe, the Far East, and Panama (Philippi, 1986–1987). It uses the results of a lengthy task analysis begun for the army in 1978 to study ninety-five military occupations. The BSEP reading program tailors instruction to the job-reading tasks common to the forty most populous military occupations overseas. More than 250 excerpts from field manuals, military forms, and training materials for those occupations were compiled into one text, along with selected articles (about the soldier as citizen, teamwork, and leadership) from military publications. By integrating knowledge of military culture and interpersonal skills with job information, the text functions as a data base. It is used in combination with exercise modules and mastery tests to teach job-specific reading-to-do and reading-to-learn tasks. Before the curriculum was developed, job-reading materials were also studied to determine how traditional, generic reading processes (such as finding the main idea, using context clues, and making inferences) are specifically used in reading military materials. The program meets the job-literacy training needs of a wide population because it provides instruction in reading processes common to many military occupations.

The job-reading materials used in BSEP are at grade levels ranging from grade 10 to grade 14.5. They are not simplified for program use because if they were, they would no longer qualify as actual job reading. Soldiers who enter the program with reading abilities at an average grade level of 8.7 are able to master reading skills using these higher-level job materials because prior job knowledge facilitates their comprehension (Sticht, 1982). Since ungraded job materials are the basis of instruction, gains are measured in percentage of job-reading process mastery rather than grade level. Soldiers who perform at levels of less than 75 percent mastery on standardized criterion-referenced job-literacy tests participate in the BSEP reading program. After sixty hours of instruction, posttest scores showed an average 36 percent gain in job-specific reading skills for these soldiers. In addition, attrition rates were 31 percent lower and reenlistment rates were 27 percent higher for BSEP participants (Harmon, 1987a). The army attributes this to the positive influence of job-literacy training on soldiers' job retention and promotion potential. In one program evaluation, the reading portion of the Test of Adult Basic Education (TABE) and a predictor version of the general technical (GT) portion of the Armed Forces Classification Test were administered to soldiers enrolled in BSEP. Soldiers demonstrated statistically significant gains of 1.8 grade levels on the TABE and 13 percent on the GT (Philippi, 1986–1987). These gains on traditional, standardized reading tests of word knowledge and paragraph comprehension, although preliminary findings, indicate a transfer of reading skills improvement from job-specific literacy training to traditional reading materials.

The civilian and military programs cited above share several features. First, they have the goal of improved job performance and promotion potential for participants. Second, they are based on prior job-task analysis to determine which reading skills are used on the job. Third, they use actual job-reading materials to derive maximum benefit from learners' existing job knowledge and to increase their job knowledge base for future use. Finally, they succeed in teaching intermediate literates reading skills in the way that the skills are used on the job.

In summary, a review of successful industry-sponsored basic skills programs leads to the conclusion that best practices are wholly dependent on the situational context in which skills are to be employed. The explicit purpose for which job-literacy training is undertaken determines the shape of its implementation design.

The most critical success factor for training in workplace basic skills is the achievement of a precise match between job-specific tasks and traditional educational instruction. Consequently, a specialized area of training expertise that combines knowledge from the fields of employment and education has recently evolved. Experts from those fields develop and implement effective curricula that use job knowledge to teach employees how to learn while simultaneously improving their ability to perform current job-reading tasks.

What Should Be Included in a
Generic Workplace Reading Curriculum?

The achievement of competency in reading, writing, and computation cannot be accomplished in a one-day or even a one-week workshop. The length of a training program depends on a number of variables, including an employee's prior knowledge in each skill area, the required skill level for the job or job family, the design of the curriculum, the commitment of management, and so on. The attainment of job-related competency in each of these skills can take anywhere from forty hours to five years and should involve follow-up and evaluation once the employee is back on the job, as well as refresher courses throughout his or her work life.

Although the curriculum guidelines in this and other chapters deal with the basic workplace skills as separate and discrete entities, when they are taught in a workplace context they are almost never taught separately; this is particularly true of reading, writing, and computation. Each incremental competency achievement by participants in any one skill area contributes to helping them achieve competency in the other two. For example, it is impossible to solve mathematical problems without having achieved some skill in reading and writing; writing clear, competent memos, reports, or bookkeeping summaries requires a certain level of reading. Only at the most rudimentary, non-literate level are skills likely to be taught completely separately, and then only for a brief period.

The reading, writing, and computation skills in Exhibit 2 have been identified as those most commonly used to perform basic job-related tasks. Research indicates that employers seek out job applicants who have mastered these processes (Pratzner, 1978; Pratzner and Russell, 1984; Smith, 1973; Wiant, 1977). For training to be effective, these skills should be presented in the context of performing simulations of job tasks.

Exhibit 2. Job-Specific Reading Processes and
Competencies Commonly Needed to Perform Job Tasks.

What are the objectives of this training?
–To improve job-related reading skills as they relate to immediate job
  requirements
–To improve job performance
–To enhance participants' chances of job stability and upward job mobility
  through improved reading skills
–To increase company productivity through improving individual reading
  capabilities

How do you develop skills in literal comprehension?
–By identifying factual details or specifications within text
–By following detailed, sequential directions to complete a task
–By determining the essential message of a paragraph or selection

What techniques are used to locate information within a text?
–Using table of contents, index, appendixes, glossary, systems or subsystems
  to locate information
–Locating page, title, paragraph, figure, or chart needed to answer questions
  to solve problems
–Using skimming or scanning to determine whether or not text contains
  relevant information
–Cross-referencing within and across source materials to select information
  to perform routine tasks
–Using a completed form to locate information needed to complete a task
  activity

What is involved in learning how to compare and contrast information?
–Combining information from multiple sources that contribute to the
  completion of a task activity
–Selecting parts of a text or visual materials to complete a task activity
–Identifying similarities and differences in objects
–Determining presence of defect or extent of damage
–Matching objects by size, color, or significant markings
–Classifying objects by size, color, or significant markings
–Distinguishing between relevant and irrelevant information in text or
  visuals

**Exhibit 2. Job-Specific Reading Processes and
Competencies Commonly Needed to Perform Job Tasks, Cont'd.**

How do you recognize cause and effect and predict outcomes?
–By using common knowledge to avoid hazard or injury
–By applying preventative measures prior to task to minimize security
or safety problems
–By selecting appropriate course of action in an emergency

How to you use charts, diagrams, and schematics?
–By obtaining a factor specification from a two-column chart to find
information
–By obtaining a factor specification from an intersection of row by column
on a table or chart; by using a complex table or chart requiring cross-
referencing within text material
–By applying information from tables or graphs to locate malfunctions or to
select a course of action
–By using a simple linear path of an organizational chart to list events in
sequential order
–By using the linear path of a flowchart to provide visual and textual
directions to a procedure, to arrive at a decision point, or to provide
alternative paths in problem solving
–By isolating each major section presented in a schematic diagram
–By identifying the components within each section of a schematic diagram
–By isolating a problem component in a schematic diagram and tracing it
to the cause of the problem
–By interpreting symbols to indicate direction of flow, text points, compo-
nents, and diagrammatic decision points
–By identifying details, labels, numbers, and parts from an illustration or
picture
–By identifying parts from a key or legend
–By interpreting a drawing of a cross section for assembly or disassembly
–By following sequenced illustrations or photographs as a guide

How do you become competent in inferential comprehension?
–By determining figurative, idiomatic, and technical meanings of terms by
means of context clues or reference sources
–By making an inference from text that does not explicitly provide required
information
–By organizing information from multiple sources into a sequenced series of
events
–By interpreting codes and symbols

How do you improve vocabulary?
–By recognizing common words and meanings
–By recognizing task-related words with technical meanings
–By identifying meanings from sentence context
–By recognizing meanings of common abbreviations and acronyms

---

Source: Adapted from Philippi, 1988.

CHAPTER 5

Writing with Impact

Every township in this Jurisdiction, after the Lord hath increased them to 50 householders, shall forthwith appoint one within their town to teach all such children as shall report to him, to write and read.

Old Deluder Satan Law
Massachusetts Bay Colony, 1647

What Is Writing?

A National Institute of Education report (Graves, 1981, p. 4) defines writing as "a series of operations leading to the solution of a problem." To resolve the "writing problem," competent writers use a two-part process. First comes a prewriting period that includes topic selection, rehearsing (that is, conscious or unconscious preparation for writing), information access, and information organization. Then comes a writing period devoted to spelling, handwriting, reading, editing, and revising.

Moreover, writing is not a single skill. It involves proficiency in the eye-hand coordination necessary for physical production of legible symbols on a page and the mental processing of information to communicate meaningful content accurately and appropriately.

What Theories Support Current Training in Writing?

To communicate effectively—whether in the limited space of prepared forms, in the condensed, telegraphic terms of memoranda, or in full-length reports — workers must employ a problem-solving process in which they activate mental diagrams or outlines (schemata) that prompt them to do the following:

- Define the anticipated readership and the purpose for addressing these readers
- Determine what form and style of communication are appropriate
- Generate and organize ideas
- Translate the message into a concise, accurate form
- Review, evaluate, and revise the written product (Mikulecky, Ehlinger, and Meenan, 1987)

In planning functional-context basic skills writing instruction, it is important to consider the potential application of recent research on written composition to curriculum design. Studies have defined the prewriting period as "that part of the composing process that extends from the time a writer begins to perceive selectively certain features of his inner and/or outer environment with a view to writing about them — usually at the instigation of a stimulus — to the time when he first puts words or phrases on paper elucidating that perception" (Emig, 1971, p. 39). The prewriting phase may only last a minute, but it is nonetheless a critical part of the writing process during which a writer uses mental strategies to recall topic background information, organize the writing task into manageable pieces, and select relevant information for inclusion in the written product (Perl, 1979). During prewriting, according to a report from the National Institute of Education (Graves, 1981, p. 14), experienced writers selectively employ mental criteria to analyze information in these categories:

- Standard
- Process
- Information
- Information process
- Experience
- Experience verification

- Audience
- Topic limitations
- Organization
- Language
- Length

A study by Hayes and Flower (1980) proved the hypothesis that competent writers use a prewriting planning process in which they take information from the task environment and from their long-term memory to establish communication goals and to translate ideas into production of a written product to meet those goals. The memory probes help writers generate and organize information relevant to the particular topic and audience. In 1981, the same researchers identified the procedural and content-specific plans that writers use to generate and refine ideas.

Knowing how to identify and eliminate irrelevant information about a topic, disrupt unuseful associative chains, and initiate new memory probes narrows the writing problem by putting boundaries on its solution and enables competent writers to be more efficient. Other studies have shown that inexperienced writers (such as those who need literacy instruction) have difficulty with memory searches (Beriter and Scardamalia, 1982). By detailing and modeling (explicitly describing and setting an example of) the mental information generation/selection process that a competent employee uses, an instructor can help employees improve the focus and organization of their written job communications.

It is believed that written composition has also demonstrated that writers carry over the use of established thinking patterns, categories, and connections built from experience and held in long-term memory (mental schemata) during the initial production and revision stages of the writing process as well as during prewriting (Rumelhart, 1980; Hayes and Flower, 1980; Stein and Glenn, 1979). Throughout the writing task, competent writers move back and forth from the abstract (high-level plans) to the concrete (specific sentences and language), while simultaneously keeping in mind the variety of plans and patterns (schemata) available. Sometimes they switch from one plan (schema) to another, merge different plans, or resolve conflicting plans (Hillocks, 1986; Flower and Hayes, 1981). Skillful writers use a variety of patterning, connections, and other schemata during the entire writing process, whereas less competent writers tend to be preoccupied with mechanics such as spelling

(Pianko, 1979; Metzger, 1977; Sawkins, 1971). Revisions made by less competent adult writers tend to concentrate on superficial changes at the sentence level and result primarily in additions to original content (Sommers, 1979). Imposing an external, concrete thinking pattern on the writing process and using criteria against which to judge a writing product lead to significant gains in writing quality (Lamberg, 1974; Young and Koen, 1973). By evaluating what has been written against specific criteria, writers can more easily recognize their writing's weaknesses and make appropriate revisions. For example, learner-writers demonstrated improvement when they used the following questions as guides (Odell, 1974).

- Does the writer state a problem?
- Are there any ambiguous terms in the statement of the problem?
- Does the writer speak to the problem posed?
- In proposing a solution to the problem, does the writer support assertions with evidence?
- Does the writer make unwarranted assumptions?

Taken together, research results strongly suggest that with training in how to plan, organize, and revise writing by using an external yardstick, learners will develop skills for accessing their internal thinking patterns in a structured way. By doing so, they will also focus more precisely on the possibilities for solution of writing problems and will improve their writing competence.

Training in how to use external criteria can best be accomplished by modeling: First, the instructor demonstrates the process, "thinking aloud" through pertinent questions; then learners gradually take responsibility for carrying out the process through self-questioning. Research shows that when learners apply learning to preselected concrete problems and activities, clear and specific objectives can be met. Instructor-led discussion and lecture should be held to a minimum so that learners spend more time learning about and practicing the skills and tasks to be mastered. This mode of instruction lends itself to the use of functional-context (simulated job-task) materials, and it has been demonstrated to be particularly effective with older learners and adults (Hillocks, 1986; Troyka, 1974; Sager, 1973).

On the basis of earlier research (Flower and Hayes, 1981, 1984; Mitchell, 1982; Odell, 1980), a functional-context model for solving writing problems on the job was created (Mikulecky, Ehlinger, and Meenan, 1987) (see Exhibit 3).

Exhibit 3. Functional-Context Model for Solving Writing Problems.

Model	*Application*
Task environment: From a job situation, an employee first identifies the general writing problem by	
–anticipating the audience,	–Who will be reading what I am going to write?
–defining the purpose,	–What is it that I need to write about?
–identifying the portion(s) of the written product developed so far.	–Has any part of this task already been completed?
Schema/Schemata (mental plan or outline/plans or outlines): From long-term memory, an employee accesses knowledge of the task, topic, audience, strategies, and plan of attack.	
	–What do I know about those who will read my communication? What do they expect? What are they able to understand?
	–What job knowledge do I need to complete the written product?
	–What do I know about effective ways to structure and produce the written product I need?
Literacy problem-solving process: Using the information gathered from the task environment and mental schemata, an employee plans and prepares a draft product.	
–The employee plans by generating ideas, organizing ideas, and setting goals for substeps to task completion, subgoals in task production, and exploration of topic.	–What is the information that I need to communicate?
–The employee translates plans to action by putting ideas on paper.	–What is the best way to communicate this information?
	–What steps will I need to take, and in what order?

Exhibit 3. Functional-Context Model
for Solving Writing Problems, Cont'd.

Model	Application
–The employee reviews by evaluating goals and revising, a continual process.	–Did I write what I needed to say clearly and accurately? –Will my reader(s) understand what I have written? –Would a particular revision improve the clarity or accuracy of what I need to say?

Monitor: Throughout the problem-solving process, an employee continually moves between text and task.

	–Am I using my job knowledge correctly in the content of my writing? –Do these words best express the information I need to communicate? –Is this what my reader needs to know? Will my reader be able to understand this? –Is there a clearer way to state my information?

Source: Adapted from Mikulecky, Ehlinger, and Meenan, 1987.

How Is Writing Taught in the Schools?

Initially, instructional writing goals center on sentence recognition and word order within sentences. From preschool through the third grade, students also are given direct instruction in handwriting: first, in the formation and refinement of printed symbols; then, in cursive lettering (except in local school jurisdictions where printing is thought to be more progressive, that is, more legible, than cursive writing, and the latter is not taught). Neatness and control of letter sizes and spacing for uniform, legible letter production are taught and practiced with the goal of having students automatically produce acceptable results after several years. Simultaneously, various strands of language learning are introduced in the classroom at increasing levels of difficulty. These strands include punctuation and capitalization, standard usage, grammar and syntax, and spelling (Prescott, Balow, Hogan, and Farr, 1978).

Punctuation and capitalization are often referred to as "writing conventions" and normally are introduced during the first grade. End punctuation (for declarative, interrogative, and exclamatory sentences) is usually introduced at this time, too, with student mastery anticipated by the end of the fourth grade. This normally is followed by instruction in the use of periods after abbreviations, the apostrophe in contractions and possessives, and commas in greetings and closings of friendly letters. By grades five and six, students should have progressed to the use of colons and the use of commas in compound sentences with subordinate clauses. Capitalization instruction follows a similar pattern, reflecting frequency of usage. Students are first taught to capitalize the first word in a sentence and the word *I,* then names of people, then rules for proper nouns (Prescott, Balow, Hogan, and Farr, 1978).

Standard usage requires substantial in-school practice to create student awareness of proper constructions and to reinforce their application in student writing. For this reason, classroom presentation of standard usage typically emphasizes a relatively small number of objectives over a long period of time; this enhances the entry of correct forms into long-term memory. In the early primary grades, objectives focus on standard usage of irregular verbs, especially the forms of *to be.* Later, students are introduced to additional irregular verbs, contractions, frequently confused words, avoidance of double negatives, and subject-verb agreement. These commonly emphasized objectives of the early grades continue to be part of the curriculum through junior high school. This is because the skill objectives within the standard usage strand are thought to be specific and nongeneralizable (Prescott, Balow, Hogan, and Farr, 1978); that is, learning to accomplish one skill objective (such as capitalizing properly) does not contribute to a learner's accomplishment of another objective (such as conjugating a proper verb).

Approaches to teaching grammar are *traditional/prescriptive,* focusing on rules for correct use; *structural/linguistic,* based on the way language is actually used rather than how it ought to be used; and *generative/transformational,* accounting for the way sentences are produced and understood.

Even with differing approaches, the order and grade levels at which the content of writing instruction is introduced are very similar. As noted earlier in this chapter, initial instruction centers on sentence recognition and word order within sentences. By third grade, lessons usually include parts of speech and their functions as sentence parts. In higher grades, compound/complex sentences or sentence transformations are taught, with students progressing from production of sentences to paragraphs to essays (Prescott, Balow, Hogan, and Farr, 1978).

Spelling instruction normally follows structured methods because incidental learning on this topic is seldom adequate. This is because of the irregularities in the sound-symbol relationships of the English language. Students notice the lack of consistency in these relationships and find spelling difficult when guided only by word sounds. Therefore, teachers usually concentrate on presenting the structured spelling patterns of the approximately 3,000 words people typically use most often in writing. The overriding objective across grade levels is for students to learn to spell these frequently used words correctly (Prescott, Balow, Hogan, and Farr, 1978).

Beyond the junior high school level, writing instruction becomes incidental and, even in English classes, is given in response to specific subject-content instruction. A prominent report on secondary school writing (Applebee, 1981) found that most student writing is in response to textbook or worksheet questions and that only 3 percent of student writing at the high school level is as long as one paragraph.

Instruction in writing skills for students participating in Adult Basic Education (ABE) programs usually follows the sequence of objectives detailed above. The main difference between this instruction and traditional kindergarten-through-grade-twelve writing curricula is that ABE programs are built on functional writing-task competencies identified from everyday life. A typical ABE instructional program for writing skills has been outlined in detail by the Utah State Office of Education (Hall, Worthington, Carruth, and Cubler, 1982). Representative competencies and objectives include the following:

- Writing grocery and "to do" lists (categorization, capitalization of proper nouns, handwriting legibility)
- Sequencing and outlining as preparation for doing household chores (outline format, capitalization, abbreviation and punctuation of dates, translation from Arabic to Roman numerals)
- Filling out forms and applications for taxes, jobs, Social Security, insurance, mail orders, driver's licenses, banking services, and so on (legibility, vocabulary, spelling)
- Identifying the main ideas in paragraphs from commercial reading texts or newspapers (finding the main idea, rewriting the main idea in simple sentence format)
- Writing business letters to order products or complain about them (standard format, capitalization of titles, punctuation, folding of business letters)

Despite an attempt to relate instruction to adult experiences, the competencies listed above merely echo traditional academic objectives for the development of writing conventions (punctuation and capitalization) and basic grammar and syntax. Guidelines and materials for teaching writing skills to vocational students, prepared by the National Center for Research in Vocational Education (NCRVE) (1985, p. 13), address similarly traditional goals:

- Student writing is legible.
- All words are correctly spelled.
- Words are capitalized correctly.
- Form of writing is appropriate to the circumstances.
- Style of writing is appropriate to the situation.
- Words used are accurate, clear, appropriate for expected readership.
- Writing is grammatically correct.
- Writing is properly punctuated.

In the NCRVE program, students are also taught proofreaders' marks, which instructors use as a vehicle for providing instruction on how to revise writing products.

Instructions for teachers using these materials suggest showing students samples of forms and reports from their occupational areas so they will see that writing skills are used on the job and will be motivated to improve their skills. The instructions also suggest assigning vocationally related writing (for example, asking an auto mechanics student to write a report on antique cars) (National Center for Research in Vocational Education, 1985). Like the adult-experience-based assignments in ABE materials, these references to learners' interests are somewhat contrived and fall far short of being the functional-context materials that workers need to learn from if they are to apply writing skills successfully on the job.

For example, commercially produced, generic writing materials may ask students to compose a sentence or paragraph about Betty the Doll Doctor, who fixes broken dolls. In an attempt to make the assignment job-related for adult or vocational students, an instructor might alter the assignment by asking students to compose a sentence or paragraph about Betty the Paramedic. Yet for the assignment to be truly job-specific, it would have to ask students to fill in the actual forms Betty the Paramedic uses on the job or to write a concise, clear, and accurate report to her immediate supervisor describing the treatment she provided to patients during her shift. Only in these last examples does the assignment become task oriented and call on students to use the problem-solving and thinking processes that are the basis of on-the-job writing skills application.

How Should Writing Be Taught in the Workplace?

Physically locating traditional ABE basic-skills writing programs in the workplace is not synonymous with conducting training in workplace literacy. If the purpose of providing employees basic-skills writing courses is to improve performance on job-writing tasks, instruction should focus on objectives that most nearly match job processes and activities as they are performed by a highly competent worker. This requires that instruction center on writing tasks and materials actually used on the job. Commercial materials may be used to provide supplemental exercises for subtask skills (such as learning correct spelling patterns or how to identify key words or phrases), but subtasks should always be correlated to mastery of the total job-writing task (Drew and Mikulecky, 1988).

Again, as when teaching job-related reading, the most effective way to teach these job competencies so that learning will be retained and transferred to job performance is by the functional-context method (Sticht, 1982). Job-writing tasks are identified through a literacy task analysis at the work site (Mikulecky, 1986). While this process of interviewing and observing is being carried out, actual job materials are also gathered to be used as the basis for constructing simulated job tasks that will function as pretests and posttests (for needs assessment and evaluation of learners' progress) and as core curriculum exercises. It is important to note that it is job-related basic skills that will be taught, not job content (Philippi, 1988). To meet employees' needs, job-writing tasks selected for instruction should be those found in entry-level positions or in middle-level positions to which entry-level workers may be promoted and should concentrate on job tasks workers report having difficulty with or simply want to do better. To meet employers' needs, job-writing tasks selected for instruction should include those for which performance results are critical to safety, upgrading, or production and those in which employees frequently make mistakes (Drew and Mikulecky, 1988).

What Are the Essential Elements of Training in Writing?

According to studies conducted by Diehl (1980) and Mikulecky (1982a), the majority of occupational-writing tasks involve completing simple forms and preparing brief memos. The latter study determined that of 276 writing tasks required to perform jobs listed in the *Dictionary of Occupational Titles* (published by the U.S. Department of Labor), more than 42 percent involved filling out prepared forms and more than 22 percent involve generating memos or letters. Another 25 percent of job-writing tasks require recording, summarizing, or noting work completed. Task-related writing (such as producing blue-

prints) accounts for another 11 percent, while only 10.5 percent deal with writing reports or articles like the ones students
in academic settings are taught to prepare.

Another report (Rush, Moe, and Storlie, 1986) indicated
that, other than in writing tasks performed by secretarial employees, clarity is the chief requirement of on-the-job writing.
Information often must be boiled down to concise communication containing only the essentials. In job training, too, the report
found that accuracy of information is considered more important than standard English usage. Further support of this contention comes from the U.S. Army, which in June 1986
disseminated new regulations emphasizing the need for clarity
and brevity in soldiers' writing.

This telegraphic style is also frequently used in business and
industrial communications. The terse style workers must use to
complete forms or produce brief memos or summaries appears
simple. But appearance is misleading; although the succinct style
of clear occupational writing is easy to read and understand, it is
not easy to write. A person must perform highly complex processing to accomplish the tasks that result in brief, accurate writing.

Companies commonly identify grammar as what they
want their employees to be taught in writing courses. By grammar, they usually mean correct writing that is clear and readable.
Organizations frequently classify employee-produced writing as
having bad grammar when it shows the symptoms of vague dic-
tion, faulty punctuation, lack of clarity, lack of focus, wordiness,
or lack of purpose. In fact, these common errors are directly
related to workers' inability to use processing and organizational
skills (Anderson, 1986). To be effective, instruction in workplace
writing should not center on grammatical exercises that treat
these inaccurately labeled symptoms but should address the
symptoms' cause by making explicit the mental processes one
needs to perform writing tasks.

What Constitutes Competency in Writing? What Constitutes Mastery?

As in reading, an adult writer's progress in writing should
be measured by ability to master necessary processes. Since writ-

ing is a paper-and-pencil (or word processor) exercise, any tests given should be in that form. If a participant demonstrates correct performance of a particular skill or process 75 to 80 percent of the time, mastery has been achieved.

What Are Examples of Workplace Training Programs in Writing?

For almost twenty years, companies such as Polaroid, Planters LifeSavers Company, Aetna Life and Casualty, and the Onan Corporation have been providing basic courses to help employees improve their on-the-job writing skills. In-house trainers or contracted local providers (such as community colleges and consultants) design skills enhancement curricula tailored to individual jobs within particular companies. As technology has been upgraded, these programs have shifted from providing basic skills training by means of traditional, generic practice materials to the use of functional-context materials representing actual on-the-job applications of those skills. Courses are designed to meet the needs of all employees — from the barely literate to those with threshold literacy to those with advanced skills.

Travelers Insurance Company. The MOST/BEST (Modern Office Skills Training/Business English for Spanish-Speaking Trainees) program offered by Travelers Insurance Company of Hartford, Connecticut, is an example of an industry-sponsored, functional-context, basic-writing training program. Travelers has modified its original program, which began operation nearly twenty years ago. In a structured work-simulated environment, the company now offers an eighteen-week training course in basic skills as they are used on the job, including writing. The course has two phases. The first is an eight-week segment (seven and one-half hours per workday) of intensive work in basics with a transition into practice in using the skills on actual job materials in simulated job activities. That phase is followed by a ten-week work-study period (four and one-half hours each morning) combined with on-the-job training (every afternoon) for specific positions, such as file clerk, records manager, telephone answerer, computer terminal operator, proofreader, typist, or word processor. Because of the makeup of the local work force, instruction also emphasizes the use of business English as a second language. During the eighteen weeks of customized preemployment training, participants are paid a stipend of $3.75 per hour, and they are guaranteed job placement upon successful completion of the course. At each week's end, department supervisors evaluate the progress of trainees with whom they are assigned to work. Class size is limited to twenty-five to thirty participants. An advisory council analyzes and recommends for instruction the skills found necessary for competent job performance and also helps with trainees' postcourse placement.

In addition to demonstrating the writing competencies required for a particular position, a trainee must show ability to perform certain tasks at company-set competency levels before he or she is placed in a job. The trainee must be able to read and follow instructions; exercise independent judgment; carry out a task efficiently, thoroughly, neatly, and with a minimum of supervision; and perform job tasks adequately.

These additional requirements reflect the independent thinking and problem-solving strategies that should be incorporated into instruction in workplace writing to demonstrate to employees that they are learning skills applicable across all subject areas, but skills that are better retained when learned in a functional context.

The U.S. Army. Another example of effective basic skills training that lends itself to emulation is the functional-context training conducted by the U.S. Army. In the Basic Skills Education Program (BSEP) (described in more detail in Chapter Four), soldiers receive twenty to forty hours of writing instruction as part of on-duty time, at an average of four hours daily. Instruction focuses on the forms and brief reports soldiers use on the job. Guided instruction, including explanation of the use of an external model (Who? What? How? How Well?), teaches soldiers occupational-writing processes one step at a time, using simulated military scenarios and actual job materials. The forms and reports covered during instruction are those that the soldiers use in their current rank or that they will use immediately after promotion: disposition forms, enlisted evaluation reports, counseling forms, and so on.

What Should Be Included in a Generic Workplace Writing Curriculum?

Exhibit 4 lists items to consider when designing a workplace writing curriculum.

Exhibit 4. Job-Specific Writing Processes and Competencies Commonly Needed to Perform Job Tasks.

What are the objectives of this training?
- To improve job-related writing skills as they relate to immediate job requirements
- To improve overall job performance
- To enhance participants' chances of job stability and upward job mobility through improved writing skills
- To increase company productivity through improving individual writing capabilities

What are the key production competencies?
- Writing key technical words accurately on forms
- Spelling task-related words and abbreviations correctly

What is the process for entering and performing single-step activities?
- Entering appropriate information onto a form
- Recording essential information in phrases or simple sentences accurately and precisely
- Recording information that involves more than one sentence

What is the process for entering and performing multiple-step activities and sourcing?
- Transferring numbers, codes, dates, figures from equipment or written sources onto appropriate sections of forms
- Writing a report including necessary support documentation or classification

How do you learn to translate action/transactions to paper?
- By writing brief descriptive accounts of activities or transactions performed
- By outlining a situation by identifying key ideas and supporting details

Exhibit 4. Job-Specific Writing Processes and
Competencies Commonly Needed to Perform Job Tasks, Cont'd.

-By summarizing essential details for a written communication according to
  problem-solving or newswriting guidelines (Who? What? Where? When?
  How?)
-By selecting relevant details for a written communication
-By stating general impression of an event or situation as it relates to
  specific reporting goals
-By summarizing events and precise dialogue in an accurate, complete,
  and objective manner
-By summarizing major points presented in a written communication
-By generating a written communication according to a specific format
  (that is, memo, letter, and so on)

How do you learn interpretation?
-By identifying objectives, intent, target audience, and all essential and
  supporting details of a written communication
-By generating a written communication with sequentially arranged events
-By writing brief justifications for actions taken and providing good
  reasons for rejecting alternative actions
-By appraising a written communication and making adjustments to
  improve clarity

Source: Adapted from task analyses of civilian and military occupations,
U.S. Department of the Army, 1988; Mikulecky, 1982a; and Diehl, 1980.

CHAPTER 6

Computation in a Technological Workplace

When you can measure what you are speaking about and express it in numbers, you know something about it; but when you cannot measure it, when you cannot express it in numbers, your knowledge is of a meager and unsatisfactory kind.

Lord Kelvin
Popular Lectures and Addresses, 1891–1894

What Is Computation?

In elementary schools, basic mathematics includes comprehensive thinking about quantification and subsidiary skills in addition, subtraction, multiplication, and division. On the job, the skills set that underlies an employee's ability to perform mathematical tasks successfully includes the following (Cornell Institute for Occupational Education, 1980):

- *Quantification,* the ability to read and write numbers, count, and put numbers in sequence, recognizing whether one number is larger or smaller than another
- *Computation,* the ability to add, subtract, multiply, and divide with single- and multiple-digit whole numbers, mixed numbers, fractions, and decimals
- *Measurement and estimation,* the ability to take measurements of time, temperature, distance, length, volume, height,

weight, velocity, and speed and to use these measures and report them correctly; or when exact measurements are unnecessary or impractical, the ability to apply simple techniques for estimating quantities, lengths, distances, and so on, with a sense of the accuracy needed for the purpose

- *Problem solving,* the ability to employ the skills listed above as they are called for in situations outside the classroom by
   recognizing the problem,
   distinguishing between useful and irrelevant information,
   determining whether more information is needed,
   determining which mathematical steps should be used to solve the problem,
   setting up the problem in a workable format, and
   computing the answer.
- *Comprehension,* the ability to draw on knowledge and skill in the areas of
   equivalents (relating measurements on different scales),
   organization of data (understanding the ways data are displayed and collecting and interpreting data),
   algebra (setting up and solving equations), and
   geometry (using principles and formulas).

As indicated in Chapter Two, for purposes of discussion throughout this book, the term *computation* is used interchangeably with *mathematics* and should be viewed in that broader context.

What Theories Support
Current Training in Computation?

Since early civilization, people have recognized mathematics as a necessary component of human knowledge. In ancient Greece, the philosopher Plato, building on the work of Pythagoras (c. 500 B.C.), expounded on computation as a bridge between the concrete, real world of experiences and the abstract world of thinking and learning within the mind. Plato stated that using mathematics to describe the forms and functions of things around us leads us to infer intangible principles that we can apply to new situations. His writings probably represent the first recorded expression of the time-honored educational belief that the study of mathematics develops people's ability to reason, thus enabling them to solve problems and learn how to learn.

Because skills in computation are of strategic relevance in the workplace (Henry and Raymond, 1983), they (like reading skills) should be taught contextually, that is, in a way that reflects their on-the-job use. Such teaching is the quickest, most effective route to improved employee performance. Over the past twenty-five years, Sticht, Mickulecky, and other experts in the field of functional-context learning have repeatedly documented the value and validity of this kind of instruction. As noted earlier, their work has demonstrated the wide difference between the on-the-job application of basic skills and the way skills are traditionally taught and used in academic environments. Their work has also shown the successful skills transfer to job performance and the long-lasting effectiveness of instruction that uses job-specific materials to activate employees' existing job knowledge while providing more training time on task.

How Is Computation Taught in the Schools?

More than fifty years ago, researchers concluded that generic, school-based mathematics instruction did not improve performance in specific content areas. In the middle to late 1980s, in numerous surveys and interviews, employers reinforced this contention by stating that the computational skills their employees were taught in school are not sufficient to meet job needs.

Because the development of computational skills depends on an understanding of numeration concepts, elementary-level mathematics instruction focuses on counting with the decimal system. In the primary grades, the most critical stages of skill development relate to work with whole numbers: digits, decades, hundreds, thousands, and so on. Fundamental concepts and operations practice with algorithms (addition, subtraction, multiplication, and division) need to be mastered before students progress to work on operations with rational numbers (fractions and decimals), which usually occurs in the intermediate school years. At higher levels, advanced concepts — such as prime numbers, exponents, greatest common factors, linear equations — are introduced.

Mathematical goals, unlike those in reading, usually are objective and discrete, hierarchical, and easily measured (Prescott, Balow, Hogan, and Farr, 1978). In most mathematics curricula, the teaching of basic operations begins with simple facts about whole numbers. Students then progress beyond facts to computation with no regrouping, to computations with regrouping in simple problems, to more complex computations, and then to computations without restrictions. Basic laws and properties are also presented sequentially, beginning in the lower grades with the properties associated with basic addition and subtraction (commutative, inverse, and identity properties), then progressing to properties related to multiplication and division.

In the intermediate grades, the emphasis shifts from whole-number operations to those with rational numbers. In the lower intermediate grades, students are taught to extend and apply their understanding of operations. They are given instruction in distributive and closure properties, exponents, and denominate numbers, and they begin intensive work with fractions and decimals, including the application of percentages, at about the fifth grade level.

As instruction continues through the intermediate grades to the high school level, objectives become increasingly abstract. In high school, graphing and statistics, the average and the mean, probability, and ratio and proportion are topics frequently found in basic mathematics instruction (Prescott, Balow, Hogan, and Farr, 1978).

In addition to covering numeration and operations, contemporary school mathematics curricula extend to skills development in geometry, measurement, and problem solving. Skills in geometry and measurement are taught in three stages: basic concepts and common terms, elements of the system for formalizing knowledge, and varied applications and implications of the systems. The metric system is usually covered as a part of measurement instruction. Typically, instruction in problem solving is limited to the application of basic operations to solve verbally stated (word) problems. Curricula traditionally focus on teaching students about the types of computation to be employed, the information contained in a problem that will help one solve it, and the ordering of steps to be taken to research a solution (Prescott, Balow, Hogan, and Farr, 1978).

Normally, adults who enroll in basic-mathematics education programs are tested to determine their level of proficiency. Most programs' curricula are drill based and geared to helping a learner pass the mathematics portion of the General Education Development test. Functional-context concepts are often employed in working with adults whose computational abilities are in the low-level range. The context used, however, has a life-skill rather than work-skill orientation. For women, these curricula tend to feature household tasks, such as computing amounts in recipes or on cleaning supply labels, while men are often given exercises requiring them to compute weights and measurements for automotive or home maintenance chores. The problem solving introduced in such courses usually requires only basic mathematical operations (Ulmer, 1969).

How Should Computation Be Taught in the Workplace?

Testimony from employer surveys and interviews indicates that workplace applications of computational skills require employees to have proficiency levels in reasoning and problem solving beyond the basic use of computation algorithms mastered in school. This is not to say that workers are quantitatively illiterate in a generic sense. In fact, the Educational Testing Service in its 1986 National Assessment of Educational Progress report found that approximately 75 percent of young adults tested performed quantitative literacy tasks at the intermediate-to-adept level or better (p. 35).

The serious problems lie in workers' inability to determine *which* computational algorithm(s) to apply to a particular job problem or to recognize errors resulting from inappropriate applications because they do not understand *why* specific computations should be used (Kloosterman and Harty, 1986). Neither time-consuming skill drills nor the use of calculators is an effective remedy because, while either can correct the problem of computational errors, neither helps a person understand which computation is needed to solve an on-the-job problem (Kloosterman and Gillie, 1987, 1988). Furthermore, the difficulty of a computational task increases if workers must apply more than one numerical operation in an appropriate sequence or must use information that is embedded in printed materials (Kirsch and Jungeblut, 1986). The most effective way to teach the skills and strategies that will equip workers to solve mathematics problems in the workplace is through the use of contextual materials that simulate job situations (King-Fitch, 1985).

What Are the Essential Elements of Training in Computation?

Studies of the occupational use of mathematical skills indicate that most jobs, regardless of their field, require employees to apply the higher-order thinking strategies of problem solving and interpretation, even when working with the most basic levels of number concepts and calculations found in job tasks (Greenan, 1984; Smith, 1973; Wiant, 1977).

A report prepared for the National Center for Research in Vocational Education cites diagnosis, estimation, and problem solving as fundamental reasoning skills used in the workplace. "In mathematics, recent research suggests that the most successful learners . . . understand the task to be one of interpreting numbers, not just doing routine calculations. . . . Failure to engage in 'higher order reasoning' about quantities is related to failures in learning the 'basic' skills of calculation and number usage" (Resnick, 1987a).

Drawing similar conclusions, a report prepared for the Indiana State Board of Vocational and Technical Education (Kloosterman and Gillie, 1987, 1988) details the need for mathematics instruction in problem solving and interpretation skills. Examining the effectiveness of various curricula for teaching workplace mathematics skills, this report demonstrates the need for instructional materials that provide instruction in the basic skill of problem solving/logical thinking in ways that promote transfer of knowledge about one problem to a new problem. Such materials stand in contrast to traditional instructional materials, which rely heavily on drill that results in specific, nontransferable mathematical skills. The report suggests incorporating in curricula for teaching basic skills in workplace mathematics a step-by-step problem-solving model that uses brainstorming, activates learners' prior knowledge, and involves group cooperation. The report emphasizes that problem-solving strategies can and should be taught contextually as applied skills for the workplace. This recommendation is echoed by the National Advisory Committee on Mathematical Education, the National Council of Teachers of Mathematics, the National Council of Supervisors of Mathematics, and the Center for Occupational Research and Development, all of which have issued publications urging educators to focus basic mathematics instruction on problem solving and interpretation of computational functions. (For a list of workplace computation skills, see "What Should Be Included in a Generic Workplace Computation Curriculum?" at the end of this chapter.)

What Constitutes Competency in Computation? What Constitutes Mastery?

As noted throughout this chapter, even entry-level job tasks require the application of complex clusters of mathematical skills. Following are two examples from the fieldwork of Larry Mikulecky, director of the Learning Skills Center, Indiana University-Bloomington (personal telephone interviews, 1988).

Example 1. Workers on loading platforms must not only know how to calculate the total weight allowance for loading units (skids) and partial units per truck, but they also must be able to compute quickly the fractional unit weights of other products to fill out each truckload, maximizing use of space and minimizing transportation costs. At the same time, the loading plan must be arranged and rearranged so that the weight and volume of final distribution will be balanced to meet safety regulations.

This entry-level task demands more than simple facility and accuracy in applying basic computation of fractions to measured weights and volumes; it requires workers to use the results of their calculations in conjunction with higher-level thinking skills of interpretation, problem solving, and decision making. The correct solution for each occurrence of the job-task procedure is based on a particular shipping order and a particular truck, and so is different each time. Therefore, it is the process for achieving various solutions that must be taught and mastered, not merely the discrete computational skills involved.

Example 2. A worker on a food-packaging assembly line that uses statistical process control (SPC) must be able to remove a sample from the line every X minutes, weigh it, record its weight (to hundredths of an ounce) on a chart, calculate (from the sample weights charted for a given period) the average weight of a package on the line, and determine whether or not that average weight falls within an allowable range of error for the weights printed on individual packages. The results of this employee's work are used to decide whether the assembly line must shut down to readjust the filling machines — a costly procedure. A next-higher-level worker interprets the data prepared by the entry-level worker and recalibrates the line machines whenever data indicate this is necessary.

The complex, yet somewhat discrete, nature of the job tasks for these workers' positions makes it difficult to find people who can perform the tasks successfully at the time of hiring. Both positions require interpretive, decision-making, and problem-solving skills beyond basic computation and measurement. In all likelihood, their employer must therefore provide or arrange for new employees' training in applied skills. Moreover, entry-level workers would need additional training to be qualified for promotion to the higher position.

It is important to note that an entry-level worker, along with mastering multiple-step processes, must make decisions based on the interpretation of completed computations. Training for this added dimension of skill application requires situational/contextual instruction that includes task analysis of each job, design of instructional materials that simulate specific job tasks, and teaching of skills as they are applied on the job. Such instruction fosters motivated workers whose learning is relevant to their everyday needs and the transfer of learning to successful job performance.

What Are Examples of Successful Workplace Training Programs in Computation?

Delco Products. Delco Products, a division of General Motors, manufactures such car components as motors, suspension systems, transmissions, engine cooling systems, and several power accessories. The Rochester plant, one of Delco's eleven manufacturing locations in five countries, is the site of the program discussed here. This plant employs 3,528 workers, of whom 3,105 are hourly wage employees.

Delco offers its technical mathematics course through a workplace literacy program begun in January 1988 and jointly conducted by Delco and the International Union of Electrical Workers (IUEW). Delco hired an educational consultant to write a proposal for program funds from the state of New York. Through the Workplace Literacy Special Grants Fund authorized by the New York State legislature, $2 million was made available to employers in 1988. More than fifteen projects were funded, Delco's among them. Delco retained the educational consultant to administer its program. The state pays the program's administrative costs, and the company pays participants' wages—they attend classes on company time—and provides classroom facilities.

Technical mathematics is one of three courses offered through the workplace literacy program; the other two are communications and a combined reading and writing course. These courses prepare participants for taking apprenticeship tests, participating in quality-of-work-life (QWL) projects, understanding statistical process control (SPC), and continuing their learning through college courses.

Delco's need for a literary program came to light when two operational changes were being carried out. First, Delco was consolidating its trades so that the manufacturing operation would be more efficient and less costly. For example, all line workers were to be trained to resolve commonplace problems occurring at their workstations. By eliminating the wait for another employee to arrive to fix things, this training would shorten production downtime. Second, Delco had to train line workers in its new statistical quality control system.

In both cases, the company discovered that workers lacked the basic skills needed for successful participation in advanced training leading to an update of the manufacturing process. Updating was especially important because the economic situation in the auto parts industry was not good; Delco is one of the few companies in that industry to have survived recent difficulties. At the time, it had experienced relatively few layoffs (only 200) and was showing a profit. Further, Delco wanted to stay in western New York. In order for the company to remain competitive and profitable in that location, training for the manufacturing update was essential.

Twelve Delco employees in the technical training area were responsible for helping to set up the program and are still actively involved in its administration. The educational consultant hired to implement the program works closely with this technical training group, and all instructor and class coordination is done through them. The IUEW president signed the workplace literacy grant awarded by the state, and the union and management each have a representative in program planning and administration.

Top management and most employees supported the program from the start, but some foremen and supervisors have resisted it. Employees are committed to the program to the extent that many will report to class even if they have been absent from work. Despite top management support and encouragement for continuing the program, foremen and supervisors are sometimes reluctant to release employees from their jobs to attend class. The program is open to all plant employees, although currently only hourly union workers are participating. The program is also voluntary, but changing plant needs eventually may lead to mandatory attendance.

The program runs for eighteen weeks (with six weeks devoted to each of the three subjects). Employees attend once a week for four hours and are given assignments to complete between sessions. To serve all employees who want to attend, there are classes for all three shifts. From January 1988 to the 1988–89 academic year, 185 people participated in the program, and for the 1988–89 academic year, Delco expects to have two twenty-one-week sessions (one per semester), with 200 people in each. Over the next five years, Delco expects to train 2,000 people through this program.

Delco's workplace literacy program is not prepackaged, and the company prides itself on offering its employees customized, functional-context training programs. At the outset, the educational consultant met with employees and managers to find out what skills training they thought was needed. The curriculum was developed from their comments and, before implementation, was presented to them for further response.

The instructors, a dozen consultants hired from outside the company, are required to attend in-service training sessions before the program begins. Although classes meet at all hours of the day and night, Delco has had no problem signing up competent, enthusiastic instructors. Instructors evaluate each of their students after each class session. Students also write a self-evaluation, giving their perceptions of what they have learned and how they are progressing. All aspects of the course are well documented, but no records are supplied to the union or management. Program reports are given only to the state of New York and remain anonymous.

No long-term evaluation of students has been done, although employees are tracked after their program participation to find out what their next educational step will be. The state of New York's grant does not require a long-term evaluation, but Delco believes one should be done and is working to determine how to do it. For now, the most significant change instructors have noticed is in participants' attitudes. The employees have become excited about learning and obviously look forward to their next class.

When employees enter the mathematics portion of the Delco workplace literacy program, they are given a test developed by the educational consultant to determine at what level they need to begin their individual programs. At the end of the mathematics portion of the program, they are given another test to show how they have progressed. Because the union does not want the program to be based on a pass-fail system, however, the tests are for evaluation purposes only. The union wants the employees to have the opportunity to learn as much as possible without the fear of failure.

To help employees feel more at ease with the skills they will be learning, instructors begin the course by addressing the issue of math anxiety. Then, before beginning work on skills, students develop mathematics goals they wish to accomplish by the end of the course. Next, on the basis of their pretest results, students are placed individually in skill areas ranging from addition of whole numbers to trigonometry and calculus. This method of placing students provides each of them with an individualized educational program (IEP). The instructors have developed a three-sheet instructional guide for each skill. The guides explain the skills and give examples of problems involving skill application. All of the skills are presented in the context of an industrial work environment, so students solve problems that they are likely to encounter on the job. Each student works at his or her individual skill level and pace.

After a student has completed each IEP guide and feels comfortable with the particular skill involved, he or she is given a mastery test. A 90 percent pass rate demonstrates that the student has competency in that skill and thus may move on. If the pass rate is not met, the student revisits the skill sheet, referring to numerous texts that offer further guidance in the skill.

Students are not grouped according to ability, but classes are kept small (sixteen students each) so that employees can receive individual attention. Additional instructors are assigned to classes that have many employees with special needs. During class, the instructors make the rounds to help each student with his or her work in individual skill areas.

One-quarter of the mathematics course is devoted to physics. The concepts of motion, fields, conservation of matter and energy, friction, and machines are presented on videotape and in lectures. Because of students' low math skills, the depth with which the concepts can be covered is limited (Susan McLean, telephone interviews, May, July, and August 1988).

The U.S. Army. Many workplace programs have been designed to improve workers' computation skills, but few of the programs incorporate the functional-context philosophy described above, with the notable exception of vendor-provided instruction on how to operate specific pieces of equipment. One of the best-known programs in functional-context training, the Job Skills Education Program (JSEP), has been sponsored by the U.S. Army. JSEP is a computer-based basic skills program developed by Florida State University and Ford Aerospace and Communications Corporation. JSEP is based on an instructional system design (ISD) model. Skills chosen for instruction are those that have been identified by means of a task analysis of high-density military occupation specialties (MOSs). The competency-based program's curriculum uses actual MOS job material, is computer assisted, and deals with skills in reading, writing, and mathematics. Instruction in mathematics competencies is delivered in units of three to ten sequential lessons for each of the following:

Numbering and counting	Addition and subtraction
Linear, weight, and volume measures	Multiplication and division
	Fractions and decimals
Degree measures	Geometry
Time-telling measures	Combination of processing
Gauge measures	(problem solving and interpretation)
Spatial measures	
Lines	Graphing in the coordinate plane
Planes	
Angles and triangles	Algebra
Solids	Trigonometry
Terminology	

The program emphasizes processes and job-usage skills and is designed for use by soldiers who test below the acceptable level of mathematics ability (estimated grade level 10.2 on the Test of Adult Basic Education), who need to retake the

Armed Forces Classification Test to raise their scores to the eligibility level for reenlistment or promotion, or who are recommended for the program by their commanding officers.

In May 1988, the U.S. Department of Education awarded Florida State University a $628,000 seventeen-month contract to adapt this successful army program for civilian use. Florida State will again be collaborating with Ford Aerospace and the New York Department of Education to develop a program appropriate for use in general vocational education curricula. Because of the strong applicability to workplace basics, the U.S. Department of Labor has selected California, Delaware, and Indiana as demonstration sites in which the new civilian form of the JSEP curriculum will be tried out.

What Should Be Included in a Generic Workplace Computation Curriculum?

A study of more than 130 different vocational areas showed high to moderate generalizability (transfer from one occupational area to another) of the mathematics skills shown in Exhibit 5.

Exhibit 5. Job-Specific Computational Processes and Competencies Commonly Needed to Perform Job Tasks.

What are the objectives of this training?
–To improve job-related computational skills as they relate to immediate job requirements
–To improve overall job performance
–To enhance participants' chances of job stability and upward job mobility through improved computation skills
–To increase company productivity through improving individual computational capabilities

What procedures do you need to learn to understand how to use whole numbers in the workplace?
–Reading, writing, and counting single- and multiple-digit whole numbers
–Adding and subtracting single- and multiple-digit whole numbers
–Multiplying and dividing single- and multiple-digit whole numbers
–*Using addition, subtraction, multiplication, and division to solve problems with single- and multiple-digit whole numbers
–*Rounding off single- and multiple-digit whole numbers

**Exhibit 5. Job-Specific Computational Processes and
Competencies Commonly Needed to Perform Job Tasks, Cont'd.**

What procedures do you need to learn to understand how to use fractions in
the workplace?
–Reading and writing common fractions
–Adding and subtracting common fractions
–Multiplying and dividing common fractions
–*Solving problems with common fractions

What procedures do you need to learn to understand how to use decimals in
the workplace?
–Carrying out arithmetic computations involving dollars and cents
–Reading and writing decimals in one or more places
–*Rounding off decimals in one or more places
–Multiplying and dividing decimals in one or more places
–Adding and subtracting decimals in one or more places
–*Solving problems with decimals in one or more places

What procedures do you need to learn to understand how to use percent in
the workplace?
–Reading and writing percentages
–Computing percentages

What procedures do you need to learn to understand how to use mixed
operations in the workplace?
–*Converting fractions to decimals, percentages to fractions, fractions to
  percents, percentages to decimals, decimals to percentages, common fractions and mixed numbers to decimal fractions, and decimal fractions to
  common fractions and mixed numbers
–*Solving problems by selecting and using correct order of operations
–Performing written calculations quickly
–Computing averages

What procedures do you need to learn to understand how to use
measurements and calculations in the workplace?
–*Reading numbers or symbols from time, weight, distance, and volume
  measuring scales
–*Using a measuring device to determine an object's weight, distance, or
  volume in standard (English) units
–*Using a measuring device to determine an object's weight, distance, or
  volume in metric units
–*Performing basic metric conversions involving weight, distance, and
  volume
–*Solving problems involving time, weight, distance, and volume
–*Using a calculator to perform basic arithmetic operations to solve
  problems

Exhibit 5. Job-Specific Computational Processes and
Competencies Commonly Needed to Perform Job Tasks, Cont'd.

What procedure do you need to learn to understand how to use estimation
in the workplace?
-*Determining whether a solution to a mathematical problem is reasonable

---

Source: Adapted from Greenan, 1984, Appendix C, p. 28.

Note: Those items with an asterisk (*) indicate skills directly involving
the use of problem solving or interpretation.

PART 4

Communication Skills: Speaking and Listening Effectively

Communication is central to the smooth operation of a competitive venture. Communication skills are at the heart of getting and keeping customers. Pitching innovation, contributing to quality circles, resolving conflict, and providing meaningful feedback all hinge on effective communication skills.

Without communication, an organization cannot function. If an organization's workers cannot communicate, little real progress can be made toward achieving strategic objectives. It is impossible to imagine that coordinated effort will occur except through communication or through the unlikeliest of coincidences (Lesikar, 1976).

Ironically, American schools offer scant instruction in oral communication and virtually none in listening. While they provide extensive formal training in reading and writing, the schools generally provide instruction in oral skills only in an elective course linked to public presentation techniques such as debate, drama, and so on.

To understand human communication, it is helpful to know some fundamentals.

Communication Is Imperfect

Because of the *human filter* of past experiences and resulting values, expectations, and so on, communication is not the highly precise activity that many people think it ought to be. Since meaning is always perceived differently depending on which

125

filter one uses (that is, which person is sending or receiving the communication), people are likely to assign various meanings to any particular set of symbols. Symbols themselves often have multiple and vague meanings and are not consistently used by message senders. Further, not everyone is proficient in encoding (that is, in selecting and putting together symbols for use in messages).

We Communicate About Ourselves

In the process of symbolizing, we often select symbols that tell more about our internal states than about any independent, external "reality." Actually, we tell how we perceive or react to the stimuli that we receive. For example, if two people view an objective composition of matter — a painting — one person may think that it is beautiful and the other think that it is hideous. In reality, the painting is not inherently beautiful or hideous. The reality that is communicated is "As I view this painting's information, as picked up by my sensory receptors, relayed through my nervous system, and strained through my filter, the painting appears to be beautiful (or hideous) to me."

Meaning Is in the Mind

Symbols do not, in and of themselves, have meaning. Meaning is in the mind of a person sending or receiving a message. The similarity of the interpretation that those involved in the communication give to symbols is a measure of the success of the communication effort (Lesikar, 1976, pp. 27–29). If we considered these fundamentals whenever we became involved in communication activity, we would ask ourselves "What did he or she mean when using those symbols?" rather than "What do those symbols mean in my mind?"

Workers spend most of their day in some form of communication. They communicate with each other about procedures and problems, and they relay information to and receive it from customers. Employees who lack proficiency in oral communication and listening are handicapped in enhancing their personal and professional development. Moreover, business leaders estimate that deficiencies in these skills cost employers millions of dollars each year in lost productivity through error.

CHAPTER 7

Oral Communication

"That's what's wrong with us! . . . We can't talk. Nobody but writers know how to put things into words and everybody goes around stuffed up with things they want to say and can't." It seemed to him that he had put his finger on the secret of all human sorrow.

Rebecca West
Life Sentence, 1935

What Is Oral Communication?

Oral communication is no longer considered the mere transmission of information or messages, sender to receiver, as theorists in the 1960s and early 1970s proposed. Rather, it is, as psychologist Carl Jung defined it, the "sharing of meaning." Communication in general and oral communication in particular involve an exchange of thoughts, ideas, and messages (Burgoon and Saine, 1978). Oral communication is a dynamic process, an ongoing interaction of elements that change as they interact.

What Theories Support Current Training in Oral Communication?

The notion of oral communication as a dynamic process suggests that an act of communication cannot be reversed or exactly repeated because communication evolves. Previous communication encounters affect the ones that follow. Some theorists assert that communication is an evolutionary process affecting

127

us as individuals and as members of social systems. Through communication, both individuals and social systems evolve and change, are replaced, or become obsolete.

Further, contemporary scholars suggest that communication is a transactional process because we constantly send and receive messages simultaneously as we atttempt to share meaning. A systematic theory, this implies an interrelationship or interdependence among elements in communication.

Figure 2 illustrates elements of an interpersonal communication process: sender and receiver, message and means of communication (channel), sources of interference (communication barriers), and feedback (responsive communication).

Figure 2 illustrates the fact that a person (whether acting as a sender or a receiver) brings an individual background or field of experience (see #1 and #2 of Figure 2) to communication interactions. The influences of a person's gender, ethnicity, age, socioeconomic status, birth order, place(s) of upbringing, spiritual and political beliefs, educational history, work experience, sense of personal power or status, sexual orientation, language skills, mental and physical health, and so on affect communication.

Current theory, confirming the beliefs of the ancient Greeks, suggests that people tend to manifest their combination of these influences in one of four visible and dominant styles of communication (Jung, 1964; Klein, 1970; Boyatzis, 1982; Harrison and Bramson, 1983). Each of these basic styles has characteristic body language, vocal patterns, and language usage. Although experts differ about what to call each style, they agree that each is based on a particular set of values that manifests itself in a visible mode of behavior and that how a person approaches a situation is based on that person's individual field of experience, which often will conflict with other people's experiences, values, and styles. The four dominant styles are found in action-oriented, process-oriented, people-oriented, and idea-oriented communicators.

Action-oriented communicators talk about getting things done, the "bottom line," moving ahead, decisions, and achievements. They tend to be direct, impatient, decisive, quick, and energetic. They have short attention spans, tend to interrupt others, and

Figure 2. Complete Process of Communication.

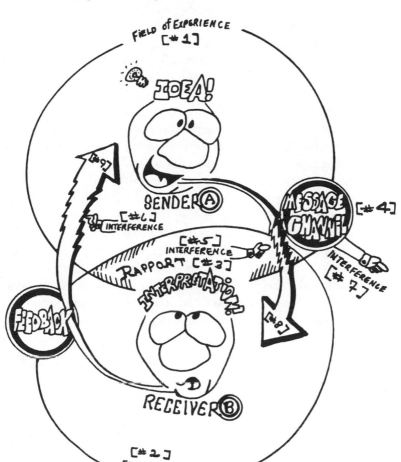

hate small talk. Their body language and vocal cues tend to be accurate indicators of what they are feeling.

Process-oriented communicators talk about facts and figures, policies and procedures, analysis, and planning. They tend to be systematic, patient, unemotional, cautious, and logical. They have long attention spans, hate off-the-cuff reactions, and offer minimal body language and vocal cues about their feelings.

People-oriented communicators talk about needs, motivations, teamwork, values, feelings, and beliefs. They are spontaneous, empathetic, and subjective, and they hate rigid procedures that fail to take into account human elements. Their body language tends to be open and their voices varied.

Idea-oriented communicators talk about innovation and change, new ways of doing things, concepts, and possibilities. They tend to be full of ideas, provocative, and difficult to understand. They like to challenge others and hate rules and regulations. Their nonverbal and vocal cues vary substantially. When gathering ideas, they like privacy and may be withdrawn; when promoting ideas, their energy level increases.

Communication occurs when styles overlap, when there is something in one person's values and experiences with which another person can identify. This identification may be called common ground or rapport (see #3 of Figure 2), and it is essential to communication. The extent to which receivers have *codes* with meanings similar to those of a message's sender is the extent to which they can communicate (LaRusso, 1977; Wolvin and Coakley, 1982; Elsea, 1986).

To share meaning through exchanged messages, most of us use, intentionally or unintentionally, what are referred to as "message channels" (see #4 of Figure 2). In adult communication, first and foremost is the message channel of the body. We use and interpret bodily nonverbal communication such as smiles, looks, nods, touches, even styles of dress. We do not need to speak another person's language to communicate with that person; a welcoming smile is universal. But nonverbal communication may not always translate; for example, the friendly hand gesture of people in one country may be considered rude or insulting by people in another country.

Researchers tend to classify body language in terms of nine components. Evidence indicates (Elsea, 1986) that this is the order in which an American processes information about another person upon meeting for the first time:

1. Color of skin
2. Gender
3. Age
4. Appearance
5. Facial expression
6. Eye behavior
7. Movement
8. Personal space
9. Touch

So much meaning is conveyed by these nine aspects of body language that many communication specialists believe that body language and appearance constitute more than half of the meaning of a sender's total message (Mehrabian, 1972; Knapp, 1978).

The second message channel involves the voice and is called *paralanguage* or vocal communication. When a person speaks, the voice has such characteristics as tone, volume, pitch, rhythm, tempo, pauses, and articulation. A voice—excluding words—may transmit as much as 38 percent of the meaning in face-to-face interactions and 70 to 90 percent in telephone conversations (Elsea, 1986). For example, the rates at which people speak and their levels of loudness have physiological effects on them and on receivers. For instance, a rapid pace of speaking increases a listener's heartbeat and adrenaline flow, and shouting may increase blood pressure; a calm, soft, and slow voice has the opposite effects. Neurolinguists are experimenting with pacing or *mirroring* techniques that may help a person control a conversation by voice variety alone (Grinder and Bandler, 1975, 1977; Bandler and Grinder, 1979; Goleman, 1979). For example, they suggest that when talking on the telephone to someone whose rate differs from yours, you should try to match the other person's rate because this may help to raise his or her comfort level quickly. Although their methods are controversial and their findings still subject to external verification, neurolinguistic programmers offer intriguing information on the power of the human voice (Goleman, 1979; Darling, 1988).

The third message channel is words. In the first two to four minutes of a new interaction, words (verbal communication) contribute only 7 percent to communication (Mehrabian, 1972). A person's choice of words, arrangement or pattern of ideas, and choices of evidence or supporting material make up a verbal message, whether spoken or written. Words are important, but in oral communication, if receivers do not like what they see in the message sender's body language or appearance or are stopped by something in the sender's voice, evidence suggests that they may not care about the words. Regardless of the verbal message conveyed, receivers' minds may already be made up because of an impression formed from nonverbal communication. There is ample evidence that when there is a contradiction between *what* we say and *how* we say it, most adults believe our manner and disregard the words we use (Mehrabian, 1972; Rosenthal and DePaulo, 1979).

When body language and vocal characteristics are appropriate and meet receivers' expectations, receivers move more quickly to act on the words. At that point, language that is congruent with nonverbal communication, appropriate to the situation, and powerful enough will sustain receivers' attention and contribute to the sharing of meaning. For example, an effective repair person avoids technical jargon when talking to an appliance owner who does not have a technical background, and an effective customer service representative understands the importance of using customers' names and courtesy titles correctly. In such cases, the initial 7 percent's worth of communication value of words may grow much larger, until words may carry most of the message.

How people use and respond to the three message channels depends on four variables: power or status, culture, gender, and physical response. The facial expression of smiling provides an example: High-status people smile less than low-status people. A smile in an American-influenced culture may mean something different from a smile in an Asian one. Women smile more than men, often in direct contradiction to the message they are conveying. A natural smile creates positive chemical changes in the body; a forced smile makes tension worse (Ekman, 1985; Ekman, Levenson, and Friesen, 1983).

The more a communicator knows about the fields of experience of other people in an interaction, the more prepared the communicator can be to control the effect of those variables on the communication process.

The communication process is also complicated by the barriers that may stand in the way of a message's being received as intended. *Interference,* or *noise,* as researchers term it, is information not wanted at a given point in the process because at that point it is not pertinent and impedes communication of information that is pertinent. Interference may originate from the sender (#5 of Figure 2), receiver (#6 of Figure 2), or message channel (#7 of Figure 2). For example, a sender's skin color, ethnicity, gender, or age may be a barrier and so, too, may nonverbal or vocal idiosyncrasies, word choice (one person's "sink" is another person's "basin"), or what an individual is believed to represent. If a sender works for an unpopular organization such as the Internal Revenue Service, a receiver may not get past that fact to the substance of the sender's message.

On the other hand, if a receiver is prejudiced, biased, ignorant, stressed, or fatigued, has language differences with a message's sender, or is a chronically inattentive listener, the sender's message may not be received as intended. For example, workers who are under stress and tension simply do not listen as accurately as they would without those barriers.

In terms of the message channel, if a workspace is crowded, poorly ventilated, or badly lit, if it has much traffic and literal noise, and many interruptions, workers may not work and communicate well. If a receiver cannot see body language or hear paralanguage and words clearly, the physical environment can be a major stumbling block to communication. Unless barriers are removed or at least lowered, a communication interaction will be only minimally effective.

Completing the complicated and unpredictable process of communication is feedback or response (see #8 and #9 of Figure 2). Feedback is both given and received when messages are exchanged, although meaning certainly can be conveyed without a receiver's showing his or her response. There are three aspects of feedback: type, form, and timing.

In terms of type, feedback may be positive or negative. Evidence from studies and observations by industrial psychologists and personnel experts show that when employees receive positive feedback or a mixture of positive and negative rather than just negative feedback, their morale is higher and their productivity greater (Skinner, 1953; Kohn, 1986a, 1986b).

In terms of form, feedback may be verbal, nonverbal, or a combination of the two. Good communicators tailor their feedback to the needs of the recipient. Some people respond better to a smile or a handshake, others to tone of voice, while still others prefer words, either oral or written.

In terms of timing, feedback may be given immediately or delayed. Again, people differ from one another and from situation to situation. Some people want to give or receive immediate responses. Others prefer that some time elapse before they respond to communication or have their communications responded to. The more communicators know about each other's field of experience, the more accurately they can time their responses.

What Are the Essential Elements of Training in Oral Communication?

To be effective communicators, people must understand their own basic communication style, understand and value different styles, and adjust their own style to others' styles. Let's consider each of these basic skills.

Awareness and Understanding of Our Own Dominant Style of Communication. Excellent and relatively inexpensive instruments are available to help in assessing styles of communication, among them the Myers Introduction to Type, Performax's Persona Matrix System, and Communication Skills, Inc.'s Self-Assessment Exercise. Such instruments provide useful information by helping identify people's personality traits or social styles. Keep in mind, however, that although proponents claim statistical validity for these instruments, critics doubt such validity. The value of the instruments lies in the increased self-awareness of people who assess their styles and in the way people can use the instruments' results to raise and resolve problems related to style conflicts and needs.

A person who has ascertained his or her dominant style needs to learn how it is manifested in body language, voice, and verbal language. Key questions to ask and answer are "What do I look like, sound like, and say?"

Each style tends to display its own set of cues, and nonverbal characteristics are crucial because more than half of a message's meaning is conveyed by them. An "action" person may manifest anger in facial expressions or gestures quite different from those of a "people" person. An "idea" person's eye behavior will likely differ from that of a "process" communicator. Good communicators know what they look like when they are angry, confident, upset, or happy. Videotaping is the fastest and most accurate way to learn these things about oneself.

Vocal characteristics also provide important information about how people communicate. If a person sounds harsh and abrasive, other people probably will perceive that person as harsh and abrasive. If a person sounds timid and insecure, he or she probably will be considered as such. A tape recording, preferably made in a real situation or in a realistic role play, accurately answers the question "What do I sound like?"

Finally, each communication style has distinctive verbal characteristics. Effective communicators understand that some word choices have more power or authority than others; that some styles value an arrangement of ideas that is linear, while others prefer a more random patterning; that some people value supporting material that is empirical (based on observation and experiment), while others prefer analogies or testimony from authority figures. An analysis of how a person writes may begin to answer the question "What do I say?" but it is also helpful to listen to audiotapes of meetings, presentations, briefings, and telephone conversations.

Ability to Understand and Value Different Communication Styles. Teams are predicated on acceptance; and as the business literature reports, teams are more productive, have higher morale, and produce better products than individuals or noncohesive groups (Hoerr, Pollock, and Whiteside, 1986; Waterman, 1987). Understanding and valuing human differences is a basic skill in conflict resolution, leadership, persuasion, and negotiation. Among the training approaches used to foster the understanding that leads to appreciation of diversity are brainstorming; group problem solving; group analysis of case studies, simulations, and role playing; and use of communication-style assessment instruments.

Ability to Adjust One's Personal Style to the Styles of Others. Most people have a backup style, a secondary style that allows a natural degree of adjustment in communication. Forced style adjustments may not be effective or may be overly manipulative of other people. But the more a person understands the communication styles of others, the easier it is to work within a natural range of responses, tailoring them to communicate sincere feelings and gain desired effects. Adjustments may be nonverbal (such as making direct eye contact), vocal (such as speaking more slowly and softly), or verbal (such as using certain words and avoiding others).

In brief training sessions, employees can learn how to adjust their communication styles. These sessions usually involve role playing and may be videotaped. When role-play scenarios are realistic, employees tend to learn quickly how to use their full style range. Some trainees use a type of theater called *trigger scripting* to supplement role playing (Valentine, 1979, 1986). Trigger scripting involves "the use of carefully selected scripts of literature intended to kindle (or 'trigger') planned-for responses from specialized audiences" (Valentine, 1979, p. 7).

What Constitutes Competency in Oral Communication? What Constitutes Mastery?

Nearly any worker can achieve competency in oral communication by taking training in how to communicate better. People whose jobs require that they make a good first impression and communicate publicly—broadcasters, ministers, recep-

tionists, performing artists, lawyers, trainers—have a special
incentive for assessing their oral communication strengths and
weaknesses and mastering their communication styles. Bank
tellers, hair stylists, bartenders, librarians, retail clerks, first-
line supervisors, manufacturing/engineering/design team members, secretaries, and social workers are among the employees
who must interact closely with other people and who need competency in their own communication styles and in understanding and valuing the communication styles of others. Finally,
workers whose jobs depend on establishing rapport, trust, and
credibility with other people must learn to master the skill of
adjusting their communication style to work well with people
whose styles differ from their own. Clearly, this is a skill requirement for good supervisors and managers. Among others
who need this skill are lawyers, physicians, customer service
representatives, waiters and waitresses, temporary office workers, repair people, insurance agents, consultants, executive
secretaries, stock brokers, salespeople, architects, and human
resource experts.

Competence and mastery in oral communication are assessed by the facility with which a person operates in human
communication interactions. Assessment of competence in oral
communication is based on observation of demonstrated behavior. For example, from an employer's perspective, an employee's
competency in or mastery of oral communication skills may be
demonstrated by ability to handle complaints satisfactorily.

What Are Examples of Successful Workplace
Training Programs in Oral Communication?

Outstanding training and development work in oral communication skills is being done by large and small firms throughout the country. Xerox is among the companies that have
benefited from taking employee training in teamwork and communication skills seriously (Samuelson, 1988). It and other companies like Digital Corporation and IBM have large, sophisticated training delivery systems. In other companies, training
staffers such as those in Gannett Corporation's training depart-

ment and Greyhound's department of career and management development act as brokers for other organizational units by providing them with names of consultants, training materials, staff assistance in assessment and program design, assistance in seminar registration, and advice.

Successful training in oral communication skills is exemplified by programs in organizations of notably different size, which are described below.

Valley National Bank. Headquartered in Phoenix, Valley National Bank (VNB) is Arizona's largest bank. VNB has assets of more than $11 billion and has over 7,000 employees in more than 200 branches in Arizona with other services throughout the Southwest. Its training staff arranges for the delivery of more than 200 courses, about one-third of which are recycled every six months. With courses ranging from basic teller training to executive development, the current training program's design was developed in the mid-1980s in response to a philosophy called *managing performance.* This philosophy calls for ongoing employee development rather than limiting development discussions to performance evaluation reviews.

VNB's leaders developed this philosophy as a part of a major shift in the bank's strategic plan. Individual employees and their managers now use achievement plans to set employee development goals. Achievement plans are constructed for each employee for a six- to twelve-month period and address four major development areas: professional, personal, management, and executive. The achievement plan does not specify the number of days an employee will spend in training, and both the employee and the supervisor must sign the plan.

VNB's training and development department is a centralized operation that receives its funding from top management. Specific technical training related to branch operations, sales, and computer applications is managed by the line organizations in consultation with the corporate training and development staff. Historically, VNB's senior management has taken personal interest in the training unit, with each succeeding CEO working with the vice president of training and development to ensure ample staffing and resources for the department. To help ensure that its training courses are needs-driven, VNB's training and development department conducts ongoing assessment of course offerings, trainers, vendors, and consultants. VNB's vice president/manager of training and development says the department can offer as much or as little training as the line requires.

The training department publishes an annual *Training Resources Directory* along with an *Employee Development Planner* to inform employees of the educational opportunities and in-house courses available to them. The directory describes each course, its goals and objectives, and its eligibility requirements. The planner communicates the training schedule and the available curricula (that is, management, supervisory, administrative support, and job effectiveness). More than half the courses are available to all employees — not just managers — and thousands of employees receive training each year. VNB refers to its *shared development* in which both employer and employee play roles. Because VNB encourages and supports ongoing employee education, it makes courses available in the evening and on weekends, as well as during the regular workday.

Training is provided through in-house trainers, external consultants (sole practitioners and companies), associations (such as the American Institute of Banking), local colleges and universities (such as Phoenix College and the Arizona State University Center for Executive Development), and vendors of interactive videos, computer programs, and workbooks (such as those for Xerox's Professional Selling Skills course). Much of the training of nonexempt employees is conducted by other nonexempt employees who have completed "train the trainer" courses. Oral communication skills constitute a significant portion of this type of training.

According to VNB's vice president for training, communication training is viewed as "a core competency" in and of itself. It is embedded in most of the courses, usually by specific mention. Banking is an interpersonal business, and even technical jobs require communication skills. A review of the course descriptions in the 1987 *Training Resources Directory* bears out this claim; for more than half the courses, "communication" is mentioned in either the course title, description, or objectives. For example, each of these courses pays attention to nonverbal communication, use of language, and listening skills:

> Negotiating Skills
> Face-to-Face Selling Skills
> Verbal and Nonverbal Communication Skills
> Conflict Resolution
> Problem Solving and Decision Making
> Communication Skills for Managers
> Moving Up to Supervision
> Functioning as a Team Member

A representative of popular courses is Communication Skills for Managers, now in its seventh year and third revision. This one-day course taught by an external consultant enrolls twenty-five to thirty participants who have completed a prerequisite course in management skills. The course has three parts. Part I reviews the communication process and the power of body language, vocal characteristics, and language choices in the creation of first impressions. In Part II, participants complete a communication-style assessment instrument and work through a series of exercises that profile each style and provide strategies for adjusting style to the requirements of different situations. Part III deals with persuasion. Participants select among timely topics (such as automatic teller machines or checking account charges) and work in teams to draw up an *influence strategy* for changing the attitudes or behaviors of a target audience.

Once a year, an employee meets with his or her supervisor to select appropriate training course(s) for the employee. To help ensure appropriate departmental planning, each supervisor for his or her function fills out a development planner (learning contract) that becomes a working departmental plan for development and course attendance and completion. As long as a course is preapproved as part of an employee's yearly achievement plan, any tuition is paid by the bank directly or through employee reimbursement. Because employees' participation in these courses is voluntary (although, admittedly, with considerable persuasion from supervisors), VNB schedules most courses during employees' work hours, although recently there has been some movement toward weekend and evening programs.

Evaluation is ongoing, with each course's specific evaluation instrument designed in concert with the managers who requested the course. In most cases, a two-part evaluation form is used: one section uses a quantitative rating system, and the second asks participants to respond to a series of open-ended questions (Elizabeth Scharfman, telephone interview, February 1988).

Harris Design Group. A small Washington, D.C., architectural firm, Harris Design Group put a communication consultant under contract to provide training in presentation skills, interpersonal communication, and related personnel matters.

Founder and president Robert Harris decided his small firm could compete more effectively if support-level staffers and professionals were trained in listening skills, communication styles, and conflict resolution. After Harris read and was favorably impressed by a local communication consultant's book, he asked her to design a training program for his staff.

Together, Harris and the consultant created a one-year action plan with specific goals and objectives. The consultant then met individually with every member of the twenty-person firm and used information from those confidential interviews to shape the design of bimonthly, half-day courses. The program design used videotaping, communication-style instruments, role playing, and small-group problem solving extensively.

Throughout the program, the consultant met weekly with Harris and his three-person executive team to assess results, monitor personnel problems, and design specific one-on-one interventions as required. Harris relied on the consultant as a sounding board, and often consulted her before meeting clients or visiting construction sites. According to Harris, the program was the best per dollar investment he ever made. Firm members still use information they learned about communication styles and remind one another about it whenever listening problems crop up (Robert Harris, personal interview, March 1988).

Tucson Fire Department. Many city and county governments have training departments. Increasingly, these are staffed by professionals with backgrounds in organizational development or training. Large departments often have their own training officer(s). One innovative public-sector training program is for fire fighters in the city of Tucson, Arizona. In 1982, under the leadership of its fire chief, the department began a major overhaul of its training program for first-line fire fighters and their supervisors and battalion chiefs. Courses now include communication skills, conflict resolution, community relations, and supervisory skills. A variety of trainers — including faculty members from the Department of Communication at the University of Arizona and local and other consultants — provide programs tailored to fire fighters. Financial support comes from the city manager's office and the fire department's own budget. Even in the face of current budget-cutting measures, Chief Richard Moreno insists that all new officers receive communication skills training.

His insistence on communication training is part of a trend: More training in communication skills is being provided as the sources of organizational return on investment (ROI) are better documented. In a tight labor market, employers are coming to realize that their employees are not expendable but are resources that need to be developed. Communication training helps organizations achieve the goal of having articulate workers who are motivated and equipped to serve customers and to participate fully in organizational life (Richard Moreno, telephone interview, April 1988).

What Should Be Included in a Generic Workplace Oral Communication Curriculum?

Exhibit 6 lists items to consider in designing an oral communication curriculum.

Exhibit 6. The Importance of Oral Communication.

What are the objectives of this training?
-To make participants aware of the importance of oral communication in
their everyday work life
-To improve participants' on-the-job oral communication skills
-To teach techniques for ongoing individual self-development of oral
communication skills
-To increase participants' value to the organization by helping them to do
their job better

Skill One: Know Your Own Style of Communication

How can you *not* communicate?
-Facts about amount of time spent communicating
-Why it is important to make good first impressions
-Explanation of how first impressions are formed in the first two to four
minutes of a communication exchange
-Three key questions effective communicators ask and answer
  -What do you *look* like? — Nonverbal Communication
    -Discussion of body language and appearance and the fact that these
    nonverbals constitute 55 percent of the meaning of the message; im-
    portance of culture, gender, authority/status
    -Practical exercise that highlights importance of nonverbals (for exam-
    ple, participants may check out personal space or whether they like to
    be touched)
  -What do you *sound* like? — Vocal Communication
    -Discussion of voice characteristics such as rate, pitch, and loudness;
    how the voice contributes 38 percent of the meaning in face-to-face in-
    teractions and 70–90 percent when one is on the phone
    -Practical exercise that demonstrates how rate or loudness can energize
    or calm people down (if group is small, get brief sample of voice on
    tape recorder)
  -What do you *say*? — Verbal Communication
    -While language is worth only 7 percent in first few moments, it will be
    worth more if and when the receiver gets past the nonverbal and vocal
    to choice of words, arrangement of and support for ideas.
    -Some word choices are more powerful than others.
    -Consistency between *what* is said and *how* it is said is important; if
    there is a discrepancy, people believe the *how*.

Are you what you value? Assessing Your Style of Communication
-Option A: Distribute a self-assessment instrument (SAI) that "measures"
each participant's style of communication. Score SAIs with the group so
that each participant knows his or her dominant and backup styles.
-Option B: Videotape some participants (or all, if the group is small) in a
brief role-playing situation where they respond to a typical job-related
situation.

Exhibit 6. The Importance of Oral Communication, Cont'd.

What kind of action styles do you use to communicate?
–Profiles of four styles of communication
  –Describe each style briefly, or show video if Option B is used.
  –Have group draw up nonverbal, vocal, and verbal characteristics for each style.
  –Have participants discuss the kind of physical environment each style prefers (for example, pictures of family, tidy desk, lots of light).
–Brainstorming session on the strengths and weaknesses of each style on the job
–Tips on improving body language and/or voice
–Practical exercise using audio or video
  –Focus on one change participants think should be made in their voice or body language.
  –Give some or all participants one to two minutes before a camera or microphone to try out new behaviors.
  –Replay tape and reinforce results; make suggestions for further change. Consider having a brief critique sheet available for participants to fill out.
–Activity plan to improve participants' oral communication skills

Skills Two and Three: Understand and Adjust
to Other Styles of Communication

How can you *not* communicate? Power of Communication
–Facts about interpersonal communication and success in the workplace
–*First* impression, *best* impression: How impressions are formed and why they are important
–Three key questions effective communicators ask and answer
  –What do you *look* like?—Nonverbal Communication
  –What do you *sound* like?—Vocal Communication
  –What do you *say?*—Verbal Communication
–Brief synopsis of each of these three channels of communication, noting importance of culture, gender, power, physical response, and *where* interactions take place
–Self-assessment instrument

Are you what you value? Assessing Your Style of Communication
–Scoring of self-assessment instrument
–Profile of four styles of communication—brief overview of each style

How do you value others? Understanding Other Styles of Communication
–Problem-solving exercise (those with each style meet in a small group to draw up a profile of what they look like, sound like, and say and their environmental preferences—for example, messy desk, plants and pictures, chair for guests)

Exhibit 6. The Importance of Oral Communication, Cont'd.

-Debriefing (each style reports out its profile)
-Discussion period (may include contributions and weaknesses of each
 style in the workplace)

What happens when styles collide? Adjusting Your Style to the Communica-
tion Styles of Others
-Small group exercise
   -Assign each group a style unlike its own.
   -Have each group draw up a plan of action to adjust its style to the one
    assigned (some adjustments might be nonverbal, others vocal, and still
    others verbal).
   -Have each group also note what "bugs" its members about the assigned
    style.
-Have each group report out its plan and the participants representing that
 style react to the "adjustments."
-Tips on expanding your range of styles and using backup style(s)

What action styles do you use to communicate?
-Case study (assign participants to groups composed of representatives of
 the four styles; give each a brief case study; groups must first discuss solution from point of view of each of the four styles, then pick best style or
 combination of styles)
-Role playing (using case study as scenario, either in small groups or before
 entire group) with focus on making adjustments in your own style (this can
 be videotaped)
-Discussion (replay video or rework role-playing scenes)

Source: Adapted from Elsea, 1988a.

CHAPTER 8

Principles of Good Listening

The reason we have two ears but one mouth is so we might
listen more and talk less.

Zeno of Citium, 2 B.C.

What Is Listening?

The word *listen* derives from two Anglo-Saxon words:
hlystan, which means "hearing," and *hlosian,* which means "to
wait in suspense." Listening, then, as communication authority
Robert Bolton (1979, p. 32) notes, "is the combination of hearing what the other person says *and* a suspenseful waiting, an
intense, psychological involvement with others." In more academic terms, listening may be defined as "the process of receiving, attending to, and assigning meaning to aural stimuli"
(Wolvin and Coakley, 1982, p. 53). To this definition, communication expert Janet Elsea (1988b) adds visual stimuli as
a consideration equal to aural stimuli in importance.

What Theories Support Current
Training in Listening?

The pioneering work on listening behavior was conducted
by the University of Minnesota's Ralph Nichols in the 1940s.
He drew an important distinction — one that subsequent researchers have agreed with — between *hearing* and *listening.* Hearing is
a complicated process in which sound waves are received by

the ear and transmitted to the brain. Most people hear sounds all the time, but only when they attend to a particular sound and give it meaning have they listened.

In addition to aural stimuli, listening involves attention to visual stimuli, especially nonverbal cues. For people who are hearing impaired, visual cues are crucial to their ability to respond to messages, just as auditory stimuli are crucial for people who are blind.

The listening process begins when sound or sight stimuli or both have been received and identified as symbols. The sounds people utter will differ from culture to culture and language to language and even within a given language's dialects. But when a speaker utters a sound group (such as a word or sigh) recognizable to a listener, meaning begins to occur for the listener. As the listener's brain begins to recognize the symbols being communicated, it attaches importance to them and searches memory for past experiences that help assign meaning to them. The process of assigning meaning involves "analyzing, understanding, registering, interpreting, relating to past and future expectancies, engaging in further mental activity, assimilating, converting meaning to mind, receiving, identifying, recognizing, and comprehending" (Wolvin and Coakley, 1982, p. 49). The listening process also involves storing information about the stimuli and their meaning in long- or short-term memory for later recall.

Many theorists believe that the listening process ends when a listener brings meaning to aural and visual symbols, but other theorists argue that the process must include a listener's reaction or response. The latter theorists assert that "the *response* stage of listening is especially crucial for judging the success of the listening act as a whole" (Watson and Barker, 1984, p. 182).

Given the transactional nature of the communication process, when listeners respond overtly, they become communication senders. For example, if the word *come* is spoken as a command, the listening process is not concerned with whether or not a listener obeys. The concern is with whether the listener has "received and attended to the data. The listening process concerns only the selecting of such stimulus data in order to 'receive' it and the cognitive structuring of it" (Weaver, 1972, p. 6).

The listening process's complexity is one reason why, without instruction, most people lack listening skills. Other reasons relate to listener, speaker, message, and environmental characteristics.

• *Listener characteristics.* Among the variables that affect people's listening abilities are culture, past experiences, gender, age, ego involvement, personal anxieties, fatigue level, attention span, intelligence, linguistic aptitude, reading skill, organizational abilities, extrinsic motivations, level of apprehension, and note taking (Nichols, 1948; Barker, 1971).

• *Speaker characteristics.* Key variables relating to speakers include a speaker's credibility, degree of attractiveness, vocal variables (such as rate of speech, loudness, pitch, and tone), fluency, facial expressions, and likability (Watson and Barker, 1984, pp. 184–185). For example, the disparity between a speaker's rate of speech and the speed of a listener's thought processes can create problems. Studies have found that for rates of speech of 120 to 250 words per minute, listeners have *reasonable* comprehension. Because the brain processes information three to five times faster than most people can talk, however, a speaker who talks too slowly or a listener who does not work to stay mentally engaged runs the risk of having the listener's attention lapse. There is also a correlation between listening attentiveness and the authority a speaker wields. To be blunt, people do not listen well to people they consider unattractive, inferior, or not credible.

• *Message characteristics.* Among the variables that appear to increase listeners' comprehension are a speaker's use of clear, unambiguous statements, use of the active voice, expression of views or viewpoints similar to those of the audience, message organization, and the violation or disconfirmation of audience expectations (Watson and Barker, 1984, pp. 184–185).

• *Environmental characteristics.* Variables in the environment such as temperature, seating arrangement, noise level, and room ventilation affect listening comprehension (Watson and Barker, 1984, pp. 184–185).

How people listen depends on *why* they listen. Reasons for listening include appreciation, information, conversation, classification, problem solving, reinforcement, empathy, stimulation, evaluation, and comprehension. President William Arnold of the International Listening Association boils all of these reasons down to two: people listen for information or to build relationships with others (telephone interview, February 1988).

An important new research area seeks to measure how people manifest their listening habits in terms of body language, voice characteristics, heart rate, and blood pressure. This area's findings, which are quantitative rather than based on the anecdotal narratives or rhetorical analyses that have marked the field of study for decades, suggest that people's listening styles fall along an energy continuum (Lynch, 1985b).

At one end of the continuum is a quiet, relaxed style of listening in which the listener's focus is on something or someone other than himself or herself. Termed the *orienting response,* this was first discovered by Pavlov in the early 1900s. This style helps bring down a listener's blood pressure and slows the heartbeat. Experimenters at the University of Pennsylvania charted the blood pressure of various people during three activities: reading aloud, staring at a blank wall, and watching fish swim in a tank. Each subject's blood pressure was highest when speaking, but lowest when watching the fish rather than when merely staring at the wall (Lynch, 1985b).

Led by the pioneering work of Father James Lynch at the University of Maryland Hospital, researchers also discovered that interacting with a pet triggered the orienting response. The key to a quiet, relaxed style of listening seems to be empathy with someone or something other than oneself. The body language of a quiet listener tends to be open and relaxed, with minimal facial expressions and movements and just an occasional nod or leaning in. Vocal responses tend to be brief, encouraging sounds now and then. As our society wrestles with high health care costs, the implication that this mode of listening is a means for stress reduction that might help people avoid strokes and heart attacks is an important avenue to explore.

At the other end of the energy continuum is a defensive, agitated, hypertensive style of listening termed *defensive, judgmental, evaluative,* or *argumentative* listening. For hypertensive people, says Lynch, "Communication with others is a *desperate* struggle.

Inside their adult bodies is a baby crying, terrified because no one can hear it. To protect themselves from the terror, they keep others at a distance. Their weapon is a defensive way of speaking and listening. But the strategy backfires; it just makes their blood pressure climb even higher" (Lynch, 1985b, p. 49). Lynch also notes that hypertensive people tend to talk fast and loud, interrupting and speaking over others, gesturing emphatically. Fortunately, defensive listeners can be taught to breathe slowly and regularly, to relax their nonverbal behaviors, and to speak more slowly. More important, however, if their physiology is to change (for lowered blood pressure, slower heartbeat, and healthful endocrinological changes), these people must solve the communication problems that prevent them from listening to and empathizing with another person; they must learn, as Lynch characterizes it, "the language of the heart" (Lynch, 1985b, p. 49).

Two styles of listening fall along the middle of the continuum. One is *social* or *conversational* listening. According to research dating from the 1920s, we spend most of our listening time in conversations with other people. So it behooves us to polish our listening skills for use in work-related, information-sharing conversations and interviews and at social events where we meet and converse with strangers, acquaintances, and friends. Typically, a social listener's body language is open and friendly, eye contact is direct, and there is frequent smiling, nodding, and appropriate touching. In this mode, a person makes encouraging, approving sounds. Social listeners act courteous, polite, and pleasant, whether they feel like it or not.

The remaining style is *active* listening, a more comprehensive approach that involves listening with ears and eyes, taking into account not just the words spoken but the way in which they are spoken (Elsea, 1986). Active listeners "people read" by looking at other people's nonverbal cues and listening for the vocal indicators that, together, reveal the message "between the lines." Active listeners capitalize on the speech-thought speed difference by using spare thinking time to summarize mentally, to listen for main ideas, to draw inferences, or to formulate questions. Their listening tracks along with a speaker's communication. They do not jump ahead to prepare a rebuttal or defense but withhold judgment and evaluation until an appropriate point in the interaction.

Active listeners give a speaker accurate and ample feedback by nodding, displaying appropriate facial expressions, asking questions, and rephrasing or paraphrasing the speaker's comments. They wait to understand a speaker's point rather than reacting to emotional trigger words (in business, for example, the word *cost* will not deafen an active listener to subsequent information on benefits). Active listeners work to find common ground, to identify with a speaker but still remain objective. Active listeners try to remove communication barriers whether environmental (such as noise, immoderate temperature, an uncomfortable seating arrangement) or interpersonal (such as language problems, cultural differences, high stress or fatigue levels).

Effective listeners decide their listening purpose on the basis of the situation, occasion, and content of a speaker's message. They then select an appropriate style, usually passive in the first few moments, but becoming more dynamic as they adjust the style at various points to mesh in interaction with a speaker. Poor listeners, on the other hand, tend to persist in using their dominant style of listening, which may be at odds with the situation, occasion, or type of message being conveyed. For example, a supervisor who feels "too busy" to engage in conversation with employees will have body language and tone of voice that give employees a clear message to "get on with important matters; I do not have time to listen to your personal problems." In fact, those rejected personal messages might provide the supervisor with vital information for dealing with "important matters." In that sense, they too are important.

What Are the Essential Elements of Training in Listening?

Listening research and educational materials have concentrated on skills for retention and comprehension of messages, primarily in the classroom. Little has been done in a quantitative, verifiable fashion to survey the range of skills people use in the workplace, much less to measure the extent to which each skill is employed, by whom, and under what circumstances. In fact, research on listening has been so narrow in its focus that, as an article in the *Journal of Business Communication* points out, "little information available can be applied to business settings. A typical business setting is more likely to be a two-way process involving questions and summarization than a lecture, which has been the focus of listening research" (Smeltzer and Watson, 1985, p. 34).

Although the attention scholars pay to listening in business settings is discouragingly little, evidence suggests that there are three basic listening skills relevant for all levels of employees in many business settings.

Adapt the Style of Listening to Fit the Situation and the Content of the Message Being Conveyed. Poor listeners lack listening flexibility; they tend to respond with their dominant style, even if that style is inappropriate or counterproductive. A stereotypical example is an employee who argues with everything he hears and often interrupts to offer judgments. Some managers fit the stereotype of a person who is so unconcerned, unresponsive, and nonassertive that employees must go to extreme lengths to get managerial attention.

A fundamental technique of effective listening is the ability to select an appropriate style: An effective listener usually is passive in at least the first few moments while assessing the situation; then he or she settles on a style to meet the situation and responds accordingly. As the listener gains information about the speaker, his or her expectations, and the context of the communication, the listener adjusts the listening style to accommodate the speaker's needs. Sometimes this means continuing the original style choice throughout the interaction; at other times, subtle changes in body language, vocal characteristics, verbal response, or energy level are required. For example, a customer service representative may need to listen with quiet empathy to an irate customer — in effect, giving the customer permission to vent negative feelings. After hearing out the customer's complaints, the service representative probably will shift to a more active problem-solving demeanor.

People who apply this skill are better communicators and, as discussed earlier, are probably less stressed. They will be more adept at a range of activities from customer service to sales, from supervision of others to performance evaluation, from teamwork to conflict resolution.

In *First Impression, Best Impression,* communication expert Janet Elsea (1986, p. 112) recommends these adjustment strategies for expanding listening styles:

- Separate the person from the words, and react to ideas, not to the person.
- Find a reason to listen; for example, if the listener is not interested in what the speaker is saying, the listener should, if necessary, create a reason to listen. For instance, a listener may listen simply because a speaker needs to be listened to.
- Resist being judgmental; even if something in the speaker's content, delivery, or appearance tempts a listener to evaluate the speaker negatively, a good listener withholds judgment. By doing so, the listener may learn something of value and at the same time helps the other person successfully communicate his or her full message.
- Do not react to a speaker's emotionally loaded language or inflammatory delivery style. Reacting to such language and style only arouses a listener's anger, lowering his or her ability to process accurately what there is to see and hear.

Reduce Barriers or Interference That May Impede the Communication Process. Some barriers to listening are environmental (poor seating arrangement, immoderate room temperature, high noise level, lack of privacy, interruptions). Others are interpersonal (cultural differences, language problems, high stress levels, differences in attitudes and expectations, nonverbal or verbal idiosyncrasies). Effective listeners use several techniques to reduce such barriers.

One technique is to heed the physical environment. For instance, effective listeners may make certain that there is adequate ventilation and light (because without them people's attention spans will be reduced), a comfortable temperature, and a seating pattern that meets the goals of the interaction (studies show that the closer people sit to one another, the more they tend to listen). Another technique is to concentrate one's mental and physical energies. After shutting out distractions, perhaps by closing the door, forwarding telephone calls, or going to a more private place, an effective listener works to resist the distractions of remaining stimuli not related to the communication. A third technique is to find common ground with the speaker. A listener should try to identify with the speaker but maintain objectivity. A fourth technique is to reduce one's stress or anxiety. There is a direct, inverse correlation between a listener's level of stress or anxiety and his or her ability to attend to, respond to, and retain a message (Elsea, 1986; Barker, 1971).

Listen Actively. Active listening is the style most often used on the job. As discussed in the section on theory, active listeners employ their ears and eyes as they attend to changes in a speaker's voice and body language. Besides watching a speaker's face, they watch the rest of the body because most speakers are spontaneous in their communication from the neck down. Tension, anxiety, deception, interest, relaxation, or confidence may be seen in a speaker's gestures, posture, use of space, movements, and touching behaviors (Ekman, 1985). Active listeners also give a speaker accurate and timely feedback — sometimes nonverbal, sometimes verbal, often a combination.

What Constitutes Competency in Listening? What Constitutes Mastery?

Until recently, research in testing listening skill has focused on listening comprehension, with much research centered on the Brown-Carlsen and STEP tests, two of the oldest and best known. The Brown-Carlsen Listening Comprehension Test, developed in 1955 by J. I. Brown and G. R. Carlsen, was designed for testing students in grades nine through twelve. It includes a series of items divided in relation to subtasks used in the comprehension of the spoken word—subtasks such as immediate recall, following directions, recognizing transitions, recognizing meaning, and lecture comprehension.

In the 1950s, other theorists devised tests that added variables such as reflective and receptive listening skills and factors ranging from listening to music for main ideas to traditional lecture retention and comprehension. The Educational Testing Service's Sequential Test of Educational Progress: Listening Test (STEP), first introduced in 1957, is still on the market. However, Brown-Carlsen and STEP may not measure listening ability but intelligence, according to some experts. Moreover, key business skills related to listening effectiveness—such as asking questions, taking notes, and summarizing information—are not measured by these traditional tests.

In the 1960s, several tests focused on children's listening comprehension were marketed, including the Orr-Graham Listening Test, the Assessment of Children's Language Comprehension (ACLA), and the Education Development Laboratories' Listen and Think modules. By the early 1970s, researchers began to modify existing instruments and create new ones in response to the "criticisms about test construction and administration procedures" (Watson and Barker, 1984, p. 181). One such instrument, designed in 1972 by the New Zealand Council for Educational Research, was called the Progressive Achievement Tests of Listening Comprehension (PAT). Tests to examine the interpersonal factors of listening as well as lecture retention were also introduced. The Jones-Mohr Listening Test, for example, measures the effects of nonverbal cues on listening comprehension.

The Watson-Barker Listening Test (WBLT) was the first test of any statistical significance that was designed specifically for adults in business settings. In its original 1983 version, this test's instructions, content, material, and test questions were on audiotape, but the test's authors have since added a videotape (Watson and Barker, 1987). The WBLT focuses on business-related topics and uses speakers with different regional accents. Fifty items measure five interpersonal skills: interpretive short-term listening, interpretive dialogue short-term listening, short-

term lecture listening, interpretive-emotional-connotative meaning short-term listening, and short- and long-term instruction-
following listening (Watson and Barker, 1987).

The 1980s also brought a number of commercial programs
that claim to measure listeners' attitudes and styles and to improve employees' listening skills. Among the most visible on the
market are Performax's Attitudinal Listening Profile System,
Telestar's Successful Listening, and Unisys Corporation's CAUSE
for Listening.

The problem with listening tests is that they may not be
measuring what they claim. As Watson and Barker (1984, p.
187) found in their extensive review of listening behavior, published in *Communication Yearbook 8,* "Most listening tests currently
on the market have been criticized by communication scholars
and educators. Critics have questioned the tests' validity, the
relations among types of listening required, generalizability to
the real world, norming procedures, passage lengths, and methods of administration." Watson and Barker (1984, p. 189) also
note that listening is a complex process, not a single skill, and
"therefore, listening tests must be identified and/or constructed
to meet the complexities and challenges of such a construct."

This is not to say that people cannot learn a great deal
about themselves as listeners from the tests currently available,
from videotaped exercises, or even from feedback from a trusted
person. But until more evidence is compiled on adult listeners
in actual work-related settings, "let the buyer beware" of tests'
claims of precise measurement of listening skills.

Ford and Xerox are examples of corporations that have
had success as a result of emphasizing listening skills mastery.
A few years ago, both had economic problems and poor public
images. Their comebacks have been, in the words of *Washington
Post* economic columnist Robert J. Samuelson (1988, p. B1),
"spectacular . . . their quality is higher, their costs have been
trimmed."

Both companies drew heavily on Japanese methods. Xerox
practices competitive benchmarking; that is, it evaluates the best
features of the competition's products and services, then tries
to exceed them. A basic tactic of this strategy is training employ-

ees to "listen" to customers by sending out 50,000 questionnaires monthly, asking customers to rate equipment reliability, service responsiveness, and copy quality. According to Samuelson (1988, p. B4) the results are impressive: In the past three years, customer service ratings have improved by a third. Since 1982, average manufacturing costs per unit have dropped 20 percent. The average period for developing a new product has decreased by as much as 60 percent.

At Ford, labor and management work closely together. For example, design and production engineers work in teams and have been able to reduce defects. Car designers work with the goal of ease of manufacturing in mind. The number of parts suppliers has been reduced, which makes components more reliable. In short, "the company listens to workers' suggestions for quality improvement" (Samuelson, 1988, p. B4).

On a smaller scale, Arizona Public Service — that state's largest public utility company — offers a course entitled Effective Listening Skills for all performance review employees. The manager for corporate employee development, Charles Richards, states that the company believes that "employees who take this course make better team players. . . . They are not so inclined to be Lone Rangers or heroes or fire fighters, but to be developers and inspirers of others" (personal interview, February 1988).

What Are Examples of Successful Workplace Training Programs in Listening?

Unisys Corporation (Formerly Sperry Corporation, Now Merged with Burroughs). Throughout the 1980s, the role model for in-house listening programs was the one instituted by the Sperry Corporation's management development program department in the late 1970s. By early 1983, Sperry had trained more than 10,000 of its employees and customers. Its program focuses on awareness rather than skill building, although several effective listening techniques are explained.

When Sperry merged with Burroughs in 1986 to become Unisys, it phased out its company-wide listening skills program in order to concentrate resources on other, more immediately critical factors affecting the merger. Course content was put into a videotape called CAUSE for Listening, which currently is sold throughout the company and to the general public. The title's acronym "CAUSE" stands for five listening skills: *c*hoose to listen, *a*ttend to the speaker, *u*nderstand the speaker's point of view, *s*ift through what is listened to, and *e*xpress understanding by paraphrasing or summarizing what the speaker has said and reflecting meaning to that person.

At Unisys, individual divisions or departments now have responsibility for deciding whether to provide listening training; those that do base their programs on the CAUSE model. For example, Unisys's defense systems division conducts regular courses in communication skills for its 32,000 employees. In 1987, the management and organizational development unit of the human resource development department initiated this program on a charge-back basis for user departments.

Two courses are offered at Unisys's Valley Forge (Pennsylvania) Training Center: A half-day seminar using the CAUSE videotape and training materials is open to first-level supervisors and all hourly wage employees; and a full-day course is open to managers. Two in-house trainers teach each course every second week, with a typical enrollment of twenty participants. According to the manager of management and organizational development for defense systems, these core courses are more skill-based than awareness-focused ones. A month after participants complete a course, they are sent a checklist of effective listening behaviors and asked to indicate their progress. Two months later, trainers call each participant to talk about the course's impact on his or her job (Paula Kirby, telephone interviews, May and June 1988).

Ford Motor Company. One of the most comprehensive and best-documented training programs is that of Ford Motor Company. One of its major training resources is the management and technical training department at its North American Human Resources Development (HRD) Center in Dearborn, Michigan.

After Ford sustained major losses in 1979, 1980, and 1981, its management decided to focus on improving product quality. Ford determined that this strategic focus would require changes in how people were managed and how they participated on the job. In 1983, despite company losses of billions of dollars, Ford quadrupled its training budget and created the Dearborn HRD Center.

Ford's strategic plan for the upcoming five years was based on team building and featured listening as a key to effective team interaction. The teamwork training involved all levels of workers from United Auto Workers line workers to supervisors and plant managers. One of the management specialists from the management and technical training department stated, "Communication skills are deeply intertwined in our team training because if the culture is to change, people need to know how to understand each other, communicate their own thoughts and beliefs, and listen to what others have to say" (Richard Donakowski, telephone interview, June 1988).

Training is decentralized at Ford: Each division has its own training function, as does each plant. The Dearborn HRD Center is called on to provide a great deal of the training for employees at all levels. The center's staff frequently tailors courses to a specific division's or plant's request, often training individuals who come to the center. Each plant, department, and division receives a semiannual catalogue that describes courses available at the center. Within a ten-week period, employees or their supervisors submit training requests; then the center staff allocates space on the basis of those requests. Current demand is so great that some courses can meet only 65 to 70 percent of the requests. Depending on the situation, the center staff handles overflow requests either by creating a second section of a course or by putting some requesters on a waiting list for the next course running.

Special requests (for example, from line workers who want help in improving their listening skills) are considered, and the center's staff and/or consultants may go to plants and divisions to provide on-site training. The management training area employs sixteen full-time specialists who work not as trainers but as supervisors. Their work is supplemented by that of training professionals who must be certified as being knowledgeable about Ford's corporate culture. All courses must be customized to meet Ford-specific needs because the intention is to provide training directly related to skill building for Ford employees' use on the job.

A recent Ford catalogue lists and describes four courses that deal specifically with listening skills and are open to managers, supervisors, or nonsupervisory workers. The Managing Conflict Workshop is a three-day workshop whose objectives include the "practice [of] listening skills in conflict situations . . . through discussion, problem-solving exercises, and video role playing." The workshop is run fifty times a year, and enrollment is limited to thirty people per running.

The Effective Listening Seminar is a one-day seminar focusing on "the four purposes of communication and the four states of listening. Participants are provided with listening history, self-assessment opportunities, and the key to effective listening. Various individual and group exercises are employed to increase awareness and build listening skills." Course objectives for participants include becoming knowledgeable about the nature and importance of listening; becoming aware of personal listening strengths, weaknesses, habits, and needs; and developing skills and techniques that will improve listening effectiveness. According to the contracting services and program administrator for the Ford courses, this seminar was developed in 1985 as a direct result of requests from both Ford's worldwide headquarters and from the Employee Involvement and Participative Management (EIPM) program. The seminar is so popular that, in 1987, it was offered ninety times at the Dearborn HRD Center, and it was also offered at several other sites.

The one-day version of the Interpersonal Skills Workshop provides participants "an opportunity to practice and improve such skills as effective listening, dealing with anger, providing and receiving feedback, and learning the benefits of assertive language." The expanded (two-day) version of the Interpersonal Skills Workshop uses team-oriented case studies and role playing to develop participants' skills in assertive and active listening. The center schedules this two-day course more than seventy times each year and also presents it several times by special request.

In courses, participants receive an evaluation form based on "the smile factor." The entire system by which Ford evaluates training is in the process of being changed. At the moment, however, training follow-up is handled much the same as at Unisys. Rosters are pulled six to eight weeks after a course, and six to eight randomly chosen participants are called and asked how they are using the skills, what skills and techniques help them on the job, and what course changes they would recommend.

Participants are not given special credit for attending most courses. If a course has certified a participant for a special job classification, however, a plant or division official notes this on a form. Each employee is allotted $1,500 for attending professional development courses, whether on-site, at local colleges, at professional seminars, or through the development centers.

Ford's commitment to training has led employees to refer to it as "a different company," one that rewards quality, appropriate risk taking, entrepreneurial spirit, and teamwork (Ron Smith and Richard Donakowski, telephone interviews, May and June 1988).

What Should Be Included in a Generic Workplace Listening Curriculum?

Exhibit 7 lists items to consider in designing a listening curriculum.

Exhibit 7. Workshop: How to Combat "the Disease of Not Listening."

What are the objectives of this training?
–To make participants aware of the importance of listening in their everyday work life
–To improve participants' listening skills as they directly relate to participants' jobs
–To teach participants techniques for ongoing individual self-development of listening skills

–To increase participants' value to the organization by helping them to do
their job better

Was what you heard really what the speaker meant? Facts About Listening
Skills
–Discussion about human beings as listeners
–Discussion of the listening process: percentage of time spent in listening
activities, listening versus hearing, factors that affect listening, and so on
–Videotaping of participants, replaying of video, and discussion of what
participants see in themselves as listeners

How do you know which of the four styles of listening (relaxed listening,
social listening, active listening, defensive listening) is your most dominant?
–Presentation of the continuum of the four styles of listening
–Group problem-solving exercise (for example, trainer divides participants
into four groups and assigns one style to each; groups must draw up a profile of their assigned style—body language cues, vocal indicators, and
typical verbal responses—and be prepared to demonstrate that style)
–Debriefing and demonstration of each style and discussion as to when each
is appropriate and when inappropriate

What are the barriers to effective listening, and do you remove/reduce
them?
–Discussion of sender barriers, listener barriers, and environmental barriers
–Group brainstorming session followed by problem-solving exercise (trainer
divides participants into at least three groups, reviews rules of brainstorming, assigns time frame for each phase, tells each group to select one or
two key barriers from list and draw up a plan of action for remov-
ing/reducing those barriers)

What are strategies for better listening?
–Presentation of four basic strategies for improving listening skills: (1) learn
to empathize and read people, (2) be flexible in your styles of listening, (3)
pay closer heed to the environment, and (4) get feedback about your listening pattern/tendencies from people whose opinion you value
–Practical exercise to increase skills (video, if possible)
–Replay of video and/or discussion of how to measure improvement

How does listening improve or weaken your health?
–Discussion of medical findings regarding listening styles
–Formulation of a plan of action for improving an individual's listening skills
and/or those of the team or unit

Source: Adapted from Elsea, 1988b.

PART 5

Adaptability Skills: Solving Problems and Thinking Creatively

Life offers countless challenges and opportunities. To meet those challenges and turn those opportunities to advantage — whether at work or in our personal lives — we need to be able to adapt to each situation by using such skills as problem solving and creative thinking.

Some problems, great and small, recur and are subject to solution through a standard formula or procedure imposed on changing information that falls into familiar and regularized categories. In such instances, problem solving consists mainly of identifying which standard formula or procedure applies. But even when this approach results in a solution, one should consider the possibility that a variation on the standard could provide a *better* solution. Moreover, a problem may include new, possibly unique aspects that demand modification or outright abandonment of the standard approach before a solution can be achieved. In such circumstances, problem solving's first cousin, creative thinking, comes into play.

Today American business is increasingly placing a premium on finding the individual who is both a problem solver and a creative thinker. As decision making is moved closer to the point of actual production or service delivery, a company's very competitive position may hinge on its workers' ability to overcome barriers quickly. Certainly, it is easier to control costs and decrease error rates when a work force feels equipped and empowered to solve problems as they arise. Moreover, competitive advantage is frequently tied to a company's capacity to innovate quickly. And that capacity rests, in large part, on the skills that employees have to free themselves from linear thinking in order to make the creative leap.

Recent investigations have demonstrated the feasibility of enhancing a person's creative behaviors through a systematic training program based on reinforcement, instruction, and practice. A 1980 study conducted by John A. Glover of the University of Nebraska seemed to demonstrate that an increase in creative thinking capabilities can enhance real-life problem-solving efforts as well as a transfer of creative behavior to everyday life (Glover, 1981).

CHAPTER 9

Resourcefulness

Nothing is more interesting for humans than human
activity—and the most characteristically human activity is
solving problems, thinking for a purpose, devising means to
some desired end.

> George Polya
> *How to Solve It,* 1973

What Is Problem Solving?

Problem solving is the process of bridging a perceived gap
between *what is* and *what ought to be.* Problem solving involves
systematic processes used to guide both individual and group
efforts. It divides naturally into three sequential stages: problem
identification, problem analysis, and problem resolution.

Everyone, whether alone or as a member of a group, experiences problems at one time or another. A person realizes
that a problem exists when he or she feels frustration, anger,
fright, or anxiety about a situation. In the workplace, problems
within groups are evident when output or productivity is not
what it should be, when communication and cooperation seem
to be lacking, or when conflict appears to be out of control.

There are three general ingredients of successful problem
solving: skill in individual problem solving, skill in group problem solving, and practical ability in combining individual and
group skills.

Problem-solving techniques are based on a variety of
theoretical propositions that explain how individuals and groups

process information in the identification, analysis, and solution
of problems. Training techniques for improving individual problem-solving capabilities usually involve (1) building a person's
awareness of his or her own problem-solving style, (2) developing a person's awareness of the effect that individual style has
on other people, and (3) applying techniques tailored to individual styles and capacities for improved problem-solving ability.

Models for improving group problem-solving capabilities
are founded on individual skill-building techniques. However,
such models also address the need to create group appreciation
for the individual problem-solving styles of others, examine
group processes that inhibit problem solving, and encourage
group acceptance and use of diverse problem-solving styles.

What Theories Support Current
Training in Problem Solving?

Effective problem-solving theories deal with two fundamental categories of mental functioning: analytical thinking and
intuitive thinking.

The separation of thinking into these categories is a classic
distinction. The notion of opposing but complementary mental capacities is deeply rooted in Western philosophy, religion,
and science. Greek mythology expresses a strongly held belief
in the duality of human nature as symbolized by the rationalism
of the Greek god Apollo and the amoral, intuitive, and irra-
tional powers of the god Dionysius.

The concept of duality in the human spirit is also prominent in the writings of early Eastern philosophers. The earliest
recorded documentation of this concept is the Chinese *I-Ching,*
or *Book of Changes,* which is attributed to Confucius and his
disciples and dates back to approximately 500 B.C. The wisdom
of the *I-Ching* relates to the interplay between two fundamental
human capacities represented by the rational *yang* and the intuitive *yin.*

This distinction between the rational and the intuitive
engendered creative tension in the development of Western
philosophy and political thought. One stream of thinkers has

emphasized the intuitive over the rational. Jean Jacques Rousseau's celebration of the *state of nature,* Nietzsche's *superman,* and Tolstoy's adulation of the common folk are all examples of placing higher value on the intuitive side of human nature. The complementary but opposing view can be found among the works of prominent thinkers from Aristotle to Bertrand Russell. They assert the need to subjugate the intuitive to the rational aspect of human nature (see Figure 3), blaming the intuitive philosophers for horrors ranging from the bloodshed after the French Revolution to the rise of modern fascism.

Not until the "enlightened" nineteenth century was the idea of humanity's twofold nature subjected to scientific inquiry and rational proof. Darwin established a biological basis for man's dual nature by demonstrating that *Homo sapiens* probably evolved from lower-order animals rather than appearing in nature in the fully developed form of the modern male and female. This gave credence to the theory that the intuitive or instinctual aspect of human nature, which is closely aligned with lower-order animal behavior, is an inherited and integral part of people, a legacy inherited from our animal forebears.

Sigmund Freud developed a coherent, if often disputed, behavioral theory predicated on the belief that the existence of both the intuitive and the rational is basic to the makeup of human personality. The Freudian model depicts a mind that operates at three levels: the intellectual, the emotional, and the instinctual. Freud and Jung introduced the idea that (1) although these aspects of human nature are essentially stable, the balance between them varies from person to person; and (2) this variation in the mix of aspects accounts for individual differences in personality and style.

In the early 1900s, researchers began direct experimentation and testing in an attempt to relate the individual mix of rational and intuitive attributes to psychological types. Their results tended to articulate and multiply the number of human capacities that theorists relate to the basic duality of intuition and rationality.

In the early 1970s, researchers began to suggest that intuitive and rational mental functions actually reside in separate

Figure 3. Intellect Versus Intuition.

Source: Reprinted by permission. Tribune Media Services.

hemispheres of the brain. Their studies propose that the left side of the brain is the seat of logic and rationality, and the right side is the seat of intuition and emotion.

Whatever their scientific merit, these philosophies and scientific inquiries have similar implications for problem solving. They support the idea that each person's intellectual faculties are organized around a unique, predetermined mix of intuitive and analytic processing powers as expressed through a distinctive personality. They hold that each person engages his or her environment using a weighted ratio of intuitive to analytical character traits. Thought and research on mental functioning tend to support the idea that problem-solving techniques can be tailored to individual psychological profiles and thereby enhance people's problem-solving capabilities.

Many current instruments for assessing individual problem-solving profiles have been modeled after the Myers-Briggs Type Indicator (MBTI) (Myers and Briggs, 1976). The MBTI measures and sorts individual problem-solving styles into four categories of personality style: extraversion or introversion, sensing or intuiting, thinking or feeling, and judging or perceiving. A person is profiled in each of these four categories, so the MBTI yields sixteen possible combinations of personality type and sixteen corresponding problem-solving styles. Drawing, as did the MBTI, on Jung's work, psychologists Keirsey and Bates (1978) describe four *temperaments* of problem-solving style: Dionysian (sensing-perceiving/impulsive), Epimethian (sensing-judging/seeking to be useful), Promethean (intuiting-thinking/seeking competence or power over objects and events), and Apollonian (intuitive-feeling/seeking self-understanding or identity).

Other instruments for assessing problem-solving style relate personal psychological profiles to hemispheric specialization in the brain. The Herrmann Brain Dominance Instrument (Herrmann, 1983) assesses levels of preference related to dominant traits in the quadrants of the brain and indicates specialization in different styles of thinking and problem solving: logical, intuitive, organized, and emotional.

Use of such instruments provides individual problem-solving profiles that can be matched to specific techniques for enhancing individuals' problem-solving capacities. When these instruments are administered to individuals in a group and the results are shared, they often help group members gain new understanding and acceptance of the many possible ways in which people approach the solving of a problem.

What Are the Essential Elements of *Individual* Problem-Solving Skills?

Some people are better problem solvers than others in part because of their superior ability to identify and analyze a problem's source. In most cases, more experience is what makes a master problem solver out of a competent one. However, experience provides informal learning in the art of problem solving and thus is not the most effective or, in many instances, the fairest teacher. Unstructured experiential learning is slow, haphazard, and constrained by a person's individual interaction with the daily environment and individual prior history. On the other hand, structured learning in a work-related context takes advantage of a person's prior knowledge and experience to validate familiar processes as they are applied to new problems, but it is not constrained by them. Moreover, such learning is reproducible and consistent among many levels of learners and is systematic. The latter means that it lends itself more easily to an organized process of evaluation and measurement of training success.

Training for improved problem-solving skills usually involves two skill categories: individual cognitive abilities and group-interaction skills.

Individual cognitive abilities are in a broad category of learned abilities that involve many essential skills and processes. For example, a problem solver needs to understand *classification,* the thinking skill of placing items in categories or classes on the following bases:

- Order: understanding of the sequence or arrangement of things and ideas

- Structure: understanding of the interrelationships of parts of a whole
- Relation: understanding of how things affect one another

For instance, a river illustrates order, structure, and relation (Nierenberg, 1982). Its order is controlled by the water flow, which constantly changes the configuration of the riverbed and may alter the river's structure if it ceases or overflows the riverbanks. In this example, the structure is the river, composed of water and its channel (bed and banks). These are related because the channel holds the water. But by its constant movement, the water *changes* the channel's characteristics. To appreciate the full complexity of this example, a person may consider other factors (such as current, eddies, tributaries), which have their own interrelationships and which also contribute to the overall order, structure, and relation of the river.

In addition to skills related to the primary classifications of order, structure, and relation, a person needs skills that relate to levels and points of view. Levels represent the ability to change the focus of analysis to increase one's depth of understanding. Using the river example again, a person who is able to broaden analysis from the river alone to the river and its surrounding geography or to the river in relation to its indigenous flora and fauna will acquire a deeper level of understanding. Points of view represent the ability to gain insight by experiencing alternative perspectives. For example, one can achieve a greater understanding of the river by alternatively examining its order, structure, and relation from the perspective of a boat on the river or a person in the boat on the river and putting the various perspectives together for a multidimensional view.

Other essential problem-solving skills involve the following:

- *Deductive thinking:* the process of drawing a specific conclusion from a set of general observations
- *Inductive thinking:* the process of drawing a general conclusion from a set of specific facts
- *Lateral thinking:* the formation of new relationships among

existing ideas. This skill often requires the suspension of logic to facilitate new paths of analysis. This can be considered improving intuitive skills.

- *Dialectical thinking:* the ability to maintain different points of view simultaneously. This skill requires a tolerance for ambiguity and the capacity to withhold judgment until all information is gathered and evaluated.
- *Unfreezing and reframing:* the ability to come to terms with the unsatisfactory aspects of a particular situation to free oneself to examine faulty assumptions (unfreezing), and the ability to create a situation (reframing). Reframing may involve a change in context, interpretation, a meaning, and so on — to discover the validity and pertinence of their underlying assumptions (Bandler and Grinder, 1982).
- *Critical/reflective thinking:* individual effort to widen viewpoints and examine underlying assumptions that may be limiting; also referred to as the ability to *reflect-in-action* (Schön, 1987)

What Are the Essential Elements of *Group* Problem-Solving Skills?

The second category of elements essential to the development of problem-solving skills arises in group settings. Workplace productivity and product quality are related to the ability of both formal and informal work teams. The successful problem-solving efforts of work teams are synergistic. That is, their members' combined knowledge and skills contribute to a better solution than any one person could devise. As the maxim says, "Two heads are better than one."

For group problem solving, mastery of certain dynamic techniques — including those discussed below (Ulschak, Nathanson, and Gillan, 1981) — is particularly relevant.

Brainstorming, a technique developed in 1957 by Osborne, encourages the generation and sharing of ideas and information in a nonthreatening atmosphere. Brainstorming helps uncover ideas and facts in situations where complexity or other restraints would ordinarily inhibit free discussion. The technique promotes people's free exploration of new ideas and possible solutions without fear of criticism. Use of the brainstorming technique encourages a person to develop lateral thinking skills (tolerance for ambiguity) and an ability to withhold judgment until all possible information has been gathered. A frequent criticism of the brainstorming process is that although it generates many creative ideas, they usually need considerable work before they can be implemented as practical solutions.

Synectics, a technique developed by Gordon (1961), provides an environment that encourages creative but guided approaches to problem solving. Synectics is characterized by clearly defined roles for a leader, clients, and participants; techniques for detaching participants' minds from consciously thinking about a problem, thereby allowing their unconscious minds the freedom to explore possible solutions; and specific ways of reflecting on ideas (that is, ways of responding to old ideas in new ways).

Nominal group techniques, developed in 1968 by Delbecq and Van de Ven, are used in a structured problem-solving process specifically designed for use in situations where a lone person is unlikely to be able to arrive at a solution. This process's strength is that it quickly achieves results because it forces problem identification or a solution through the use of a quiet time for generating new ideas, followed by a forced interaction period. It normally takes about two and a half hours to run a nominal process meeting. The facilitator does not need extensive experience, and the technique provides an opportunity for each person to become involved because the leader encourages open discussion and clarification of all generated ideas.

Systems analysis, developed in 1968 by von Bertalanffy, is an excellent technique to use when a review of a problem's total context is called for, as opposed to times when a problem seems to be an isolated element. A systems approach is open; that is, it considers that a system interacts with its environment. Three representational models clarify how a system exists in its surroundings:

- In the hierarchical model, a system is described in terms of the systems above and below it (for example, "ground

transportation systems" fall below the category "human transportation systems," and above "rail systems," "bus systems,"
and so on).
- In the input-output model, a system is seen in terms of the
  resources that go into it and its subsequent outcomes.
- In the entities model, the group looks at the system's elements
  and attributes and at the relationships among them.

A systems approach also looks at multiple causes for problems, which keeps the problem solver from having "tunnel vision," and examines the whole picture rather than only one or
a few parts or elements. This technique offers a good process
for structuring problem analysis and discovering alternative solutions. Its weakness is that it offers no structure for participants'
roles.

Force field analysis, developed in 1947 by Lewin, is a process used to identify the dimensions of a problem and strategies
for solving it. Two main sets of forces are identified: inhibiting
forces that resist the problem's resolution and facilitating forces
that push the problem toward resolution. This, too, is an excellent analytic tool. It is useful for reviewing a problem that
involves a whole group and is easily combined with other problem-solving techniques to generate ideas for long-term planning.

The technique of basic-assumption mental states, developed by
Bion (1959), is an approach to improving group functioning
based on psychodynamics (which relates people's behavior to
their motivations and drives). The approach's premise is that
impaired work groups are characterized by one of three dysfunctional assumptions. This means that an impaired work group
has a tacit negative agreement (assumption) that prevents its
members from accomplishing their tasks.

- A dependency assumption group manifests needs for dependency and security by looking to its leader for decisions and
  authority. Because these needs can never be fully met, the
  group cannot accomplish its work tasks, which leads to failure
  for which the leader is blamed.
- A fight-or-flight assumption group may, in the fight mode,
  be characterized by energy devoted to attack or resistance

or, in the flight mode, by joking, intellectualizing, or leaving. The underlying need is for self-preservation, which is frequently subtly expressed. For example, group members may engage in busywork not essential to their tasks.

- A pairing assumption group's members are characterized by expressions of warmth and support for each other and the group as a whole; often new leaders are promoted and new ideas are embraced. However, the group's tasks are avoided through passive, hopeful expectations of things to come.

In contrast, a positive work-state group is characterized by a focus on accomplishing the tasks at hand. Each group member retains an identity based on individual abilities. Anxiety is low, and there is inquiry coupled with decision making and action. Specific skills are required to use basic assumption techniques to transform a malfunctioning group into a functional, positive work-state group. These skills are knowledge of individual preferences, which are assessable through the Reactions to Group Situations Test (Stock, 1974), and the ability to identify the faulty basic assumptions described above so that those barriers may be brought to conscious awareness and overcome.

Control orientation techniques, developed by Argyris and Schön (1978), attempt to move groups from Model I (unilateral control) to Model II (bilateral control) behavior. Model I behavior is impaired behavior by a person in a group. A person who behaves this way focuses on convincing others of his or her view without being open to changing that view or considering the validity of other views. This behavior is characterized by a unilateral attempt to achieve individual goals, maximize personal "winning," and minimize personal negative feelings. It inhibits group exploration of issues and alternatives in deference to achieving the objectives of a particular person.

Model II behavior is characterized by bilateral, shared control of a task and responsibility for its outcome. Defensiveness and negative feelings are seen as areas to explore, and the focus is on valid information and inquiry. Public development and testing of hypotheses are an integral part of this technique and decrease the likelihood of decision errors.

What Are the Essential Elements of
Training in the Problem-Solving Process?

Individual and group skills in problem solving are necessary but not sufficient for successful practice of problem solving in the workplace. Both individuals and groups need a *process
structure* for using their skills. There are many problem-solving
models. Selection of the best model depends on the many factors that make each problem, work team, and organization
unique. There is rarely a best way to approach even a specific
problem; any of several methods can be successful. Selection
of a model also depends in part on the level of sophistication
of the individuals and groups who are to perform as problem
solvers and in part on the complexity of the problem or problems being addressed. Below are descriptions of several problem-
solving models that have received favorable responses from people who have used them.

The *eight-step model* was developed by quality expert Joseph
Juran (1988) and includes the potential to

1.   identify potential problems,
2.   select potential problems for analysis,
3.   analyze root causes,
4.   identify possible solutions,
5.   select solutions,
6.   test solutions,
7.   implement solutions, and
8.   track solutions' effectiveness.

In the problem phases of this process, people are taught
techniques such as brainstorming and information gathering.
They are also taught to draw up workflow diagrams, which are
graphic depictions of work processes that may reveal built-in
production bottlenecks or conflicts, and to prioritize through
voting and consensus.

In the problem phases, people are also taught specific data-
reduction techniques (ways to organize data), such as graphing;
Pareto diagramming, which sorts out for priority treatment the

few major problems — in terms of frequency, seriousness, cost —
from the many important but lesser problems; and cost estimation.

Analytic tools used to help people learn how to trace back
to and identify problems' causes include the following:

- Fishbone diagrams, which depict contributing causes as ribs
  leading into a spine problem, or negative effect
- Structure trees, which sketch the hierarchy of root causes;
  the trunk, or main problem; and the branches, or secondary problems and symptoms
- Scattergrams, which plot dots representing the correlation
  of two variables; for example, a scattergram may show that
  people who do X are likely to have Y happen, although the
  correlation does not necessarily equal cause and effect.

In the eight-step model's solution phase, participants learn
additional techniques, including force field analysis, cost-benefit
analysis, and group presentation skills. They are also trained
in how to participate effectively in work groups, primarily by
using a set of technical problem-solving skills.

The *comprehensive model* (Friedman and Yarbrough, 1985)
includes techniques such as the following:

> Becoming aware of a need
> Analyzing the problem
> Knowing the options
> Adopting a solution
> Implementing the solution
> Integrating the solution into the system

The problem-analysis phase of the comprehensive model
incorporates an additional sequential model that relates to
thinking skills. These skills include identifying basic organizational goals, identifying obstructing and enabling forces,
disentangling interrelated difficulties, identifying the "players"
and their points of view and vested interests, distinguishing
factual from inferred information, and identifying alternative
strategies.

The comprehensive model also provides suggestions (such as brainstorming) for enhancing the creative nature of the process and a recommendation to would-be problem solvers to think very positively about the ideal outcomes — as an aid to achieving them. The primary methodology for training in this technique is the use of case studies to provide concrete examples of ambiguous, multifaceted, real-world problems that do not have readily apparent or easy solutions. The intent is to help learners acquire a long-range outlook that incorporates many viewpoints.

The *POWER model* (Mink, Mink, and Owen, 1987) uses the acronym POWER to describe the key elements in each step of the model and to reflect the confidence that a problem-solving group may feel when successful. A variety of methods may be used in this process; its major steps are as follows:

> *P*roject a vision of how the situation should be different.
> *O*bserve the discrepancy between what exists and what should be.
> *W*ork out, after considering choices, an action plan and implement it.
> *E*valuate/monitor progress and achievement.
> *R*evise plans as indicated by evaluation findings.

Behaviors that may interfere with the process include discounting the value or importance of people, the problem itself, the possibility of defining or solving the problem, and the particular context in which the problem occurs.

Several of these models for learning about problem solving go beyond refining techniques for problem identification, analysis, and resolution. Other more complex models concentrate on methods that allow people to step out of their frames of reference to examine the underlying assumptions that cause them to view problems in a particular way. This often results in people's realization that the problems they have been attempting to solve are only symptomatic of other, more complex, underlying problems. This leads to a more sophisticated problem-identification process. Also, people may realize how certain assumptions have caused them to have difficulty in implementing the original solutions they devised.

An example of higher-order problem solving appears in the story of the passengers on the *Titanic,* who when the ship began to list badly, rejected the ineffective proposal that they move deck chairs to the ship's other side to correct the capsize. They immediately realized that this would be a futile gesture; they understood that the builders and promoters of the world's first "unsinkable" ship were tragically wrong and that the appropriate strategy was to get out the lifeboats to try to save as many lives as possible.

In the models discussed above, problem-solving processes may appear very complex, with a cumbersome number of steps to follow. However, most problem-solving processes fit into a generic model that can be replicated with good results no matter what the substantive problem is (see Figure 4).

Following is a discussion of how a generic problem-solving model works.

Problem Analysis. John Dewey said that a problem well defined is half solved. Problem analysis begins with the recognition that a problem exists and that it is necessary to define it accurately. Even when an analytical system is in place, accurate problem identification is often difficult because symptoms may be confused with causes. As mentioned earlier in this chapter, some people are better problem solvers than others in part because they are better able to identify a problem's true source; usually, people become better at problem identification when they have had more experience. One way to improve problem identification skills is to emphasize the gathering of information that shows not only the existence of a problem but also its nature and extent.

Discussion and Analysis of Assumptions. Each person brings a set of assumptions to each problem-solving situation. The quality of the solutions generated is affected by the appropriateness of the assumptions. These assumptions may include *structural assumptions* related to the problem's context—

Figure 4. Problem Analysis/Solution Model.

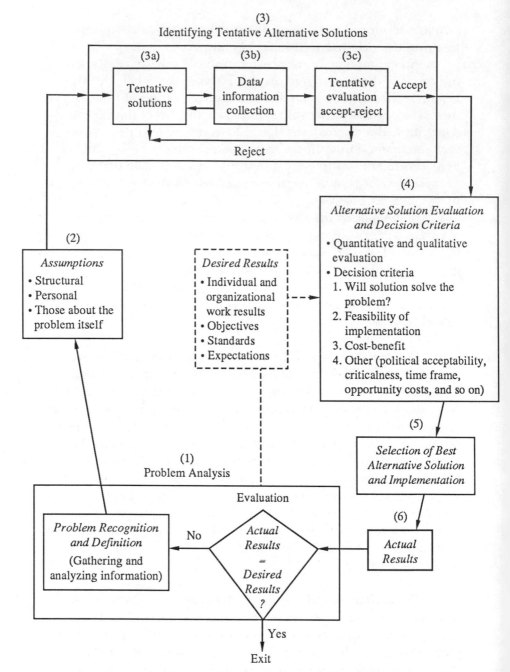

Source: J. S. Rakich, B. B. Longest, and K. Darr, *Managing Health Service Organizations,* © 1985, Philadelphia: W. B. Saunders Company. Reprinted by permission.

controllable and uncontrollable variables-related areas of responsibility, availability of additional resources, deployment and use of personnel, job design, and so on; *personal assumptions* unique to an individual's experience and personality — a person may hold such assumptions in either an open-minded or restrictive way; and *problem assumptions* related to such things as the problem's importance, its political implications, and one's anticipation of management's acceptance or rejection of solutions.

Identification of Tentative Alternative Solutions. Identifying possible alternative solutions is a repetitive process in which people are encouraged to identify and assess a wide range of solutions. Skills and techniques that come into play include those for innovation, creativity, and brainstorming. The amount of time, energy, and resources devoted to each tentative solution depends heavily on the quality and precision of the initial problem definition and the degree to which assumptions are not overly restrictive. There are two potential hazards: excessive concern with selecting the best alternative when a less-than-optimal solution would do, and procrastination rather than action.

Alternative Solution Evaluation. Evaluating alternative solutions involves measuring, against predetermined standards and criteria (such as feasibility, rationality, acceptability, and so on), the reasonable tentative solutions that have emerged.

Selection, Implementation, and Feedback. From the feasible alternatives that meet evaluative criteria, one or more may be selected for implementation. At this point, the two most important requirements for success are (1) management-employee commitment to implementation and (2) continuation of the problem-solving process to ensure desired results and to solve new problems that may arise.

As individuals or groups become more skillful in problem-solving techniques, they may only need to carry out one or two of the model's steps to manage a problem. No real-world situation requires absolute adherence to a rigid set of steps. A model's usefulness lies in its provision of a series of guidelines and a range of strategies and tools for selection and deployment as specific situations demand.

Figure 5 illustrates how the major elements of problem solving — individual cognitive abilities, group interaction techniques, and the problem-solving process — interact.

What Constitutes Competency in Problem Solving? What Constitutes Mastery?

Following is an illustrative list of generalized evaluative criteria for determining individual and group competency and mastery in problem solving.

Competency. Competency includes the ability to do the following:

- Represent a problem (Can this person/group identify and define a problem in a way that allows for solution?)
- Apply logic (Does this person/group analyze a problem's structure in a way that allows appropriate data to be obtained?)
- Formulate a solution (Can this person/group devise a solution on the basis of available data?)
- Create a feedback mechanism(s) (Can this person/group monitor a solution effectively to evaluate its implementation?)
- Provide summative evaluation (Can this person/group assess the final outcome in comparison with the original problem?)

Mastery. Mastery includes the ability to do the following:

- Redefine/reframe a problem (Has the appropriate problem been identified and addressed?)
- Analyze underlying assumptions (What are the underlying factors that affect framing of the problem and its possible resolution?)
- Suspend logic (Have counterintuitive approaches been considered?)

Figure 5. Generic Model of Problem-Solving Skills.

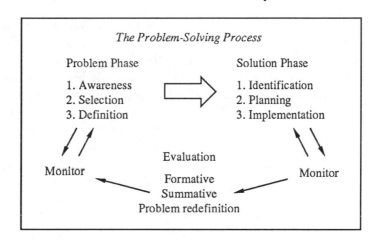

Individual Cognitive Skills
1. Classification, order, structure, relation, levels, points of view
2. Deductive thinking
3. Inductive reasoning
4. Lateral thinking
5. Ambiguity tolerance/dialectic
6. Unfreezing/reframing
7. Critical/reflective thought

The Problem-Solving Process

Problem Phase

1. Awareness
2. Selection
3. Definition

Monitor

Solution Phase

1. Identification
2. Planning
3. Implementation

Monitor

Evaluation
Formative
Summative
Problem redefinition

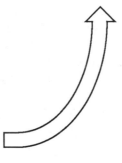

Group Interaction Skills
Brainstorming
Synectics
Nominal group technique
Systems analysis
Force field analysis
Basic assumption mental states
Control orientation

- Put the problem in a systems perspective (Is there a projection at each stage to the intermediate and final outcomes?)
- Provide formative evaluation (Is there an ongoing evaluation of the process at each stage?)

As a result of research, psychologists have come to recognize that both competency and mastery in problem solving require acquisition of relevant knowledge *and* an awareness of how to organize that knowledge efficiently so that it is available for problem solving.

What Is an Example of a Successful Workplace Training Program in Problem Solving?

Xerox Corporation is a $15 billion company that does business in over 130 countries and has numerous offices and manufacturing plants around the world. Xerox has two major business areas: Financial Services and Business Products and Systems. Although almost half of its profits and 30 percent of its revenues come from the Financial Services area, that part of the corporation has not begun to implement the problem-solving training discussed here for its 12,000 employees. However, nearly all of the Business Products and Systems' 100,000 employees have participated in this training. Business Products and Systems manufactures products that meet the document-processing needs of Xerox customers: copiers/duplicators, electronic typewriters, software, printers, professional workstations, communication networks, and reproduction services and supplies.

Xerox problem-solving training is an integral part of its Leadership Through Quality strategy. Training addresses three corporate priorities: satisfying customers, improving return on assets, and increasing market share. These priorities are aimed at ensuring that Xerox remains a financially healthy company through its ability to maintain a competitive edge. For that purpose, Leadership Through Quality was developed in direct response to increasing competition from Japan. In the early 1980s, Xerox became concerned about maintaining its quality standards and determined that an operational change was needed to reflect its already high commitment to quality production. David Kearns, Xerox's chief executive officer, was favorably impressed with the quality programs in operation in Xerox's Japanese affiliate, Fuji Xerox, and believed that instituting the same practices in other locations would benefit the company. So in 1983, the corporation began developing a strategy for implementing quality improvement throughout the company. A major element of the strategy was the establishment of a training process to reach every employee of the Business Products and Systems side of the corporation. A team of key training people from Xerox was assembled to develop the new training programs.

Enhancing individual problem-solving capabilities was thought to be a major factor in Xerox's effort to improve product and service quality. Therefore, training program development included a quality-improvement component (concepts, measurements, and definitions of quality, and interactive skills such as oral communication and behavioral styles) and a problem-solving component.

Program participants are given a reference manual that details a six-step problem-solving process:

1. Identifying and selecting the problem
2. Analyzing the problem
3. Generating potential solutions
4. Selecting and planning the solution
5. Implementing the solution
6. Evaluating the solution

For each step, the manual shows an objective, guidelines, activities necessary to achieve the objective, tools needed, and end-of-step questions to answer to aid progress toward the next step.

The manual also contains information about problem-solving tools and techniques—such as brainstorming to generate ideas, using list reduction to reach a consensus, and using charts and graphs to analyze and display data or plan actions. Each tool or technique is defined, described, and clarified by examples of its use.

During a training session, participants are often divided into small groups and given case studies to work on. The case studies are representative of problems that a Xerox family group (functional work group, that is, employees who work in the same job area) or an employee involvement group might encounter on the job. People may refer to their manuals at any time while working to solve their assigned problems. The manuals have also proven to be useful later, when employee involvement groups are solving actual workplace problems. On the job, it is through employee involvement groups and family work groups that the problem-solving skills learned in training are applied. These groups are supported by quality specialists and managers who serve as problem-solving and quality-improvement facilitators, encouraging employee participation and involvement. A problem-solving group may consist of the manager and employees within a family group , or it may cut across family groups.

When the training program began, it started with Xerox's president, then reached downward to involve every manager in the training program twice: They met once with peers, then assisted in training their subordinates. By the end of summer 1988, nearly all the originally targeted employees had been trained in the Leadership Through Quality processes.

To ensure the best participation in and timing for the training, each operating unit determined how it wanted the program administered. Most units had family group members attend the program together. As often as possible, Xerox prefers to train its employees by family group since that is how people work on a daily basis. New hires are mixed together, however, because company guidelines require that all new employees be trained within ninety days of their starting dates and because it takes a "critical mass" of people to conduct the program.

Although the training was initiated and developed at the corporate level and the development was originally funded through the corporate budget, today each operating unit has taken over financial responsibility for putting its employees through the required training. The employees pay nothing. Each operating unit, in addition to being responsible for funding its own employees' participation, has a great deal of autonomy in determining how and when training is delivered. For the most part, in-house trainers are used, but some units choose to hire outside deliverers, usually former Xerox employees. Most of the curriculum is developed at the corporate level by an in-house staff with the help of consultants (again, often former Xerox employees).

Each operating unit also determines its training schedule. Five to six days are needed to train each employee, but some units spread the training out over a longer period rather than experience significant downtime because of employees' absence on consecutive days. Spreading training out also allows employees time to absorb information and to apply their new skills to the job between sessions. Besides the basic problem-solving training developed at the corporate level, many units have developed supplemental courses, and some units offer refresher programs for employees who went through the beginning phases of the training. Xerox is receiving more and more requests from employees for these courses.

Because almost all the targeted employees have completed the program, a special version of the problem-solving training has been designed within Xerox's New Employee Orientation and Quality Training program, which is specifically geared toward the new hires' needs. This program includes one and a half days of orientation to Xerox and three and a half days focusing on problem solving and quality improvement. The course is required because Xerox has found that new employees need to understand Xerox's common language and processes of quality in order to join the trained work groups.

Xerox has also begun to encourage its suppliers, vendors, and dealers to participate in quality training. In fact, Xerox has reduced the number of suppliers with which it will do business, keeping only those that can meet Xerox's quality requirements.

Program evaluation is done through opinion polls of participants. Each unit evaluates its own programs. No criterion-referenced tests or other formal methods are used to evaluate how well individuals learn the skills. Review tests may be given, but they are not used for grading.

Many changes have taken place in Xerox since the launching of the Leadership Through Quality strategy. It is credited with positive changes in the ways that employees interact: Meetings have become more structured and more effective; there is more emphasis on data collection and data analysis to substantiate recommendations and support findings; and evaluation is more prevalent. These changes have occurred gradually, overcoming resistance by employees who did not want the changes.

The training is coordinated by a corporate manager of quality training. Each operating unit has a quality training manager, who oversees the unit's programs. The unit quality training managers meet once a quarter with the corporate manager to discuss proposed program changes and how to avoid duplicating work efforts. For example, if a unit is making a program adaptation, related information and materials are made available to the other units (Sarah Turner, telephone interview, April 1988).

What Should Be Included in a Generic Workplace Problem-Solving Curriculum?

Exhibit 8 provides a list of items to consider when devising a problem-solving curriculum, and Exhibit 9 shows the steps to describe the deviation when analyzing a problem.

Exhibit 8. Group Process Approach to Problem Solving/Problem Analysis.

What are the objectives of this training?
–To increase participants' skills in problem solving
–To clarify techniques for individual problem solving
–To introduce new techniques for group problem solving
–To improve on-the-job success and productivity

How do you identify work-related problems?
–By defining the scope of the problem
–By obtaining valid information about the problem in order to identify what
  it is

**Exhibit 8. Group Process Approach
to Problem Solving/Problem Analysis, Cont'd.**

What are two alternative approaches to group problem solving?
–Fundamental group problem analysis focuses on generic group brain-storming to identify the cause of any type problem and on group input and commitment.
–Complex group problem analysis focuses on problems that have appeared recently or have always been present with no apparent cause and on group input and commitment.
–Both approaches can be used when the cause of the problem is unknown and needs to be determined and when the resources of the group rather than the skills of one individual are needed to address the issues.

How do you develop group skills in problem identification, problem solving, and decision making?
–Fundamental group problem analysis
   –Discusses facts surrounding problem
   –Silently generates causes of problem
   –Provides round-robin recording of causes
   –Clarifies and discusses causes
   –Verifies the causes
   –Carries out corrective action
   –Reports results of corrective action
   –If first cause does not check out, moves on to second most probable cause, and so on
–Complex group problem analysis uses videotape to illustrate how to do the following:
   –Set up a deviation statement (see Exhibit 9)
   –Generate facts
   –Silently generate causes of problems
   –Provide round-robin recording of causes
   –Vote to establish probable cause
   –Compare probable cause to facts
   –Verify probable cause
   –Carry out the corrective action
   –Report results of corrective action
   –If first cause does not check out, move on to second most probable cause, and so on

What practices will help you gain proficiency in problem analysis/resolution?
–Videotaping participants going through each process and group critiquing the videotape to emphasize process and conclusions
–Reviewing application of approaches by using actual case studies of work situations
–Performing three- and six-month refresher practicums to review process

Exhibit 9. Deviation Statement.

PROBLEM ANALYSIS

QUESTIONS TO DESCRIBE THE DEVIATION

WHAT IS THE DEVIATION STATEMENT?

What Is/Is Not
–The object with the defect?
–The defect?

Where Is/Is Not
–The object with the defect observed (geographic location)?
–The defect on the object?

When Is/Is Not
–The object with the defect first observed (clock, calendar time)?
–Observed since then (clock, calendar time)?
–The defect first observed in the cycle of the object?

Extent Is/Is Not
–How many units of each object have the defect?
–How much of each unit is affected?
–How many defects are on each unit?
–What is the trend?

Note: For each "is" fact, ask what (where, when, to what extent) the deviation could be, but is not.

CHAPTER **10**

Creative Thinking:
New Ideas for Old Problems

The mind is not a vessel to be filled, but a fire to be kindled.

> Plutarch
> *Morals,* 42–120 A.D.

What Is Creative Thinking?

As a subject for separate study, creative thinking is nearly forty years old (Rickards and Freedman, 1979). In the ensuing years, "Creativity and innovation have become watchwords, if not buzzwords, on the American business scene" (Gordon and Zemke, 1986, p. 30).

Appropriately, people have created hundreds of definitions for creative thinking. However, most experts agree that creativity is the ability to

use different modes of thought
come up with something new
visualize, foresee, and generate ideas
form new combinations of ideas to fulfill a need

Boiled down, most definitions of creative thinking describe mental processes leading to new and relevant ideas. "Psychologists say that a person perceives and then interprets the world as a set of relationships and patterns. A change in the pattern

191

occurs at the moment of insight" (Rickards and Freedman, 1979, p. 3). Although most definitions of creative thinking lack hard-edged certainty, there seems to be general agreement about the necessary components of the creative thinking process. Fundamentally and essentially (Marzano and others, 1988), creativity

> requires desire, preparation, hard work, and forethought,
> involves pushing the limits of knowledge and ability,
> requires strong internal rather than external motivation,
> involves the ability to reframe a problem to see it in a different light, and
> involves the capacity to block out unproductive distractions.

These conditions make it apparent that creative thinking should not be thought of as a moment in time but rather as stages in a process. The stages include preparation, unconscious incubation, the moment of insight, and finally, verification or production.

Another way of looking at creative thinking is to view it as a single position along "a continuum of circles spiraling endlessly upward" (Campbell, 1985, p. 129). Above creative thinking on the continuum is the concept of inventiveness, which involves taking a creative idea and turning it into a practical application. Moving along the spiral, the next high point is referred to as innovation. Innovation encompasses creativity and inventiveness but is primarily the act of bringing about change from an accepted way of doing things to a new way of doing things. Finally, to bring the process to a useful resolution before the spiral extends into new creative thinking, the ideas generated thus far must demonstrate a productive outcome. Productive innovation implies that "a new development adds something to or improves the way we currently do something" (McTague, 1987, p. 23).

What Theories Support Current Training in Creative Thinking?

Historically, creative thinking has been identified as characteristic only of geniuses. Since the boom in creativity training, however, a sense of the universality of creative potential has evolved, and effective techniques to assist in unblocking the individual's creative thinking processes have been developed. Today typical assumptions about creativity include the following:

- Everyone has the potential for creative action, although for many people this potential is never fulfilled.
- Blocked potential for creativity can be tapped if individuals can be helped to behave in ways associated with people who are widely acknowledged as being creative.
- A powerful means of achieving this potential is through the use of structural aids to creativity, or creative problem-solving techniques.
- Techniques and behavior patterning can be introduced effectively through training programs.
- Through such training, individuals and their organizations will benefit considerably (Rickards and Freedman, 1979).

Several techniques that enable individuals and groups to enhance their creative capabilities are based on theories developed only in this century.

• *Synectics.* Social scientist William J. J. Gordon's (1961) research tried to uncover the process constants that underlie the creative condition. His work revealed the theory of synectics. This theory is based on the idea that creative behavior can be increased if metaphor (comparison or analogy) is applied to situations where new and innovative viewpoints are needed. In his research, Gordon discovered that the most important element in innovative problem solving is "making the familiar strange" because thinking breakthroughs depend on viewing familiar problems in new contexts.

• *Lateral thinking.* Professor Edward de Bono (1970) of Cambridge University developed a theory he referred to as lateral thinking. Lateral thinking calls for an escape from habitual or *vertical* ways of thinking in order to seek novel approaches to solving problems. De Bono categorized problems as those with solutions that require the processing of information, those in which the problem is one of accepting what cannot be changed, and those that can only be solved by reorganizing information and assumptions about the problem. To solve the third type, a person has to be illogical or think laterally.

• *Personalized and developmental learning.* Basic propositions underlying training in creative thinking are that it needs to become personalized and that it ought to be developmental. These ideas are based on personal construct theory (Kelly, 1955) and learning styles theory (Kolb, 1976). The personal construct theory argues that a person views the world somewhat in the way others do and also, to a certain extent, in a uniquely personal way. It follows, then, that the effectiveness of any material presented during training will be significantly influenced by each participant's past experiences and personal point of view. Personal construct theory suggests that training material should be designed to promote this personalized learning. Kolb's Learning Styles Inventory (LSI) model suggests a method for achieving this.

According to the LSI model, a person passes through four learning stages: concrete experience, reflective observation, abstract conceptualization, and active experimentation. Each person evidences a preference for certain stages in this process. The LSI model implies incremental learning over time. Fresh stimuli are introduced at each learning session and participants develop new, personalized responses to these stimuli. The influence of this kind of developmental learning is likely to continue after training and can lead to changes in trainees' attitudes toward taking risks and their greater persistence in the management of ideas and problem solving. The result will be more creative behavior patterns (Rickards and Freedman, 1979).

• *Whole brain training.* A contemporary training approach to applied creative thinking is based on the theoretical concepts of specialized brain functioning and hemisphere lateralization. One of the major proponents of brain-dominance technology, Ned Herrmann (1983), bases his training methodology on the theory that although each brain is unique, brains in general are specialized. He also draws on expert agreement about dominance: eye dominance, hand dominance, foot dominance, ear dominance, and brain-hemisphere dominance. Within each human being, specialization and dominance produce a combination of specialized preferences that affect general behavior and, particularly, individual learning style.

The theoretical model of brain dominance divides the brain into separate quadrants, each different and equal in importance (see Figure 6). Two of the quadrants represent the more cognitive, intellectual modes of thought and behavior, whereas the other two represent the more visceral, emotional modes.

Herrmann has developed a brain-dominance testing instrument to measure a person's thinking preferences. Whole-brain training programs are designed to provide dynamic learn-

Figure 6. Thinking Processes.

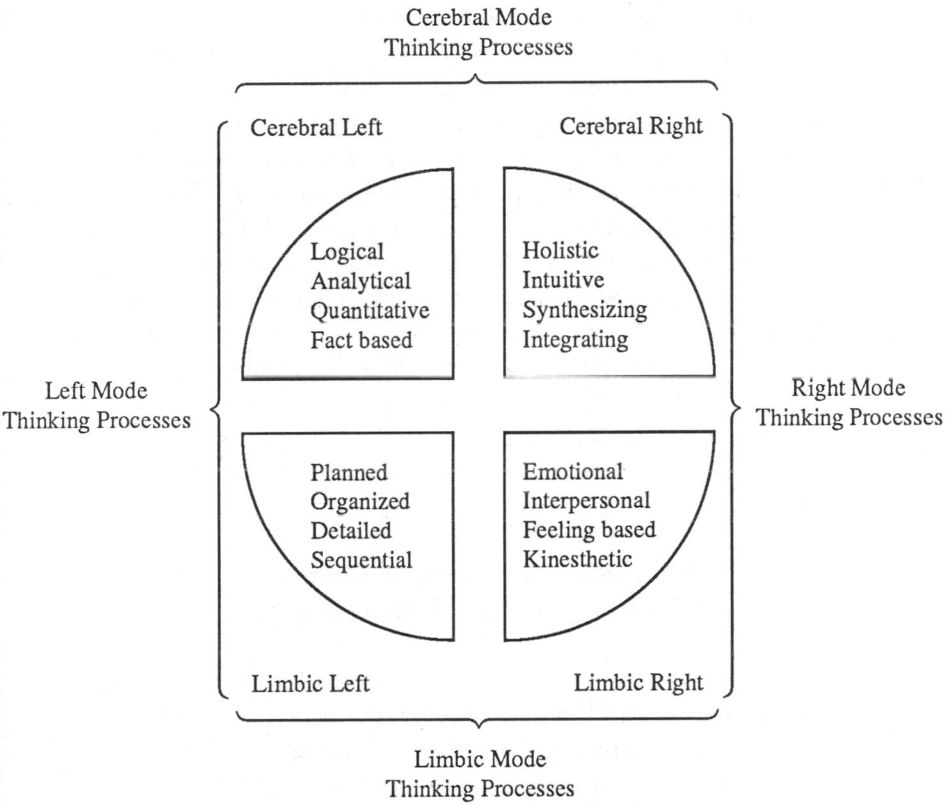

Cerebral Mode
Thinking Processes

Cerebral Left   Cerebral Right

Logical	Holistic
Analytical	Intuitive
Quantitative	Synthesizing
Fact based	Integrating

Left Mode   Right Mode
Thinking Processes   Thinking Processes

Planned	Emotional
Organized	Interpersonal
Detailed	Feeling based
Sequential	Kinesthetic

Limbic Left   Limbic Right

Limbic Mode
Thinking Processes

Source: N. Herrmann, "Brain Dominance Theory," in R. Craig (ed.), *Training and Development Handbook: A Guide to Human Resource Development* (3d. ed.), © 1987, New York: McGraw-Hill Book Company. Reprinted by permission.

ing experiences that move back and forth to distribute learning equally across all four quadrants. The theory is that to be the most creative, people need to be well developed and well integrated in the entire range of cognitive abilities.

• *Multiple intelligences.* A complementary idea to that of brain dominance is the theory of multiple intelligences (Gardner, 1985). Harvard psychologist Howard Gardner proposes that there is not simply one intelligence but seven: linguistic (verbal dexterity), musical, logical-mathematical, spatial, bodily kinesthetic (tactile), inner-directed (self-understanding), and interpersonal (empathy).

Arguments about this theory relate to the question of whether there must be integration of two or more of these cognitive activities for creative thinking to occur or whether one of these capacities alone can support creative activity. Among centuries' worth of examples that bear out the premise that creative people are often adept in several different intelligence areas are the ultimate Renaissance man, Leonardo da Vinci (writer, scientist, inventor, painter, sculptor); Manhattan modern Woody Allen (actor, writer, director, professional clarinetist); and contemporary businessman Frank Stanton (president of CBS television during its growth years and master craftsman in wood). "The benefit of mastery of multiple intelligences in one person is obvious; people who have several skills don't get locked into a single path. . . . People who are only good with hammers see every problem as a nail" (Campbell, 1985, pp. 55–56).

What Are the Essential Elements of Training in Creative Thinking?

Creative or innovative thinking is the flip side of the coin known as critical thinking. Whenever a person is formulating a question, analyzing a problem, or defining a situation with clarity, accuracy, and fair-mindedness, he or she is using the skills of critical thinking. When a person is solving an unstructured problem or planning a project, his or her creative abilities are brought into play. And when a person is imaginatively and empathically considering diverse points of view, he or she is using both creative and critical skills.

It is difficult to sort out distinct elements of the creative thinking process that lend themselves to being taught. If the objective of training in creative thinking is to increase the creative capacity or creative behavior of individuals or groups, however, there are identifiable elements that can be enhanced through practice.

The elements for improving a person's creative thinking capabilities are referred to as cognitive (thinking/knowing) skills. Many of the cognitive techniques discussed here are the same ones a person needs to solve problems effectively.

W. C. Miller (1987) discusses how to enhance creativity by using both the intuitive (creative) and the logical/rational (critical) sides of the brain. Miller's terms correspond to Herrmann's left-brain, right-brain theory, and Miller, too, believes that augmentation of both linear and intuitive elements of cognitive activity are necessary for optimal creative processing.

Techniques for learning how to generate new ideas by using a linear approach provide a base upon which to build alternative solutions. Linear techniques involve using a pattern of logical thinking such as a sequence of steps. Linear methods facilitate the act of creativity by providing ways to organize information that help focus attention on where creativity or innovation is possible.

In contrast, rather than involving a series of steps or analytical categories, the intuitive approach relies on a "leap of faith" to a whole answer all at once. There is little or no experience of moving along a path toward a solution. Instead, a person finds an intuitive solution through what is sometimes called an *aha! experience* or a *eureka! experience.* *"Eureka!"* (Greek for "I have found it!") is what the third century B.C. mathematician Archimedes supposedly exclaimed when, while bathing, he realized that the volume of an object can be calculated by the amount of water it displaces.

Learning how to be fluent in both linear and intuitive thinking leads people to the best creative results. When exploring the path from linear to intuitive thinking, W. C. Miller

(1987, p. 66) believes that "If you can determine from the beginning that your creative solutions will fall into any of *x* categories, you can focus on exploring those categories. By proceeding from specific starting points, you can take small steps from one idea to another until suddenly you are far from the original starting position. In this uncharted territory you may find the innovative solution you desire."

Below are brief descriptions, adapted from Miller (1987), of several of the many linear and intuitive thinking techniques currently being used. Although each technique can be implemented independently of the others, people frequently obtain better solutions by combining techniques.

Linear Thinking. The following techniques and processes are related to *linear* thinking.

• *Matrix analysis.* Laying out a set of constants and variables along the vertical and horizontal axes of a graph and then identifying where they intersect is known as matrix analysis. For example, Table 4 illustrates a market/technology product-packaging matrix on which every intersection represents a place to look for innovations that apply a particular technology to a particular market.

• *Morphological analysis.* A system for breaking an idea or problem into parts for study. Table 5 demonstrates a morphological analysis for inventing a new mode of transporting people

Table 4. Example of Matrix Analysis.

		Markets			
		Transport	Medical	Beverage	Industrial
Technologies	Co-extrusion				
	Resin blend		x		
	Laminates				
	Adhesives				
	Thermoform				

Source: W. C. Miller, *The Creative Edge,* © 1987, Addison-Wesley Publishing Co., Inc., Reading, Massachusetts. Figure on page 67. Reprinted with permission.

Table 5. Example of Morphological Analysis.

Driving Force	Mode of Movement	Material	Purpose
Diesel	Rail	Plastic	People
Gas turbine	Wheel	Metals	Animals
Steam	Rollers	Wood	Heavy freight
Pedal	Coasters	Stone	Baggage
Electric	Air cushion	Cloth	Foods and spices
Squirrels in a cage	Water	Glass	Plants

Source: W. C. Miller, *The Creative Edge,* © 1987, Addison-Wesley Publishing Co., Inc., Reading, Massachusetts. Figure on page 69. Reprinted with permission.

and things. If a third dimension is added, a three-dimensional cube is created rather than a two-dimensional grid.

• *Nature of the business.* Analyzing the nature of a business is a process for uncovering how an organization defines, or should define, the nature of its business in order to innovate strategy decisions. As an example, Miller (1987) cites the leaders of Southland Corporation's 7–11 stores, who realized that they were not in the grocery business but rather in the convenience business. This led them to move in an entirely different direction in terms of marketing strategy and inventory. Nature of the business may use matrix and morphological analyses to help participants determine a proper focus for action.

• *Reframing questions.* A technique in which questions are restated in different contexts so participants find new viewpoints for understanding a problem is known as reframing questions. With new viewpoints, participants can develop different problem definitions and generate new ideas in terms of each definition.

• *Force field analysis.* Force field analysis is a problem-solving technique for analyzing and dealing with resistance to change. It works to stimulate people's creative thinking by defining the organizational vision, identifying and maximizing strengths of forces, and identifying and minimizing their weaknesses. Figure 7 illustrates the tug-of-war among forces that may

Figure 7. Force Field Analysis.

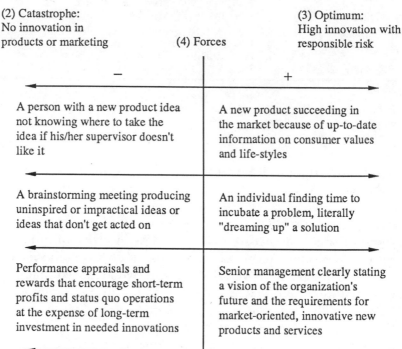

(1) Problem: How to foster
a better climate for
innovation *and* creativity

(2) Catastrophe: (3) Optimum:
No innovation in   High innovation with
products or marketing   (4) Forces   responsible risk

— +

A person with a new product idea not knowing where to take the idea if his/her supervisor doesn't like it	A new product succeeding in the market because of up-to-date information on consumer values and life-styles
A brainstorming meeting producing uninspired or impractical ideas or ideas that don't get acted on	An individual finding time to incubate a problem, literally "dreaming up" a solution
Performance appraisals and rewards that encourage short-term profits and status quo operations at the expense of long-term investment in needed innovations	Senior management clearly stating a vision of the organization's future and the requirements for market-oriented, innovative new products and services

Source: W. C. Miller, *The Creative Edge,* © 1987, p. 73, Reading:
Mass.: Addison-Wesley Publishing Co., Inc. Reprinted with permission.

inhibit a person's or an organization's ability to move toward optimal solution of a problem.

Intuitive Thinking. The following techniques and processes are related to *intuitive* thinking.
   • *Force fit/forced relationship.* Force fit/forced relationship is a process for putting together concepts that appear to have nothing in common. If a group's members are not generating new ideas, a facilitator will guide them on a *mental excursion* away from the problem. Group members will be asked to draw anal-

ogies or develop oxymorons (such as "open enclosure" or "false truth"). After a while, the facilitator asks group members to find (to force) an association between the analogies or oxymorons and the original problem. The facilitator may start a "get-fired" discussion in which the group is challenged to come up with solutions that would work but that would also lead to getting its sponsors fired. Once such a solution is identified, the group's task becomes finding ways to scale it down so that the problem is solved without jeopardizing anyone's job (Ulschak, Nathanson, and Gillan, 1981).

• *Brainstorming.* Brainstorming is a group-based, idea-generating technique. The group is led by a chairperson who controls time, presents the problem to be worked out, and controls the process. The idea-generating phase typically lasts one to one and one-half hours. Participants then categorize the ideas, evaluate their potential usefulness, and recommend the most promising ones to the "problem owner."

• *Lateral thinking.* As noted in this chapter's theory section, lateral thinking is a process used for escaping conventional ways of looking at problems. Training in this process primarily involves helping participants learn to challenge their own assumptions and to develop awareness that methods other than straight, logical reasoning can solve problems.

• *Divergent thinking.* A process for expanding the view of a problem, divergent thinking involves thinking in different ways about the problem as a whole without necessarily trying to solve it. In divergent thinking, a person tries to connect ideas for which connections are not apparent; the resulting combinations may lead to a previously unsuspected solution to a problem.

• *Synectics.* In practice, synectics is a group-based, problem-solving technique that stresses control over the creative environment and reasoning by analogy. The term *synectics* come from the Greek and means "the joining together of apparently irrelevant elements." Synectics, which was discussed more fully earlier in this chapter, involves the following:

• Presenting the problem as given
• Conducting a short analysis of the problem as given
• Clarifying and simplifying the problem as given

- Reinterpreting the problem through analogy and metaphor (making comparisons such as "the heart is a pump")
- Leaving the problem as given and playing with the analogies and metaphors
- Forcing a metaphor or analogy onto the original problem
- Redefining the problem

Creativity-Relevant Skills. Research demonstrates that there is an identifiable group of creativity-relevant skills that must be available to a person if he or she is to achieve success with the creative techniques described above. According to Amabile (1983), people demonstrate use of these skills by

> breaking the perceptual set,
> breaking the cognitive set,
> understanding complexities,
> keeping responses open as long as possible,
> suspending judgment,
> using wide categories,
> remembering accurately,
> breaking out of traditional performance modes,
> perceiving creatively,
> using idea-generating investigations,
> concentrating effort and attention for long periods,
> persisting in the face of difficulty, and
> maintaining high levels of energy and productivity.

In addition to having these behavioral skills, creative people tend to have certain correlated personality characteristics, including

> work-related self-discipline,
> ability to delay gratification,
> tolerance and perseverance in the face of frustration,
> independence of judgment,
> tolerance for ambiguity,
> high autonomy,
> absence of sex-role stereotyping,

internal control mechanism,
risk-taking orientation,
self-initiated, task-oriented striving for excellence, and
nonconformity.

Creative acts — the formation of new, useful combinations of ideas — do not happen in a vacuum. To be creative, a person first must be aware of a specific problem, task, or technology — and he or she must be motivated to work on it. Further, the person must have at hand both the working knowledge and skills that together can illuminate a new solution. Finally, the person must have the combination of behavioral and personality traits listed above to mold these attributes, knowledge, and skills into an action-oriented whole.

Even if an employee possesses all the personal elements necessary for creative output, however, nothing is likely to happen if an organization does not establish a creative climate. According to David Campbell (1985, pp. 87–99), senior fellow at the Center for Creative Leadership, there are seven organizational barriers that can hinder people's individual creativity:

1. Fear of failure
2. Preoccupation with order and tradition
3. Resource myopia (failure to see the strengths and weakness of the people around you)
4. Overcertainty ("the specialist's disease")
5. Reluctance to exert influence
6. Reluctance to play (unwillingness to cultivate fantasy)
7. Excessive reward for success (creating too much anxiety)

To be creative in an organization that has and perpetuates these barriers, a person must learn how to circumvent or change them.

In a positive vein, Miller (1987), Raudsepp (1987), and Pearson (1988) discuss the environment and opportunities that an organization can create to foster a culture that directs people's energies toward the achievement of innovative results.

Raudsepp (1987) and Pearson (1988) describe how organizations can foster innovation and creativity:

- By developing and maintaining a corporate environment that values improving performance above everything else
- By encouraging managers to experiment with new forms of organization to maximize the creative support people can give to one another
- By celebrating individual contributors and de-emphasizing the anonymity of group rewards and commendations
- By permitting innovative ideas to rise above the demands of running a business
- By recognizing that efforts to improve the creative climate will meet resistance and inertia but being persistent in encouraging it
- By clearly defining a strategic focus that lets the organization channel its innovative efforts realistically, in ways that have market payoff
- By encouraging and training subordinates to open themselves to new ideas and new experiences
- By encouraging responsible individuality and maturity throughout the organization from entry-level workers to the executive branch
- By providing a safe atmosphere for failure by regarding errors and mistakes as opportunities for learning
- By providing creativity training and workshops
- By knowing where to look for good ideas and how to build on them once they are found
- By allowing creative people to take as large a part as possible in overall decision making and in the formulation of long-term plans

What Constitutes Competency in Creative Thinking? What Constitutes Mastery?

It is not possible to measure the success of creative thinking in a way that demonstrates a person's generic competence or mastery of creative skills. This is largely because creative thinking is domain-specific; that is, it is related to a particular subject(s). For example, a person may exhibit creativity in, say, architectural design but be totally inept at writing poetry or developing a strategy to market a new product. Therefore, a person's competency or mastery may not be transferable to other subjects but may have its anchor in a particular area(s) of expertise.

It is possible, however, for individuals to demonstrate their creative competence or mastery in the workplace in two areas. The first area is creative problem solving, which refers to a person's ability (alone or in a group) to discover new solutions to existing problems or to identify problems in new ways that promote their solution. The second area is creative innovation, that is, development of new products, market strategies, packaging solutions, production processes, and so forth. Nevertheless, people will be successful in one or both of these areas only to the extent that an organization encourages a climate of creative chance taking and opportunities for implementing useful ideas.

Mastery of the creative process can be described as the integration of intellectual capabilities complemented by expertise in a wide range of subject-specific areas and fueled by intense self-motivation, resulting in high creative productivity.

What Is an Example of a Successful Workplace Training Program in Creative Thinking?

Procter & Gamble (P&G) makes home products, including synthetic detergents, soaps, cleaning products, food products, paper products, and health and personal care products. It has been estimated that 98 percent of U.S. households have two or more Procter & Gamble products at any given time. The company, which employs 78,000 people worldwide, surpassed $1 billion sales in 1987.

P&G is a progressive company that has offered training in creativity to its employees for more than twenty-five years. Creativity is ingrained in the corporate heritage and culture, as reflected in a senior manager's comment: "The first time I came to work, people were talking about change and improvement." P&G believes that it is every employee's responsibility to be creative. Thus, the purpose of its creative thinking skills course is to help employees bring about workplace innovation by finding and using "novel and useful ideas or solutions to problems that can be implemented." In other words, it is not enough for employees to generate creative ideas; their creative ideas need to be put into use.

P&G placed renewed emphasis on creativity in 1987 as part of its sesquicentennial (150th anniversary), which celebrated the theme "Excellence Through Commitment and Innovation." At that time, a new version of the creativity course was designed and developed with assistance from the Center for Creative Studies of Buffalo, New York.

All P&G's training programs are offered through the corporate training and development office located in Cincinnati, Ohio, and are open to all its U.S. employees. Programs are funded through the budgets of the locations in which the employees work, and employees attend courses on company time. The creative thinking skills course is open to employees at all levels and is voluntary, as is nearly all training at P&G. Employees usually learn of the course through word-of-mouth, through employees who have attended the course and recommend it to their peers and subordinates. Employees may also learn about the course from a course catalogue that is published every three months or from supervisors who may recommend that employees take the course.

Historically, P&G has valued employee diversity in race, gender, and age. The creativity course has helped the company appreciate more subtle differences among people because the course brings participants to a higher level of understanding about the importance of individual creativity. P&G believes that people inherently want to grow and contribute to organizational success; the skills they develop in the creativity course help them to do so.

The creative thinking skills course is a highly interactive, two-day course based on a collaborative learning model. The course is delivered by the Center for Creative Studies, but P&G employees serve as coaches who assist with the course's small group activities. The course begins by providing participants with a framework for understanding the concept of creativity. Creativity is demystified for participants as they learn that it is not magical and does not happen by accident but is a complex concept composed of four parts: person, process, product, and environment.

Participants also learn that sustaining creativity is a function of knowledge, of how well a person knows what he or she is doing. Employees learn the importance of being aware of their skills and weaknesses in terms of fluency in developing ideas, flexibility, ability to elaborate or build on ideas, and originality of thinking. To be personally creative, an employee must use a sense of curiosity by asking "Why?" An employee must also exercise imagination and be willing to take calculated risks and deal with complexity.

The course explores many avenues for expressing creativity, such as through writing, drawing, or other arts. Every participant leaves the course with something that he or she has created. The course also emphasizes that a person may need a change of mind-set in order to be creative. Employees must be deliberate about exercising creativity rather than waiting for it to happen. In the course, participants focus on the process of creative problem solving, which includes identifying and understanding a problem, generating creative ideas for its solution, and then executing and implementing one or more of those ideas.

Time is set aside for individual reflection, small group activities, and journal keeping. The course provides a wide variety of activities to meet the needs of participants' learning styles. It is designed to be effective for either a group of people who work in the same unit or department, for a group of people from different organizational levels, or for people from different units or departments. A secondary benefit of the course is the networking that begins among people during the small group activities and often continues after the course.

The majority of course time is spent on the concepts and techniques outlined above. The remainder is spent working on problems, both personal and work related, that the participants bring to the course.

Course evaluation consists of extensive research compiled one, three, and six months after the course's completion. This evaluation looks at how participants have used their newly learned skills on the job and, consequently, how their jobs have been affected (William Lambert, telephone interviews, September and October 1988).

What Should Be Included in a Generic Workplace Creative Thinking Curriculum?

Exhibit 10 provides aid in designing a creative thinking curriculum.

Exhibit 10. Creative Thinking Skills: The Problem-Solving Perspective.

Administer Torrance Test of Creative Thinking at beginning and conclusion of workshop to measure increased performance.

What are the objectives of this training?
–To demonstrate to participants why creative thinking is essential for success in the workplace
–To master some techniques of creative thinking that can be used to increase levels of creative response on the job
–To build skills in applying creative thinking to group and individual problem-solving situations through instruction, practice, and reinforcement exercises

What is involved in problem recognition and definition skills in creative problem solving?
–Trainer and participants examine intuitive problem-stating style.
–Participants practice several procedures or parts of procedures for defining problems.

What is the process for generating ideas?
–Trainer and participants examine idea-generation procedures (unusual uses for mundane items exercise).
  –Trainer selects a noun randomly and instructs participants to think of as many uses as possible.
  –Trainer has participants pick a common problem and list as many solutions to the problem as possible.
–Participants practice several idea-stimulating procedures or parts of procedures, working individually.

What is a basic creative problem-solving procedure?
–Trainer facilitates a brainstorming type of interactive group session that combines definitional and idea-generating procedures.

**Exhibit 10. Creative Thinking Skills:
The Problem-Solving Perspective, Cont'd.**

-Trainer and participants examine methods for evaluating ideas that were generated.
-Trainer encourages participants to invent their own problem-solving systems by combining parts of procedures that have been discussed and practiced.
-Trainer analyzes elements of day's activity from the participants' point of view as "what/why" statements.

What is the role of interpersonal skills awareness?
-Trainer prepares the way for interpersonal aspects of creative problem solving; exercises and discussion topics include Kolb's learning style inventory and active listening.

How do you extend and modify basic problem-solving procedures to make them useful in specific situations?
-Trainer introduces the concepts of personal accountability for and multi-dimensionality of ideas, relating these to generalized framework.
-Participants prepare and implement personal action plans.
-Using a matrix, participants combine material into "what/why" constructs and apply them to case studies in creative problem solving.

Source: Adapted from Rickards and Freedman, 1979, p. 6.

PART 6

Developmental Skills: Managing Personal and Professional Growth

Personal management skills are the building blocks for good morale, a focused work life, and even organizational productivity. A strong foundation of skills in self-esteem, motivation/goal setting, and employability/career development influences the behavior, attitudes, and desires of workers and ultimately contributes to an organization's ability to carry out its mission and strategies.

These skills form a subtle undercurrent that reaches into every aspect of an employer's organization. Therefore, they are essential for everyone in the work force, from new, entry-level employees through the experienced workers who are the backbone of every organization.

In the past, employers attempted to "cream" the best available entry-level workers from the existing labor pool. That is, they tried to identify workers who appeared to have good personal management and other basic skills, and then they hired them. Individuals who were weak in personal management skills but lucky enough to find employment were usually relegated to low-level jobs; often when the skill requirements of their jobs grew beyond their level of competence, they were simply let go.

In recent years, however, with the shrinking pool of entry-level workers and increasing competition among employers, the military, and others to hire the best of that pool, employers are facing a different dilemma. In order to fill their factories and sales counters, employers must reach below the "cream" to a second and third tier of entry-level candidates — to those individuals who often have limited personal management skills. Therefore, employers are finding that because they cannot hire workers who already possess such skills, they must invest training dollars to build the kinds of employees who have strong personal management skills.

The employer's dilemma presents tremendous new opportunities for school- and government-sponsored "second chance" training programs. These programs already offer extensive curricula in personal management skills, but now they have the potential to be used by employers in tailoring their programs to specifically meet workplace needs. Moreover, customized training programs in personal management skills would significantly improve current efforts to assist the economically and educationally disadvantaged in our society to find and hold jobs. Many members of the low-income population do not possess even rudimentary techniques for finding employment. They may have the will to work — and even many of the skills an employer seeks — but they are unlikely to be hired because they do not know how to respond effectively to job advertisements or conduct themselves in an employment interview. Often, deficiencies in personal management skills are a result of their having no effective role models and mentors who can convey these skills by example and through teaching.

Problems with personal management skills are not only surfacing at the entry level or with new hires; experienced workers may also show deficiencies, although they are often less severe than those of the entry-level worker. Experienced workers may have vague goals and ambitions but little or no real understanding of how to pursue them through appropriate training, alternative career tracks, or promotions. Circumstances outside the organization, such as mergers, layoffs, and downsizing, sometimes create feelings of powerlessness and diminish self-esteem. Declining productivity, increasing grievances, high absenteeism, and increases in injuries often result, driving employers to consider providing personal management training for experienced as well as new-hire workers.

Increasingly, employers are realizing that such training will enhance their current and future prospects. By helping their workers gain these skills, employers are developing more self-aware and satisfied employees. Ultimately, this leads to a more effective and productive work force.

CHAPTER 11

Self-Esteem:
Confidence Leads to Competence

That kind of life is most happy which affords us the most opportunities of gaining our own esteem.

Samuel Johnson, 1709–1784

What Is Self-Esteem?

A person who demonstrates a strong sense of self-worth may be characterized as possessing a positive self-concept. A positive self-concept gives people a firm foundation from which to reach their maximum potential in the workplace and in other areas of life. Self-esteem flows from a good self-concept. In fact, every person's self-concept is made up of three essential elements:

- *Self-awareness* — knowledge of one's own skills and abilities, awareness of one's own impact on others, awareness of one's own emotional capacity, and awareness of one's own needs and how to address them
- *Self-image* — one's view of oneself
- *Self-esteem* — the expression of happiness or dissatisfaction with one's own self-image

What Theories Support
Current Training in Self-Esteem?

Positive feelings about the self play an integral role in the life of every successful person. Theoretical exploration of the

215

link between positive self-perceptions and success in life, particularly success in employment, reaches at least as far back as 1890 to the work of the philosopher William James. James (1890) wrote that the self is both a knower and an object of knowledge. James further theorized that each person has three selves: (1) a *material self,* or one's body and personal possessions; (2) a *social self,* or a sense of human relations and status; and (3) a *spiritual self,* which includes desires, inclinations, and emotions.

These selves, according to James, interact dynamically as we seek to enhance our self-perceptions. Some self-perceptions develop in the context of social interaction and are largely influenced by the feedback that we get from others (Mead, 1934). Such self-perceptions are multidimensional (in that they consist of the various roles we play) and hierarchical (that is, some dimensions are more important to us than others) (Beane and Lipka, 1986). Since James's day, many philosophers and psychologists have explored the issues surrounding the concept of self-perception and its importance in a person's life. Modern theorists suggest that, for each person, positive self-perception needs to be constantly reinforced in some way.

In the early 1940s, humanistic psychologist Abraham Maslow described a *hierarchy of human needs,* which includes the following:

- Physiological needs, such as hunger, thirst, and sex, the fulfillment of which is basic to human survival
- Safety needs, such as those for security and freedom from threat
- Social needs, such as those for love, affection, and acceptance by others
- Self-esteem needs, such as those for self-respect and success
- Self-actualization, or self-realization, need, such as that for self-identity or fulfillment of personal potential

In Maslow's hierarchy, self-esteem and self-actualization are the two highest needs (see Figure 8). Self-actualization encompasses the idea that a mentally and emotionally healthy person will view himself or herself as capable of functioning adequately in any situation.

Figure 8. Maslow's Hierarchy of Needs.

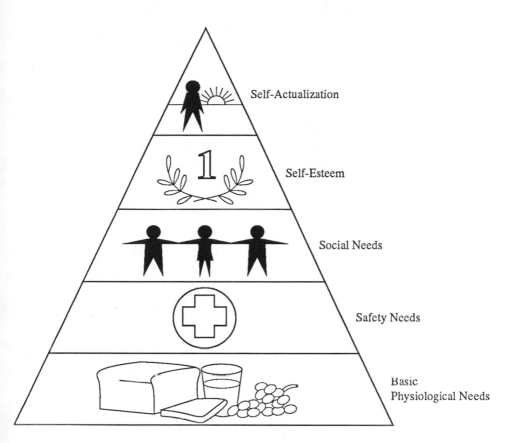

Maslow assumed that needs are fulfilled in the order presented; that is, the lowest level of needs (physiological) is at least partially fulfilled before the next level (safety) can emerge and so on. His theory is widely cited and discussed but has not been extensively tested. Questions have therefore arisen regarding people's regression or uneven movement among the levels of need, particularly in a work environment. Some psychologists and educators question whether it is necessary for a person to fulfill needs in the sequence Maslow identified, believing instead that people fulfill their needs in random sequence, depending on the situation.

Since the 1950s, theorists and researchers have specifically explored self-perception's place in human growth and development (see Figure 9). Several fairly consistent ideas about personality, behavior, and level of self-esteem have come from these theoretical observations and practical research. Among them are the following:

- Self-concept has a central place in personality, acting as a source of unity and a guide to behavior.
- Although self-perceptions are multidimensional and hierarchical, at one level they blend into a general sense of self.
- Self-perceptions seek stability, consistency, and enhancement.
- Self-perceptions may be based on roles a person plays, as well as on the attributes that a person believes he or she possesses.
- Although the self may be an initiator, self-perceptions mainly arise in a social context and are greatly influenced by feedback from significant others (Beane and Lipka, 1986).

Figure 9. Process of Self-Perceiving.

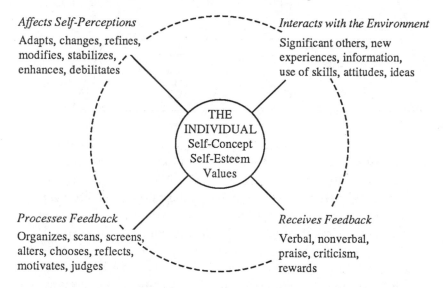

Affects Self-Perceptions

Adapts, changes, refines, modifies, stabilizes, enhances, debilitates

Interacts with the Environment

Significant others, new experiences, information, use of skills, attitudes, ideas

THE INDIVIDUAL
Self-Concept
Self-Esteem
Values

Processes Feedback

Organizes, scans, screens, alters, chooses, reflects, motivates, judges

Receives Feedback

Verbal, nonverbal, praise, criticism, rewards

Source: Reprinted by permission of the publisher. From J. A. Beane and R. P. Lipka, *Self-Concept, Self-Esteem, and the Curriculum,* © 1986, p. 17, New York: Teachers College Press, © 1984, 1986 by Teachers College, Columbia University. All rights reserved.

Donald E. Super of Columbia University has linked an individual's self-concept with how he or she goes about selecting a vocation. Super (1953) proposes the theory that people strive to implement their self-concept by choosing to enter occupations that seem most likely to permit self-expression. Therefore, according to Super, occupational behaviors can best be understood by viewing them within the context of the individual attempting to implement a self-concept.

What Are the Essential Elements of Training in Self-Esteem?

There is broad agreement on the advantages of ensuring that each person has a strong, mature, realistic self-concept that leads to positive self-esteem. However, to develop training curricula that deal with improving an individual's self-esteem, a trainer needs to analyze its component parts so that the training can be focused on those areas that will benefit most from positive reinforcement. The first element of self-concept is self-awareness.

Self-Awareness. Self-awareness derives from the satisfaction of four basic needs.

1. *Knowledge of skills and abilities.* People who know their skills and abilities are able to evaluate realistically where their talents lie, what their strengths are, and how these relate to job performance. Not all people possess this knowledge, however. For example, homemakers who wish to return to the work force or students who have never held full-time jobs may not be aware of their skills and abilities and thus their value to potential employers.

2. *Awareness of impact on others.* People with good self-perceptions know that they have an impact on others and that other people react positively or negatively toward them, depending on the signals (such as tone of voice and body language) they send out. They know that to communicate and interact well in the workplace, they need to understand the signals that provide an indication of the thoughts and feelings of others. A

major part of the training for people who have low self-esteem involves development of their social adjustment and communication skills. An employee who is able to improve these skills functions much more successfully in reciprocal friendships and in relationships with co-workers and supervisors.

3. *Awareness of emotional capacity.* A person with a positive self-concept is aware of what his or her emotional cutoff point is. This individual is better able to cope with stress, deal with change, handle criticism, and keep reactions to personal and professional tensions within a tolerable range. Problems are part of everyday living, but the inability to handle difficult situations leaves a person stressed, and stress may manifest itself in withdrawal or in angry behavior. Such behavior usually is counterproductive in a work environment, and a person who behaves negatively may lose promotions or even a job.

A corollary of the ability to handle stress is the ability to deal with change. Change, however positive, may still be stressful. For example, moving from the relative freedom of a classroom to the more restricted and high-powered demands of an office job can be stressful. In the workplace a person needs skill in learning how to cope sanely and creatively with all kinds of changes.

Along with change comes criticism. Criticism may be negative or constructive; it may depress workers or challenge them. Learning to differentiate between the two kinds of criticism is vital to achieving maturity and job growth. Learning to deal thoughtfully with both types of criticism is essential to maintaining a job and moving upward in an organization.

4. *Awareness of self-needs.* Self-awareness requires that a person have enough self-knowledge to recognize when it is time to seek more information before taking action. Effective use of this skill presupposes capabilities in the areas of critical thinking and decision making.

Critical thinking is the ability to distinguish truth from fallacy, examine alternatives, and evaluate and test the validity of claims. The steps of critical thinking (McConnell, 1983) are

identifying problems,
asking questions,

discovering plans or patterns,
linking information,
reaching conclusions, and
evaluating.

A mature individual generally follows these steps automatically.

Decision-making skills allow a person to move from identifying needs and feelings to acting on them with restraint. Sound decision making requires more than just knowing facts; it requires that a person determine the value of each piece of available information and infuse that information with a personal value system. The decision-making process involves

setting objectives,
determining strategy,
making an action plan,
implementing the plan, and
gathering informal feedback.

Once people feel capable of making their own decisions, they begin to have a sense of control over their lives.

Self-Image. The second element of self-concept is self-image. A healthy, mature person has a positive view of himself or herself: "I am a caring person," "I am a good learner," and so forth.

Self-esteem is an expression of a person's happiness or dissatisfaction with his or her self-image. For example, a worker may believe that he or she is an efficient employer, but colleagues may not regard efficiency as a positive attribute. Some people might be influenced to change to a dysfunctional mode of behavior, that is, become inefficient. A person with high self-esteem who believes that it is good to be efficient will not let the negative opinions of others influence his or her positive sense of self. An efficient worker with high self-esteem will not allow peers' opinions to destroy the positive self-image that comes from behaving in a manner consistent with personal values and workplace ethics.

Self-Esteem. The development of a positive self-image and correspondingly high self-esteem begins long before a person enters the workplace. In fact, "various vocational psychologists have long accepted the theory that self-concept is a significant factor in an adult's choice of vocation, preparation for a career, and participation in the world of work. . . . The choice of a certain occupation is an explicit statement of one's self-concept" (Holland, 1981).

A feeling of low self-worth can be changed significantly through self-esteem training. The earlier in one's life this reinforcement begins, the better; but even mature adults can learn to improve their self-perceptions. The main way to attain a better self-image is to gain a feeling of empowerment—for each individual to assert himself or herself effectively, to acquire the skills to communicate clearly what he or she wants or needs. Ultimately, people who sustain positive self-awareness and a correspondingly upbeat self-image will be capable of pursuing and obtaining a job and of moving up in the workplace.

What Constitutes Competency in Self-Esteem?
What Constitutes Mastery?

It is difficult to train one in self-esteem and even more difficult to measure it. Improving the skills that lead to greater self-esteem are highly personal and diverse; they cannot necessarily be measured with a norm-referenced, incremental growth scale. There are, however, qualitative criteria that may be used as indicators that a person is developing and maintaining clear and positive self-perceptions (Beane and Lipka, 1986):

- Demonstrating willingness to take risks
- Functioning in an ambiguous and flexible environment
- Demonstrating willingness to assume leadership and responsibility
- Following through on tasks
- Showing confidence in work and assessing it accurately

Education and training programs that reinforce positive self-esteem should be provided both in and out of the workplace.

Several process models for training in self-esteem have been used with reasonable success in enhancing participants' self-esteem.

A generic, open-ended, developmental (process) model to enhance peoples' self-esteem is concerned with improving skills and abilities and with developing general, transferable knowledge. The goal is for learners to develop desirable ways of thinking, acting, and feeling that they can use for their own purposes.

In 1978, a team of British educators led by Geoff Stanton proposed several process models that can be applied to self-esteem training (Stanton and others, 1980). Although Stanton's team developed these models for use in educational settings, they are easily adaptable to training in the workplace. Three of the models that Stanton's team developed do not offer rigid structure but rather suggest plans of action.

The *experiential model* is an open-ended model, with emphasis on participants' acquiring self-awareness rather than developing specific vocational competencies. For example, participants' activities may include working together as volunteers at a homeless shelter or becoming active in workplace politics. The goal is for participants to focus on their personal feelings about such a project rather than on mastering the vocational skills needed to do the project tasks.

This approach is very different from most classroom learning. Its advantage is that the activities are in and of the real world and therefore more motivating in terms of improving self-image than the accomplishment of a contrived task might be. A potential disadvantage is that activities may be so unstructured that learners may not learn as much as was hoped and intended; results are not easily measured.

The *reflective model* enables students to learn generic techniques for solving problems in diverse experiential situations. This personal approach uses participants' own experiences to promote their understanding of how the dynamics of one situation can be viewed and resolved in a variety of ways, depending on differing patterns and relationships. For example, a conflict between a manager and an employee may be seen as either a conflict of personalities or of roles. Participants become aware of the fact that the way in which a problem is approached often dictates the options available for its resolution. Success in completing this process generates a sense of accomplishment that leads participants to improved self-esteem.

A disadvantage of the reflective model is that it assumes that the learners have good communication skills and are able to work at an abstract level. Also, learners may not see the relevancy of "just talking." An advantage is that learners' experiences are treated as credible, and that in itself may enhance their self-esteem. This approach also offers learners constructive ways of looking at the world, and these outlooks will help them deal positively with new situations.

The *counseling model* uses group settings to evaluate trainees' personal experiences, behaviors, and understanding of other people. Participants learn from each other by describing and discussing experiences and examples from their own lives. They learn the dynamics of human relationships — the effects that a person may have on someone else, and the effects that other people may have on that person. Clearly, improving interpersonal communication skills is a vital part of increasing self-esteem.

The counseling model's advantages are that it provides recognition that behavior may be based on feelings and emotions and that it offers a structured format for learners' exploration of feelings and relationships. A disadvantage is that the experience may turn into a group therapy session in which the learning of new action skills (such as decision making) is neglected. Without a conscious effort by the trainer to tie participants' new learning to improved self-perception, that primary goal of the experience may not be achieved.

In contrast to process approaches, a product approach to teaching self-esteem primarily focuses on achievement of a tangible end product through a demonstration of skill — such as writing a job-related memo or building an engine. A product approach is useful in teaching self-esteem because demonstrable evidence of skill mastery may boost participants' self-confidence. Process and product approaches are both valid training techniques, but one may be more appropriate than the other, depending on the situation. Most successful adult training models for self-esteem incorporate process techniques into an overall product approach.

Much has been written about how adult learners are more motivated to learn when they can see the immediate applicability of what they are learning. Learning is also facilitated when learners are able to see their work's results and, consequently, feel an immediate sense of accomplishment. "The strongest and most lasting 'good' feelings come from learning and growing on the job, expanding one's competence, increasing one's mastery, becoming recognized as an expert" (Nierenberg, 1973). Teaching self-esteem skills in a job context has the advantage of linking the enhancement of positive self-image to the actual work circumstances that will most affect the participant.

What Are Examples of Successful Workplace Training Programs in Self-Esteem?

Self-esteem training is offered in many settings, from traditional public schools and "second chance" job training programs to the workplace. Below are examples of successful programs in all three areas. They show how this training challenge can be met in both preemployment and workplace environments.

Educational Institutions. It is difficult to know whether self-esteem is being addressed as a distinct skill in primary and secondary schools. Local school districts have a high degree of autonomy and may determine for themselves what to include in various curricula. Therefore, some school districts offer self-esteem enhancement training while others do not. Several national organizations and many state school boards have advocated teaching self-esteem as a part of school curricula, but it is not known how many local school districts do so. Although it is possible to find curricula for teaching self-esteem that were developed by school boards, teachers, and organizations, no reliable statistics are available to confirm the extent of their actual use.

Where it does occur, self-esteem enhancement training is most probably integrated into traditional educational curricula. That is, the skills are taught in the context of courses such as social studies or health sciences, not as a separate skill area.

One successful effort to establish an atmosphere that enhances self-esteem has taken place at Jefferson Middle School
in Olympia, Washington. For thirteen years, this school's principal has worked for and been successful in improving the self-
esteem of students and teachers. The program focuses on the
dynamic interplay between the principal and the faculty and
between the faculty and the students. All players are made to
feel important and valuable. Teachers are encouraged to try new
ideas and develop creative teaching methods, and problems are
openly discussed with teaching peers and the principal.

For students, an important aspect of the program is a daily
advisory class. When students enter the middle school, they are
assigned to small groups. Each group meets a teacher-adviser
every school day until graduation, up to three years. In this setting, issues directly related to self-esteem and self-awareness are
raised. Teachers follow the social and academic progress of their
students to the point of interacting with other teachers about
the cause of an advisory student's low grade.

But advisory classes are not the only place students find
a supportive environment. The entire school operation is a model
of positive encouragement. A key to program success is that
teachers accept accountability for students' performance. Students seldom merit failing grades, however, because teachers
make every effort to work with students to find and eliminate
the causes of their poor behavior or performance, thereby avoiding the need to assign failing grades.

Students believe that their teachers sincerely care about
them. The value of this caring environment is reflected in two
facts: More teachers request placement at Jefferson than there
are positions available, and Jefferson graduates who go on to
the local high school have a drop-out rate of less than 2 percent
(Tom Eisenmann, telephone interview, November 1987).

Private Sector. Corporations do not, as a rule, directly
address such "soft" issues as self-esteem — unless, of course, economics determine otherwise. When the existing labor pool sup-
plies sufficient numbers of exmployees who project high self-
esteem, there is little incentive for companies to hire people with

self-esteem deficiencies and train them. If, however, there is a labor shortage and the only available people exhibit self-esteem problems, an employer may have no realistic alternative but to hire them—and if the employer is wise, to train them.

One popular self-concept/self-esteem training workshop is conducted at the Washington Hospital Center (WHC), a 4,700-employee, not-for-profit, acute-care teaching hospital in the heart of Washington, D.C. The 871-bed hospital is a member of the Medlantic Healthcare Group and has approximately 32,000 in-patients per year.

Entitled "Self-Concept and Self-Esteem: Keys to Unlocking Human Potential," the workshop was developed by the hospital's human resource development (HRD) department to complement and balance the hospital's other skill-based and professional development training courses. Of the hospital's several strategic goals, the self-concept/self-esteem course directly addresses the goal of humanizing the hospital's environment for patients and employees. To provide excellent, humane patient care, HWC believes that employees need to understand the impact of their own "self-concept" and its relationship to their feelings of self-worth and the work that they do.

The workshop enhances participants' skills by helping them to (1) increase their awareness of self-concept; (2) understand, through a values clarification exercise, the personal values with which they operate; (3) look at personal life choices and how a person affects and is affected by those choices, and (4) set goals for improving their self-esteem.

Course content is related to a broad range of life and work experiences. Special focus is placed on applying these experiences to challenges in the work environment. Examples of situations that arise in each employee's work environment are used to illustrate the concepts to be learned and to provide a functional context.

The one-day workshop is experiential and interactive. It uses a variety of learning approaches, including self-reflection exercises and group and individual exercises. The course developer believes that it would be useful to expand the workshop to one and a half or two days in order to cover additional concepts and techniques for enhancing self-esteem.

To begin the workshop, the instructor has participants introduce themselves and tell others about their interests. The instructor then gives each participant a list of questions designed to provide insights into his or her personality, and the participants share their answers with the group.

Topics discussed in the course include the importance of self-concept, human potential, how people are defined, and each participant's future plans for improving his or her self-concept and self-esteem. The instructor uses several measures of self-concept or personality type to evaluate aspects of each participant's self-concept and style of self-management. These include the Myers-Briggs Type Indicator and Element "S" of the FIRO-B (Fundamental Interpersonal Relations Orientation-Behavior) instrument. On the basis of the knowledge gained from the course, participants develop individual action plans to state their goals for working toward an improved self-image.

The self-concept/self-esteem workshop was developed in 1987. Between 1987 and 1989 forty-five employees completed the course. As this book went to press, three additional courses were planned for 1989, with a projected enrollment of approximately seventy-five.

The workshop is just one of 120 courses that the HRD department offers each year. The department has grown in size and popularity since its founding in 1978, when only nine workshops were available per year. HRD courses are available to all employees, and most courses, including the self-concept/self-esteem workshop, are voluntary. All are offered on hospital time. The sessions are paid for through HRD's budget; employees attend for free.

Evaluation of the Washington Hospital Center's training programs takes on many forms. Reaction sheets are common. In addition, two or three months after a program, instructors and participants occasionally meet for lunch to discuss results. Participants also receive follow-up letters, and managers and supervisors report success stories about participants whose job performance improved after training. For the self-concept/self-esteem course, evaluation consists of a reaction sheet participants complete at the end of the course. No determination has yet been made as to the longer-term impact of the course on employees' job performance (Rosalind Jeffries and Bernard E. Robinson, telephone interviews, May and August 1988).

Public Sector. Public programs are probably the source of most training to enhance adults' self-esteem. Most of these programs have been developed under funding from the federal Job Training Partnership Act (JTPA). JTPA programs also provide other job-readiness training to targeted groups, including youth, older Americans, parents on welfare, veterans, people with disabilities, displaced homemakers, and dislocated workers. Although the various programs differ somewhat because they are run by different local agencies and organizations with diverse trainees, they all share the same objective: to help their clients become more employable. JTPA programs characteristically have well-defined curricula with tested and measured results that show them to be generally successful in improving participants' self-esteem.

In 1986, the 70001 Training and Employment Institute developed an operations manual for the California State Department of Education and the California State Job Training Coordinating Council. This manual is representative of the programs available, particularly to JTPA youth participants. The operations manual that 70001 developed for youth education and training includes a unit on how to enhance learners' self-esteem and help them achieve the self-actualized state that is an avenue to improved chances for success.

The unit deals broadly with motivating youth and developing their interpersonal relationships through the mechanism of affiliative organizations that provide recognition for positive achievement. One reason for establishing an affiliative organization is to meet participants' self-esteem needs. This is accomplished by providing structured situations in which participants are offered positive experiences and find a wealth of opportunities for success. The program includes a recognition system that helps trainees feel accepted, competent, and nondependent and to develop a better sense of who they are. As the manual explains: "[A] recognition system, like any other tool, seldom is effective when used alone. But used in conjunction with solid counseling, empathic support, and consistent guidance from staff, recognition systems can be a valuable tool in helping trainees learn to be successful" (70001 Training and Employment Institute, 1986). Recommended recognition tools include awards, photographs and newspaper articles about trainee achievements, and displays of trainee artwork and writings.

There are also other means for satisfying trainees' self-esteem needs. Peer tutoring and mentoring involve using trainees who have developed a positive self-image to help those in need of self-esteem training; this bolsters the tutor's self-esteem while simultaneously providing a positive role model for the trainee. Leadership roles enhance individuals' self-esteem, especially if program staff members carefully monitor the trainee/leader's challenges; this provides an opportunity for people at all skill levels to be challenged and grow. Success-oriented training that is the equivalent of competency-based instruction promotes pride in achievement because it provides clear proof that the trainee has achieved predetermined objectives.

Ideally, by allowing trainees to discover and develop their own strengths and abilities, this type of program will lead them to become self-actualized. Trainees are often motivated by the satisfaction that comes from reaching established goals and the pride that comes from accomplishment. The result is a positive self-perception that helps a young person adapt and make progress in society at large (Kim L. McManus, telephone interview, October 1987).

What Should Be Included in a Generic Workplace Self-Esteem Curriculum?

Exhibit 11 provides information on a self-esteem curriculum.

Exhibit 11. Self-Esteem: The Power of Positive Self-Thinking.

What are the objectives of this training?
–To teach techniques for building self-esteem

**Exhibit 11. Self-Esteem: The Power
of Positive Self-Thinking, Cont'd.**

-To demonstrate to participants how increased self-esteem will help them
 improve their work performance
-To perform real-world exercises that will incrementally build self-esteem in
 participants and help them recognize and avoid self-destructive behavior

How do you determine your self-esteem quotient?
-By making a self-concept inventory that describes each participant
 according to the following criteria and then putting a plus (+) or minus
 (–) beside each item to indicate strength or weakness:
  -Physical appearance
  -Relating to others
  -Personality
  -How others see you
  -Performance on the job
  -Performance outside the job
  -Mental functioning
  -Sexuality
-By performing an accurate self-assessment that includes acknowledging
 and remembering strengths and describing weaknesses accurately,
 specifically, and nonpejoratively
-By separating out weaknesses and rewriting them by using nonpejorative
 language, accurate language, and specific rather than general language to
 describe the self and by trying to find a corresponding strength for each
 weakness
-By acknowledging strengths through the recall of positive things others
 have said about one
-By writing a new, realistic description of the self that covers all eight areas
 of the self-concept inventory
-By acknowledging each participant's strengths through daily affirmation,
 reminder signs, and active integration

How do you combat self-distortion?
-By writing down self-statements that "murder" self-esteem
-By examining self-statements for distortions such as overgeneralization,
 global labeling, filtering, polarized thinking, self-blame, and personalization
-By writing rebuttals about the self using an imaginary support person who
 can be positive, accepting, assertive, rational, and compassionate

How do you avoid the tyranny of the "shoulds"?
-By comparing "shoulds" with their basic value systems
-By determining whether or not "shoulds" are in conflict with your values
-If "shoulds" and your values are in conflict, by revising them to reflect the
 reality of your needs

How do you handle making mistakes?
-By feeling good about yourself in spite of mistakes

**Exhibit 11. Self-Esteem: The Power
of Positive Self-Thinking, Cont'd.**

-By performing exercises such as the following to raise "mistake"
consciousness:
  -Realize that everyone makes mistakes
  -Forgive yourself for making mistakes
  -Visualize mistakes as a natural consequence of living and limited
  awareness, and affirm self-worth

How do you handle criticism?
-By discussing how reality influences each participant's view of criticism in
terms of the following:
  -Innate constitution
  -Physiological state
  -Emotional state
  -Habitual behavior patterns
  -Beliefs
-By discussing the three *ineffective* response styles to criticism: being
aggressive, being passive, or being both
-By discussing the three *effective* response styles: acknowledgment, clouding
(token agreement with a critic), and probing (clarification)
-By learning how to counter criticism effectively by removing self-esteem
from the picture and comparing the reality of what the critic is saying with
what is constructive and what is accurate

What is your wants inventory versus your needs quotient?
To answer this question, one takes the following steps:
-Develops an inventory of wants to raise awareness
-Evaluates the inventory and determines in which wants or needs assertive-
ness and self-esteem seem to desert you; and then negotiates what is impor-
tant by being clear and assertive
-Each participant should work on three requests he or she wants to make
of another person and then transfers the successful experience to someone
in one's life who really can fulfill specific wants (practice makes perfect);
guidelines include the following:
  -Keeps requests small
  -Keeps requests simple
  -Doesn't blame or attack
  -Is specific
  -Uses high self-esteem body language
  -Mentions positive consequences
  -Sets a mutually agreeable time for the conversation
-Keeps a log documenting details of improvement

Source: Adapted from McKay and Fanning, 1987.

CHAPTER 12

Motivation and Goal Setting: Developing a Personal Game Plan

You cannot *bestow* motivation on anyone; you can give an
employee a raise, or a promotion, or even a kick in the rear,
but you *cannot* "give" him the urge, the desire, the strong
wish, to achieve a goal. That must come from within.

> Lefton, Buzzotta, and Sherberg
> *Improving Productivity Through People Skills,* 1980

What Is Motivation/Goal Setting?

Motivation and its subset, goal setting, may be viewed
from two perspectives. One concerns a person's *internal* needs
and goals and the interrelationships among them; the other concerns a person's *external* behavior and how employer institutions
can motivate people toward greater goal attainment and needs
satisfaction. This discussion considers both viewpoints about people's motivations for behavior on the job and off. According to
psychologist Edwin Locke, the ability to set conscious goals is
a major determinant of a person's motivation for performing
tasks. Thus goal setting is a primary technique applied to both
internal and external motivational approaches.

People are internally motivated by the need for self-actualization that usually is demonstrated by their desire to develop
their strengths and perform to the best of their abilities. A person may feel "an unsatisfied need that creates a state of tension

causing the individual to move in a goal-directed pattern toward need satisfaction and equilibrium" (Lewis, 1983, p. 185). In other words, people "are motivated by the satisfaction that comes with reaching established goals and the pride they can take in their accomplishments" (70001 Training and Employment Institute, 1986, p. 153). Motivation/goal setting is directly related to self-interest, and when people's self-interest is stimulated and achieved, their self-esteem is enhanced, further motivating them to better performance of life tasks. As the old French proverb tells us, "Nothing succeeds like success."

Striving for successful performance in the workplace is a major life task that requires a person to be motivated to work well — to perform to the best of his or her abilities and to complete work on time, within specifications, and under supervision. A person's workplace success results from both internal and external motivation/goal setting. Internal motivation/goal setting involves the background a person brings with him or her to the workplace, including personality, attitudes, work ethic, self-esteem, and economic and psychological needs for achievement. External motivation/goal setting primarily relates to circumstances and activities — such as work environment, organizational culture, organization of work, specific job content, organizational goals, supervision, and reward structure — that are initiated or reinforced by an employer organization.

In summary, work motivation is "[a] set of energetic forces that originate both within as well as beyond an individual's being, to initiate work-related behavior, and to determine its form, direction, intensity, and duration" (Pinder, 1984, p. 8) *and* "[a] description of the forces acting on or within a person that cause the person to behave in a specific goal-directed manner" (Hellriegel, Slocum, and Woodman, 1983, p. 169).

Charles A. Garfield, a clinical professor at the University of California at San Francisco Medical School, discovered that less successful people, regardless of career field, had no regular pattern of preparation, mental attitude, and methodology that they applied to life or work situations. He believed, however, that these characteristics could be taught to and developed in a person who looked inside himself or herself for the resources to meet life's challenges (Lewis, 1983).

What Theories Support Current
Training in Motivation/Goal Setting?

Goal setting has been identified as a major motivational strategy. At its most effective, goal setting motivates an employee to perform well on the job and thereby meet organizational needs as well. Goal-setting theory states that intentions are better predictors of a person's work behavior than are perceptions, beliefs, or attitudes. Therefore, when employees at all organizational levels learn to set their own work-related goals, employers can better predict, plan for, and assess individual work behavior and its outcomes.

Other principles of goal-setting theory include the following:

- Higher and harder goals will result in higher levels of performance than easy goals will.
- Specific goals will result in higher levels of effort than vague goals will.
- Incentives such as money, feedback, and competition will have no effect on behavior unless they lead to a person's setting or acceptance of specific, hard goals (Pinder, 1984, p. 160).

Experts in goal setting, Locke and Latham (1984, p. 18) describe goal setting as a technique and identify practical ways in which goals facilitate performance by directing a person's attention and action, mobilizing a person's energy and effort, increasing a person's persistence, and motivating a person to develop appropriate task strategies.

Locke and Latham identify other benefits that goal setting may bring an employee, such as "increasing a liking for the task, relieving boredom, increasing satisfaction with performance, and increasing recognition, self-confidence, and pride" (1984, p. 26).

Goal setting, which is both a theory and a practical application, is a widely accepted motivational technique. Because of its inclusion in and applicability to several other theories of work motivation, goal setting is considered to be an *integrative* theory. Whether as a theory or a technique, goal setting can be applied to the individual at work and to organizational needs. In practice, it is individuals who can learn how to set goals and to follow through to reach them.

Latham explores the personal and organizational benefits of goal setting. "Goal setting," he states, "is important for increasing self-efficacy because without goals people have little basis for judging how they are doing. Self-motivation is sustained by adopting specific attainable subgoals that lead to large future goals. Subgoal attainment provides clear markers of progress, which in turn verifies [*sic*] a growing sense of self-efficacy" (Latham, 1988, p. 568).

Other theories of work motivation are often categorized as either content or process. The content theories describe the internal factors that influence behavior. The process theories describe how those internal factors interact in an external work setting to determine behavior (Hellriegel, Slocum, and Woodman, 1983).

Content Theory

Theory of Needs. Maslow's hierarchy of human needs theory was discussed in Chapter Eleven and illustrated in Figure 9. It concerns internal motivation (motivation arising from a person's internal needs and goals) and is frequently cited in discussions and definitions of work motivation and resulting training programs.

Motivator/Hygiene Theory. In 1959, in an attempt to gain better understanding of work satisfaction, industrial psychologist Frederick Herzberg and his colleagues investigated factors influencing external work motivation. When members of their first sample group (among which were included the nonsupervisory categories of engineers and accountants) were asked for descriptions of satisfying work situations (motivating factors), they offered such descriptions as "achievement, advancement, recognition, responsibility, and the nature of work itself" (Murrell, 1976, p. 73). In describing unsatisfying situations (hygiene factors), participants spoke of "company policy, supervision, relations with superiors, working conditions, and pay" (Murrell, 1976, p. 73).

The relationship between the two sets of factors is important to discussions of work motivation. The theory that arose from Herzberg's work proposes that company policy, supervision, relationships with superiors, and other such factors do not motivate people in the workplace but may impede motivation. The way to motivate employees, then, is by creating opportunities for achievement, recognition, and internally satisfying work, not through work conditions and external environment. In this theory, even pay levels do not motivate in and of themselves, although the perceived absence of adequate pay can demotivate employees.

The conclusions of this explanation of motivation — or lack of it — led to the practical call for *job enrichment*. Job enrichment expands a given job by providing the jobholder more opportunity for decision making and responsibility and more control over the task and its meaning. Such expansion of authority, not just *job enlargement* to increase tasks, results in additional individual work motivation. "Job enrichment involves building 'motivators' like opportunities for achievement into the job by making it more interesting and challenging. This is often accomplished by giving the worker more autonomy and by allowing the person to do much of the planning and inspection normally done by the supervisor. Job enrichment always means changing the content — the specific duties and tasks — of the job rather than changing the job's wage rate or working conditions" (Dressler, 1983, p. 121).

Process Theory

Goal setting is an aspect of job enrichment because by setting goals a person can define, develop work plans for, and assess the process and impact of additional tasks. Included in the process theories are operant learning and conditioning, expectancy, equity, management styles, and goal setting.

Operant Learning and Conditioning Theory. The theory of operant learning and conditioning also provides an explanation for work motivation. In this theory, it is most important to observe and describe only a person's behavior and to avoid guessing at why the behavior is occurring. Behavior is explained as "a function of its consequences" (Pinder, 1984, p. 187). Therefore, "operant conditioning is the process of changing the frequency of probability of occurrence of operant behaviors as a result of the consequences that follow them" (Pinder, 1984, p. 190). For example, every time a person acts in the workplace, consequences follow. For instance, if a person who is punctual is commended for that behavior, punctual behavior is reinforced. If, however, a person's punctuality gets no reinforcing response or commendation, there is no reason to assume that the behavior will continue.

Operant learning and conditioning theory has important implications for the training field. This theory reinvigorated the concept of feedback, and today many training programs focus on offering positive feedback for desirable work behaviors. This theory also supports the idea that behavioral learning objectives are needed for training programs. Descriptions of the trainee behaviors expected to result from a training program are needed so that the trainer can reinforce them during training and so that the trainee knows when success has been reached in training and thereby develops an awareness of how to reinforce successful behavior back on the job.

Goal setting can be a key ingredient in operant conditioning and behavior modification. Goal setting can describe specific desired behaviors and when they should occur. Stated goals also facilitate feedback and allow an employee an opportunity to test workplace behavior.

Expectancy Theory. Expectancy theory assumes that it is neither internal nor external factors alone that cause certain behaviors but rather a combination of the two. People make decisions about their behavior in the workplace on the basis of anticipated rewards. Most people will avoid behaviors that result in undesired outcomes (Hellriegel, Slocum, and Woodman, 1983).

Expectancy theory describes two levels of outcomes. The first level includes outcomes from the effort itself, such as the job well done. Second-level outcomes are the results that may accrue. For example, a person may work hard to perform well on the job with an expectation of promotion or bonus as a reward. It follows that if the individual sees no relationship between effort and outcome, then the effort may not be exerted.

Equity Theory. Equity theory addresses the issue of an individual's perception of fairness in comparison to others in the workplace. It includes two general concepts: (1) Individuals evaluate the present situation as an exchange ratio and make decisions as to how much effort they want to put in. (2) Individuals make decisions that are based on a comparison with the efforts (inputs) and results (outcomes) of their peers.

Management Styles Theory. Organizational behaviorist Douglas McGregor (1960) proposed that the nature of supervision or management is critical to employee motivation, and he described managerial outlook as resulting in employee motivation or demotivation. He defined two management styles, Theory X and Theory Y, in which managers' views of employees are based on completely different assumptions about employees, creating self-fulfilling prophecies about employee motivation.

In Theory X, managers have responsibility for organizing and controlling all elements of productivity — "money, materials, equipment, and people — in the interest of economic ends" (McGregor, 1966, p. 5). The external action of management is viewed as the determinant of employee behavior; therefore, control of employee behavior is seen as being within the realm of management. McGregor (1966, p. 6) based the Theory X management assumptions on managerial belief that the average employee is

- by nature indolent, working as little as possible,
- lacking in ambition, avoiding responsibility, preferring to be led [*sic*],
- inherently self-centered, indifferent to organizational needs, by nature resistant to change,
- gullible, not very bright, the ready dupe of the charlatan and the demagogue.

In Theory Y, a manager holds a different set of assumptions about employees:

- People are not by nature passive or resistant to organizational needs, although they may have become so as a result of their experiences in organizations.
- Motivation, potential for development, capacity for assuming responsibility, and readiness to direct behavior toward organizational goals are all present in people.
- Management does not put these qualities in employees, although it is the responsibility of management to make it possible for people to recognize and develop these human characteristics for themselves.
- The essential task of management is to arrange organizational conditions and methods of operation so that people can achieve their own goals best by directing their efforts toward organizational objectives. This is primarily a process of creating opportunities, releasing potential, removing obstacles, encouraging growth, and providing guidance (McGregor, 1966).

McGregor further proposed that the creation of an organizational climate based on Theory Y does not require management to become "soft" and lack leadership. Rather, this theory views management styles as a positive and motivating force on employees. The Theory Y management style, working atmosphere, trust, and assumption that employees are mature and functioning adults with a natural desire to be involved in work and to participate in a future at the workplace are all critical components to be fostered (McGregor, 1966, pp. 14–16).

Today's participative management theory and practices are consistent with Theory Y. Participation programs may include quality circles, employee survey feedback, job enrichment, work teams, union-management quality-of-work-life programs, and so on. These programs and other participative practices that give employees more autonomy and authority in their everyday work are increasing as changing technology and organizational distribution of information force more decision making to the point of production, sales, or service. Successful participative management requires skills in individual and group goal setting.

What Are the Essential Elements of Motivation/Goal Setting?

One of the most important steps in learning how to motivate oneself is to become goal conscious, that is, to accept the importance of goals and to learn how to set them. Essential elements in becoming skilled in internal motivation/goal setting include the following:

- Learning the direction to be taken and why
- Learning different kinds of goals for different situations, including routine goals for improving daily output, problem-solving goals, innovative goals, and personal goals (Quick, 1987)
- Developing long-range goals and shorter-range subgoals
- Defining strategic, practical steps to meet goals
- Developing measurements and evaluation criteria for assessment of goal attainment
- Measuring progress toward goals
- Negotiating goals with others
- Identifying resources necessary to reach goals
- Revising goals

Educators/trainers Kenneth Carlisle and Sheila Murphy (1986, p. 4) have defined the essential elements of external motivation/goal setting as requiring the following:

- Very sharp focus on individual skills
- Employees' full understanding of how to perform correctly
- Employees' participation in problem solving and decision making
- Employees' personal commitment to action
- Positive and negative results to be linked directly to performance

- Patient, persistent follow-up by supervisors
- A leader (manager/supervisor) who can use practical motivation techniques correctly

What Constitutes Competency in Motivation/Goal Setting? What Constitutes Mastery?

Competency in motivation/goal-setting skills can be described in several ways. Carlisle and Murphy (1986, p. 6) see specific motivational competencies as

being able to concentrate,
being assertive,
being diligent,
being enthusiastic,
being self-confident,
being self-disciplined,
controlling stress,
developing a good habit,
feeling good about oneself,
going the extra mile,
handling problems and
   complaints,
having a positive attitude,
having patience,
listening to directions,
looking for a better way,
maintaining good attendance,
maintaining professional grooming and appearance,
profiting from experience,
projecting a positive company image,
using good judgment,
working as a team,
working effectively in meetings, and
working quickly.

To achieve competency in goal setting, a person should be able to do the following:

- *Envision what reaching the goal would look like or feel like.* This is a very important aspect of the goal-setting process. A person should be able to close his or her eyes and imagine what will be achieved when a specific goal is met.
- *Challenge himself or herself.* Again, it is important that goals lead to increased performance levels and provide for individual growth.
- *Set specific and measurable goals.* To direct work behavior and

relate it to attainment of personal goals, a person must be able to determine when a goal has been attained and, if attainment of success is not absolute, to assess the level of success. Success can be assessed by the number of completed tasks; product completion within a certain time frame; money saved or earned, or costs avoided; or process changes and improvements.

- *Break each major goal into subgoals with the steps to be completed in each.* Dividing goals into parts and defining how to achieve the parts and, ultimately, the overall goal is a strategic process requiring that a person learn how to outline steps that he or she must take to achieve an end goal. Experience with this critical process results in a person's increased ability to think strategically.
- *Allocate the people and resources necessary for reaching end goals.*
- *Identify potential problems and obstacles to reaching goals, and identify how to avoid or overcome them.*

Skills mastery for motivation/goal setting is not demonstrated at a single point in time. Rather, it is reflected throughout a lifetime in terms of the successes each person has as measured against his or her own and society's expectations. Charles A. Garfield of the University of California at San Francisco Medical School conducted a fifteen-year study of more than 1,000 highly successful people in all walks of life and found that they shared six motivation/goal-setting characteristics that could be said to demonstrate mastery of these skills. They are

achieving progressively higher goals over a period of time,
taking their work seriously and . . . not grow[ing] complacent about their jobs,
being motivated by self-set, personal objectives (rather than goals dictated by others) and work[ing] for the pleasure of working,
attacking problems rather than the person who caused them,
assessing the worst possible results of a risky situation before proceeding,

mentally projecting themselves into upcoming situations, activities or circumstances and role [playing] how they would react (Lewis, 1983, p. 401).

What Are Examples of Successful Workplace Training Programs in Motivation/Goal Setting?

To identify successful practices in motivation/goal-setting training for nonsupervisory employees, it is important to look for programs that integrate aspects of several work motivation theories: job enrichment, employee participation practices, and integration of employees' personal and organizational goals, with adherence to strict standards of measurement of behavior and results. The following three cases incorporate and emphasize various elements of work motivation theories.

Tektronix. Tektronix, Inc., of Beaverton, Oregon, provides a self-motivation/goal-setting program called Individual Development Planning to nonsupervisory personnel in its systems group of approximately 1,000 employees. The company has approximately 16,000 workers, with 1987 sales totaling $1.4 billion. It has five major plants in Portland, Oregon, and field offices and distributors worldwide.

The decision was made to initiate individual development planning for employees because managers of the systems group believed that the division needed to do a better job of employee development. This decision came at a time when staff numbers were being cut and management wanted to develop remaining employees.

The individual development planning program, first offered in December 1987, was also consistent with Tektronix's philosophy and goal of being an "employer of choice," one that values its people as resources worthy of investment and that wants to add value to their individual jobs.

The human resource department was responsible for developing and administering the program. Program funding comes from each participant's manager's budget. Managers have been willing to support the program, and participation is growing. In fact, other departments now are requesting the program for their personnel.

Although the program is based on a packaged program entitled Managing Personal Growth (distributed by Blessing White, Inc.), it has been tailored to reflect the needs of workers in Tektronix's environment. The voluntary program is offered monthly. Prework by the manager and the employee is followed with two days of training for the employee.

The training is offered by three in-house staff and line people who were trained to use the program by its distributors. In addition, other trainers — some human resource staff members, some line managers — have expressed their strong support and would like to offer and instruct in the program.

One incentive for program participation is the spreading word that taking the program is something employees can do to help themselves. That word comes from people who have participated in the program and expressed the belief that they learned skills useful in their present jobs and for their lives outside of work.

Program evaluation is predominantly subjective. Success is measured by soliciting the opinions of participants and their managers.

The program consists of skill assessment, values identification, and goal setting. Prework for a participant and manager involves assessing the employee's current skills for the present job and ranking his or her ability to do that job. The employee and manager compare their results and jointly decide on performance priorities for the employee for the next six to twelve months.

Employees who participate benefit from reflecting on their skills in comparison with the skills needed to do their present jobs. They also learn how to set goals and are assisted in developing very clear goals for the next six months on their present jobs.

In addition, employees find it helpful to work on goal setting and plan for individual development with their managers at a time independent of performance appraisal. For many people, this is the first time that they have shared this kind of feedback and developmental work with managers outside the context of performance appraisal.

From the prework and the course work, an employee gets an assessment of his or her current skills, a positive discussion with his or her manager on skills and knowledge needed to do the present job, an opportunity to make the present job better, and development of skills that he or she can also use outside the workplace.

Overall, participants find that the experience provides an opportunity for growth. Early on, the program addresses values related specifically to work and to life in general. Reflection on and clarification of these values help employees focus their energy on goal setting for personal and organizational growth. As a result, employees perform better on their present jobs, prepare for their next jobs, and clarify and set goals for their lives outside of work.

In this program, employees are also asked to solve problems and suggest other areas in which they would like to grow and take on additional responsibilities. This aspect of the program has led to promotions and job enrichment for some participants.

Managers have found that the program results in more openness between managers and employees, increased employee commitment to present jobs, and improved employee goal-setting skills for development toward future jobs and for widespread application outside the workplace. Managers believe that the program has "tremendous value to the individual and to the organization" (Janet Maurer and Julie Errend, telephone interviews, October 1988).

Goulds Pumps. Goulds Pumps, Inc., located in Seneca Falls, New York, is a company with 4,000 employees operating out of six plants. Its business is to design, manufacture, and service centrifugal pumps and to provide their component parts for industrial, agricultural, commercial, and consumer markets.

The company provides a Performance Review and Development (PRD) program that incorporates several of the external motivational theories outlined in this chapter. As part of the PRD program, direct training in external goal setting is provided for all supervisory and nonsupervisory personnel with the exception of union personnel, who are excluded because their salary negotiations are under contract.

The training begins by building an environment based on McGregor's theory of integration, that is, an environment based on the assumption that tying organizational goals to personal goals will result in greater employee motivation and, in turn, will improve achievement of organizational objectives. The program also incorporates the concept of job enrichment. Each employee is asked to identify ways to expand his or her work and take greater responsibility for organizational problem solving. Opportunities for recognition, growth, and advancement are developed in accordance with the motivators described in the motivator/hygiene theory (discussed earlier in this chapter's section on theory). The program includes a course in work-related goal setting that is mandatory for all exempt (nonunion) employees. It also calls for an open, participatory management style, which was one of the stated major change objectives for the program. Employees learn to write goals based on measurable behaviors, and their goals then become the basis of their annual performance reviews. The program's training materials include appropriate action words for describing behavior at every personnel level. It is that behavior and its results that are measured and evaluated.

The current performance planning and review system grew out of a detailed assessment of the informal system that Goulds had in 1985. The assessment was done through an employee advisory committee (which represented the support staff to executive levels, divisional and corporate staffs, and personnel within and outside Seneca Falls). One problem that the assessment identified was an organization-wide lack of skill in goal setting for performance. In response, a new system was established in 1986, consistent with Goulds's organizational mission of having a productive work force. The system, which is still used, includes performance planning through a mutual objective-setting process; assessment of overall performance, including objectives; and identification of employees' development and career planning needs. Also as a result of the assessment, pay for performance emerged as a personnel strategy.

PRD training operates under the manager of employee development and the manager of personnel and staffing. Its funding comes from each division and from the corporate HRD department. Training is carried out by training staff members or divisional employees who have been trained in how to conduct the program. The mandatory training annually requires at least one-half day of training for every employee plus a two-hour update, and supervisors receive additional in-depth training. PRD training is implemented along with performance reviews, according to this schedule:

> January to March — training and performance reviews, goals and objective setting for the current plan year
> March 15–30 — salary review discussions
> April 1 — implementation of merit salary increases

The goal-setting training provides employees with a standard method for setting performance-based goals and receiving feedback on them. The system includes individual and group goals by correlating organizational objectives with departmental objectives and relating those to the individual's objectives.

Goulds's management believes that the program, although not quantitatively measured, motivates employees by helping them understand what they need to accomplish during the year. The openness of the program process is also thought to be motivating. The program allows for interim measures, including periodic discussion of individual and group annual goals. In fact, a performance planning and review form requires ongoing discussion between supervisors and employees. Earlier systems were informal, were not regularly conducted, and did not require supervisor-employee discussion. In the current system, participation and dialogue are key and draw on employees' trained skills in setting individual and group goals (Jeryl Mitchel, telephone interviews, October 1988).

LTV Steel Company. LTV Steel Company, a subsidiary of the LTV Corporation, has 30,000 employees in sixteen locations.

LTV Steel's motivational program includes a training course in participation for labor/management teams. The one-week course focuses on work-related improvements by team building and other basic skills topics such as problem solving and group dynamics. This training originated as part of an effort to improve the company's union-management relations in the late 1970s. The training also addressed an LTV mission to create a more participative work climate.

The training program was agreed to by management and the union and written into the 1980 labor agreement. That year, the first team was trained in the team participation process. This training is conducted at off-site locations and is provided by the employee development staff of trained facilitators, both hourly wage and annual salaried. The training is coordinated through the manager of participative programs in the industrial relations department.

Each team consists of approximately two salaried and eight hourly workers. To date, 8,200 people have been trained, and it is expected that over the next three years another 2,000 to 3,000 people will participate in this voluntary program. However, if a totally new work system involving extensive participation by all employees is initiated during this time, even more teams will be trained.

The main incentives for program participation are input in decision making, recognition, and improved work life. In addition, some participants perceive the training as a benefit because it is offered off-site on company time and builds skills useful in their personal lives.

Course content includes approximately three days on skills for group dynamics, motivation, monitoring the group for team effectiveness, maintaining the group, and developing leadership and approximately two days on skills for problem analysis and skills for effective presentations.

The program's effectiveness is evaluated on the basis of whether the trained teams continue to work together. In the participation program, a team looks at specific problems, designs solutions, and sets implementation schedules. A team may address any problem other than those covered by union contract.

Suggestions for substantial cost-saving measures have regularly resulted from this process. After setting goals for solutions to problems or for work reorganization, each team has to make a formal presentation in which all team members participate.

This training is perceived as being motivating because the group and individual participation results in a consistent balance of salaried and hourly workers. It brings together people who do not always work together and mandates coleaders: one salaried, one hourly. According to an LTV Steel manager, it also motivates employees by "providing a feeling of control over their work, over their destiny. What they contribute matters. They have a new language, a new time frame, and they think differently. They are able to analyze problems, set goals, and make presentations. Once a year, there is also a celebration where teams are brought into a conference highlighting success stories. This recognition of their work together and of a new way to work is very motivating" (Chuck Butters, telephone interviews, October 1988).

What Should Be Included in a Generic Workplace Motivation/Goal-Setting Curriculum?

The purpose of offering a training program in motivation/goal setting is twofold: to be able to predict and define future employee behavior to meet organizational needs best and to help individual employees learn techniques for enhancing their goal attainment and needs satisfaction. A model program should include all the skills of self-motivational goal setting while incorporating elements of several of the theories of external motivation, as shown in Exhibit 12.

Exhibit 12. Outline for Model Training Program.

Part I: Self-Motivation Through Goal Setting—If You Don't Know Where You're Going, You'll Never Get There

What are the objectives of this training?
–To improve participants' understanding of internal and external motivation as they relate to the work environment

Exhibit 12. Outline for Model Training Program, Cont'd.

–To help each participant define what works for him or her in motivating
for success
–To internalize techniques for goal setting to improve attitude and work
performance
–To increase productivity and thereby enhance participants' probability of
job stability and success
–To improve the bottom line of the organization through enhanced
individual motivation

What are the intangible needs that motivate internal goal setting?
–Discuss Maslow's hierarchy of needs:
  –Physiological
  –Safety
  –Social
  –Self-esteem
  –Self-actualization
–Discuss how people's behavior on the job is related to their needs.
  –People's on-the-job behavior represents the payoffs they want and seek.
  –Goal-setting activity is directly proportional to the benefits people think
    they are likely to receive from the effort expended.
–Discuss motivator/hygiene theory:
  –Job enrichment
  –Opportunities for achievement
  –Recognition
  –Internally satisfying work

How do you set internal work goals?
–Setting and achieving goals can give a big boost to self-esteem in the
workplace.
  –Develop exercises with simple, short-term goals — for example, getting to
    work on time.
  –Break the goal down into small steps.
  –Concentrate on observable behavior.
  –Visualize personal struggling.
  –Include positive consequences of accomplishing the goal.
  –Affirmatively spell out the first step.
  –Set a date to implement it.

How do you set internal personal goals?
–By crystalizing your thinking
–By developing a written plan of action with deadlines
–By deciding what you really want in life
–By developing self-esteem and learning to behave with self-confidence
–By developing the determination to follow through

How do you keep a log to track the development and success of self-
motivation through goal setting?

Exhibit 12. Outline for Model Training Program, Cont'd.

-By selecting small goals each day
-By writing out a process for achieving success
-By documenting actual performance on the road to success
-By documenting feelings and thoughts as you go along
-By sharing successes and failures with others
-By continuing to try

Part II: Motivation — Improving Productivity Through People

What are the tangible job needs that motivate external goal setting?
-Tangible needs are the substantive rewards an employee seeks for work:
  -Material payoff (a stock-option plan, a parking space, a new laboratory)
  -Situational payoff (a supervisory position, a lateral move into a new job
   area, and so on)
-Discuss the relationship of tangible needs to intangible needs.
-Optimally, individual benefits and organizational results should be able to
 mesh so that both the employer and the employee are rewarded by the
 work done.

How are people extrinsically motivated?
-Motivation is about achieving more productive performance, which trans-
 lates into achieving job goals in the most efficient way.
-Using a motivation assessment instrument, ascertain the link between each
 participant's job goals and his or her needs.
-Discuss conditions under which benefits can be realized.
  -Note need to motivate for both an intrinsic behavior change and an
   extrinsic business change; the second won't happen without the first.
  -Provide case studies that illustrate the three E's of work motivation
   (exchange, equity, and expectancy).

What other factors motivate individuals in a work setting?
-Discuss external goal setting:
  -Direct attention and action.
  -Mobilize energy and effort.
  -Increase persistence.
  -Develop appropriate task strategies.
-Discuss operant learning and conditioning:
  -Demonstrate how behavior elicits consequences.
  -Show how positive feedback leads to desirable work behaviors.
  -Illustrate how stated goals facilitate feedback.
-Discuss management styles:
  -Open and respectful
  -Employee participation
  -Self-directing
  -Trustful atmosphere

Exhibit 12. Outline for Model Training Program, Cont'd.

-Discuss participation:
  -Quality circles
  -Employee survey feedback
  -Work teams
  -Job enrichment
  -Quality of work life
  -New design of the workplace
-Discuss expectancy:
  -Rewards expected from action/results
  -Rewards received from action/results
  -Change in behaviors because of rewards
-Discuss equity:
  -Fairness perceived in relation to others
  -Increased work effort because of perceived fairness in relation to
    others

What are some successful motivation techniques?
-Carrying out exercises that require a sharp focus on individual skills
-Correctly understanding the expected performance
-Developing evaluative criteria and measurements for goal attainment
-Measuring progress toward goals
-Negotiating goals with others
-Identifying resources necessary to reach goals
-Constantly revising goals by setting new boundaries

CHAPTER 13

Career Development: Planning for Today and Tomorrow

Alice:	"Would you please tell me which way I ought to go from here?"
Cheshire Cat:	"Well, that depends a good deal on where you want to go."
Alice:	"I don't much care where."
Cheshire Cat:	"Then it doesn't much matter which way you go."

Lewis Carroll
Alice's Adventures in Wonderland, 1865

What Are Employability/Career Development Skills?

In their book *Career Development,* Leibowitz and Hirsh (1984, p. v) use the exchange between Alice and Cheshire Cat to illustrate how critical it is for all of us to acquire skills, establish goals and direction, and maintain a focus in order to achieve personal and professional success and satisfaction.

One guide to finding, getting, and keeping a job and advancing in a career is the *hierarchy of career adjustment* (see Figure 10). Researchers Oettinger, Cole, and Miller (National Alliance of Business, 1986a) and their colleagues at Colorado State University's Experimental Manpower Laboratory developed this hierarchy, which presents the employability/career development progression as a series of stages or levels through which a person moves to reach self-actualization. The hierarchy also takes into account other skills (communication, interpersonal, and human relations skills) that have been identified as basic to personal success in the workplace. Together, these identified skills should be thought of as "functionally integrated and complementary, just like limbs — arms and legs — on the human body" (National Alliance of Business, 1986a, p. 217).

Employability skills, which constitute the career acquisition and maintenance stages of the hierarchy, can be divided into two parts. The first part involves learning a clear-cut set of competencies that prepare people for employment. These competencies include people's ability to "discuss chosen occupations in terms of job requirements and available places of education, training, and preparation assistance relating to their own interests, aptitudes, values, and personal circumstances," write résumés, fill out applications, contact employers, respond appropriately in interviews, and write follow-up letters (National Alliance of Business, 1986a, p. 218).

The second part of employability competency is sometimes referred to as job keeping or work-maturity skills of personal management. Competency in personal management covers a range of personal-responsibility skills a person needs to hold and advance in a job. Among many others, these skills include those related to grooming and hygiene, following directions, personal behavior, willingness to work, truthfulness, and personableness. Personal management also covers the more practical daily living (survival) skills related to such activities as opening a bank account, renting an apartment, using public transportation, getting enough sleep, and arriving at work on time.

Employability/personal management skills usually are taught in conjunction with employment-related skills, including the self-esteem, goal-setting, and motivation skills discussed earlier. The last skill group is vital because it helps to identify and clarify for work force entrants very important but less clearly delineated skills that are absolute prerequisites for achieving employment and job success. Employability and employment-related skills help make people "self-sufficient, capable of functioning on their own, and free from job obstacles" (National Alliance of Business, 1986a, p. 219).

Figure 10. Hierarchy of Career Development.

Career Stage	Level	
Career Enhancement	16	Solidifies position Expert or consultant
	15	Top position, new career, or community leadership
	14	Increases risk-taking behaviors
	13	Seeks fulfillment and personal meaning in career
Job or Career Advancement	12	Career maturity
	11	Job or promotion getting
	10	Advancement readiness
	9	Orientation for change
Job or Career Maintenance	8	Skilled performance and job satisfaction
	7	Human relations, meets personal needs in work environment
	6	Entry-level performance, some satisfaction with work
	5	Job conformance and adaptation
Job or Career Acquisition	4	Job getting
	3	Job or career readiness
	2	Basic career seeking
	1	Work role identification

Figure 10. Hierarchy of Career Development, Cont'd.

	Successful Outcomes
↑ *Self-actualization*	Self-realization
	Successfully applies career learnings as a leader
↑ *Interdependence*	Growth, achievement, recognition Expanding opportunities
	Seeks out and participates in personal, community, and career growth
	Fully functioning and satisfied with career Intensifies skills
↑ *Human relations* *skills*	Obtains promotion or new job
	Applies for promotion or new job
	Motivated to seek responsibility and improvement
↑ *Interpersonal* *skills*	Solidifies long-term employment
	Personalizes feelings and meanings related to work and staff
	Improved skills and performance employed beyond probation period
↑ *Communication* *skills*	Demonstrated survival and adaptation skills
	Obtains job or position training
	Applies for job or enters training, education, or on-the-job training
	Identifies job or career goals and developmental pathways
	Motivated to seek work or a career

Source: Adapted from National Alliance of Business, 1986a, p. 727.

Adult career development, which comprises the top two levels of the hierarchy, is still in the process of having its boundaries defined. To the general public, the term *career development* calls to mind such things as vocational counseling, career guidance, and life skills planning. If asked where people go for help in starting a career, moving to a new job, reentering the work force, or making a transition from part-time to full-time employment, the average person is likely to name the local community college, a religious vocational service, a private career counselor, and so on. All of these possibilities are correct but limiting. Career development is a *process* of providing services to adults to help them face and negotiate career change. And employers do this, although they are often missing from people's lists of institutions involved in career development. Today an employer must create an atmosphere and opportunities for its workers to maximize career potential and, at the same time, use career development to manage their own human resources better. This discussion addresses adult career development only and, specifically, as it relates to employer organizations.

Organizational career development is defined as "the outcomes of interaction between individual career planning and institutional career management processes. Desired institutional outcomes might include the communication of career opportunities to employees and obtaining a better match between individual career interests and organizational opportunities. Individual outcomes might include better self-understanding and identification of desired career goals. It should be clear that . . . organizational career development refers to the results occurring through dual career processes and focuses on the *joint* relationships between individuals and their work environment" (Gutteridge and Otte, 1983, pp. 6–7; see Figure 11).

What Theories Support Current Training in Employability/Career Development?

Employability skills training programs are, for the most part, empirically rather than theoretically based. Teachers and trainers question employers about what constitutes success in the

Figure 11. Working Model of Organizational Career Development.

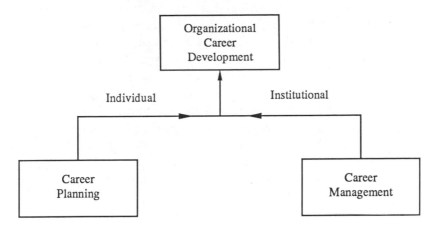

Subprocesses   *Subprocesses*

• Occupational choice   • Recruitment and selection

• Organizational choice   • Human resource allocation

• Choice of job assignment   • Appraisal and evaluation

• Career self-development   • Training and development

Career: The sequence of a person's work-related activities, behaviors, and associated attitudes, values, and aspirations over the span of one's life.

Organizational career development: The outcomes of the interaction between individual career planning and institutional career management processes.

Career planning: A deliberate process for becoming aware of self, opportunities, constraints, choices, and consequences; for identifying career-related goals; and for programming of work, education, and related developmental experiences to provide the direction, timing, and sequence of steps to attain a specific career goal.

Career management: An ongoing process of preparing, implementing, and monitoring career plans undertaken by the individual alone or in concert with the organization's career system.

Source: Gutteridge and Otte, 1983, p. 7.

workplace. Then, on the basis of employers' answers, teachers and trainers build a learning situation that mirrors the work environment and communicates as strongly as possible the skills necessary for on-the-job success. The structure of employability training depends on where each training participant is in terms of the cognitive and affective domains. The cognitive domain encompasses such skills as recall, recognition, comprehension, analysis, synthesis, thinking, and understanding, that is, how much people know when they enter training. The affective domain relates to participants' interests, attitudes, values, feelings, and emotions, that is, how they behave.

Employability skills training is normally a prejob training function. It is included here because it is one of those skills that employers are looking for and not finding in their new labor force entrants. Frequently, a limited labor pool has forced employers to pay community-based training organizations to provide this type of training for potential new hires in order to help them learn how to prepare and apply for jobs. The knowledge that one has the skills to apply for a job will have a strong positive impact on an individual's self-esteem throughout life.

Career development training, on the other hand, rests on a broad base of theory that has been evolving for nearly a century. According to Carole Minor, a faculty member in counselor education at Northern Illinois University, these theories can best be organized and discussed as follows (1985, pp. 17–39).

In the first decade of this century, vocational educator Frank Parsons (1909) developed an intervention model of vocational guidance that even today underlies most vocational selection programs. Parsons was concerned with the plight of the working class and urged a variety of reforms, one of which was encouragement of workers to choose jobs that were based on their abilities and interests. If workers could choose a vocation by first identifying their own talents, then matching those with the skills required for various jobs, Parsons believed that workers would be more satisfied with their jobs and more productive. The underlying assumption of his model was that people make an occupational choice only once in a lifetime.

In the early 1950s, however, two new theories (Ginzberg, Ginsburg, Axelrad, and Herma, 1951; Super, 1953) broadened the perspective. Their contribution is the view that career development and career choices are the result of a process rather than being a point-in-time event. Further, these theories present the idea that career choices can be identified by stages that are separate and distinct.

Other theories claim that people's career choices can be predicted from their individual characteristics. The most heavily researched of these theories (Holland, 1973) asserts that patterns emerge from what people say about themselves, their interests, and their skills. These patterns form personality typologies that have been developed into a three-digit occupational environment code called Holland's Code. Holland also hypothesizes that people will search out environments in which they can express their personalities (congruency) and that this search may explain why people change jobs.

One reason for the widespread use of Holland's theory is that he translated it into two useful instruments, the Vocational Preference Inventory and the Self-Directed Search, both of which measure personality types and relate them to specific occupations. Moreover, other highly respected instruments such as the Strong-Campbell Interest Inventory have used Holland's typology as an organizing tool.

A different theoretical construct based on social learning theory asserts that occupational choice is primarily determined by external environmental and genetic variables (father's education and occupation, educational level, race, gender, influence of significant others). This, together with Holland's personality typology, helped to form the accident theory of career behavior (Krumboltz, 1979). Basically, this theory states that interest and personality patterns develop without direction on the basis of accidental events and genetic attributes.

In recent years, taking into account all the research available, several theorists have developed new models of career choice and adjustment. One of these models (Tiedeman and O'Hara, 1963) identifies a series of phases through which a person progresses over a lifetime of career choices (see Figure 12).

The first phase is referred to as anticipation and has four stages: exploration, crystallization, choice, and clarification. In the exploration stage, a person interacts with the environment

Figure 12. Career Decision-Making Model.

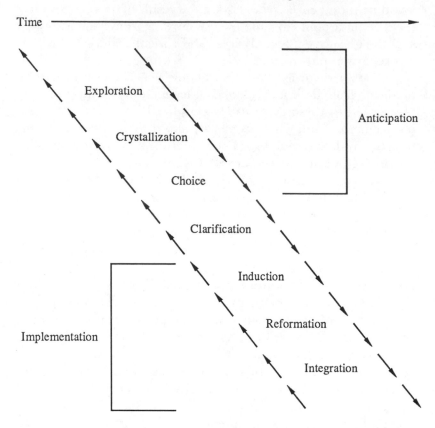

Source: Adapted from Tiedeman and O'Hara, 1963, p. 40.

and receives feedback. In the crystallization stage, the person's observations begin to form a pattern. In the choice stage, the person makes a tentative career choice and begins to act on it. Finally, in the clarification stage, the person prepares for entry into an occupation.

The second phase is referred to as implementation and has three stages: induction, reformation, and integration. In the induction stage, the person enters a job field. In the reformation stage, the person is able to act on an organization to make changes. In the integration stage, the person acts on the organization and the organization acts on the person.

Recently, theories that deal with work adjustment and job satisfaction have grown in popularity. In these, a key idea is the necessity of a match between organizational expectations and individual employees' expectations. The clearer both parties are about their expectations, the greater the satisfaction will be on both sides. Identifying problems in which unmatched expectations play a part can be a great help in counseling dissatisfied workers.

What Are the Essential Elements of Employability/Career Development Skills?

Preemployment and personal management skills cover the full range of finding, getting, and keeping a job. Exhibits 13 and 14 are extensive lists of employer-identified preemployment and personal management (work maturity) skills.

Exhibit 13. Employability Skills.

Accessing community resources
Applications
Being a consumer
Budgeting
Career planning/decision making—"pathing"
Changing jobs, companies, occupations, careers
Choosing an occupation
Contacting employers in person
Driver's license
EEO/AA concerning hiring practices
Employer expectations and obligations
Employment forms/red tape
Entering into contracts
Follow through on job leads, interview prospects, and so on
Forms in community (Social Security card, voter registration, deed, birth
   certificate, car registration, accident report)
Insurance
Interviewing
Job search
Labor market information (job opportunities, requirements, and
   descriptions)
Labor unions
Legal and financial aspects of employment (work permits, minimum wage,
   equal pay for equal work)
Letters (inquiry, cover, thanks, follow-up, resignation)

Exhibit 13. Employability Skills, Cont'd.

Loans, credit, and installment buying
Making change
Money management
Networking for occupational information and job hunting
Occupational knowledge (business/industry profiles, career data, vocational
    descriptions)
Opening banking account (checking, savings)
Payroll structure, taxes, and deductions
Personal interests, aptitudes, abilities
Personnel practices
Preparing federal/state/local taxes
Promotion from within
Reading a road map
References
Renting an apartment
Researching potential employers
Résumés
Self-assessment
Shopping
Sources of public/"hidden" job leads and openings
Telephone etiquette (initial contact, setting up appointments, thanks,
    follow-up)
Telling time
Termination of employment
Transfer of capacities
Using public transportation
Values clarification
Vocabulary/abbreviations used in world of work
Want ads
Worker rights, benefits, and responsibilities
World of work awareness concerning labor market functions (labor
    exchange, supply and demand, projections and trends, automation)

Source: Adapted from National Alliance of Business, 1986a, p. 220.

Exhibit 14. Personal Management Skills.

Abstinence from illegal, physically abusive, and violent actions	Acknowledgment of mistakes/errors	Appearance
Acceptance of assignments, guidance, criticism, and correction from supervisor	Active participation	Asking clarification questions as appropriate
	Adaptability	Assumption of responsibility
	Adherence to written/formal and unwritten/informal norms of site	Attendance
Accuracy of work		Attention to detail

Exhibit 14. Personal Management Skills, Cont'd.

Attentiveness
Attitude
Behavior
Breakdown/clean-up
  routines
Calling in sick
Care/concern for
  property of others
Cheerfulness
Command of site ter-
  minology
Common sense
Communication
Conduct
Confidence
Conscientiousness
Consideration
Consistency of effort
Cooperation
Coping with conflict
Coping with frustration
Courtesy
Dealing with the unex-
  pected
Decorum
Dedication
Demeanor
Dependability
Deportment
Desire to grow/advance
Determination
Diligence
Diplomacy
Discretion
Doing own share of
  work
Efficiency
Enthusiasm
Finishing work in
  timely manner
Flexibility
Following directions
Following "leave" pro-
  cedures
Following rules of
  workplace

Following safety
  regulations
Following through
Freedom from in-
  fluence of chemicals
  on job
Friendliness
Functioning without
  being easily
  distracted
Getting along with
  others at site
Giving feedback
Grooming
Handling boredom
Handling pressure
Helpfulness
Honesty
Honoring commitment
Hygiene
Industriousness
Informing of intention
  to quit/resign
Initiative
Integrity
Interest in job/site ac-
  tivities
Judgment
Keeping personal life
  from interfering with
  work
Leadership
Loyalty
Maintaining effort in
  spite of setbacks
Maintenance of tools,
  equipment,
  machinery, and work
  station
Management of time
Manners
Meeting deadlines
Neatness
Notification of
  lateness/absence
Openness to change

and new ideas
Organization of duties
Patience
Performance of as-
  signed work without
  prompting
Perseverance
Personableness
Poise
Politeness
Pride in work
Prioritization of tasks
Productivity of
  type/amount of work
  required
Punctuality
Quality of work
Quantity of work
Reaction to authority
Readiness to work
Redoing unacceptable
  work without com-
  plaint
Reliability
Requesting feedback
Requesting further
  assignments
Resolution of
  difficulties
Seeking advancement
Seeking ad-
  vice/assistance when
  necessary
Self-control
Self-discipline
Self-management (ade-
  quate child care,
  housing, transpor-
  tation)
Sense of humor
Sensitivity
Settlement of disputes
Showing respect for
  supervisors and
  fellow workers
Sincerity

Exhibit 14. Personal Management Skills, Cont'd.

Stability	Use of correct chain of	job repeatedly
Stopping work only at	command	Willingness to work
proper times	Utilization of materials	Working at acceptable
Suggesting im-	and supplies	speed/steady pace
provements	Volunteering extra	Working indepen-
Tact	effort when	dently/on own with
Task completion	necessary	minimal supervision
Thoroughness	Volunteering to learn	Working under close
Tolerance	new things	supervision
Truthfulness	Willingness to accept	Working under stress
Use of appropriate	additional tasks	Working within
language	Willingness to do same	"pecking order"

Source: Adapted from National Alliance of Business, 1986a, p. 231.

Although these lists may look as if the skills necessary to get and keep a job are endless, in reality, they fall into several clearly defined categories that enable them to be easily taught in a work-related context. Preemployment skills categories include world of work awareness, labor market knowledge, occupational information, career planning and decision making, and job search techniques (phone contacts, résumés, applications, interviews, and follow-up letters). Personal management (work maturity) skills categories include positive work habits, attitudes, and behaviors (such as punctuality, regular attendance, neat appearance, and good conduct) as well as daily living (survival) skills (such as using the telephone, telling time, going shopping, renting an apartment, opening a bank account, and using public transportation).

Many people might question the need for specially designated courses to train people in these skills. Their question assumes that people learn these skills as a matter of routine while growing to maturity. But that is a false assumption. The dropout, the young high school graduate, the delayed entrant into the labor market, or members of other special job-applicant groups may have had no role models or opportunities — formal or informal — from which to learn career initiating and sustaining skills. Thus, to ensure that each person has an equal opportunity to find a place in the working world, more and more training programs have been established with the sole objective of providing potential new workers with a "level playing field" on which to achieve employment success.

The skills provided through organizational career development training must benefit not only the individual trainee but also the organization that is investing time and resources to improve its human resource management. In the most successful organizational career development programs, individual and organizational interests overlap in "an implementation strategy evolving out of the integration of individual career planning goals and organizational career management objectives to assist in the acquisition of knowledge, attitudes, and values systems necessary for one's successful performance and movement within a career system" (Gutteridge and Otte, 1983, p. 9). Most career development programs aim for a systematic approach that allows employees to participate fully in their own growth and development (see Figure 13 for a model of an individual's career planning process in an organizational setting). The skills in which most employees need enhancement include self-assessment, self-determination, self-understanding, and career planning. From the organization's perspective, a career development program can enhance organizational ability to identify and develop high-potential employees, plan for succession, match individual and organizational career interests, and maximize employee productivity and retention.

Some aspects of the career planning model require further elaboration (Gutteridge and Otte, 1983). First, although career planning's focus is on how an individual fits in with the organization, most career planning activities also explore how a person performs within a broader life context. Second, career planning for employees within an organization has overtly different goals from career planning undertaken by students or unemployed people. These differences derive from the organization's preeminent need to maximize the usefulness of the individual to the institution. This need usually precludes consideration of career possibilities outside the institution's boundaries, although in some instances organizations support career planning

Figure 13. Model of Individual Career-Planning Process.

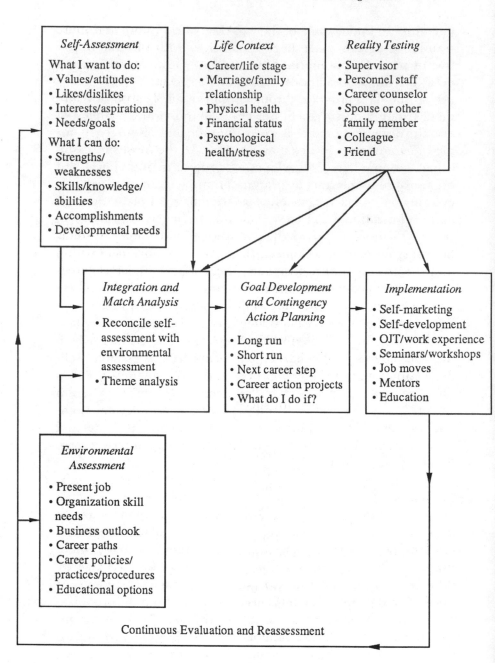

Source: Gutteridge and Otte, 1983, p. 32.

(such as outplacement counseling) that includes consideration of external alternatives. For example, in the military, officers whose careers have plateaued may be encouraged to consider alternative civilian careers. Third, a component of the model relates to enhancing individual self-assessment capabilities. In other words, employees learn how to match what they *want* to do with what they *can* do. To help employees gain a realistic view, their self-assessments frequently are accompanied by feedback from supervisors and peers. Finally, there is an attempt to clarify, through such techniques as job postings and skills inventories, how a person may link individual career plans with organizational career management goals.

For an organizational career development program to be effective, it must be tied to strategic goals and to existing organizational structures, such as organization development activities and developmental training programs. An occasional career development workshop or other one-time or uncoordinated attempts at career development will not have lasting effects. Nor will a program be effective if no other mechanisms (such as counseling) are in place to reinforce what people learn through formal career development activities. Career development activity should be an integral part of each employee's job, and it should occur regularly. At a minimum, career development should be discussed in conjunction with an annual performance review. Whatever its scope, a career development program should be flexible to allow for changes such as a move to cross training.

In organizations that offer only packaged programs, career development programs tend to look alike. An effective program will have several activity options so that it can meet each employee's needs. Designing and delivering career development training require commitment, assessments of needs and skills, knowledge of available jobs and careers, guidance, and evaluation.

For a career development program to be effective, an organization must be willing to provide time, money, and other support. Thorough planning and careful selection of a program administrator are also important. Support must come from top managers and supervisors if a program is to survive and be effective, and support from employees is also essential. Involvement of people from all organizational levels in the development of the career development plan will help build commitment.

Before an organization can institute an effective career development program, it must determine the needs of the organization and of the individual people within it. One of the first steps of program planning is identification of target populations because career development skills can be taught to several different audiences, each of whom may have different concerns:

- Entry-level employees, especially those who are first-time workers
- Midcareer employees
- Preretirement employees who may need career development information to help them prepare for a transition to life outside the organization
- Women, members of ethnic minorities, people with disabilities, and others who may face societal barriers to career development
- Employees facing job loss who need outplacement services

A career development program for employees facing layoff can be beneficial for an employer because such a program serves to enhance a company's image and lessens the likelihood of layoff-related lawsuits and bad publicity. In particular, it is important for employees who are not laid off to maintain a positive image of the company and, consequently, to maintain their work motivation (Latack and Dozier, 1986).

An employer must have means by which to determine employees' skills. To develop realistic career development strategies, employees need to know their strengths, weaknesses, abilities, and interests—work related and otherwise. An assessment center is one tool that an organization may use to determine its employees' skills and to inform itself of the talent and potential within employee ranks. An assessment center is designed to determine the developmental needs of employees by observing their behavior as they participate in a variety of situational exercises, games, tests, and interviews (Bray, 1981, p. 315). For companies that cannot afford to send employees to assessment centers but wish to offer customized on-site assessments, commercially prepared skills-inventory instruments are available for use at significantly lower cost.

Employees need to know how they fit into the organizational structure and what opportunities are available to them within the organization. These opportunities should be described realistically, or employees will become frustrated when their post-training expectations exceed the organization's ability to deliver. Employers can make employees aware of opportunities for advancement within the organization by posting position announcements as jobs become available. Position announcements inform employees of the skills and skill levels required to gain entry to advertised jobs. In many cases, the jobs that an employee aspires to may not be viable options unless the employee undertakes additional, significant — and often time-consuming — training or education.

Employees should be made aware of nontraditional career paths open to them (Hall, 1986, p. 8). Many people would be content despite not moving up in an organization as long as they could grow and develop in their current or lateral positions. Opportunities should therefore be available for employees to gain broader knowledge and take on more responsibility even if they are not moving up the ladder. Moreover, employers should develop multiple career paths that allow employees to move laterally as well as upward if they wish to do so.

Guidance is the critical link between organizational career development activities and an employee's implementation of career development skills learned in training. To move employees to act on the career development skills they have learned, supervisors or a guidance counselor should provide follow-up guidance and encouragement. Guidance helps address professional and personal attitudes and behaviors that may prevent an employee from satisfying identified developmental needs. Guidance may take the form of career counseling provided by a trained career development counselor, or supervisors and managers may serve as counselor/coaches, a role they play in many organizations. Because supervisors have more contact with employees than a career counselor, the dialogue between an employee and his or her supervisor may be one of the most effective elements of a career development program. The more open both an employee and a manager are, the more effective the dialogue and therefore the career development program.

Using supervisors in a counseling/coaching role requires that they be trained in counseling, interpersonal skills, and performance appraisal techniques. Guidance in career development may be most effective when it is tied to performance appraisals because then career development goals can be examined and addressed with employees individually on a regular basis. Discussions should not occur only at performance appraisal time, however; they should also take place whenever an employee has completed training or wants to discuss career development.

Supervisors often must be provided incentives to take on the counseling/coaching role. They may be reluctant to perform this role because their subordinates might choose to leave if they discover that, with their skills and the opportunities available to them within the organization, they cannot meet their professional and personal goals (Cairo, 1985, p. 243). Yet there may be benefits if this happens — because only employees who have a genuine interest in their positions and the organization and who have the skills to match their given jobs will remain. These remaining employees are likely to have high motivation and productivity.

Not only should employees be encouraged to develop career development goals and plans based on their skills and the jobs available, but their goals should be readdressed periodically and progress toward them measured. Program effectiveness should also be evaluated to ensure that the career development program is addressing the needs of its targeted audiences and the organization.

What Constitutes Competency in Employability/Career Development Skills? What Constitutes Mastery?

It is difficult to separate competency from mastery in employability or organizational career development. In employability, the difference may be demonstrated by the person who makes half-hearted efforts to obtain employment that provides no real personal and professional growth versus the person who actively plans, organizes, and seeks a job that he or she perceives as a career stepping-stone. The ability to master job search and personal management skills is particularly vital in contemporary society, where it is predicted that a person will change jobs an average of five to seven times during his or her work life.

Because preemployment and personal management skills are for the most part taught to people before they are employed, the training format usually is a simulated work-site situation for which behaviors can be measured by an instructor/trainer in a classroom. There are many ways to measure achievement of competency. The most comprehensive and sophisticated have been developed under such programs as the federal Job Training Partnership Act (JTPA) and the school-to-work transition programs offered through public secondary schools and post-secondary institutions that work with adults. Exhibits 15 and 16 show how one of these programs sets competency measurement standards, and the beginning of a sample training plan for assessing a person's skills related to getting and succeeding in a job interview. One measure of mastery might be that a person received a job offer as a result of a successful interview.

Exhibit 15. Developing Performance Objectives for Competency Statements.

For skill acquisition to be measured, competencies must be stated in terms of performance objectives that involve three elements: indicator, means of measurement, and benchmark or standard of performance.

For example, if the competency statement is "To exhibit acceptable hygiene and grooming," a related objective might be: "Given a list that combines descriptions of a well-groomed person and a poorly groomed person, the trainee will, with 100 percent accuracy, check the phrases that describe a well-groomed person."

In this case, the *indicator* is "the trainee will . . . check the phrases that describe a well-groomed person."

The *means of measurement* is "Given a list that combines descriptions of a well-groomed person and a poorly groomed person."

And the *benchmark* or *standard of performance* is "with 100 percent accuracy."

Another objective for the competency statement above might be: "Given the headings *interview, office, fast-food restaurant, and construction site,* the trainee

**Exhibit 15. Developing Performance
Objectives for Competency Statements, Cont'd.**

---

will list four examples of appropriate dress under each, with no errors."

The *indicator* is "the trainee will list four examples of appropriate dress under each."

The *means of measurement* is "Given the headings *interview, office, fast-food restaurant,* and *construction site."*

And the *benchmark* or *standard of performance* is "with no errors."

Source: 70001 Training and Employment Institute, *Eight Common Ingredients of Successful Programs,* © 1986, 70001 Training and Employment Institute, Washington, D.C. Reprinted with permission.

**Exhibit 16. Sample Curriculum Goal and Related
Competency Statement and Performance Objectives.**

Goal: Demonstrates skill in seeking employment

Competency Statement:
1.1 Identifies and uses sources of employment information

Performance Objectives:
1.1.1 Given vocabulary words and definitions related to employment sources, the trainee will match the words to their meanings with 90 percent accuracy.
1.1.2 Given a newspaper "want ad" section and a list of jobs the trainee has expressed interest in, the trainee will circle all advertisements for job openings that match his or her personal interest list.
1.1.3 After studying job-finding techniques, the trainee will demonstrate ability to use a newspaper and telephone directory business listings (the "Yellow Pages") by locating and writing the names of two potential employers, their telephone numbers, and their addresses.
1.1.4 After studying ways to seek employment, the trainee will list, with 100 percent accuracy, five sources for locating employment opportunities.
1.1.5 Given a list of employment information sources, the trainee will write, with 100 percent accuracy, an advantage and a disadvantage of each.

Source: 70001 Training and Employment Institute, *Eight Common Ingredients of Successful Programs,* © 1986, 70001 Training and Employment Institute, Washington, D.C. Reprinted with permission.

The ability to measure change in a person's attitudes and behaviors that occurs as a result of participation in career development events is very limited. The available standardized tests are limited to vocational maturity, decision-making behavior, and attitude change.

Organizations usually try to measure participants' changes in career knowledge and skills, career behavior, attitudes toward the training intervention and career choices, and functioning in certain roles. Competency or mastery often is measured through behavioral samplings and observations to assess improvements in morale, productivity, use of career planning and job search skills, and supervisory ratings of subordinates' job adjustments.

What Are Examples of Successful Workplace Training Programs in Employability/Career Development Skills?

Because employability skills training usually takes place prior to employment, many effective programs are found in organizations designed specifically to address the needs of people who desire employment but lack employability skills.

Inner City, Inc., a Wholly Owned Subsidiary of Polaroid Corporation. Inner City's Boston-area program is somewhat similar to programs offered through public job training (under the Job Training Partnership Act), but it is operated by a team of Polaroid and non-Polaroid staffers and uses no public funds. The program provides no profit for the company, and its graduates have been placed in jobs with approximately 300 other Boston-area companies.

Inner City was founded in 1968 and is based on the philosophy that economically and educationally disadvantaged people do not need technical skills training as much as they need to learn good work habits, basic skills, and job responsibility. However, in order to help close the gap between employer requirements and labor force qualifications, Inner City has added some higher-level skills training (for example, offset printing, word processing, and so on) to its program. Initially, Polaroid Corporation financed the program, but it is now self-sufficient. While in training, participants manufacture products that are sold to Polaroid and other organizations. The profits provide the program's operating budget.

Anyone eighteen years of age or older who can complete the application, submit employment eligibility proof, and pass a physical examination is automatically accepted into the program or, if necessary, placed on a waiting list. As openings become available, applicants are called in. Their waiting period may be from several days to as long as a few months.

The average training period is five months. The program is rigorous, and nearly one-third of the participants drop out without finishing the program, although a job is guaranteed to every trainee who adheres to the rules and completes the program.

The program is divided into four phases that consist of both on-the-job experience (approximately six and one-half hours per day) and classroom instruction (approximately one and one-half hours per day). Participants are paid between $4.00 and $5.10 an hour for an eight-hour day. Phase I of the program is a six-week orientation in which basic work skills (such as regular attendance, punctuality, performance, discipline, motivation, interpersonal relations, and self-esteem) are stressed. Trainees also receive actual varied work assignments during this phase and can enroll in a computer-assisted basic education component.

Phase II of the program, in addition to the work assignments, requires trainee involvement in seminars and individual and group counseling/support sessions. Mandatory seminars, 50 percent of which trainees attend on their own time, cover fifteen topics, such as life skills and how to get and keep a job, goal setting, career exploration, upward mobility, and communications.

In Phase III, trainees prepare for job placement by participating in mock interviews with actual employers. After reviewing their techniques, personal appearance, and presentation skills, trainees are sent to actual interviews until they are able to find jobs. A recently added Phase IV provides additional training and work experience opportunities for trainees with little or no job history.

Inner City's record is impressive. Over 100 graduates a year are placed in jobs, and 60 percent of those placed remain in that placement for at least a year (Tim Moore, telephone interviews, October 1988).

Eastman Kodak Company. More companies are establishing career development programs as the needs of the work force and the changes of the marketplace compel both employers and employees to map out their long- and short-term objectives in order to achieve personal and institutional goals.

Eastman Kodak is a *Fortune* 500 company with $13.3 billion in reported sales and 100 new products in 1987 alone. The company has 145,000 employees worldwide, 86,800 of whom are in the United States. The company has manufacturing and marketing facilities in 45 countries and sales outlets in 150 countries. Kodak's Copy Products Division employs about 5,000 people in the United States. The division produces a wide variety of copiers and printers, from midsize convenience copiers to high-volume electrophotographic copiers/duplicators. Its other products include a fully integrated turnkey electronic publishing system and two families of nonimpact printers.

The company has undergone a restructuring that resulted in a shift from a centralized to a decentralized organization with separate business units, each headed by a general manager. To make these business units more efficient, some have been aligned with a research laboratory because this allows new products to be introduced to the marketplace faster. Previously, the production cycle—from the inception of an idea to the marketing of a product—took up to four years. Since the restructuring, it frequently takes less than two years. Other major changes include the slashing of product prices with concomitant product quality improvement, the encouragement of risk taking to move products out faster, and the fostering of new-found entrepreneurial energy. Under the restructuring, Kodak has seen major improvements in the manufacturing process, a 20 percent reduction in waste, an increase of research and development expenditures to 7.5 percent of sales, a 15 percent increase in overall productivity, and development of joint ventures with Japanese companies.

Kodak believes that it needs to make maximum use of its people's skills. In the spring of 1987, the Copy Products Personnel Development Steering Committee recommended that the division implement a career development initiative. Subsequently, a career development program was begun with the goal of creating a vehicle for planning purposes. The program increases employees' job satisfaction and allows Copy Products to meet future human resource needs better because the company has a clear picture of employees' skills and talents. The program's emphasis is on each employee's responsibility for his or her own career development. Copy Products believes that the success of the individual and the organization depends on the effective placement and full development of the abilities of all employees. Therefore, its career development program's objectives are to

> encourage employees to think about their careers,
>
> provide a mechanism for an employee's realistic career self-assessment and goal setting,
>
> find a mechanism to maximize individual potential by providing goals,
>
> commit employees to take action toward developmental goals,
>
> provide a skills and interest inventory of all division employees,
>
> objectively match individual employees' skills to the needs of the division, and
>
> show that managers and supervisors care about employees' career development.

The division investigated various alternatives for meeting its program goal and objectives and, in May of 1987, selected an outside vendor who could supply a suitable career development program. Before the program was implemented, Copy Products prepared a description of every job in the division. These descriptions were gathered into a job summary catalogue to inform employees of division jobs and the skills required for each.

Beginning in the fall of 1987, the program was phased in through four steps. Supervisors were the first group to be trained. Exempt employees were next, with their training beginning in the spring of 1988. In September 1988, nonexempt technical and administrative personnel began the program, and finally in March 1989, the program was introduced to production personnel.

Supervisors were chosen to enter the program first because of their important role in the career development program. They

are expected to lead discussions with each of their employees
to help them set and achieve career development goals. A mandatory workshop was designed for supervisors, in which they
learn techniques for performing their roles of coaches, appraisers,
advisers, and referral agents. By February 1988, all 300 supervisors had completed the program.

The coach/adviser role of supervisors is not new at Kodak,
although the career development program has formalized it.
Supervisors have always been expected to discuss their employees' career plans with them, but before this program, employees
were not always prepared to discuss their skills and plans. Now,
after completing the career development workshop, employees
are better prepared for productive discussions.

A voluntary workshop was designed specifically for nonsupervisory employees. In it, they define their interests, skills,
and values; learn how to enhance their present jobs; and set
realistic goals. Employees must also meet with their supervisors
to discuss the employees' skills and developmental needs and
the resources necessary to meet them.

Employee reactions to the meetings with their supervisors
have generated such comments as "The session with my supervisor was very constructive" and "For the first time, I know where
I stand with my supervisor." Supervisors and employees are expected to talk together at least once a year, but more frequent
meetings are encouraged. Kodak's Copy Products Division has
experienced little resistance from the supervisors serving in this
capacity.

In the first six months of the program, 350 exempt employees, who represent 35 percent of the eligible population,
went through the program, and there were about 100 names
on the waiting list.

The career development workshops for supervisors are
delivered jointly by the vendor and Copy Products Personnel
Relations. The vendor is the specialist in the area of career
development, while the staff addresses the specifics of Eastman
Kodak. For the nonsupervisory employees' course, instructors
are chosen from the Copy Products Division employees who have
previous training experience.

Both supervisors and nonsupervisory employees have eight-hour career development programs. Nonsupervisory employees take the course in two four-hour segments, held two weeks apart. The first session is devoted to self-assessment, and the second concentrates on setting goals. The two-week gap allows time for employees to meet with their supervisors to discuss individual employees' skills and available opportunities. The supervisors' course meets for one eight-hour session, although Copy Products management believes that there is enough information in this session to warrant possible expansion of the workshop. This "extra time" would be used for more skill-building exercises.

The division plans to provide refresher courses. For supervisors, the refresher will consist of a videotape; for other employees, it will consist of a shortened version of their original course. The present career development workshop will continue to be offered as long as a demand for it exists.

At this time, the program is too new to be measured for long-term results, but positive responses from participants provide early indications of the program's impact. Their comments have included the following: "I feel better prepared to discuss my career," "I will use the course to enrich my current job," and "It shed new light on how I can change things." A preliminary six-month, follow-up evaluation has shown that most employees feel that they are better able to assess their skills, interests, and values and that most have scheduled career planning discussions with their supervisors. Three-fourths of the participants feel that their supervisors now have a better appreciation of their skills and interests. Thirty-eight percent of the participants have made changes in their current jobs to make better use of their skills and interests.

In addition to the workshop, other organizational structures support career development. A skills data base is maintained by Personnel Relations to assess skills available and needed in the division. Employees have access to the job summary catalogue, job-opening requisition information, a tuition aid plan, a training course catalogue, and two career resource centers. The centers are in Rochester, New York, each in a major manufacturing unit of Kodak. Each center contains more than 500 books and periodicals on careers and related topics. The centers also contain software programs that help employees with skills self-assessment that may take from four to six hours to complete (Richard H. Clute, telephone interviews, September 1988).

What Should Be Included in a Generic Workplace Employability Skills Curriculum?

Exhibit 17 provides guidelines for designing an employability skills curriculum.

Exhibit 17. Employability Skills Training: The First Step Toward Job Success.

What are the objectives of this training?
–To improve participants' lifetime skills for getting and keeping a job
–To teach techniques for daily living that will lead to lessened stress in the workplace
–To help participants understand the benefits and obligations of being employed
–To help participants learn to think ahead about what is required to meet employer rules and standards

When you complete this training, what will you be able to do?
–Use multiple sources of job information such as classified ads
–Identify a prospective employer's products and services
–Determine key contacts within a perspective employer's organization
–Identify the free services provided by the state employment agency in helping people find jobs and training
–Determine how private employment agencies operate to help people find jobs for a fee
–Identify the procedures involved in applying directly for jobs at a company personnel office
–Prepare for common types of employment tests
–Identify the purpose of job application forms
–Read and complete those parts of a job application asking for personal facts, job interests and job skills, references, and education and employment records
–Prepare letters of inquiry or application
–Compile a list of references
–Apply for a social security card, work permit, licenses
–Prepare a résumé summarizing experience, education, and job training

**Exhibit 17. Employability Skills Training:
The First Step Toward Job Success, Cont'd.**

-Identify the purpose of job interviews
-Identify the necessary steps in getting ready for a job interview
-Assess prior work experience, career goals and personal character, job references and personal aptitudes
-Discuss wages and salaries with prospective employer
-Define basic terms about wages and salary, identify standard paycheck deductions, and do simple computations related to salary
-Identify and describe common company benefits
-Identify the purpose of worker's compensation and describe the benefits it provides
-Identify the purpose of unemployment insurance and of disability insurance and describe the benefits they provide

For what work and career-planning skills will this training prepare you?
-Correlating the relationship between job and academic skills
-Demonstrating an accurate employment market knowledge of occupational requirements and trends
-Describing what various fields of work are like and what kinds of people are successful in them
-Evaluating the chances of getting a job now and in the future in the field of work that interests the individual
-Determining how many and what kind of workers will be needed (in the short term and long term) in the local area
-Identifying where and how to get specific local labor market information
-Determining the kind of preparation and training needed to get an entry-level job and subsequent promotions
-Identifying occupations and professions through appropriate information sources
-Evaluating occupational apprenticeships and other training opportunities
-Evaluating educational opportunities (college, vocational training, home study, lifelong learning programs)

What life skills will you be knowledgeable about when exiting this training?
-Using the telephone correctly
-Telling time correctly
-Knowing how to use the local public transportation system
-Practicing appropriate hygiene and dress
-Using money effectively
-Understanding the need for income tax returns and how to compute tax returns
-Knowing the major points to consider in renting an apartment
-Knowing what banking and financial services are available in the community
-Using sound buying principles for purchasing goods and services
-Understanding credit and using it judiciously
-Knowing what contracts are for and what their elements are

**Exhibit 17. Employability Skills Training:
The First Step Toward Job Success, Cont'd.**

-Buying and maintaining a car
-Appraising personal insurance needs
-Identifying and understanding appropriate child-care services

What does it mean to be reliable at work?
-Accrue an acceptable attendance record by being on the job regularly and
  promptly
-Record timely notice if late or absent
-Complete tasks on time
-Demonstrate responsibility and dependability by carrying out assigned tasks

What kind of attitude/behavior should you display at work?
-Arrive at work clean and dressed properly
-Solve personal business problems outside of work
-Arrange for adequate child care
-Demonstrate self-control
-Accept responsibility for one's own actions
-Use appropriate language
-Maintain a sense of congeniality

What work habits will serve you best in the workplace?
-Preparing, planning, and organizing job responsibilities
-Arranging materials, tools, workstation
-Demonstrating consistency in task completion
-Using appropriate job techniques
-Planning time effectively
-Planning reasonable work goals

What will your supervisor expect of you at work?
-To be attentive and cooperative
-To request clarification when needed
-To negotiate differences of opinion
-To accept guidance or correction and constructive criticism
-To recognize and respect another's authority
-To complete instructions and work under supervision

What should you expect of your employer?
-To assess employment conditions
-To evaluate work standards and schedules
-To state clearly personnel procedures
-To identify clearly emergency and safety procedures
-To define loyalty

Source: Adapted from National Alliance of Business, 1986a, pp. 791-794.

What Should Be Included in a Generic
Workplace Career Development Skills Curriculum?

Exhibit 18 provides guidance in designing a career development skills curriculum.

**Exhibit 18. Organizational Career
Development Training: Moving Up the Ladder.**

What are the objectives of this training?
–To empower participants to take charge of their own careers
–To explore the meaning and practice of career development
–To learn techniques for ongoing evaluation of a career
–To plan for employment future

How do you do an initial self-assessment?
–Who am I? What do I want to do?
  –Self-concept
  –Values clarification
  –Personality characteristics and personal style
  –Motivational patterns
  –Occupational interests
  –Personal preferences
–Where have I been?
  –Personal and educational background
  –Work history and experience
  –Key accomplishments and successes
  –Peak experiences
  –Significant life decisions
  –Satisfying and dissatisfying experiences

What is a future self-assessment?
–Where am I now? What can I do?
  –Analysis of current job: behavioral demands, importance of various job
    elements, likes and dislikes
  –Values skills and abilities: professional/technical, managerial, personal,
  –Special knowledge and capabilities: personal qualities, developmental
    needs, sources of satisfaction and dissatisfaction
–Where do I want to be?
  –Occupational daydreams, ideal job description
  –Desired future accomplishments
  –Preferred working environment
  –Ideal life-style
  –Career goals
  –Personal goals

**Exhibit 18. Organizational Career
Development Training: Moving Up the Ladder, Cont'd.**

How do you conduct an environmental assessment?
–What's out there?
  –Organization profile, business outlook
  –Opportunity structure, job requirements, selection standards
  –Available career paths or options
  –Developmental policies
  –Other resources and information

How do you develop a goal-directed action plan?
–What's the next step?
  –Reconciling self-assessment with environmental assessment
  –Identifying long-range alternatives
  –Specifying short-range goals
  –Setting priorities
  –Preparing an action plan
  –Developing a contingency plan

How do you implement your action plan?
–How do I get there?
  –Develop marketing techniques
  –Establish career action projects with time frame for completion

---

Source: Adapted from Gutteridge and Otte, with Williamson, 1983, pp. 37–39.

PART 7

Group Effectiveness Skills: Working with Others

People constantly interact with other people. At work, people associate with each other as superiors, co-workers, subordinates, professional colleagues, consultants, suppliers, prospective customers, and customers — and may act as friends, allies, or opponents. To perform work roles effectively without sacrificing our essential individuality or productive human relationships requires the application of good group effectiveness techniques such as interpersonal, teamwork, and negotiation skills.

CHAPTER 14

Interpersonal Skills

Remember that the entire population of the universe, with
one trifling exception, is composed of others.

> John Andrew Holmes
> *Barnes & Noble Book of Quotations*

What Are Interpersonal Skills?

Everyone has a need for affiliation and association. Life
is full of interdependent relationships that, to work successfully,
take coordination, patience, and communication. People who
are perceived as highly accomplished in getting along well with
other people in most situations are said to have good interpersonal skills. Interpersonal skills combine an ability to be proactive with a capacity for sustaining effective and productive
interaction between and among group members. A person who
demonstrates effective interpersonal behavior has acquired the
ability to sustain trust, openness, emotional support, and the
expression of strong feelings.

Interpersonal skills cannot be clearly separated from activities carried on in everyday life. They are reflected in such
factors as the following:

- How a person chooses to motivate others (in a caring or a
  punishing way)
- How secure a person is about appropriately disclosing his
  or her needs

289

- Whether or not a person feels free to express warmth and caring
- How positively a person can undertake to confront someone at the appropriate moment
- Whether or not a person chooses to convey openly an understanding of others

What Theories Support Current Training in Interpersonal Skills?

Many theories about how people interact impact significantly on the techniques currently used to conduct training in human relations. The theories discussed below represent several schools of thought that when applied successfully can lead to enhanced interaction between individuals and within and among work groups.

The Fundamental Interpersonal Relations Orientation-Behavior (FIRO-B) Scales Theory. The FIRO-B theory is a three-dimensional theory of interpersonal behavior (Schutz, 1958). Its three behavior types are inclusion, control, and affection (see Figure 14).

"The literature supporting reasonableness of postulating these three interpersonal needs and the FIRO-B instrument as a tool to measure individual characteristics of these needs is compelling" (Mink, Mink and Owen, 1987, p. 9). Inclusion, according to Schutz (1958, p. 22), deals with such things as attention, acknowledgment, recognition, prominence, identity, and participation. Control is communicated by behaviors expressing leadership, power, accomplishment, and intellectual superiority, among other things (p. 23). Positive affection is embodied in "situations of love, emotional closeness, personal confidences, and intimacy, while negative affection is characterized by hate, hostility, and emotional rejection" (p. 24). The scale used in the FIRO-B was specifically designed to measure interpersonal relationships in order to provide feedback for understanding group members' interaction.

The FIRO-B theory is commonly used in human relations training as an exercise to measure expressed or wanted

Figure 14. Questions Related to Entry into a Group.

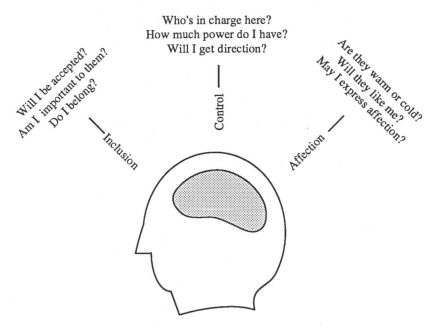

Source: R. S. Ross and R. M. Ross, *Relating and Interacting: An Introduction to Interpersonal Communication,* © 1982, p. 7. Reprinted by permission of Prentice-Hall, Inc., Englewood Cliffs, N.J.

inclusion, control, and affection. If the FIRO-B activity is presented correctly, an increase in openness will occur along with other positive behavioral changes that can enhance each member's contribution to a group and make the group as a whole a more effective vehicle for achieving its objective(s).

Gestalt Theory. Gestalt theory is frequently the basis for training techniques that have demonstrated great success in improving individual competence in human interaction skills. The Gestalt principle, simply stated, is that the whole is greater than the sum of its parts. The first person to apply this principle to social units or groups was psychologist Kurt Lewin, whose research findings suggested that a group does, indeed, take on a distinct personality that supersedes the personalities of its members.

Much of the activity that has grown up around the ideas of Gestalt was guided for many years by humanistic psychologist Fritz Perls. Perls was one of the key innovators of the human relations movement during the 1950s and 1960s.

Gestalt theory is especially relevant to interpersonal skills training because many people are not particularly aware of their internal events, and Gestalt-based techniques focus on increasing self-awareness. Once awareness is achieved, excitement and energy emerge; these, in turn, can lead to action resulting in contact. *Contact* is defined as "the coming together of me with something or someone that is not me; . . . an appreciation of the uniqueness and difference of the other" (Karp, 1976, p. 203). In Gestalt theory, this process is known as the *contact cycle* (see Figure 15) and is the key concept in Gestalt psychology (Pfeiffer and Pfeiffer, 1975).

Figure 15. Contact Cycle and Gestalt Psychology.

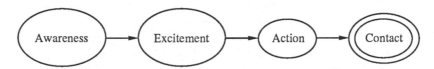

Source: Reprinted from J. William Pfeiffer and John E. Jones (eds.), *The 1975 Annual Handbook for Group Facilitators,* San Diego, Calif.: University Associates, Inc., 1975. Used with permission.

For example, suppose someone is walking down the street one morning and comes upon a bakery that radiates a wonderful smell of freshly baked goods. The person's mind creates a fantasy of delicious pastries, prompting a decisive move to make fantasy a reality by entering the bakery and making a purchase. Finally, settling on a nearby bench, the person proceeds to eat (make contact with) the purchased pastries.

While contact is normally seen as a good or desirable end, too much contact (satiation) dulls the senses and diminishes awareness, the critical first step in the contact cycle. To sustain the cycle's forward movement — to keep desire and interest alive — each person develops a rhythm of contact and withdrawal. In terms of food, for example, although it is desirable to convert fantasies into actual consumption (contact), there is also an obvious need to avoid overindulgence so that food can be digested properly and one's weight controlled. To do this, people set up food rhythm cycles (such as eating only two or three times daily) and indulge in fulfilling special food fantasies only occasionally. In the same fashion, they establish a rhythm of contact and withdrawal from other people, depending on how often and how intensely they want to make contact. At times, they do not want any interpersonal contact.

Another impediment to a fulfilled contact cycle is resistance. Resistance occurs between the excitement and awareness stages of the contact cycle. In the bakery example, although a person is stimulated by fantasies of how tasty the baked goods will be and takes action by starting to enter the store, resistance — the voice of experience and conscience — may say, "You weigh too much. Stop before you ruin your diet. Turn away." Thus, resistance may break the contact cycle despite awareness and excitement to action. Although resistance is frequently seen as bad, it often serves to stop us from making contact with undesirable events or people. Contact and contract are concepts that are also used to describe elements of teamwork and negotiation, as we shall see later in this chapter.

Another Gestalt theory concept that plays a major role in interpersonal training is called figure/ground. When something is a figure — an issue that is clearly and sharply focused — its very presence and clarity justify the need to deal with it. Once an issue (figure) is laid to rest, it can be moved to the background (ground), and another important issue can be addressed. However, until and unless a figure (issue) is dealt with, it is always present and influential.

For example, if two groups meet, lack of knowledge about the people in the other group may be the issue (figure) for one group. Not until someone in that group acknowledges anxiety does this issue (figure) begin to pass into the background. Fortunately, many issues (figures) can be released simply by acknowledging them.

At the individual level, an example of figure/ground relates to Dale Doe, a member of a work group in an interpersonal skills workshop. Dale's issue (figure) is anger that Dale denies rather than acknowledges. To get rid of that anger, Dale would need to admit to it (unblock it) and begin to understand its origins. To do so, Dale would need to answer such questions as "What am I doing? How am I doing it? What do I want? What do I need? What am I pretending? What do I feel angry about? With whom am I most angry?"

A concept unique to Gestalt theory is that of experiment. An *experiment* is the opposite of a structured approach in that a structured experience offers some expectation of what the outcome might be, whereas the experimental approach is totally free of expectations. The experimental approach is used within the framework of the contact cycle. A person or group is asked to take on an activity and to allow the action to lead it without any preconceptions about the outcome. This resembles a laboratory experiment in which a new combination of chemicals is mixed to see what will result.

Jungian Theory of Personality Types. A third theory found in many human interaction skills training programs is the Jungian theory of personality types. Swiss psychiatrist Carl Jung developed a theory that states that apparently random variations in human behavior are actually orderly and consistent and result from basic differences in the way people use their perceptions and judgment. According to Jung, each person uses all four of the processes (sensing and intuiting, thinking and feeling) identified by his typology, but each person's personality type is distinguished by a relative preference for each of the processes.

The Johari Window. The Johari Window (named after its creators, *Jo*seph Luft and *Har*ry *I*ngham) gives a slightly different theoretical perspective to viewing interpersonal skills. It relates to concepts of disclosure, feedback, and revelation (see Figure 16). The window's four quadrants or areas represent a whole person in relation to others.

Area I (free activity) represents behavior and motivation known to the self and known to others. It shows the extent to which a person is involved in give-and-take, working with others, and enjoying experiences with others. The larger this area, the

Figure 16. Johari Window.

	Known to Self	Not Known to Self
Known to Others	I. Area of Free Activity (Public Self)	II. Blind Area ("Bad-Breath" Area)
Not Known to Others	III. Avoided or Hidden Area (Private Self)	IV. Area of Unknown Activity

The following charts illustrate the effects of self-disclosure and feedback.

Under conditions of self-disclosure

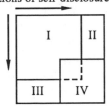

Under conditions of feedback

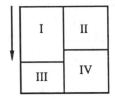

Under conditions of self-disclosure and feedback

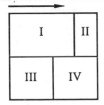

Source: J. Luft, *Group Processes: An Introduction to Group Dynamics,* by permission of Mayfield Publishing. Copyright © 1984, 1970, 1963 by Joseph Luft.

greater the person's contact with the real world and the more available the person's abilities are both to self and others. The more the free self coincides with the whole self, the more the true self is communicated with others and the less tension there is for a person. Complete coincidence is not possible, or necessarily desirable, for anyone. But (as illustrated in Figure 19) through self-disclosure and feedback, a person can expand the boundaries of the free area to encompass more situations and relationships.

Area II (blind area) represents behavior and motivation not known to oneself but apparent to others. For example, a person may have a mannerism in speech or gesture but be unaware of it even though it is quite obvious to others. Feedback is one way in which others can help a person to open up to the blind self by letting the person know what they see that he or she cannot. If offered in a supportive and responsible way, feedback can inform a person of the effect that certain behaviors have — of how actions, attitudes, and ideas are having a positive or negative effect on others, and how the person is conditioning his or her life.

Area III (private self) represents behavior and motivation known to the self but kept from others. In a group coming together for the first time, this quadrant is large because a person does not know much about new acquaintances. This area, which remains large if a person keeps thoughts and feelings inside, is the site of what is known as the *hidden agenda*. Disclosure is one way of sharing the private, hidden self with others. But the choice of disclosure belongs to the individuals; no one has the right to force a person to disclose the hidden self.

Area IV (unknown activity) represents behavior and motivation not known to oneself or to others. We know this area exists because a person and the other people with whom the person interacts sometimes discover new behavior or motives that were present all along. Revelation is the means by which the unknown self is unveiled. For example, a slip of the tongue may reveal something formerly unknown about a person. Revelation comes spontaneously; it cannot be planned.

Delivery Modes. Several delivery modes based on the theories described above lend themselves to training in interpersonal skills. The overriding theme is that working alone no one can make himself or herself skillful in interpersonal relations. The idea is to provide opportunities for two or more people to become aware of new ideas, to experiment to enlarge their repertoire of skills, and to improve their competency by using each other as sounding boards that reflect how each is doing in putting ideas into practice. One of the most successful ways to do this is by training in a functional context, exploring application of concepts in the context of real-world situations and materials through modeling, role playing, case studies, and other similar activities.

What Are the Essential Elements of Training in Interpersonal Skills?

A relatively new theory, the *relationship life cycle* (Portnoy, 1986), provides us with a paradigm for discussing how to achieve competence in the area of interpersonal skills. Robert A. Portnoy, administrator for human resources development at McDonnell Douglas Astronautics Company, developed this theory to explain how working relationships develop and adapt to the changing needs of groups (Portnoy, 1986, pp. 23–56). The relationship life cycle model (see Figure 17) illustrates how people develop working relationships and either learn to cope with differences or face disintegration of a relationship because of conflicts that could not be resolved.

When a group comes together for the express purpose of performing a task, achieving task completion may be more important than immediate concern with improving the group's interpersonal relations. "However, when a group has come together for the purpose of developing and improving interactive skills, human behavior must become the most important factor in performance and the consequent observation" (Rae, 1985, p. 30). By discussing and observing human behavior—within groups, between groups, and between individuals—in each stage of the relationship life cycle model, it is possible to identify and build incrementally the essential skills that can lead to competency in interpersonal skills.

Figure 17. Relationship Life Cycle Model.

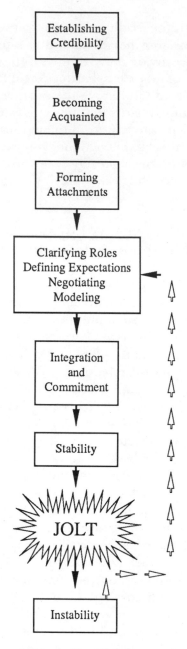

Source: Robert Portnoy, *Leadership: What Every Leader Should Know About People,* © 1986, p. 41. Reprinted by permission of Prentice-Hall, Inc., Englewood Cliffs, N.J.

On the job, establishing credibility, the first stage in forming a relationship, can be formal (such as an exchange of written personnel information) or informal (such as a recommendation or words of support from a colleague). Basically, a transaction takes place prior to any face-to-face meeting between principal parties, and credibility results when each party sees the other's credentials or claim as appropriate for the purpose of the potential relationship. Areas of training related to this stage are as follows:

- Cross-cultural awareness (differences among people from dissimilar backgrounds)
- Job skills knowledge (competent job performance)
- Written communication (accurate expression on paper)

The second stage, becoming acquainted, may be initiated formally through interviews and group meetings within a job setting or informally in a more relaxed, social environment. This interaction moves beyond the basic credentials of the first stage, going into additional qualifications that become important in the potential relationship. Each party evaluates the other on how well both's expectations and personal wants match. Areas of training related to this stage are as follows:

- Interview skills (asking and responding to questions)
- Active listening (responding nonjudgmentally to a speaker's content and feeling, thereby building rapport)
- Values clarification (discovering whatever is so important to a person that it is unlikely to be compromised)
- Interest identification (learning what each person likes)
- Learning styles (finding out how each person learns best: by seeing, hearing, talking, and so on)
- Nonverbal communication (observing and interpreting body language)

If there are going to be any attachments, they begin to develop at the third stage, forming attachments, and a certain amount of energy will be devoted to the prospect of forming the relationship. As trust begins to emerge, a shell of bonding and relationship forms. Areas of training related to this stage are as follows:

- Disclosure (opening up to another)
- Process observation (understanding and describing the action in the immediate environment)
- Feedback (giving and receiving responses)
- Oral communication skills (saying well what one really means)
- Self-insight skills (understanding the thoughts, feelings, motives, and so forth that are inside oneself)

The fourth stage—clarifying roles, defining expectations, negotiating, and modeling—is characterized by people's active participation in formulating the functions expected to be performed by each member in a relationship. Individual roles and functions are usually classified and agreed on through one of two channels: negotiation or modeling (an unconscious process based on patterns of behavior acquired from previous experience in relationships). The areas of training related to this stage are as follows:

- Negotiation skills (giving and taking to reach consensus)
- Role negotiating (positioning with regard to others)
- Modeling (setting an example and learning from others' examples)
- Mental flexibility (adapting to the needs of the moment)
- Goal setting (establishing objectives)

In Portnoy's words, "Once roles have been clarified and mutually understood, the individuals strengthen their attachment to one another, forming what becomes a sense of integration and commitment" (1986, p. 31). At this stage, they behave as members of a functioning unit with a sense of camaraderie and loyalty to the group and to the greater organization. Others perceive them as having established a relationship separate and apart from other relationships. The areas of training related to the integration and commitment stage are as follows:

- Group processing skills (how individuals react in groups)
- Group dynamics skills (what happens in a group: cohesiveness, conflict, communication rates, and so on)
- Coaching (consultation for reaffirmation or criticism of performance)

In the stability stage, each member of the relationship performs in a way that meets the other's expectations, and everything is running smoothly, with individual, group, and organizational objectives being met. Areas of training related to this stage are as follows:

- Teamwork training (working together)
- Group growth skills (enhancing group performance)
- Risk taking (performing creatively)
- Consensus building (gaining support for ideas and actions)

A jolt is a disturbance that interferes with the relationship's operations. A jolt occurs when one person's behavior is inconsistent with the expectations of another. When changes occur in a person's role performance, tension between that person and another may result, disrupting their relationship's stability. Misunderstandings will arise in even the most fully realized relationship. Jolts occur in every relationship and may simply reflect the fact that human beings are not static. Areas of training related to the jolt stage are as follows:

- Patience and flexibility (learning how to deal with discontinuity of expectations)
- Brainstorming and synectics (techniques for new ways of thinking to solve problems)
- Tolerance for ambiguity (ability to function in uncertainty)

During the stage of instability, a relationship is strained because individual and group needs are not being met. There is defensive behavior and avoidance (emotional withdrawal). Efficiency suffers when people have difficulty dealing with the problem or problems that create instability and engage in blam-

ing and hostile projections. Areas of training related to this stage
are as follows:

- Conflict management (techniques for reaching mutual agreement from opposing viewpoints)
- Repair strategies (learning how to "make up" after disagreement)
- Force field analysis (a problem-solving technique for analyzing and dealing with resistance to change)

Perhaps the most important skills to master in the general
area of human relations training (interpersonal, negotiation, and
teamwork skills) have to do with conflict management. In the
working world, success largely depends on the ability of individuals at all levels of the work force to get along with each
other. Situations in which people treat each other like objects
rather than thinking, feeling human beings inevitably lead to
retaliation of some sort. If people are made aware of the fact
that differences in human operating modes are a regular, normal part of human interaction, it becomes possible to create
training experiences that help them defuse potentially counterproductive situations. Portnoy's relationship life cycle provides
one skills training model for addressing the many aspects of interpersonal skills training.

What Constitutes Competency in Interpersonal Skills? What Constitutes Mastery?

A person who has developed credibility and competency in
interpersonal skills is a person who has the capacity and inclina-
tion to be proactive. A proactive person is aware of how changes
in his or her behavior act as a catalyst for change in the behavior
of others. In our culture, this awareness is often difficult to acquire.
Our general culture and, in particular, our formal schooling in-
cline us to act through the use of organizational tools in an attempt to bring about change in others rather than to sensitize
us to our ability to change situations through personal action.

The disposition to act through an external medium seems to be built into the way we are taught to think about social reality and, more concretely, built into the manner in which we learn to talk to each other. We tend to give credence to our perceptions of others and to feel justified in generalizing from these even though we know that perceptions are inevitably biased by our internal views. It is rare to find a person who is aware of his or her internal biases and can therefore control personal behavior in a way that produces effective change.

The ultimate interpersonal skill is the skill of personal action. This is a complex skill that requires an inventory of learnable behavioral skills such as self-disclosure, empathy, listening, feedback, and challenge (asking for feedback). Personal action is not attainable without this inventory of interpersonal skill behaviors; separately, however, these behaviors do not guarantee successful acquisition of the skill of personal action. The successful blending and stylizing of these skills is analogous to a pianist's acquiring virtuoso status. All skills required to play a Beethoven concerto can be identified and learned, but virtuosity only comes through a personalized, stylized integration of skills. The essence of the skill of personal action is embodied in what psychologists refer to as the *proactive personality*. The proactive person has the courage to face the consequences of individual decisions. Further, he or she assumes that we are all born with some degree of intentional forward thrust, just as we are all born with some degree of intelligence. As with intelligence, proaction can be modified by circumstances, individual effort, or social/environmental conditions.

What Is an Example of a Successful Workplace Training Program in Interpersonal Skills?

Duke Power Company, headquartered in Charlotte, North Carolina, is a large utility company that provides electricity to 1.5 million residential, commercial, and industrial customers in the central portion of North Carolina and the northwestern section of South Carolina. In 1987, 64 percent of the electricity generated by Duke Power came from nuclear sources, 34 percent from coal, and 2 percent from hydroelectric and other sources. In 1987, the company, which then employed 20,000 people, had revenues of $3.7 billion.

Duke Power offers many professional development courses to exempt and nonexempt (hourly wage) employees. Before 1988, few professional development courses were open to nonexempt employees, but in that year, all courses were opened to every employee. Managers who believed that their nonexempt employees needed training in the same skills as managers and other exempt employees requested the change. Now, although all employees receive the same training, employees attend courses with their peers; different levels of employees are not mixed unless the demand for a particular class is low.

The professional development courses were opened to all employees not only because of the managers' request but also because Duke Power saw the strategic need for all employees to gain a broader perspective of their jobs, to have a greater appreciation of their organizational roles, and to possess strong management skills. The company is flattening its organization, and with fewer managers, employees at lower levels need to have skills that traditionally were associated with management-level positions.

Duke Power pays for the professional development courses and course materials. Individual departments, however, are responsible for the costs of getting their employees to the training site and for their lodging and meals during training. All courses are conducted on company time.

Managers and supervisors are sent catalogues that list the training programs that they may nominate employees to attend. Employees may also ask to attend specific courses, but the employees must be nominated by their supervisors. In general, training programs are voluntary, although managers may require that employees attend. The training department prioritizes all of the requests for training and places employees in courses according to the slots that are open.

Interpersonal skills are taught in the Professional Development Core Curriculum, a series of three courses: Personal Development, Relationship Development, and Career Development. Each course lasts two days, for a total of six days of training spread out over a six-month period. Two hundred employees complete the series of courses each year. Nearly all employees who attend are professional employees below the supervisory level, usually those who may eventually become supervisors. The courses were designed and developed with the aid of an outside consulting firm. Two of the three courses are taught by a consultant and the other by Duke Power trainers. Duke Power expects to have its own trainers soon teaching all three courses.

Duke Power teaches little theory in its courses; rather, course content focuses on practical techniques. Interpersonal skills are the primary focus of the first two courses. Participants in them are introduced to the interpersonal skills necessary for personal and relationship development. Participants are given ample opportunity to divide into small groups to role play and practice new skills with guidance from trained facilitators.

The objectives of the personal development courses are for participants to determine their personal work styles and learn what work styles others may have, learn how behaviors are related to stress, learn the important elements of a supervisor-employee relationship, and determine their individual supervisors' work styles.

The goal is for the participants to understand themselves and what they bring to the work setting and to understand their supervisors. Participants also learn which work or job situations best match their behavioral life-styles.

To promote achievement of goals and objectives, participants carry out exercises related to two instruments. The first instrument is designed to interpret each participant's work style and to help participants understand the implications of one's work style and the work styles of others. A second instrument assesses the behavior style of a participant's supervisor. By comparing the two instruments' results, participants learn the value of complementary work styles.

This part of the course also addresses the way that participants may manage their relationships with their supervisors. To do so requires that an employee understand the supervisor and the work environment and also know his or her own strengths, limitations, needs, and tendencies toward dependency on authority figures. Participants also need to become aware of their own and their bosses' communication styles because it is important to know how people receive information — especially to know the degree of involvement in day-to-day functions that supervisors want and how to deal with disagreements with supervisors.

The second course of the core curriculum, Relationship Development, is designed to enable participants to handle workplace relationships. Participants begin this course by learning relationship management theory and the myths and realities of relationship management. Through lectures and group activities, participants then learn to handle difficult interpersonal situations. The first step in doing this is to diagnose interpersonal situations by identifying and analyzing them; the second is to create strategies for managing interpersonal situations; and the third is to anticipate and handle disruptive communication by using effective tactics.

This course also addresses the way to deal with special situations, such as those involving conflict, confrontation, and negotiation. Participants improve their interpersonal skills by learning how to avoid or heal damage, such as anger and mistrust, that may occur in interpersonal relations.

Clearly, Duke Power teaches interpersonal skills in a functional context: Participants learn interpersonal skills as they relate to their specific work environments and their relationships with supervisors (Phillip M. Plott, telephone interviews, April, July, and October 1988).

What Should Be Included in a Generic Workplace Interpersonal Skills Curriculum?

Exhibit 19 provides an outline for developing an interpersonal skills curriculum.

Exhibit 19. Basic Interpersonal Skills
Training Workshop: A Three-Phase Model.

What are the objectives of this training?
–To improve the skills necessary to interact constructively in a one-on-one
  and group situation
–To practice these skills until proficiency is achieved
–To help each participant understand his or her strengths and weaknesses in
  interpersonal skills
–To learn how to continue to grow and master these skills

How do you learn to build the skills of relationship, trust, and risk?
–The individual skill-training phase to establish and develop mutual relationships through the core skills of relationship building includes the following:
    –Self-preservation: determining what you need to function effectively
    –Self-disclosure: an examination of interpersonal style
    –Concreteness: the more concrete the statements, the more immediate the
      interaction with others becomes
    –The expression of feeling: discover the place of emotion in interpersonal
      dialogues
    –Responding
    –Accurate empathy: the ability to respond actively and with under-
      standing to those who disclose themselves
    –Respect: examining the quality of respect for others

What are the skills of challenge?
–New skills to enhance the ability to engage in the process of feedback and
  to challenge responsibly include the following:
    –Strength identification: recognize the strengths of others and let them
      know you appreciate them
    –Advanced accurate empathy: communicate to the other person not only
      what he or she says but what he or she is implying; make the connection
      between seemingly isolated statements
    –Confrontation: acknowledge what a person says versus what is actually
      done
    –Immediacy: examine what is happening in the here and now (process
      observation)

What are group-specific skills?
–Individual skills do not necessarily generalize to group situations, and it is
  sometimes necessary to learn how to use a variety of skills in a variety of
  combinations actively in a group.
    –Active response: when contacted by someone in the group, the par-
      ticipant contributes actively to the dialogue (active listening)
    –Taking the initiative: contacting others actively and not merely waiting
      to be contacted in order to establish and develop a relationship

**Exhibit 19. Basic Interpersonal Skills
Training Workshop: A Three-Phase Model, Cont'd.**

-Primary: level accurate empathy—spontaneous, accurate, empathic
understanding, unforced
-Self-disclosing: revealing the self without actively being requested to do
so
-Owning the interaction of others: acting as a catalyst in the conversation
of others in order to help them achieve their goal
-Using challenge skills: checking to see what is happening in each of the
relationships being developed ("Where do you and I stand now in our
relationship?")
-Calling for feedback: asking others for confrontation or any other interaction necessary to achieve goals

Why do you develop a core contract?
-Training structure is reduced to a minimum; pursuit of goals is achieved
through an open group experience by using newly acquired skills. The core
contract is used to provide structure to examine each interpersonal style,
observe self-behavior and receive feedback, acquire or strengthen basic interpersonal skills, and begin to alter interpersonal style to enhance lifestyle.

Why do you keep a log?
-To enter experiences, behaviors, and feelings that will help improve skills
outside of the group experience
-Hints for keeping a successful log include making entries concrete, keeping
track of what one needs to work on, keeping a page for each group
member, and deciding what one wants to accomplish in each following
group meeting.

Source: Adapted from Egan, 1976, pp. 27–33.

CHAPTER 15

Teamwork

Mori Motonari (1497–1571), a Japanese warlord, when he
was on his deathbed, assembled his three children. He gave
each child an arrow to break, which each child did. He then
asked that three other arrows be bound together, then each
child took a turn at trying to break the bound arrows, but
without success. Individually, the arrows offered no
resistance, but together they were formidable. That lesson
was not forgotten by the Mori heirs, and certainly not by the
rest of the country in the generations to come.

D. J. Lu
Inside Corporate Japan, 1987

What Is Teamwork?

"Teams are collections of people who must rely on group
collaboration if each member is to experience the optimum of
success and goal achievement" (Dyer, 1987, p. 4). Further,
"teamwork is managed, planned, systematic coordination of
effort by a group with a common goal in an optimally productive way" (Lefton, Buzzotta, and Sherberg, 1980, p. 388). Teamwork is managed because someone—officially or unofficially,
formally or informally—exercises control. Teamwork is planned
because it results from preparation and organization. It is systematic because its components, the team members, act as a
unit and share a common goal. Also, a team's shared purpose
and its coordinated efforts work to get the most output per unit

309

of input (Lefton, Buzzotta, and Sherberg, 1980, pp. 388–389). Underlying these descriptions of teamwork is a concept of co-operation in which individuals' interests are subordinated to group unity and efficiency.

In the workplace, teams are organized so that individuals' talents and skills can be directed through group effort to the accomplishment of vital tasks and goals. This pooling of human resources frequently requires people to display the flexibility and versatility that allow team members to "play off" or complement each other's skills.

Quality teamwork results when team members know how to recognize and work with a wide variety of unique personalities and when each team member has a sense of the cultures and approaches that other members represent. Successful teamwork only occurs when team members understand the dynamic interaction among members and how the dynamics evolve as a team moves toward its goal.

Each team member needs to be aware of the skills that other team members have and how those skills can be applied to help reach the group goal. To have this awareness, team members need to provide and receive feedback in a focused manner. When team members communicate, they need to appreciate the fact that people gather and process information in personalized ways. Good teamwork is grounded in recognition and use of the valuable differences among team members' strengths.

What Theories Support
Current Training in Teamwork?

The concept of teamwork has a historic tradition in the United States, but the idea of training to improve teamwork skills is relatively new. Because team members must exercise interpersonal and negotiation skills, teamwork training shares some of the same theoretical bases as those skills. Training to improve team performance, particularly of task-oriented groups, draws on experience with and research on the ways in which individuals behave in small groups in an organizational environment. Several major theories and research efforts are important in teamwork training.

The Hawthorne Studies. The breakthrough studies of how people work together came in the late 1920s and early 1930s with the Hawthorne studies. In this research, a group of Harvard University professors at the Hawthorne, Illinois, plant of Western Electric set out to test the hypothesis that work output was connected with work-area lighting. The results were not what researchers had anticipated. Instead, they found that productivity rose whether lighting was increased or decreased as long as workers still had enough light to see. Further analysis revealed that the most significant independent variable influencing productivity was a sense of *group identity,* a sense of "social support and cohesion that came with increased co-worker interaction" (Dyer, 1987, p. 8)—that is, with teamwork.

Since the Hawthorne studies, countless studies of group behavior and team effectiveness have encouraged the belief that it is reasonable and worthwhile to think of teamwork as a trainable skill.

Jungian Theory and the Myers-Briggs Type Indicator. Today most training programs that provide insight into enhancing individual teamwork skills are based on what works in practice, with relatively few programs based explicitly on theory. But one of the instruments most widely used in developing successful teamwork training programs, the Myers-Briggs Type Indicator (MBTI), has an explicit theoretical framework supporting its objectives. Isabel Briggs Myers, chief architect of the MBTI, intended to implement Carl Jung's theories through the use of the indicator. The MBTI is one of a growing number of psychological instruments concerned primarily with normal behaviors (McCaulley, 1981).

People's preferences in perception and judgment, as measured by the MBTI, come into play in the two major aspects of teamwork: communicating and problem solving. All of a team's problem-solving efforts can be reduced to the gathering of information and the translation of information into plans of action for the scientific pursuit of knowledge, seeking of solutions to technical problems, resolution of moral issues, or conduct of day-to-day business.

Myers's (1974) results suggest that good teamwork calls for

team members' recognition and use of certain valuable differences among them. These differences result from the four basic preferences about the use of perception (sensing and intuiting) and judgment (thinking and feeling).

Individuals exercise a preference for one of the two perceiving functions and one of the two judging functions. The less-preferred function from each pair is used less and is accordingly not as developed or trusted as the preferred function. A person can be associated with pairs of functions, then described as a person who either

> perceives primarily through sensing and judges primarily through thinking,
> perceives primarily through sensing and judges primarily through feeling,
> perceives primarily through intuition and judges primarily through thinking, or
> perceives primarily through intuition and judges primarily through feeling.

The MBTI also indicates whether a respondent has a preference for an attitude of extraversion (a focus on the world of people and things) or introversion (a focus on the world of ideas and concepts). Then the MBTI categorizes a person according to one of sixteen possible combinations of preferences (see Table 6).

The MBTI is a nonjudgmental instrument through which people report on themselves in order to learn about themselves and their preferences. It is extremely well researched and offers a logical and orderly model of human behavior.

Several benefits accrue to organizations that use the MBTI as a tool for improving teamwork skills (Hirsch, 1985). First and foremost, it identifies the strengths and weaknesses of people working together on projects and teams. This enables decision makers to parcel out assignments in a more productive way. By identifying individual preferences, the MBTI enables managers to put together working groups that have fewer interpersonal conflicts. It can also help people deal more effectively with other levels of intraorganizational conflict.

Table 6. Examples of Contributions Made by Each Preference to Each Type of the Myers-Briggs Type Indicator.

ISTJ		ISFJ		INFJ		INTJ	
I	Depth of concentration	I	Depth of concentration	I	Depth of concentration	I	Depth of concentration
S	Reliance on facts	S	Reliance on facts	N	Grasp of possibilities	N	Grasp of possibilities
T	Logic and analysis	F	Warmth and sympathy	F	Warmth and sympathy	T	Logic and analysis
J	Organization	J	Organization	J	Organization	J	Organization

ISTP		ISFP		INFP		INTP	
I	Depth of concentration	I	Depth of concentration	I	Depth of concentration	I	Depth of concentration
S	Reliance on facts	S	Reliance on facts	N	Grasp of possibilities	N	Grasp of possibilities
T	Logic and analysis	F	Warmth and sympathy	F	Warmth and sympathy	T	Logic and analysis
P	Adaptability	P	Adaptability	P	Adaptability	P	Adaptability

ESTP		ESFP		ENFP		ENTP	
E	Breadth of interests	E	Breadth of interests	E	Breadth of interests	E	Breadth of interests
S	Reliance on facts	S	Reliance on facts	N	Grasp of possibilities	N	Grasp of possibilities
T	Logic and analysis	F	Warmth and sympathy	F	Warmth and sympathy	T	Logic and analysis
P	Adaptability	P	Adaptability	P	Adaptability	P	Adaptability

ESTJ		ESFJ		ENFJ		ENTJ	
E	Breadth of interests	E	Breadth of interests	E	Breadth of interests	E	Breadth of interests
S	Reliance on facts	S	Reliance on facts	N	Grasp of possibilities	N	Grasp of possibilities
T	Logic and analysis	F	Warmth and sympathy	F	Warmth and sympathy	T	Logic and analysis
J	Organization	J	Organization	J	Organization	J	Organization

Source: M. H. McCaulley, *Jung's Theory of Psychological Types and the Myers-Briggs Type Indicator,* © 1981, Center for Applications of Psychological Type, Gainesville, Florida. Reprinted with permission.

Note: E = extroversion, I = introversion; S = sensing, N = intuition; T = thinking, F = feeling; J = judgment, P = perception.

Gestalt Theory. When the principles of Gestalt theory (discussed in Chapter Fourteen) are applied to an organizational environment, the objective is to achieve collaboration that produces the best results in terms of workers' satisfaction and productivity. These results occur when each person is clear and concise about what he or she wants for himself or herself and for the organization and each person can effect and maintain good contact with the other members of the organization (Karp, 1976).

The principle of negotiating for contact is an alternative to negotiating for contract (both of which are discussed more fully in Chapter Sixteen). Negotiating for contact is the essence of team relationship building because it is a collaborative effort based on the recognition that power resides in individuals and that each person has a right to maintain individuality while contributing to the team effort rather than an obligation to go "underground" in order to "play the game" (Karp, 1976).

Disclosure of Internal Frames of Reference Theory. The theory of disclosure of internal frames of reference is one of several more recent teamwork theories substantiated through empirical research (Culbert and McDonough, 1980). It asserts that people may improve their abilities to work together once they become more skilled at viewing each other "in the proper context." This theory's central premise is that each person finds a unique way of aligning self-interests with a job's requirements. Further, the theory states that work teams whose members understand and respect these alignments function more effectively. This approach seeks to help team members understand what another person wishes to accomplish through his or her behavior rather than projecting potentially inaccurate intentions onto the other person's actions (Mitchell, 1986).

Use of teamwork training as a tool for improving organizational productivity is likely to grow in the years ahead. When theories as yet unheard of are developed and applied, their success will depend on how carefully the essential skills needed to be an effective team player can be matched with the particular requirements of different organizations.

What Are the Essential Elements
of Training in Teamwork?

"Productive team members share information, exchange ideas, contribute new directions, and solve problems" (Miskin and Gmelch, 1985, p. 127). Effective team membership requires mastering many areas of expertise: task-oriented skills, generic problem-solving skills, group-processing skills, and interpersonal relations skills.

Every group or team passes through generic stages of development. Below is an overview of these stages and the problems inherent in each. It is to resolve these problems that organizations provide training in teamwork skills. Left unsettled, the problems can and do result in significant obstacles to effective team functioning and ultimately affect an organization's productive capacity.

The first stage of team development is building a new team. All teams face the challenge of turning diverse individuals into a functioning group with mechanisms and processes for goal setting, problem solving, decision making, task completion, communication, and support. The advantage of building a new team is that it offers an opportunity to set up processes properly from the outset. Doing so requires an initial team-building effort that concentrates on the following process issues (Dyer, 1987):

- Consensus (agreement by all members) on the level of priority of organizational needs to be addressed by the team
- Consensus on shared expectations of the team members
- Clarification of the goals that the team wishes to accomplish
- Agreement on work guidelines

The second stage of team development is resolving conflict within an existing team. Sometimes team members have difficulty arriving at a common understanding of the foregoing issue. This may happen when new members with a different understanding are added to an existing team (for example, following the acquisition of another firm whose members must be assimilated) or when an ongoing team generates unresolved internal conflict.

Whenever and for whatever reason conflict arises, it must be resolved before a team can function effectively. The first step in resolving conflict must be a commitment by all team members to ending it. With this fundamental agreement, members can then negotiate over specific areas of dispute. If a conflict is severe, the use of an outside mediator may be necessary.

The third stage of development is consolidating the team. After a team has worked on interpersonal relationships by resolving any major conflicts, it begins to build the trust and confidence to examine its operating methods. This usually results in the adoption of clearer, more systematic approaches that lead to clearer, more methodical ways of working. The improved relationships of the preceding stage are the basis for establishing the team's ground rules and working procedures.

Yet another stage of development may involve revitalizing the complacent team. Sometimes an effective team slips into an attitude of complacency until a challenge jolts the group into reaction. Typically, the challenge requires more creative thinking and innovative problem solving than the team is used to generating.

Figure 18 illustrates the kind of questions that need to be asked at each stage of group development to ensure that the team-building process remains on track.

The quality of teamwork is governed by the extent to which members are able to achieve operational competency in five structural areas:

1. Accommodating the individual personalities of team members
2. Understanding individual members' communication patterns
3. Accommodating each member's cultural differences
4. Understanding the dynamics of the team as it progresses through the growth cycle
5. Being aware of and using each member's job-specific skills and abilities

Teams are most frequently organized around this last area while the influence that the first four areas have on a team's

Figure 18. Diagnosing the Stages of Group Development.

Forming ⟶ *Storming* ⟶ *Norming* ⟶ *Performing*

	Will I Be Accepted?	Will I Be Respected?	How Can I Help the Group?	How Can We Do Better?

Personal	• Who's here?
	• What role can I play?
	  – Gatekeeper
	  – Harmonizer
	  – Organizer
	  – Leader
	  – Fact finder
	• Feel uncertain, tentative
		• What ideas, experiences, expertise can I contribute?
		• Do I agree or disagree?
		• What's in it for me?
		• The credentials game
		• What do I like? dislike? accept?
			• Here's how I do it on my job
			• Feel comfort, or discomfort, about role I'm playing
			• Want to help
			
			"I"
				• Free to share ideas, opinions, feelings
				• Unselfish enthusiasm for group members, the task
				• Feel need for closure
				
				"We"

	Politeness	Bid for Power	Cooperation	Enthusiasm
Interpersonal	• Small talk • Generalities • Limited disclosure • Relationships begin to form	• Who will lead? • With whom can I align myself? • Compete with others based on personal agendas • Fight or flight • Quiet apprehensions	• Self disclosure • Here's how I do it • Recognizing other ideas • Listening more carefully • Commitment to emerging leadership	• Praise and criticism • Straight talk • Having fun too • Paraphrasing, perception checking occur more naturally
	Orientation	Organizing	Data Flow	Creative Problem Solving
Group	• Why are we here? • What's our assigned task? • Identify strengths of the group	• What's the real problem? • Resistance to others' ideas • What's our mission, goals, strategy? • How will we proceed?	• Open exchange of ideas and information • Problem definition • More trust • Urgency to identify, evaluate solutions	• Decision making • Intensity about task completion • Relationship and results oriented • Shared responsibility for group process
	Why	How	What	Criteria

Source: 3M and Doug Peters and Associates, © 1988, p. 10. Reprinted with permission.

success or failure at task achievement is ignored. Regardless of each team member's level of expertise, it is how each succeeds in team member interactions (the first four factors) that will define and control the team's working relationship.

Perhaps the most important of the first four areas is understanding the communication patterns that individuals use to format their conversations in groups. Because the ways in which people communicate strongly influence a team's potential for success, effective communication should be considered the foundation on which other teamwork skills such as leadership, problem solving, conflict resolution, group processing, interpersonal relations, and task-oriented productivity skills are constructed.

One approach to effective teamwork — team relationship building (White and McKeen, 1987) — relates to all five structural areas, but particularly to communication patterns. This approach is essentially a matter of reaching agreements with others about how each member wants them to behave toward him or her in the work setting. It involves identifying what one person wants another to start doing, do more of, do less of, stop, or continue doing. These requests are made for the purpose of increasing the requester's individual effectiveness. To be successful in this effort, a person needs to develop an understanding of process observation, giving and receiving feedback, active listening, depth interviewing, and negotiating for contact.

Process observation is the ability to record what is going on at the surface of the group interaction. This task involves being able to describe objectively the actions of an individual or a group as they occurred during a given period of observation. This is a difficult skill to master, but it is of generic importance to team effectiveness.

Giving and receiving feedback involve skill in "the process of exchange through which people communicate their intentions and make their intentions and behavior congruent" (Mink, Mink, and Owen, 1987, p. 163). Two types of feedback are essential to effective teamwork: performance feedback (on individual productivity) and interpersonal feedback (on how a person's actions are affecting other team members).

Active listening is a skill technique for helping people solve their own problems. The active listener focuses on and is involved with a speaker's need to communicate. The listener takes active responsibility for understanding both the content and the feelings being expressed by the speaker's words, tone, and actions.

Depth interviewing involves a facilitator's open-ended, individual interviews with all team members. After the interviewing and a third-party analysis, each team member is given the collective information derived from other team members. Each person is then allowed time and opportunity to respond regarding his or her specific behaviors as they relate to group functioning and task accomplishment and to receive additional feedback from other members.

Negotiation for contact is authentic communication about what a person wants. As noted earlier, this skill is the essence of team relationships because negotiating through contact is meant to satisfy the underlying wants of the parties involved.

The advantage a person gains from understanding and being able to use this particular set of skills is the ability to maintain effective work relations with colleagues. To talk usefully about how we are working together, we must be able to *see* in concrete terms what is going on, *describe* it in a way that others will receive nondefensively, *disclose* and *listen* effectively to the feelings that people in the work relationship have, *test* others' perceptions about the situation, and *negotiate* new, more productive work relationships. Each of these factors of team relationship building is designed to enhance the ability of teams and individuals to work at avoiding negative processes that inhibit good teamwork.

A slightly different methodology for enhancing practical group process skills (Harvill, West, Jacobs, and Masson, 1985) is aimed specifically at maintaining productive communication between and among group participants through the use of the following communication tools.

- *Cutting off* is used to stop group members who ramble or become boring and to help members learn to be more concise.

- *Drawing out* is used to encourage reluctant participants to be more vocal.
- *Holding the focus* is used to maintain attention on a specific topic or person.
- *Shifting the focus* is applied when group energy is dragging or when emotional issues have been discussed and concluded, or it is used to bring a rambling conversation to an end and to move on to something else.

Among the important skills that team members need to learn is leadership, an essential element of effective group functioning. According to Case Western Reserve University's David Kolb and his colleagues, in this society we often fail to differentiate between leaders as people and leadership as a function. Kolb develops the idea that there is no reason that only one team member should be given or take on the responsibility for worrying about how a group is progressing. Leadership, Kolb believes, is best thought of as a group function in which most members will contribute to the achievement of goals and to the maintenance and growth of the group. From a practical standpoint, delegating the role of leader to only one person is a highly inefficient use of resources. Team participants can learn to be both effective managers and participants. If an issue is raised that a team member disagrees with, he or she should take the initiative in raising the disagreement for the whole group to examine. "In a well-functioning group . . . an observer looking in from the outside might not be able to pick out the formal leadership. The 'leadership function' could pass around according to the group's need at a particular point" (Kolb, Rubin, and McIntyre, 1984, p. 143).

Building an effective team requires that individual members identify and work through their differences rather than ignore and suppress them or allow them to turn into conflict. Members must understand and accept the changing nature of their roles on the team task functions, group building and maintenance functions, and individual functions (see Exhibit 20 for explanatory definitions) and understand how they fit into the overall organizational framework.

Exhibit 20. Definitions of Group Member Roles.

Task Functions

1. Defines problems — group problem is defined: overall purpose of group is outlined.
2. Seeks information — requests factual information about group problem or methods of procedure, or for clarification of suggestions.
3. Gives information — offers facts or general information about group problem, methods to be used, or clarifies a suggestion.
4. Seeks opinions — asks for the opinions of others relevant to discussion.
5. Gives opinions — states beliefs or opinions relevant to discussion.
6. Tests feasibility — questions reality, checks practicality of suggested solutions.

Group-Building and Maintenance Functions

7. Coordinating — a recent statement is clarified and related to another statement in such a way as to bring them together. Proposed alternatives are reviewed.
8. Mediating-harmonizing — interceding in disputes or disagreements and attempting to reconcile them. Highlights similarities in views.
9. Orienting-facilitating — keeps group on the track, points out deviations from agreed-upon procedures or from direction of group discussion. Helping group process along, proposing other procedures to make group more effective.
10. Supporting-encouraging — expressing approval of another's suggestion, praising others' ideas, being warm and responsive to ideas of others.
11. Following — going along with the movement of the group, accepting ideas of others, expressing agreement.

Individual Functions

12. Blocking — interfering with the progress of the group by arguing, resisting, and disagreeing beyond reason. Or, by coming back to same "dead" issue later.
13. Out of field — withdrawing from discussion, daydreaming, doing something else, whispering to others, leaving room, etc.
14. Digressing — getting off the subject, leading discussion in some "personally oriented direction," or making a brief statement into a long nebulous speech.

Source: Dimock, H. G. *Groups: Leadership and Group Development,* © 1987, p. 95. University Associates, San Diego, California. Reprinted with permission.

Conflict resolution strategies fall into three categories (see Figure 19): avoidance, in which a person tends to hold feelings back or tries to ignore them or to leave the conflict; delay, in which a person waits for the situation to "cool off" or keeps the issues so unclear that attempts at confrontation are not possible; or confrontation, in which a person may use power strategies (such as physical force, bribery, threats, punishment) or may use negotiation that can lead to compromise for a "win-win" solution.

Figure 19. Conflict Situation Categories.

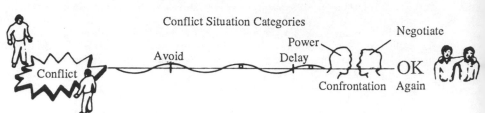

Source: Texas Instruments, "Team Maintenance," in *Team Leader Manual: Effectiveness Teams Programs,* © 1984. Reprinted with permission.

Problem-solving skills are also needed for good teamwork. Because information gathering and processing are critical to the functioning of a team effort, team members need to recognize that each person gathers and processes information differently, perceiving situations in a very personalized way. These individual differences often create barriers to a group's ability to solve problems. When left unidentified, the differences can become the basis for hostile projections and antagonistic interactions among group members. Yet these same individual differences have potential utility for helping a group develop creative solutions to problems. So beyond being able to recognize individual differences, each team member must understand that each person's approach has inherent strengths and weaknesses. This general understanding, together with specific understanding (gained through the Myers-Briggs Type Indicator) of how each team member approaches problem solving, provides each member with information and strategies for enhancing personal and team performance.

Looking at the various skills essential to good teamwork reveals that they are primarily dependent on each person's ability to observe accurately what is happening on and below the surface. Work relationships most often go bad when people who act together on a job lack perceptual observation skills. For example, a person may see others in terms of evaluative categories (authoritarian, lazy, and so on) and then give feedback couched in these broad, frequently negative terms. This, in turn, creates feelings in the recipient that are difficult to resolve. The result is that the work relationship worsens and affects the team's ability to reach its stated goals. In an attempt to avoid this outcome, the unspoken rule guiding some teams is "It is best not to talk about these things." The negative undercurrent created by this tacit agreement dissipates the positive energy that a team needs if it is to engage in productive problem solving.

In summary, research on how people operate effectively in a team environment indicates that individual group members need to develop a consciousness about and competency in a set of behavioral skills and a set of conceptual skills.

The behavioral skills include

> process observation,
> active listening,
> giving and receiving feedback,
> negotiating for contact,
> self-assessment,
> ability to intervene in the group process,
> goal setting,
> action planning,
> communicating, and
> modeling (setting or providing an example).

The conceptual skills include understanding the

> group development process,
> adult development process,
> creative problem-solving process,
> organization's operational culture,
> value of personality differences, and
> constraints of communication patterns.

For the most part, translating any one of these skills into learnable behaviors and attitudes is difficult. Probably the most highly regarded diagnostic tool trainers use for enhancing people's individual abilities in these skill areas is the Myers-Briggs Type Indicator.

What Constitutes Competency in Teamwork? What Constitutes Mastery?

Effective team members are good problem solvers, negotiators, planners, communicators, and motivators who are able to create and maintain an open, trusting environment while participating in group work. A skilled team player understands the principles of group processing and has the ability to intervene when group behavior interferes with the achievement of group goals. Effective team members can perform well in the position of leader since "sharing leadership functions is the typical mode of operation in high-performing groups. It encourages much greater involvement of the individual team members and is much more rewarding for them" (Ends and Page, 1977, p. 66). Those who have achieved mastery in teamwork skills are capable of performing the following functions in a group setting when the need arises or the opportunity is appropriate.

- *Establishing, communicating, and clarifying goals:* Goals must be clear and precise in each team member's mind. When this is not the case, it is extremely difficult to develop plans to accomplish the group task, and commitment among team members will be weak.
- *Securing commitment to goals:* Each team member must be able to see that the goals are worth the effort; otherwise, the best that can be hoped for is uninspired, mediocre team performance.
- *Defining and negotiating roles:* Each team member must be able to take on the roles that are required for task accomplishment, and team members need to identify and agree about the relationships among those roles before tackling group tasks. Advance agreement on ground rules for interaction is needed too. Negotiation is often required to obtain the necessary agreements.

- *Securing commitment to roles assigned:* Commitment is stronger when each team member has some say in establishing roles and some opportunities to negotiate the specifics of his or her own roles.
- *Planning activity:* Each member must have a clear idea of all parts of the action plan, especially of how his or her roles and activities fit into the overall plan.
- *Setting performance standards:* Each team member must be able to communicate performance standards clearly to increase the probability of positive performance and morale. Whoever takes on a leadership role must communicate to other team members how well they are expected to perform as individuals and as team members.
- *Providing feedback to individuals and to the group:* Each team member should be able to provide feedback that is formative (promotes needed changes in behavior), summative (assesses quality and character of completed task), and appreciative (recognizes satisfactory or exemplary work done by individuals).
- *Providing coaching:* An effective team member must be able to reinforce the standards that help other team members increase and improve their skills. He or she must be able to clarify the importance of each team member's contribution and to facilitate colleagues' individual development.
- *Providing motivation:* Mastery of teamwork skills involves motivating others by example, that is, by demonstrations of enthusiasm, initiative, openness, and trust.

What Is an Example of a Successful Workplace Training Program in Teamwork?

Texas Instruments (TI) manufactures semiconductor products, computers, defense electronics systems, industrial automation and control systems, metallurgical materials, and consumer electronic products. The company has approximately fifty manufacturing plants in fifteen countries, and had sales of $5.6 billion in 1987. TI employs 75,000 people worldwide.

TI's progressive management has been developing new means for employee involvement in production and decision-making processes for nearly forty years. Currently, it has a corporate initiative, People and Asset Effectiveness (P&AE), to promote employee involvement. P&AE consists of various team activities organized into a structure that includes a formal training program.

In the 1960s, the idea of teamwork was somewhat formalized at TI when a psychologist in the personnel department (there was no training department at that time) began experimenting with ways to encourage employees to think beyond their own jobs. The goal was to encourage each person to take more responsibility for the work he or she was doing and to work cooperatively with his or her natural work group to solve problems and discuss productivity issues. No formal training was done; rather, an institutional approach was taken, with the concepts of teamwork and cooperation integrated into the corporate culture at all levels.

In the early 1980s, the corporate manager for education, training, and development decided TI should provide formal training in teamwork. Based on the P&AE initiative, a formal training program, called Effectiveness Teams (ET), was launched. The training program's aim is to provide employees with the necessary tools and skills for performance as effective team members. The program was developed and implemented on an experimental basis for a year or two but is now a permanent, integral part of TI's institutional structure. The goals of the ET program are to improve the quality of TI products, increase TI's profits, and make working at TI enjoyable.

Training at TI is completely decentralized. Although the central training department developed the ET program and makes it available to operating units that want to conduct the program and implement the team concept, units are not required to implement the program. Funding for the program's initial development came from the corporate budget, but today each employee's cost center pays for his or her participation in the course. Most units have elected to provide this program to their employees, although training varies widely by operating unit because each has a training department with the autonomy to conduct training when and how it wishes.

The employees targeted for training also vary by operating unit. Units that have been conducting the program for a while only need to train new hires. Other units are just starting the program and need to train all their employees. In that case, employees may be trained with their natural work groups (vertical grouping) or they may be trained with their peers (horizontal grouping). Usually, managers and supervisors are trained together and participate in a train-the-trainer program. The frequency with which ET training is offered is driven by demand.

Definite changes in management style have been attributed to the teamwork training, but changes in individual performance have been more difficult to measure, although TI believes that significant, positive changes have occurred.

The Effectiveness Teams' concepts are taught in a functional context; each work unit customizes the training to address the specific needs of the employees being trained and ensures that the training is relevant to the unit's activities. Because its training programs are customized and closely tied to the corporate culture, TI infrequently uses outside training providers.

Usually, units begin ET training with a train-the-trainer session for team leaders who later conduct ET training for the employees in their work groups. Whether for team leaders or team members, the ET program is normally a five-day course, although a shortened three-day format is available. Team leaders may participate in their course for five consecutive days, but taking an entire work team off the line for five days would be very disruptive, so nonsupervisory employees are likely to participate once or twice a week.

The team leaders' course is more organized and standardized than the course for nonsupervisory employees. Participants in this course receive a notebook containing information on the important teamwork skills. One chapter is devoted to detailing the skills necessary to be an effective group leader. The logistics of ET implementation, such as keeping schedules and maintaining records, are also discussed. Another chapter outlines individual communication skills that facilitate teamwork. A chapter on team building looks at individual team members' necessary roles and tasks. Also provided are tools and methods (such as dealing with anger, brainstorming, and avoiding groupthink) that are useful to team interaction and functioning. Most of the rest of the notebook discusses seven steps to problem solving, a process TI deems central to teamwork.

The corporate training department has developed a course-book that team leaders may use when teaching their employees, but few units use the book in its entirety. Most team leaders develop their own courses, using the corporate material as a guideline for developing material tailored to their own particular functional areas and employees.

The teamwork course involves little lecture. Instead, group interaction through discussions and exercises is used extensively. Approximately 60 to 70 percent of ET training is interactive, while only 30 to 40 percent is instructor led.

Evaluation of the Effectiveness Teams training takes place informally. Supervisors advise the training department of what is working and what is not, but there is no long-term follow-up of the program's effect on employees (Ralph Dosher, telephone interview, May 1988).

What Should Be Included in a Generic Workplace Teamwork Curriculum?

Exhibit 21 provides guidance in developing a teamwork curriculum.

Exhibit 21. Building Team Effectiveness Skills.

What are the objectives of this training?
–To present participants with an overview of the importance of effective teamwork
–To enhance teamwork in order to resolve specific organizational problems
–To explore the need for improvement in teamwork
–To explore ways in which participants can strengthen their teamwork skills

What is teamwork?
–Explain basic teamwork theory
–Consider issues of management style, support, trust, cooperation, and conflict
–Assess individual teamwork styles (MBTI)
–Explore the characteristics of personal effectiveness ("intimacy exercise" – openness and confrontation)

Exhibit 21. Building Team Effectiveness Skills, Cont'd.

What are the issues around team leadership?
–Discuss concepts of participative leadership
–Complete and analyze team leadership style questionnaire
–Discuss the impact of leader's actions on activity of the team

How do you prepare an action plan for teamwork improvement?
–Prepare action plans for individual development and group development
 by splitting participants into small groups
–Present plans to all participants
–Comment on plans and review events

What are the skills particularly relevant to becoming an effective team member?
–Communication skills
　–Oral communication (distribute a self-assessment instrument that
　 measures each member's style of communication)
　–Listening: key ideas
　–Active listening techniques
–Feedback skills
　–Concept of feedback
　–Guidelines for giving feedback
　–Guidelines for receiving feedback
–Problem-solving skills
　–Defining the critical issues
　–Selecting the problem for resolution
　–Exploring the causes
　–Analyzing the data
　–Examining the results
　–Selecting the solution
　–Developing an action plan
–Conflict resolution skills
　–Dealing with feelings
　–Determining the cause of the conflict
　–Choosing a strategy to resolve the conflict (active listening, assertion,
　 confrontation, creative problem solving)
–Team task skills
　–Setting goals and objectives
　–Setting standards
　–Getting and giving information
　–Processing information
　–Planning for action
–Team maintenance skills
　–Keeping communication lines open
　–Managing conflict
　–Evaluating team process
　–Providing for the team's physical needs

CHAPTER 16

Negotiation

Let us never negotiate out of fear, but let us never fear to
negotiate.

John F. Kennedy
Inaugural Address, 1961

What Is Negotiation?

Negotiation is one among several possibilities for settling disagreements. If the conflict management and resolution
process is viewed as a continuum, one end of the scale is an
attempt to avoid potential conflict altogether. When the disagreeing parties are not able to eliminate potential conflict, the situation usually gains intensity and complexity, leading to the other
end of the continuum — conflict.

There are many interim stops along the way between the
extremes of conflict avoidance and outright conflict (private decision making, informal discussions, negotiation, nonviolent mediation). Failure to resolve a disagreement at any one of these
points may trigger violence (see Figure 20). As disagreements
outgrow the reasonable discussion phase and depending on the
situation, negotiation may prove to be the least intrusive of the
resolution possibilities.

One definition of negotiation useful for this discussion talks
about it as "a bargaining relationship between parties who have
a perceived or actual conflict of interest. The participants volun-
tarily join in a temporary relationship designed to educate

Figure 20. Continuum of Conflict Management and Resolution Approaches.

Conflict avoidance	Informal discussion and problem solving	Negotiation	Mediation	Administrative decision	Arbitration	Judicial decision	Legislative decision	Nonviolent direct action	Violence

Private decision making by parties

Private third-party decision making

Legal (public), authoritative third-party decision making

Extralegal coerced decision making

Increased coercion and likelihood of win-lose outcome

Source: Moore, 1986, p. 5.

each other about their needs and interests, to exchange specific resources, or to resolve one or more tangible issues such as the form their relationship will take in the future or the procedures by which problems are to be solved" (Moore, 1986, p. 6).

The success of a private decision-making negotiation effort will depend on how skilled participants are at using one or more of four basic negotiating styles: forcing, compromising, accommodating, and collaborating (see Table 7). Each of these approaches has its place and can produce resolution, amicable or otherwise, if used appropriately.

What Theories Support Current Training in Negotiation?

Although much thought has gone into definitions of negotiation and despite voluminous literature on the negotiation process, theoretical models based on good empirical evidence are not plentiful. Nonetheless, several theories of negotiation have demonstrated some success in practice.

Need Theory of Negotiation. A useful and practical theory for resolving conflict called the Need Theory of Negotiation was developed in 1968 by Gerard I. Nierenberg, author, lawyer, and founder of the Negotiation Institute. Nierenberg's theory was modeled after humanistic psychologist Abraham Maslow's hierarchy of needs (see Chapter Eleven, Figure 9). Nierenberg's theory expresses the belief that participants in a negotiation are motivated by certain paramount needs and that discovering how to satisfy those needs provides the foundation for true resolution of conflict. The theory is premised on the idea that if people learn to understand each other's needs, they will understand what motivates the opposition in a conflict and what strategies to adopt to reach consensus.

Nierenberg translates his theory into practical application through diagrams and extensive discussion of his three-dimensional need theory model (see Figure 21). This model includes six varieties of application, seven basic needs, and three levels of approach. The result is 126 individual cubes, each of which represents a different negotiating gambit. The strength

Table 7. Basic Negotiating Styles.

Style	Advantages	Disadvantages
Forcing	normally uses less time leads to total victory if you have more power than other side	can lead to stalemate if the other side uses the same approach other side can become resentful and vengeful
Compromising	natural style for most people appears to be fair because both sides win and lose	can lead to extreme initial positions since both sides anticipate "splitting the difference" may result in agreements that truly satisfy neither side
Accommodating	when the other side is right, you should give in when the relationship with the other side is more important than negotiating issues creates potential IOUs for future negotiations	may result in a major loss to your side on important issues can lead to a habit of giving in on all issues that can result in a significant loss of power and reputation
Collaborating	both sides can "win big" personal relationships can be improved rather than harmed	can be extremely time consuming negotiators with a forcing style may interpret this approach as weakness

Source: Byrnes, Joseph F., Ph.D., "Creative Confrontations: The Art of Negotiating," *Trainer's Workshop,* New York: American Management Association, August 1987. Reprinted by permission.

and ease of application of each gambit can be determined by its relative position within the model; the greater the number of alternatives for handling a negotiation, the greater is the chance of success. The need theory model establishes a probable order of importance in negotiation maneuvers. The more basic the need gambit, the more probable is the chance of a successful outcome (Nierenberg, 1973).

Figure 21. Structure and Order of
Gambits in the Need Theory of Negotiation.

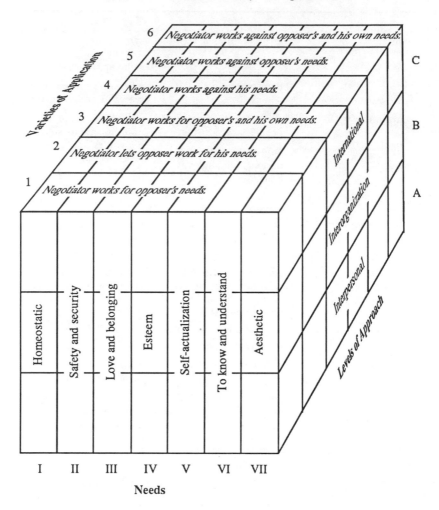

Source: G. I. Nierenberg, *The Complete Negotiator,* p. 101, © 1986, New
York: Nierenberg, Zief. Reprinted by permission.

Each of the theories described below contains elements
similar to Nierenberg's need theory.

Contract Versus Contact Theory. As with other group effectiveness skills, the part of Gestalt theory that deals with con-

tact provides a viable alternative to contracting when settling disputes or disagreements through a negotiation process. Americans tend to view negotiation as involving a compromise, a trade-off, or more commonly, a contract. Our idea of a good compromise is one in which each party believes he or she has won because each has received a desired outcome, whether tangible or intangible. An example frequently used to illustrate this point describes two girls squabbling over leftover pie, each arguing that she should have a larger slice. Neither can agree how to ensure an even split. Enter mother, the mediator, who suggests that one girl cut the pie any way she likes, and the other girl have first choice of the piece she wants. The girls think that this appears to be a fair contract, and they accept it, each feeling she has gotten an equitable deal.

Superficially, this example of contracting appears in a positive context of toleration and respect, but in actuality, it assumes mutual mistrust and conceals implications of separation and distance that lead to continuing problems. Analysis of this example and other similar negotiations reveals that the result focuses on the "thing" that gets traded rather than on the more important relationship that develops between parties during the negotiation process.

There are several long-term difficulties with this type of negotiation. First, it creates a false sense that everything has been settled when, in fact, that is almost never true. Therefore, when further disagreements occur, as they undoubtedly will, frustration and disappointment are apt to ensue. Second, it overstresses reliance on clear meanings of words. Words are not very clear conveyors of meaning but inevitably give rise to varying definitions and interpretations. Yet words serve as motivators for action, so negotiated agreements often give rise to more diverse behavior patterns rather than making behavior more uniform. Third, this type of negotiation is expensive, and maintenance of the contracts that result from it are costly to service over time.

Although these difficulties place contractual negotiations in a poor light, given the present social order, negotiated contracts are essential to the operation of most formal organizations. If, however, we carry this culturally dominant model down to the level of interpersonal relationships in organizations, expense and proscription of free activity escalate. Contractual negotiations cannot carry the load of collaborative choice making that is characteristic of day-to-day organizational work.

An alternative to contract negotiation is *contact* negotiation. In this context, contact signifies that authentic communication about what a person wants has occurred. In contrast with contractual negotiations, in contact negotiations each side describes what it really wants, then works to meet expressed wants and needs. Gestalt psychology is a major influence on contact negotiations because it helps uncover the unconscious social, cultural, and psychological histories and influences that each person — including oneself — brings to the negotiation process. This creates a need for training to increase people's physiological and psychological self-awareness and understanding of how individuals operate in groups.

In contact negotiation, there is often a great deal of movement in position because each party's initial proposal is subject to change as discussion reveals deeper wants and needs. As a contact negotiation moves forward and the underlying wants of the involved parties are revealed, new possibilities for achieving satisfaction arise. When this happens, an agreement founded on satisfying real needs (making contact) is negotiated, as opposed to contracting a resolution that is only an agreement of words. Thus, although the two kinds of negotiation may have results that look the same, the contact process is substantially different, and its product is qualitatively better and more sustainable over time.

Interest Versus Position Theory. In their book *Getting to Yes* (1987), Fisher and Ury propose a series of negotiating techniques collectively referred to as *principled negotiation*. This theory provides a framework that allows a problem-solving approach to the negotiation process. Fisher and Ury, respectively director and assistant director of the Harvard Negotiation Project, believe that "the basic problem in negotiation lies not in conflicting positions, but in the conflict between each side's needs, desires, concerns, and fears" (p. 42). They premise their theory on the idea that when negotiation focuses on positions, it fails to meet the basic criteria for producing wise agreements efficiently and amicably. Moreover, such negotiation endangers the building of ongoing relationships.

Further, when the positions rather than the interests of negotiating parties are emphasized, people find themselves in a dilemma. They perceive only two ways to negotiate, the "hard sell" versus the "soft sell." Fisher and Ury (1987, p. 9) maintain that hard and soft sell positions produce the following results:

- Participants are considered adversaries rather than friends.
- The only goal is victory rather than agreement.
- Concessions are demanded as a condition rather than a cultivation of the relationship.
- There is distrust rather than trust of others.
- The process involves threats rather than offers.
- There is an insistence on position rather than agreement and other like positions.

The dilemma of these positions creates the need for a trade-off between getting something wanted (position) and getting along with others (relationships, mutual gain).

To stress interests and approximate a "soft" approach gets to the very heart of negotiation — addressing the vital interests and desires of the parties involved. According to Fisher and Ury, the satisfaction or achievement of these is the end goal of the negotiation process. In other words, interests and desires make up the "psychological bottom line" of negotiating (White, 1985).

What Are the Essential Elements of Negotiation?

In their techniques of *principled negotiation,* Fisher and Ury (1987) pinpoint four skill areas that they consider essential for successful conflict resolution through negotiation.

Separating the People from the Problem. Above all, negotiators are people. The people in the negotiation process create
relationships in which there are differences separate and apart
from the substantive issues being addressed. These human
differences stem from the interplay of emotions, values, backgrounds, and viewpoints of the individuals involved. For negotiations to be successful, everyone involved must pay constant
attention to understanding and resolving "people" problems. To
separate the people from the problem, good negotiators learn
how to deal with their own perceptions and emotions as well
as those of others. To do this effectively requires skills in self-
insight, personal interaction, cross-cultural awareness, communication, and problem solving.

To interact effectively with others and with their environment, people must learn how to access their own "internal
data" and to interpret accurately what is going on around
them. Despite an abundance of third-party evaluations and
appraisals, people do not, as a rule, perceive their own behavior accurately; nor are they often aware of the subtext
of what occurs around them. For the self-insight that enables
one to reflect on and learn from experience, a person needs skills
in process observation and active listening. When used together,
these skills provide information that can tell a negotiator whether
the direction of negotiation needs to be changed. The information that these skills provide is more important than messages'
stated contents because the most important part of what people
say is conveyed in voice tone, body posture, and other nonverbal communication; words are often the least important carrier
of meaning.

Process observation is people's ability to understand and
describe accurately actions occurring around them so that they
can respond quickly and precisely to situational needs. For example, in a business meeting, a person skilled in process observation will notice and draw information from each participant's
body posture and use of space, conversational pauses or indications of subject closure, who talked to whom and how frequently,
attitudes of receptivity, and so on.

Active listening is a process whereby an empathetic listener allows a speaker to talk through a problem for himself or herself without necessarily establishing a dialogue. In negotiation, this listening skill helps one party refrain from intervention while the other is speaking and in the midst of resolving what may be a block to agreement. The listener becomes a mirror for the speaker, reflecting as much as possible of the total picture the speaker is communicating. The listener does this neutrally, projecting neither a negative nor a positive view. The objective is for the listener to understand the situation under discussion from the speaker's point of view and to convince the speaker that the listener does understand before dealing with whether or not the two agree. Examples of active listening techniques include paraphrasing the speaker's statements to verify the listener's accuracy of interpretation; avoiding responses that imply evaluation, analysis, or advice; omitting questions that show sympathy or caution, and so on. "Active listening skills, implemented in a climate of genuine concern and acceptance, help both parties in an interpersonal exchange understand, as fully as possible, the relevant content — facts and feelings — floating around on top and underneath the table" (Kolb, Rubin, and McIntyre, 1984, p. 208).

A competent negotiator possesses flexibility, creativity, and patience. Flexibility allows a person to adjust quickly to new developments, to move beyond the boundaries of a stated problem to a new formulation that may not have been readily apparent, and to adopt different reactions and approaches as a situation requires. Flexibility allows negotiators to stop acting as adversaries and to begin approaching negotiation as a process for mutual gain. The notion of mutual gain is easier to promote if the interests and goals are similar and if the benefits are directly dependent on a degree of interdependence.

Mastenbroek (1983) developed four scales that represent certain negotiating dilemmas that can be dealt with more or less creatively. For each dilemma, he describes creative approaches for resolution. The approaches run on a sliding scale from cooperation to fighting (see Figure 22).

Figure 22. Scales of the Four Major Negotiation Dilemmas.

Jovial Versus Hostile

1	2	3	4	5
Genial, confidential		Credible, solid		Hostile, irritated
Relying on personal charm, tendency to tell lots of jokes, likes to become very close		Promoting informal discussions, showing interest in personal matters, moderate use of humor, consistent behavior		Keeps the opponent at length, formal behavior, sometimes sarcastic, shows irritation, seems unpredictable
Dependent: "Your interest is my interest"		Shows interdependence: "What solution will we find?"		Shows independence: "What can *I* get out of this?"

Conceding Versus Stubborn

1	2	3	4	5
Lenient, indulgent		Tenacious, testing		Hard, stubborn
One presents information and arguments as open for discussion		Firm presentation of facts and arguments, but margins are self-understood		One presents information and arguments as self-evident and unassailable
One accepts the interests of the other side as they are described		One tests the interests of the other party to get to his or her priorities		One challenges the interests of the opponent to discard them
One promotes a smooth and gradual working out of a compromise; one is prepared to make generous concessions		One allows impasses to occur and uses them as a test; relatively small concessions are part of the game		One provokes crisis situations; a tendency toward "final offer, first bid"

Bending Versus Domineering

1	2	3	4	5
Minimal resistance		Preserving a balance		Aggressive, trying to dominate
Inhibited use of favorable facts		One tries to adjust the balance by means of facts and restrained pressure		Adjustment by arrogance, threats, emotional outbursts and manipulations
When challenged, not much resistance		When challenged, one reacts proportionally		When challenged, one attacks
No active interest in alternatives to current relations		One is alert to alternatives to improve one's position *within* the present relation		One behaves as having other attractive alternatives which one is ready to use at the least sign of trouble

Figure 22. Scales of the Four Major Negotiation Dilemmas, Cont'd.

Uncommitted Versus Overcommitted

1	2	3	4	5
No commitment to rank and file		Tries to enlarge the maneuvering space		Is just carrying out instructions
Takes freedom of action but risks losing rank and file support		Avoids a strict mandate but stays in contact and influences "opinion leaders"		Asks for and "obeys" mandate
Independent thinking but too detached from constituents		Prevents stereotyping, is moderating expectations		Goes along with stereotyping, is raising expectations of the outcome

Source: Mastenbroek, 1983.

Mastenbroek believes that each midpoint on the scale represents the "optimal balance between cooperation and fighting — which is the approach most likely to lead to successful negotiations" (p. 77). For negotiators to operate at these midpoints, they must have a high degree of creativity — to understand common dilemmas and to have enough insight to read their own reactions as well as those of others.

Learning new ways to perceive the self, others, and the environment requires unusual patience. A negotiator should have patience and a tolerance for ambiguity that enables him or her to withstand the pressures for immediate answers to questions or problems (Lipitt, 1983). The skilled negotiator patiently attempts to reduce disorder and to find sense and meaning in apparent contradictions.

Cross-cultural issues are not limited to the dramatic differences between countries. Many of the worst cases of cultural misunderstanding occur closer to home and the workplace. Even in outwardly homogeneous small groups, people's norms, values, and behavioral codes vary widely. To perform well in the context of negotiation, a person must be particularly sensitive to cultural differences — even among players from the same organization. For example, labor and management will have differing perspectives on some issues.

Cultural sensitivity is the ability to detect the ruling values that motivate other people's actions and the subtleties of how they perceive situations. Because cultural differences are inherent in all negotiations, there needs to be strong emphasis on sensitivity to structure (rules) and process. When in place, structure and process are the mechanisms for dealing with whatever differences arise over substantive interpretation. If negotiating parties have similar cultural points of view, the process level of negotiation is decided on almost without conscious decision. When parties are from markedly different cultural backgrounds, however, agreement on a process within which to discuss substantive issues becomes crucial to the negotiation's outcome.

As people become more proficient in dealing with the substantive and process levels of negotiation, they also need to pay attention to basic communication patterns. They particularly need to learn how to use self-disclosure to their advantage and to be aware of the importance of interpersonal tact. Schein (1981a) refers to these as *verbal articulation skills* and indicates that the ability to use these skills well helps a negotiator establish the degree of openness that best serves the negotiation process. Schein says that "one of the ways that relationships become more intimate is through successive minimal self-disclosures which constitute interpersonal tests of acceptance."

In terms of self-disclosure, Fisher and Ury (1987) suggest that one way to deal with differing perceptions during the negotiation process is to make them explicit and discuss them. Fisher and Ury also believe that communicating loudly and convincingly things that most people are willing to say (unimportant things, if you will) or that others would like to hear sets an agreeable tone and can be one of the best investments toward securing a mutually agreeable outcome.

The key to verbal articulation skills is tact. Language management dictates that communication in negotiation needs to be frank and honest without either side blaming the other for the problem. Tact has been described as the behavioral manifestation of cultural and moral humility that leads a person to believe that since "there is genuinely room for different values in this world, then we have the basis for showing in our speech and behavior an adequate level of respect for others in negotiating with them" (Schein, 1981a, p. 45).

Another skill set essential to the art of successful negotiation relates to problem solving. Problem solving begins before actual negotiation starts and is ongoing until agreement is reached or the negotiating parties decide to break off the effort. To be an effective problem solver, a negotiator will plan carefully, beginning by deciding how to handle the opening pleasantries because "even the exchange of greetings is a form of negotiation" (Rand, 1987, p. 94).

Problem-solving skills related to negotiation fall into two categories: proactive and "repair." Proactive problem solving involves analysis and planning before negotiation begins — for example, researching the opposition, researching the history of the conflict, researching its present condition, formulating requirements, assessing motivations, considering time and timing, identifying all the players, identifying the powerful figures on each side, determining all the costs of stalemate, and choosing strategy or tactics (Shea, 1983). Repair strategies and skills are used throughout the negotiation process. They include clarifying the problem, proposing and examining possible solutions, resolving the problem by a mutually agreeable decision, creating an implementation strategy, and evaluating the plan after implementation.

Focusing on Interests, Not Positions. The next skill area addressed in the theory of principled negotiation involves the conflict between positions and the goal of agreeing on a position (Fisher and Ury, 1987). Nierenberg (1973) also emphasizes that fixating on taking a position rather than focusing on interests often leads to an impasse. The basic problem is not with conflicting positions in and of themselves but in the discrepancies between people's needs, desires, concerns, and fears. These necessitate identification of the interests of the other party involved in the negotiation. Nierenberg and Fisher and Ury state that the most powerful interests are basic human needs and that if negotiators can reach consensus on issues of common human need, the opposing parties can move on to agreement on other, more difficult issues.

Experience suggests that, depending on requirements of the moment, negotiators need to look at a variety of options, such as identifying interests, realizing that each side has more than one interest, establishing commonality of interest around basic human needs, talking about interests with the other party, talking about interests as part of the problem, being concrete but flexible, and being firm about the problem but separating the problem from the people.

     Inventing Options for Mutual Gain. Fisher and Ury further believe that to be successful at negotiations, people need to be able to invent options for mutual gain (see Figure 23).

Figure 23. Four Basic Steps in
Inventing Options for Mutual Gain.

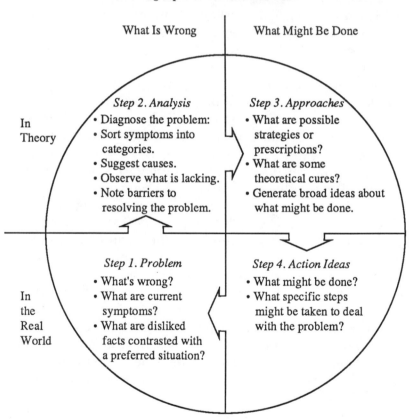

As people begin to invent options for mutual gain, it is suggested that negotiators should protect against making an agreement that ought to be rejected and to help make the most of assets so that any agreement reached will satisfy the interests involved.

The best protection against accepting an agreement that should be rejected or rejecting an agreement that should be accepted is referred to as a BATNA (*best alternative to a negotiated agreement*). By developing BATNAs, effective negotiators increase their bargaining power — because power directly relates to willingness to tolerate no agreement and ensure themselves against agreeing to an inferior settlement just to end negotiations. It is true that "if you can walk away from a bad deal, you are in a strong, intelligent position during the negotiations" (Byrnes, 1987b, p. 23).

Using Objective Criteria. Using objective criteria (such as standard specifications, market values, replacement costs, and so forth) produces wiser agreements, more amicably and efficiently. To develop such criteria, negotiators need to use fair standards and procedures based on the following:

- Framing each issue as a joint search
- Being open to reason about which standards are most appropriate and about the manner in which they will be applied
- Yielding only to principle and never to pressure

What Constitutes Competency in Negotiation? What Constitutes Mastery?

Competency and mastery in the art of negotiation come from understanding and gaining proficiency in eliminating obstacles that block movement toward successful conflict resolution. A skilled negotiator avoids judging prematurely, searching for a single answer, resorting to an "either/or" mentality, or expecting the other party to solve "your" problems. A negotiator who is able to recognize and work through obstacles has achieved mastery. As with any skill, however, the learning and fine-tuning of negotiation skills never stop. According to Chester Karrass in *The Negotiating Game* (1970), certain "traits" characterize a successful negotiator. These include planning skills, ability to think clearly under stress, verbal ability, practical intelligence (street or world wise), personal integrity, knowledge of yourself, and ability to perceive and exploit power.

Knowing in theory what makes a good negotiator is different from actually dealing with other human beings in an adversarial relationship. Mastery of the skilled art of negotiation comes from practicing skills over and over again and learning from each success and mistake or missed opportunity.

What Is an Example of a Successful Workplace Training Program in Negotiation?

Michigan Consolidated Gas Company (MichCon) is a utility company that transmits, stores, and distributes natural gas to over a million customers in Michigan. MichCon is a wholly owned subsidiary of MCN Corporation. At the end of 1987, MichCon had assets of $1.2 billion and employed 3,478 people. Approximately half of these employees are professionals (overtime exempt and nonexempt), while the other half are unionized workers (hourly wage).

MichCon has several plant locations; training takes place in its three major installations. In the past, MichCon did not put much emphasis on nonsupervisory training; it was an exception, not the rule. Now the company is committed to all employees' development and, consequently, is paying more attention to the training of nonsupervisory employees.

In 1987, MichCon began to require negotiation skills training for collectors in the account services department and for buyers and supervisors in the purchasing department. Collectors need these skills to negotiate larger payments from customers who are delinquent in paying their bills. Purchasing buyers and supervisors need the skills to negotiate the best prices for goods and services purchased for the company. Courses for the two groups cover similar negotiation skills but use job-specific case studies to illustrate problems that collectors and purchasing personnel may encounter.

MichCon is still in the process of putting all of its collectors through the program. Eventually, the program will only be offered to new hires, although a refresher course may be offered every three years or so. The program is now offered approximately every six months, and so far ninety employees have completed it; another fifty to sixty employees are expected to complete it in the next one to three years.

The need for negotiation skills training was identified by both the purchasing management and the operating departments. In the course of discussions with training department staff members (who act as internal consultants), the decision was made to develop the program. The employee development department's budget pays for the program, which is conducted on company time at no cost to employees.

The two-day course is purchased from an outside consultant, who tailors it to the context of jobs in individual departments and also performs course delivery. In many cases, participants' education levels are an issue that must be addressed because many collectors are high school graduates whereas purchasing personnel, who are learning similar negotiating skills, often have undergraduate degrees or other formal education.

Several practical techniques important to negotiation skills are presented at the beginning of the course: setting the stage physically (Where will the meeting be?), analyzing the authority of the person with whom negotiation is taking place (Does this person have the authority to make a decision on the case?), identifying/creating deadlines, and so on. Participants also learn which situations require the application of negotiation skills and which do not and the desired outcomes of negotiation. In addition, participants learn skills needed to negotiate well, such as oral communication and listening skills and problem-solving skills. Participants learn to analyze the interests and needs of a client or the opposition and how to devise a negotiation strategy. Future negotiators also learn that they need to be able to identify the other party's problem and work to solve it — because for negotiation to remain productive, a tug-of-war must be avoided.

Role play is used extensively in the course. The scenarios are situations that participants will actually encounter on the job. After techniques have been presented, participants are given issues to negotiate. The participants usually pair up or form groups to role play, although they sometimes practice individually. By facing different numbers of negotiators, participants learn the advantages and disadvantages of working with and opposite more or fewer negotiators. Participants are videotaped as they act out negotiations, and later the participants and instructor review and constructively criticize the tape.

MichCon conducts both short- and long-term evaluations of its negotiation skills program. Short-term evaluation takes the form of a test given at the course's conclusion to measure how much employees learned. The National Association of Personnel Managers offers purchasing personnel the Certified Purchasing Managers exam to measure the continuing effects of negotiation skills training. For account collectors, looking at whether or not delinquent customers have made larger initial payments gives an indication of the training's effects on actual job performance. Recent evaluations show that larger payments have resulted, indicating that the training was effective (Roberta Henrichs, Kelley Dillon, and Ken Huskey telephone interviews, May and July 1988).

What Should Be Included in a Generic Workplace Negotiation Curriculum?

Exhibit 22 lists items to consider in designing a workplace negotiation curriculum.

Exhibit 22. Managing Conflict: The Negotiation Process.

What are the objectives of this training?
–To cover the basics of negotiation
–To better understand how a negotiating session works and what its key elements are
–To help participants understand their own strengths and weaknesses in a negotiating posture
–To help participants strengthen their own negotiating skills
–To explore how a positive negotiating position will sustain a positive collaborative atmosphere after negotiations have concluded

Exhibit 22. Managing Conflict: The Negotiation Process, Cont'd.

What is conflict?
–Two opposed parties actively seeking their own end goal
–Positive and negative uses of conflict in an organization
–Principal causes of conflict

How do you manage conflict?
–By identifying the problem(s)
–By selecting a strategy for resolution (avoidance, delay, confrontation,
  negotiation, collaboration)

When is negotiation appropriate?
–When there is leeway to give
–When resources are limited
–When a win/lose stance is undesirable

What are the benefits of effective negotiation?
–Improved working relationships
–Enhanced organizational effectiveness
–Enhanced personal effectiveness
–Ability to make better deals
–Techniques for breaking through standoffs and stalemates

How do you prepare for the negotiation process?
–By determining the degree of seriousness of the conflict
–By identifying organizational and individual self-interest in resolving the
  conflict
–By establishing mutually acceptable negotiating guidelines
–By establishing ground rules (time, commitment, mediator, place, food and
  drink, recording, confidentiality)

How do you analyze an opponent?
–By determining the BATNA (*best alternative to a negotiated agreement*)
  –Your own and your opponent's mini-max position
  –What each side is willing and able to walk away with
–By choosing an appropriate strategy and tactics and negotiating a win/win
  resolution based on this information

What are the traits of a successful negotiator?
–Evaluating yourself as a negotiator
  –Planning skills
  –Ability to think clearly under stress
  –Verbal ability
  –Practical intelligence (street or world wise)
  –Personal integrity
  –Knowledge of yourself
  –Ability to perceive and exploit power

Exhibit 22. Managing Conflict: The Negotiation Process, Cont'd.

What are some effective negotiating approaches for resolving conflict?
-Needs theory of negotiation (Nierenberg)
-Contract versus contact (Gestalt theory)
-Interest versus position (Fisher and Ury)

What are some negotiation skills exercises?
-One-on-one activity (solo approach) with feedback from an observer
-Team negotiation with evaluation and debriefing from each team observer
  -Enumeration of learning points
  -Discussion of elements of activity

PART 8

Influencing Skills: Making a Difference

Organizations are a maze of explicit and implicit structures that make up their "culture." Understanding how to operate within this maze can spell the difference between career growth and failure in the workplace.

An organization's culture consists of shared beliefs and values, common symbols and rituals, and even the use of specialized jargon. Its rules for success are often formal, but informal influences run like an undercurrent throughout. Similarly, its behavioral and attitudinal taboos are both obvious and subtle. Further complicating the picture are subcultures that spring up at various organizational and departmental levels, each of which has its own set of expectations and taboos.

Employees need to have a sense of how to maneuver effectively within an organization's culture and subcultures. Increasingly, a major part of that maneuvering includes having a sense of when it is appropriate to assume a leadership role, as well as how to mobilize the group for better team performance when taking on that role.

Peak performance can only occur when employees are well equipped to navigate the organizational waters. However, many of today's workers do not have the tools necessary to meet this challenge. They need training in the skills necessary to influence successfully the inner workings of their organization: organizational effectiveness and leadership.

351

CHAPTER 17

Understanding Organizational Culture

The company management never told me about the corporate
culture or the unspoken rules. The old-timers let me know
where to sleep on what shifts and which foreman to avoid.
They told me how much work I was supposed to do and
which shop steward I was to speak with if I had a problem.

Gene Geromel
Nation's Business, January 1989

What Is Organizational Effectiveness?

Embedded in every organizational structure are compet-
ing and complex social orders, each with its own values and rules
of conduct. Consequently, effective participation in organizational life requires all involved to acquire certain specialized
skills. According to Edgar H. Schein (1981b, p. 266), professor
of management at the Sloan School of Management, Massachusetts Institute of Technology, "Each of us learns to construct
somewhat different selves for the different kinds of situations
in which we are called on to perform and for the different kinds
of roles we are expected to take."

These skills include the behaviors, attitudes, and knowledge an employee needs to achieve success on the job both as
an individual and as a member of an organization. Each worker
uses these skills to adapt to organizational expectations, including
expected job performance levels. Therefore, the skills are viewed
as necessary to help people align themselves with an organiza-

tion's culture, that is, with "the philosophy or style of a company; its technological origins, which might provide clues as to its basic assumptions; and its beliefs about its mission and its future" (Schein, 1985, p. 34).

Organizational effectiveness skills help employees learn how to behave moment by moment, day by day to measure up to an organization's internal rules and regulations. These skills provide the guidelines for establishing appropriate and effective interrelationships. Specifically, they enable a person to do the following:

- Empower self and others to achieve individual and organizational effectiveness
- Use power and influence to meet job requirements and to align personal and professional vision with the organizational mission
- Use personal resources to manage diversity—of culture, age, gender, and so on—among co-workers
- Use transformational skills (personal and interpersonal behaviors) to interpret information data bases and political substructures and to influence and adapt to changes in the organization's basic business
- Facilitate self and others to achieve credibility and effectiveness
- Behave appropriately in relating to others at all levels (subordinates, peers, and superiors)

Employees who succeed in using organizational effectiveness skills are perceived as competent and satisfied with their careers and in control of their professional development.

What Theories Support Current
Training in Organizational Effectiveness?

In every workplace, there is both an explicit or formal structure and an implicit or informal structure. The formal structure is represented by organization charts with clearly defined chains of command and delegation of duties. Research shows, however, that groups within an organization depart from formal structure to create their own channels of communication and dependence on the basis of people's proximity, tasks, common interests, personalities, or social classes (Lewis, 1983). In an informal organizational structure, there may be no clear lines of authority, delegation, or responsibility. Strongly implied in the epigraph at the beginning of this chapter is the idea that employees will create informal structures to satisfy unmet needs. Employers must therefore come to terms with the legitimacy of informal as well as formal structures in order to help employees achieve success on the job, which in turn leads to a more productive work force.

Organizational structure theories are useful for helping employees understand how different kinds of organizations function and what is acceptable employee behavior in these different environments. Various theories have concluded that organizations can be viewed in different ways; they can be *mechanistic* or *organic,* or they can be *markets, bureaucracies,* or *clans.*

A typical mechanistic-type organization has many precisely designed tasks, well-defined rules and procedures, tight control from top management, and emphasis on communicating only through a formal chain of command. On the other hand, an organic organization is typically more flexible, allowing a higher degree of adaptability to change. Its characteristics include loosely defined task activities, few rules and procedures, more emphasis on self-control through the problem-solving process, and emphasis on horizontal communication.

A different perspective views organizational structures in terms of the interdependence of relationships (Ouchi, 1980). For example, in a market relationship (such as in Mary Kay Products), an employer and workers negotiate a mutually determined equitable compensation based on an external competitive market pricing mechanism. In a bureaucratic relationship (such as in government agencies), each worker contributes labor to a corporate body that places an independent value on each position's contribution and then compensates on the basis of these value guidelines. In a clan relationship (such as in the U.S. Marine Corps, Japanese automobile industries, and Hewlett-Packard), workers are socialized to accept the company goals as their own, and they are rewarded for this acceptance on the basis of nonperformance criteria such as length of service or number of dependents.

An individual's ability to adapt to an organization's particular operating culture is perhaps the single most helpful skill in the search to achieve workplace success. Organizational effectiveness skills are different from job skills. They relate to how an employee chooses to respond to the pressures of organizational life. From studies conducted in organizational culture, Schein (1981b) has provided some useful insights into specific skills that can help employees integrate into a group or organization. These include skills related to understanding an organization such as the following:

- *Common language and conceptual categories.* If members cannot communicate with and understand each other, a group is impossible by definition.
- *Group boundaries and criteria for inclusion and exclusion.* One of the most important areas of culture is the shared consensus of who is in and who is out and by what criteria one determines membership.
- *Power and status.* Every organization must work out its pecking order, its criteria and rules for how one gets, maintains, and loses power; consensus in this area is crucial to help members manage feelings of aggression.
- *Intimacy, friendship, and love.* Every organization must work out its rules of the game for peer relationships, for relationships between the sexes, and for the manner in which openness and intimacy are to be handled in the context of managing the organization's tasks.
- *Rewards and punishments.* Every group must know what its heroic and sinful behaviors are; what gets rewarded with property, status and power; and what gets punished in the form of withdrawal of the rewards and, ultimately, excommunication.
- *Ideology and "religion."* Every organization, like every society, faces unexplainable events, which must be given meaning so that members can respond to them and avoid the anx-

iety of dealing with the unexplainable and uncontrollable (Schein, 1985, p. 66).

Part of the work environment, which is created by the culture, is the overall "feeling" or impression that people have about an organization. Views vary as to exactly what components go into the composition of organizational climates. Malcolm Knowles, one of the nation's leading authorities on adult education and training, has identified what he believes are some major factors: personnel development philosophy; management philosophy and style; organizational structure, whether functional or hierarchical; financial policies; and reward systems.

From a slightly different perspective, W. Charles Redding, in the book *People at Work* (Timm, 1982), identifies five elements that, taken together, he believes determine organizational climate:

1. Degree to which management is supportive of its employees' efforts
2. Extent of participative decision making
3. Degree of trust employees have in management
4. Freedom to communicate openly
5. Emphasis on high performance goals

Familiarizing workers with concepts such as those noted above, which go into the makeup of the "ideal" organizational climate, can help determine whether or not a specific organization is one in which an employee will be able to function effectively. Research has borne out the idea that many of the factors Redding lists do play a major role in determining how positive an organization's climate will be.

Employees also need to develop an easily accessed reference system for looking at and analyzing an organization's climate. One analytical approach for doing this is called *frames*.

The *structural frame* describes an organization that stresses formal roles and relationships, such as McDonald's or Digital Equipment Corporation (DEC). McDonald's is a classic structuralist organization because it manages through the following means:

- A variety of structural mechanisms created to protect central activities from fluctuation and uncertainty (such as coding, stockpiling, leveling, forecasting, growth)
- A high degree of role differentiation
- Standard rules and policies, along with operating procedures that limit discretion and ensure predictability and uniformity

DEC adopted a more structuralist approach as it matured and began to slow in growth. DEC had thrived with a very informal and flexible structure during the company's early years, but the same structure produced major problems when DEC grew into a multibillion-dollar corporation. These problems were interpreted as structural, and DEC adopted more formal procedures and relationships.

For an employee to be successful in this kind of organization, he or she must be able to adapt to certain realities:

- The organization primarily exists to accomplish established goals.
- There is a structure that is formally designed and implemented for establishing the goals, environment, technology, and participants; and that structure will be rigidly adhered to.
- The organization will avoid environmental turbulence and disruptive personalities by constraining workers through norms and rationality.
- Because specialization improves organizational performance, workers are more likely to hold onto their jobs.
- Control will be exercised through authority and rules.

The *political frame* characterizes an organization that is basically a place where divergent views are the norm, such as in universities and labor unions. Universities operate through the classical political approach to management because they are organizational coalitions of interest groups at different hierarchical levels, and their goals and decisions emerge from ongoing processes of bargaining, negotiation, and jockeying for position. Labor unions, likewise, epitomize the political frame tenet that the pursuit of self-interest and power is the basic process in organizations. Change occurs only when an interest group can impose its agenda on the organization, creating a significant shift in the balance of power.

To be comfortable in such an atmosphere, an employee must assume the following:

- Most important decisions will involve the allocation of scarce resources.
- Within the organization there will be many opposing coalitions composed of a number of individuals and interest groups.
- Individuals and interest groups will differ in their values, preferences, beliefs, information, and perceptions. Such differences will change slowly, if at all.
- Organizational goals and decisions arise from constant processes of bargaining and jockeying for position.

The *human resource frame* starts from the premise that people are an organization's most critical resource, such as in the United States Postal Service and Texas Instruments. These two organizations subscribe to the human resource approach to management because of their significant investments in organizational development that seeks to find the most mutually beneficial fit between the organization and its most critical resource — people.

To be at ease in this frame, a worker must fit into a pattern that assumes the following:

- The organization exists to serve human needs.
- The organization and its people need each other.
- If there is a poor fit between an individual and the organization, one or both will suffer.
- When the fit between an individual and the organization is a good one, both benefit.

The *symbolic frame* is closely related to the human resource frame and centers on the concept of meaning, belief, and faith in an organization, such as in the U.S. military and Procter & Gamble. The United States military relies on the symbolic approach to management because of the presence of strong organizational myths and sagas that hold its institutions together and infuse activities with passion and meaning.

Procter & Gamble's use of the Ivory soap "99 and 44/100s percent pure" story illustrates the purpose that such myths are supposed to serve in symbolic organizations, that is, to communicate and perpetuate organizational tradition and meaning to both insiders and outsiders.

The symbolic frame assumes that organizations are full of questions that cannot be answered and problems that cannot be managed or understood. To help alleviate this uncertainty and mystery, symbols are created. Among the most common symbols are myths, rituals, ceremonies, fairy tales, stories, humor, and play. For individual success in this type of organization, an employee must adopt these attitudes:

- What is most important about any event is not what happened but the meaning of what happened.
- The meaning of an event depends heavily on human interpretation of it.
- Many of the most significant organizational events and processes are ambiguous and uncertain; that is, what happened and why are both unclear.
- Ambiguity and uncertainty tend to undermine rational approaches to analysis, problem solving, and decision making.

Table 8 illustrates how different organizational concerns, activities, and processes are interpreted according to the four different frames or approaches described above.

What Are the Essential Elements of Training in Organizational Effectiveness?

The need for the individual worker to realign personal behaviors and preferences to meet the requirements of a particular employer has existed for as long as there have been people working for other people. The exact relationship between the individual and the organization is difficult to pinpoint because it is continually changing. In fact, during the twentieth century the relationship has undergone a rather dramatic transformation that raises a crucial question: How do two very different entities — the individual and the organization — which have dissimilar needs that frequently work at cross-purposes, work out their differences and learn to realize their needs to achieve mutually rewarding results? This question has become particularly pertinent as rapid changes in the global marketplace have forced organizations to restructure and redefine the nature and intent of their businesses in a way that has completely changed the historical pattern that led employees to believe that "the organization will take care of me." Directly or indirectly, restructuring has affected all industries and continues to influence individuals and organizations as world economic conditions change and become less predictable.

Since 1925 (during the life spans of many people currently in the work force), four distinct historical stages have affected the individual-organizational relationship:

The Depression–World War II era, 1925 to 1945
Postwar industrial period, 1945 to 1960
Governmental-industrial influence, 1960 to 1975
Evolution to a service economy, 1975 to present

Although the exact dates and descriptions of these stages vary, depending on the authority providing an opinion, there is general agreement that they represent general trends in our economy since the mid-1920s. During the entire period from 1925 to 1975, the concept of training in skills that would help to make employees more effective in their organizational interactions was not very much in evidence. Not until around 1975 did the business world begin to recognize organizational effectiveness as a skill that might contribute to improving productivity and competitiveness.

Most economists agree that this change coincided with America's continuing evolution from an industry-based to a service-based economy. The result of this evolution led to a restructuring of organizations to more competitive — that is,

Table 8. Four Interpretations of Organizational Processes.

Process	Frame			
	Structural	Human Resource	Political	Symbolic
Planning	Strategies to set objectives and coordinate resources	Gatherings to promote participation	Arenas to air conflicts and realign power	Ritual to signal responsibility, produce a symbol, and negotiate meaning
Decision making	Rational sequence to produce right decision	Open process to produce commitment	Opportunity to gain or exercise power	Ritual to provide comfort and support until decision happens
Reorganizing	Realign roles and responsibilities to fit tasks and environment	Maintain a balance between human needs and formal roles	Redistribute power and form new coalitions	Maintain an image of accountability and responsiveness; negotiate new social order
Evaluating	Basis for distributing rewards or penalties to control performance	Basis for helping individuals grow and improve	Opportunity to exercise power	Occasion to play roles in a shared ritual
Approaching conflict	Maintain organizational goals by having authorities resolve conflict	Develop relationships by having individuals confront conflict	Develop power by bargaining, forcing, or manipulating to win	Develop shared values and use conflict to negotiate meaning

Goal setting	Keep organization headed in a direction	Keep people involved and communication open	Provide opportunity for individuals or groups to make interests known	Develop symbols and shared values
Communication	Transmit facts and information	Exchange information, needs, feelings	Vehicle for influencing or manipulating others	Telling stories
Meeting	Formalized place to make decisions	Informal place to be involved, share feelings	Competitive place to win points	Sacred place to celebrate and transform the culture
Motivating	Monetary rewards	Growth, self-actualization	Coercion, manipulation, seduction	Symbols – plaques – perks – T-shirts

Source: Bolman and Deal, 1984, p. 247.

lower—staffing levels. In this context, tying organizational effectiveness training to the human resource development system was an idea whose time had come. Organizations were and are being encouraged to change existing systems and to add new structures that equip employees to take personal responsibility for developing their skills in understanding and adapting to organizational norms.

Most programs that provide formal training in organizational effectiveness seek to help people discover and utilize information that will help ease the relationship between the individual worker and his or her organization. Frequently training in the skill of organizational effectiveness is presented as a part of a larger training effort in the area of career development. A person's ability to use organizational skills effectively depends on establishing a presence in the workplace and maintaining consistency in the following areas:

- *Volition,* the willingness to conduct professional activities with interest, awareness, and enthusiasm
- *Value,* the appraisal of self-worth in terms of profession, career, current position, and current organization, including the planned or future contributions a person can make
- *Versatility,* the ability to adapt to a variety of organizational frames
- *Visibility,* the skills and behavior that allow a person to attain and maintain position in a chosen organization and/or profession
- *Vision,* the ability to create desirable outcomes and results for both self and organization by choosing to align personal vision with organizational vision rather than seek other employment

One career development study of what constitutes effective on-the-job behavior (Merman and Clark, 1985) uncovered sixteen behavioral outputs that help employees adapt effectively to organizational demands. These behavioral outputs relate to the development of organizational adaptability, professional effectiveness, and job performance (see Table 9).

Table 9. Behavioral Outcomes of
Organizational Adaptability.

Developmental Aspect	Behavioral Outcomees	Organizational Skill
Career Assessment	Past forces and influences understood	Understanding of needs, values, and beliefs that form behavior in organizations.
	Identified and appreciated one's own career values	Knowing what's important in work life.
	Identified desired organizational values met	Selecting the right organization to individual needs, values, and talents.
	Adapted to changes and took responsibility for personal choices	Being flexible, fitting in, and aligning self to organizational cultures.
Self-Assessment	Understood and appreciated personal strengths and abilities	Knowing and using strengths.
	Understood how one is perceived by others	Asking for and receiving feedback.
	Identified and created a personally satisfying and productive work environment	Creating and maintaining a productive work environment for self.
	Realistically compared career appropriateness to performance feedback	Understands reality of performance in relation to goals.
Professional Growth	Took an enabling approach to self and others	Influences growth of self and others.
	Updated professional behavior within a career field	Knows what is expected professionally.

Table 9. Behavioral Outcomes of
Organizational Adaptability, Cont'd.

Developmental Aspect	Behavioral Outcomees	Organizational Skill
	Gathered and applied information related to careers	Resourceful in getting and using information. Using political substructures to gain information.
	Created interdependent win-win relationships	Uses others to achieve mutual goals. Achieving common vision with others to transform the organization.
Organizational Effectiveness	Understood industry changes and their impact on career effectiveness	Knows what's happening in the industry.
	Understood future options and opportunities	Understands that organizational life will be different in the future.
	Took advantage of support systems	Uses others to support attainment of the vision.
	Balanced the personal, professional, and social aspects of one's life	Knows priorities in life and integrates them with organizational needs.

Source: Merman and Clark, 1985.

What Constitutes Competency in Organizational Effectiveness? What Constitutes Mastery?

How does an employee demonstrate competency in organizational effectiveness? The skills involved in organizational effectiveness are not taught in school, but they *are* critical to an individual's successful performance on the job. Competency covers a variety of personal and professional capabilities that have been tested by observing employees who show positive results by understanding and taking charge of their work lives regardless of the conditions under which they are asked to perform.

A further review of the behavioral outcomes uncovered by Merman and Clark (1985) revealed that employees usually operated along a competency continuum that ranged from usually considered not as effective to usually considered somewhat effective to usually considered most effective.

From a counseling or training standpoint, classification of each desirable outcome makes it easier to identify the areas in which a person needs development to use organizational effectiveness skills. Very few people perform at the level "usually considered most effective" from the time they begin a job; fewer ever achieve mastery of all sixteen behavioral outcomes. Competency, however, represents knowledge of essential concepts plus forward movement in the organizational socialization process and a growth and improvement curve that eventually leads to mastery.

A sample description of a continuum related to the behavioral outcome "Taking an Enabling Approach to Self and Others" and a corresponding behavioral descriptor, impact statement, and short case study are presented in Table 10.

The relationship between career mastery and behavioral outcomes is important for determining what additional training in organizational effectiveness skills will be helpful to an employee at different career stages.

Several instruments for measuring career development are useful for determining progress in mastering organizational effectiveness. One instrument developed by career development specialist John O. Crites (1988) has been particularly good. This is his updated 1978 career assessment instrument, the Career Mastery Inventory. This instrument is based on the premise that a worker needs to master six career development tasks to maximize career potential during the period that begins with job entry and ends at midcareer. The six tasks are as follows:

1. *Organizational adaptability* — getting into an organization, "learning the ropes," becoming socialized to expectations and norms

Table 10. Example of a Behavioral Outcome: "Taking an Enabling Approach to Self and Others."

Usually Considered Not as Effective	Usually Considered Somewhat Effective	Usually Considered Most Effective
Descriptive behavior: Individuals influence others in a way that meets their needs rather than the needs of others or the organization. They want their lives to run smoothly so they will be efficient and have a high need to look, and be thought of as, productive.	**Descriptive behavior:** Individuals try to be "right" above all else. They believe that, by doing so, they will stay safe and secure. They often seek approval from others. They are often confused about how to handle their feelings and attitudes.	**Descriptive behavior:** Individuals are known as effective problem solvers. They are open and honest in their communication, and always seek clarity and agreement from others. They realize when their criticism is not productive, and they turn negatives into positives.
Impact statements: If the organization allows this behavior to continue, it may become lax in its standards. Norms that discourage effective team building, risk taking, and innovation may develop.	**Impact statements:** Individuals may influence their productivity because of a high need for approval. Organization risks effective and timely completion of its mission and purpose.	**Impact statements:** Openness of this type helps reduce conflict and foster good communication between and among departments. However, it may be difficult for the organization and others to accept.
Case example: No matter what happens, Donna, an inventory data entry clerk, will find fault with it. Her behavior demonstrates	**Case example:** George, a middle manager for a major public utility, fears any type of change. His attitude is to protect himself by	**Case example:** Gordon, a customer service representative for a waste disposal firm, is in

a feeling that nothing is right with anything, especially the organization. Although she is competent and continues to meet and sometimes exceed her job expectations, her attitude often "gets in the way" in terms of the effectiveness of the department. Her supervisor perceives her as a person who will sabotage change in any way possible.

making certain that those he perceives as powerful like him.

Whenever he is in meetings, he supports decisions that are the most popular. He places others' needs ahead of his own. He can disable organizational effectiveness by his political maneuvering or enable its effectiveness through his positive, friendly attitude.

a position of high visibility to the customer. He handles all the complaints and makes sure that the trucks are properly scheduled and on time.

Not only does he have a positive attitude toward people, he is also very aware of the mission of the organization. When people talk to him in negative or less productive ways, Gordon is quick to find the positive elements in the situation and thus help the person feel better about it. In this way, Gordon is able to further the organization's goals and mission plus meet his own needs as well.

Source: Merman and Clark, 1985.

2. *Positional performance*—learning the job, accomplishing job duties and tasks

3. *Work habits and attitude*—being dependable, having a positive approach, accepting supervision

4. *Co-worker relationships*—getting along with others, dealing effectively with interpersonal problems on the job

5. *Advancement*—getting ahead, moving up the organizational ladder

6. *Career choice and plans*—looking ahead, establishing goals for the future, identifying career paths

A comparative analysis of the items in Crites's instrument with the sixteen behavioral outcomes that Merman and Clark (1985) discussed reveals a distinct correlation between them (see Figure 24).

What Is an Example of a Successful Workplace Training Program in Organizational Effectiveness?

The Monsanto Company of St. Louis, Missouri, is a multinational company engaged in researching, manufacturing, and marketing a widely diversified line of high-quality products, including chemical and agricultural products, pharmaceuticals, low-calorie sweeteners, industrial process controls, synthetic fibers, and plastics.

Monsanto has more than 100 plant and facility locations throughout the world and employs nearly 50,000 people. Its annual revenue is more than $7.6 billion.

Like many organizations, Monsanto experienced rapid change in the late 1970s and early 1980s. Responding to market-place changes, the company elected to reduce costs and increase profitability. One organizational strategy was to exit the commodity chemical business in favor of high-value chemical products, pharmaceuticals, and life science products. In the 1980s, Monsanto's board of directors set in motion actions that would transform the organization, with new rules and new ways of communicating its basic business operations. Industry analysts agree that Monsanto has earned high marks for its adaptation to change and predict continued growth for the company in the coming years.

Figure 24. Career Mastery and Behavioral Outcomes Matrix.

Behavioral Outcomes	Organizational Adaptability	Position Performance	Work Habits and Attitudes	Co-Worker Relationships	Advancement	Career Choice and Plans
Part I: Career Assessment						
Understood past forces and influences		●	●	●	●	●
Identified and appreciated career values	●	●			●	●
Identified desired organizational values	●	●				
Adapted to changes and took responsibility for choices	●		●	●	●	
Part II: Self-Assessment						
Understood personal strengths and weaknesses		●	●	●	●	
Understood how one is perceived by others		●	●	●		
Identified and created satisfying work environment	●	●	●	●		
Realistically compared career to feedback	●				●	●
Part III: Professional Growth						
Took enabling approach to self and others	●			●		
Updated professional behavior in career	●	●	●		●	●
Gathered and applied information to career	●				●	●
Created interdependent relationships			●	●	●	
Part IV: Career Effectiveness						
Understood industry changes and impact					●	
Understood future options and opportunities		●			●	●
Took advantage of support systems	●			●	●	●
Balanced personal, social, and professional life	●		●		●	●

Source: Adapted from Merman and Clark, 1985.

To cope with its changing environment, Monsanto's corporate finance group began offering organizational effectiveness training in July 1987. Currently, all its organizational effectiveness training is conducted in St. Louis, although the training is also available to employees from other locations.

Organizational effectiveness training was begun in response to the organization's need to help employees take personal responsibility for adjusting to the demands of the "new" organization. Senior management is placing a greater emphasis on entrepreneurial thinking down the line, along with creativity and the production of higher-quality products and services. Life at the new Monsanto created a great many challenges, some simply because most employees were accustomed to the old way of doing things. When employees were asked to create career paths consistent with Monsanto's new structure and aligned with its organizational mission and purpose, many employees found the request difficult because they believed they lacked the necessary skills. What used to be normal ways of achieving career success by relating to a centralized system were no longer possible.

To succeed under the decentralized system, employees need to learn new adaptation skills: how to catch the supervisor's eye by being innovative and creative and yet work within the corporate culture to achieve harmony and unity. These skills are now critical to employee success and satisfaction — and vital to the achievement of Monsanto's strategic goal of improving its competitive edge. All of these concerns are being addressed in training.

The corporate finance staff developed a plan to implement organizational skills training within their function, and the costs of developing the training program were funded by the corporate finance group. However, each business unit is responsible for funding the costs of its employees' attendance at training.

By its first anniversary, the program had already experienced changes based on active employee participation and a review of program materials to improve their fit to Monsanto's corporate culture. The program's positive impact is most noticeable in affirmative feedback from managers, employees' better understanding of career realities in Monsanto, good word-of-mouth advertising from former program participants, increased numbers of employees seeking to attend the program, and former participants' stronger commitment to Monsanto and their jobs.

The training is delivered by an outside provider that specializes in helping individuals and organizations adapt to change. An internal Monsanto coordinator is also available to arrange seminar activities, evaluate results, coordinate prework assignments, and consult with business units to determine their needs in terms of employee attendance and desired results.

Participants in the voluntary two-and-a-half-day program come from a variety of business units and include managerial and professional employees. For the most part, participants are employees who are determined to achieve more personal control by learning how to adapt to organizational restructuring and the uncertainty of organizational change. To date, most volunteers have come from the finance and information systems departments.

As of 1989, the program was being offered once every four months. Although most people who have asked to take the course have been from Monsanto's professional-technical-managerial level, the program is open to everyone, and nonsupervisory employees are encouraged to attend.

The program's success is measured in terms of noticeable changes in employee attitudes and behaviors in moving toward career self-management and improved adaptability to organizational change. At the discretion of the trainers, tests based on the Career Mastery Inventory (Crites, 1988) have been administered prior to the program and just following the training. An additional program evaluation is conducted three months following training's conclusion. The purpose of this evaluation is to determine whether participants have implemented actions relating to key organizational skills, and if so, what the results have been. Another evaluation is conducted one year after participation in the program to determine participants' continued retention and use of information learned in the training.

Indicators of program success include the following:

- Participants' enhanced job satisfaction, performance, and success
- Behaviors that enable employees and the organization to grow
- Individual participants' greater self-control in terms of meeting personal, professional, and social needs
- Evidence that people know what they want from the organization and how to obtain it

The program is designed as a highly participative workshop. Prior to a workshop, five people who know a prospective participant provide information about that person. As a participant completes each training unit, he or she is provided feedback based on the information the five people provided earlier. Workshop activities, exercises, homework, participant interaction, and individualized attention characterize the training.

To help employees implement more effective self-management techniques and adapt to new or changing internal corporate environments, the program specifically addresses positive behaviors and explores their value to workers who want to enhance their determination to conduct career self-management activities, develop options to improve their versatility, make their professional and self-worth more visible, and develop the ability to visualize new carer possibilities (M. A. Fetters, personal and telephone interviews, 1988).

What Should Be Included in a Generic Workplace Organizational Effectiveness Curriculum?

Exhibit 23 presents items to consider in designing an organizational effectiveness curriculum.

**Exhibit 23. Organizational Effectiveness:
Understanding "Who's on First and What's on Second!"**

What are the objectives of this training?
-To increase participants' understanding of explicit and implicit organizational norms, structures, and codes and how they shape the work environment
-To improve participants' skills and abilities to function in an organizational environment in an effective and job-enhancing manner
-To understand how each participant is perceived by others (peers and supervisors) in a way that helps or hinders his or her organizational effectiveness
-To help participants understand the impact of their personal and professional values, choices, and behaviors on their effectiveness in an organization

What are organizational effectiveness skills?
-The ability to read and understand organizational cues to better understand the organization's directions and values
-The ability to understand the explicit and implicit structures and codes of an organization to better comprehend its culture and succeed within it
-The ability to understand how compatible or incompatible personal and organizational values and behavior patterns will enable you to succeed in a particular organization, make a decision to leave, or modify your beliefs and style of operating in order to stay and achieve your objectives
-The skill to develop an action plan that identifies how you can use available organizational mechanisms to help increase organizational effectiveness

What will a self-assessment process contribute to improving my organizational effectiveness skills?
-Provide a knowledge of work-related skills and abilities such as vocational/occupational skills, strengths, personal and professional values, relationships, and interests
-Help in understanding what one does best and enjoys doing, as well as in making a determination of how marketable these preferences are in today's organizations
-Help to uncover one's personal vision of the ideal work environment by answering the following questions:
  -What am I doing in my ideal job environment?
  -Where am I doing this?
  -What skills do I bring to the job?
  -What results can I achieve?
-Answer the questions "How prepared am I to meet the challenge of achieving my vision?" and "What do I need to learn and know to achieve my vision in this organizational structure?"

Exhibit 23. Organizational Effectiveness:
Understanding "Who's on First and What's on Second!", Cont'd.

-Uncover resources, training and/or educational needs, and ways you and/or
the organization can best help you fulfill the vision

How will improving my understanding of how I can grow professionally
impact on my organizational effectiveness skills?
-It will help to match opportunities with career interests.
-It will develop skills to uncover and create new job opportunities within
and outside an organization.
-It will change attitudes toward wanting more responsibility—from a feeling
of powerlessness to a desire to assume control.
-It will broaden focus and perspectives of what is important in terms of
career and personal life.
-It will explore how normative behavior standards differ from organization
to organization and how behavior impacts on the ability to do a job successfully.

What will this knowledge enable you to do?
-Understand my own *value*
-Enhance my determination *(volition)* to conduct self-management activities
-Develop options to enhance my *versatility*
-Make my personal and professional worth more *visible* to others
-Develop my ability to *visualize* desirable job and career outcomes

---

CHAPTER 18

Sharing Leadership

[T]he most successful leader of all is one who sees another picture not yet actualized. He sees the things which belong in his present picture but which are not yet there. . . . Above all, he should make his co-workers see that it is not *his* purpose which is to be achieved, but a common purpose born of the desires and the activities of the group.

Mary Parker Follett
Dynamic Administration, 1941

What Is Leadership?

In their book *Leaders,* Warren Bennis and Burt Nanus (1985) tell of decades of academic analysis that have provided us with more than 350 definitions of leadership. They mention the thousands of empirical investigations conducted in the past seventy-five years to discover what leadership is, investigations that have not yielded an unequivocal understanding of what distinguishes effective leaders from ineffective leaders (p. 4). Frequently, the definitions that emerged merely reflected fads, fashions, politics, or academic trends and represent nonsense rather than reality (p. 5).

While it is difficult to construct a precise definition of leadership, it is helpful to begin by differentiating leadership and management. Management entails a process of initiating, delegating, directing, motivating, and evaluating. Management is a control process, "the administrative ordering of things"

(Zenger, 1985, p. 44). Managers typically use a well-defined and existing structure for controlling people's activities in producing goods or services. Managers carry out objectives, but leadership involves a process of guiding others toward defining what objectives should be.

Even so, managing and leading cannot be sharply distinguished. As John Gardner, former secretary of Health, Education and Welfare and founder of Common Cause, put it: "Every time I encounter an utterly first-class manager he turns out to have quite a lot of leader in him" (Gardner, 1987, p. 5).

Leadership at each level — group, organization, nation, world — may encompass all the functions and competencies required of a manager and, at times, exceeds them (see Figure 25). Being a leader is a complex activity because it emerges out of the values and vision of the person exercising leadership skills and demonstrating mastery of intricate interpersonal skills. In very broad terms, leadership is a visionary activity that communicates goals and secures behavioral commitment.

Within organizations, distinction needs to be made between leadership that is appointive and leadership that is shared.

Figure 25. Management-Leadership Continuum.

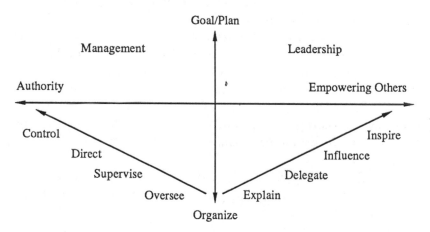

An appointed leader occupies a position because he or she has been designated or elected to take charge. An appointed leader is empowered with the broad authority and extensive resources to make decisions that are quite likely to affect the entire organization. To appointed leaders, at all organizational levels, belong the tasks of providing a transforming vision of what the organization or work group should be about, creating a structure to realize that vision, creating an environment in which both subordinates and colleagues are intrinsically motivated, and demonstrating the links between and among organizational units.

The idea of shared leadership, on the other hand, has emerged and is gaining respect because, practically speaking, large organizations are such complex organisms that decision making cannot be limited to the chief executives but must be dispersed horizontally and vertically throughout the company. As yet, however, we give little credit or encouragement to the literally hundreds of thousands of people exercising dispersed or shared leadership.

Shared leadership has two meanings. The first refers to the functional roles that group members perform. All group members can and should perform leadership functions appropriate to each person and to group needs. "To see the need and fail to respond can be viewed as a failure to fulfill membership responsibilities" (Kolb, Rubin, and McIntyre, 1984, p. 143). Any member can influence group behavior. For example, shared leadership in a quality circle entails having all members perform various roles necessary to completing a task and to maintaining working relationships among group members. The person designated leader at any given point does not so much direct discussion and decision making as facilitate the group's forward movement in achieving tasks that lead to a desired objective.

The second meaning of shared leadership refers to leadership responsibilities that an appointed leader delegates to subordinates. Individually or in a group, subordinates may be encouraged to make decisions and initiate action without seeking the appointed leader's approval. For example, a production work group may be empowered to modify processes to cut production time or improve product quality and asked merely to keep the supervisor informed.

Today's large corporations are "moving in the direction of creating more shared leadership roles through what is referred to as 'intrapreneurship,' the creation of small entrepreneurial units within the organization with the freedom and flexibility to operate virtually as small independent businesses. . . . [For example,] General Motors has thousands of leadership roles available to its employees, and MCI has hundreds" (Bennis and Nanus, 1985, p. 224). As organizations become more comfortable with the concept of shared leadership, an explosion of leadership roles will undoubtedly be available to all levels of employees.

What Theories Support Current Training in Leadership?

Leadership is a behavior or set of behaviors that can be observed and learned. There is, however, no single leadership theory that is appropriate to all situations. Before providing training in shared leadership practices, decision makers therefore need to identify the kinds of leadership situations employees at each organizational level can be expected to encounter.

Leadership theories abound. The theories discussed below were selected because they are more easily adapted to the practice of shared leadership. That is, their component parts lend themselves to the development of practical exercises for communicating the concepts of shared leadership to individuals at all organizational levels as contrasted with theories whose implementation would, in general, limit practice to the upper echelons of management.

Functional Leadership Theory. Functional leadership theory was derived from the group dynamics research done in the late 1940s and early 1950s (Miles, 1981). It rests on three basic tenets: (1) functional leadership is a behavior or set of behaviors that occurs in a group; (2) there are shared functions that can be performed by an appointed leader or by any or all of the group members, depending on the requirements of the situation; and (3) the key leadership functions are facilitating the accomplishment of tasks and maintaining the group relationship.

Training in functional leadership occurs in a group where members, guided by a trainer, simulate real-life experiences and receive feedback on how they behaved during the simulations. The training group provides a psychologically safe environment for members to experiment with new behaviors that they might not feel comfortable practicing in the workplace. The learning process entails several steps:

- Group members experience dissatisfaction with their behaviors.
- Members move on to selecting new behaviors.
- Members practice new behaviors.
- Members get evidence on the results.
- Members generalize, apply, and integrate successful new behaviors.

The content of training in functional leadership includes identifying the properties of groups (such as norms, goals, membership, leadership, and communication); developing skills in diagnosing group problems; and practicing skills in leading groups. Theory about group process is integrated with real-world learning activities (experiential learning). Group members improve their functional leadership skills through the medium of group learning activities.

Contingency Leadership Theory. Contingency (situational) leadership theory correlates effective leadership style with the preparedness of a group to accept the particular style the leader chooses. The contingency model describes situations in which the ability to be effective as a leader depends on whether the leader is task centered or human relations centered. What the group wants and is ready to receive determines which leadership style will be most effective.

Problems occur when the person providing leadership favors one orientation over the other and is unable to change orientation as a situation requires. Within this perspective, functional leadership training provides people with the skills to diagnose a situation and change the situation to fit their leadership style or to adapt their leadership style to fit the situation more comfortably.

Paul Hersey, from the University of Massachusetts, and Kenneth H. Blanchard, author of *The One Minute Manager,* propose a leader effectiveness model (1982) based on the concept of adaptive (contingency style) leader behavior. In the Hersey-Blanchard theory, leadership style entails identifying task and relationship behavior or some combination of behaviors. For leaders to be effective, their styles must be appropriate for the situation in a specific environment (leader, leader's followers, superiors, associates, organizational and job demands) and for the level of maturity (ability and willingness of people to take responsibility for directing their own behavior) of group members.

Training in leadership effectiveness starts with the administration of the Leadership Effectiveness and Adaptability Description (LEAD), an instrument developed by Hersey and Blanchard. This assessment describes twelve situations and four possible leadership actions for each situation. Respondents are asked to select from these alternative actions the one that they believe best reflects their own leadership style. This self-diagnostic activity is the starting point for helping participants enlarge their behavioral capabilities in terms of the connection between task and relationship. In the Hersey-Blanchard model, there are four possible task-relationship links: high task/low relationship; high task/high relationship, high relationship/low task, and low relationship/low task (see Table 11). The appropriate style depends on the maturity/immaturity level of the group (see Figure 26).

Organizational Development Leadership Theory. The organizational development (OD) approach to leadership is based on open systems theory, concepts from group dynamics (team building, conflict resolution, interpersonal relationships, and others), and theories of human organizations (Olmstead, 1980). Basically, OD leadership theory relies on the leader to have a vision (goal) about the group's potential and a commitment to the group's success. Leaders need the ability to identify elements

Table 11. Changes in the Leadership Situation
Expressed in Terms of Task and Relationship.

Variable Being Changed	Change Made	
	Style Favors	
	Task	Relationship
Leader-member Relations	Leaders could be given: 1. Followers who are quite different from them in a number of ways. 2. Followers who are notorious for their conflict.	Leaders could be given: 1. Followers who are very similar to them in attitude, opinion, technical background, race, etc. 2. Followers who generally get along well with their superiors.
Position Power of the Leader	Leaders could be given: 1. High rank and corresponding recognition, i.e., a vice-presidency. 2. Followers who are two or three ranks below them. 3. Followers who are dependent upon their leader for guidance and instruction. 4. Final authority in making all the decisions for the group. 5. All information about organizational plans, thus making them expert in their group.	Leaders could be given: 1. Little rank (office) or official recognition. 2. Followers who are equal to them in rank. 3. Followers who are experts in their field and are independent of their leader. 4. No authority in making decisions for the group. 5. No more information about organizational plans than their followers get, placing the followers on an equal "footing" with the leaders.
Task Structure	Leaders could be given: 1. A structured production task that has specific instructions on what they and their followers should do.	Leaders could be given: 1. An unstructured policy-making task that has no prescribed operating procedures.

Source: P. Hersey and K. H. Blanchard, *Management of Organizational Behavior: Utilizing Human Resources,* 4/e, © 1982, p. 144. Reprinted by permission of Prentice-Hall, Inc., Englewood Cliffs, N.J.

that hinder or help groups develop, and they must be willing to work toward personal development for themselves and others in the group. To be able to deal with any and all situations that might arise, a leader must have a flexible response strategy

Figure 26. Changes in the Leadership Situation
Expressed in Terms of Maturity of Followers.

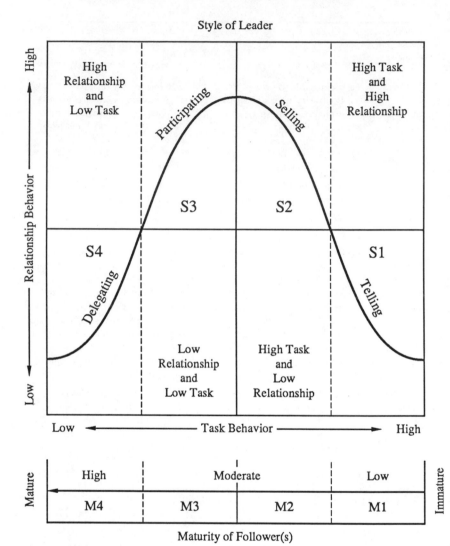

Source: P. Hersey and K. H. Blanchard, *Management of Organizational Behavior: Utilizing Human Resources,* 4th ed., © 1982, p. 152. Reprinted by permission of Prentice-Hall, Inc., Englewood Cliffs, N.J.

because organizations (groups) are dynamic and interactive systems.

Harvard professor Chris Argyris's theory of leadership behavior provides a good example of this approach. In his theory, an effective leader must have skillful diagnostic capabilities in order to be responsive to group needs. Training subject matter includes what to look for in terms of a group's environment and interaction, techniques for identifying what is going on, and learning how to react appropriately to events. Argyris has incorporated his early studies on leadership or professional effectiveness (Argyris and Schön, 1974) in an approach he calls *action science* (Argyris, Putnam, and Smith, 1985).

In action science, a leader's behavior is said to depend on what he or she believes will bring about a desired result. Argyris and Schön (1974) have identified two basic patterns of behavior. In the first behavioral pattern (Model I), leaders design and manage a given situation unilaterally; that is, they own and control the task(s) themselves, they require only their own skills for self-protection, and they stand alone in protecting others. A good example of this type of a role model is an army sergeant. When other people resist this kind of leader's behavior, the leader becomes defensive.

In a different model of behavior (Model II), the leader creates a situation in which the leader and others share in decision making. That is, the task is jointly owned, and there is collaboration to accomplish it. As a consequence, defensive behavior is reduced, and both parties are able to engage in effective problem identification and solving.

Training for more effective behavior usually occurs in a seminar. The basic teaching tool is the case study, frequently prepared by seminar members who record on one side of a sheet of paper a conversation they have had. On the other side, they record each exchange in the conversation, the assumptions they had about the situation, their behavior, and the other party's behavior. The conversation is then analyzed for Model I or Model II behavior to try to determine what is dysfunctional. Training also occurs by examining the interactions of the ongoing group. The specific training content is examination of the behavioral assumptions that people use in their interaction with others. The content is learned experientially as people diagnose their own behaviors and begin to move from Model I to Model II behavior.

Applied Psychoanalytic Leadership Theory. Robert A. Portnoy (1986) of McDonnell Douglas Astronautics Company interprets leadership from the perspective of applied psycho-analysis. For Portnoy, the key factor in effective leadership is avoidance of counterproductive behavior caused by impulsive power (arising from the id) or crippling anxiety and fear (from the superego). Portnoy used this theory of human behavior to develop the *relationship life cycle*. Basically, the relationship life cycle provides a model that helps a leader understand how members of a work team can use conflict to strengthen their commitment to team relationships and to the organization. "Once leaders recognize the presence of conflict, they can redirect energies from defensive and self-serving behaviors into discussion that can help to reclarify roles and redefine expectations" (Portnoy, 1986, p. 55). Portnoy's model (see Chapter Fourteen for a discussion of the essential elements of interpersonal skills and Figure 20 on the relationship life cycle) can be used as the basis for group discussion and analysis of case studies. The specific training content revolves around the application of the psychoanalytical theory of personality to leadership.

Interpersonal, Personal, and Cognitive Leadership Theory. According to the interpersonal, personal, and cognitive theory of leadership, a leader relies on expertise in interpersonal skills to work effectively with people and to move their behavior in the direction of achieving organizational goals. Leadership entails a high order of personal skills: independence, courage of judgment, and ability to tolerate ambiguity and stress.

Training for this type of leadership combines several activities ranging from prescriptive (didactic) sessions to experiential (reality-based) learning, and from apprenticeship to mastery levels (Strong, 1986; Zenger, 1985). Specific content includes theoretical material on leadership and human behavior and training in group leadership techniques, presentation skills, interpersonal communication, decision making, and organizational development.

As noted earlier, all of these leadership theories lend themselves, without great distortion of their basic tenets, to the development of training programs that help empower people throughout an organization, including its nonsupervisory workers, through the acquisition of transferable leadership skills (shared leadership). There are other theories that, although significant in the developing history of leadership theory, depend heavily, if not exclusively, on the top-down exercise of power and the control of significant resources. Therefore, without significant reinterpretation of their basic meanings, they do not lend themselves to adaptation for training of nonsupervisory employees. Such theories are founded on concepts of *power* leadership rather than on the precept of *empowering* leadership. Two of these power leadership theories, however, deserve mention.

Transformational Leadership Theory. The transformational leadership approach has recently captured the corporate and public imaginations. A transformational leader pays attention to what is going on, determines what part of the events at hand are important for an organization's future, sets a new direction, and concentrates the attention of everyone in the organization on it (Bennis and Nanus, 1985, p. 88). The transformational leader imposes a vision on the organization and leads by example.

Transformational leadership is about change, innovation, and entrepreneurship. "This brand of leadership is a behavioral process capable of being learned and managed. It is a leadership process that is systematic, consisting of purposeful and organized search for changes, systematic analysis, and the capacity to move resources from areas of lesser to greater productivity. . . . The challenge is for transformational leadership at all levels in an organization. Rosabeth Kanter's *Change Masters* (1983) focused our attention on such leaders in the middle of an organization. She focused new insights into the role of middle

level leaders in transforming an organization" (Tichy and De-
vanna, 1986, pp. viii and x).

Training in transformational leadership is derived from
study of best practices and presents, in effect, the art of leadership. It is focused on and designed for organizational decision
makers at the supervisory level and above. The delivery modes
for training in transformational leadership have been consulta-
tions, seminars, and articles and books of specific case studies
representing best practices.

Liberal Education Leadership Theory. Liberal education
leadership theory asserts that all good leaders must have a base
of good liberal education because "it is when you get into areas
of leadership that you begin to truly appreciate a liberal education" (Johnston and Associates, 1986, p. 66). Liberal education
theory is a broad and open-minded approach to subject matter, with an active and questioning role for the learner and the
exercise of individual judgment and the application of broadly
applicable skills (pp. 16–17). In other words, the concept of
liberal education leadership training is process oriented rather
than subject oriented. From a theoretical perspective, liberal
education embraces a study of the structure of knowledge underlying functional disciplines as well as the knowledge perspectives that each functional discipline provides on the world; skills
in reasoning, communication, and inquiry; and a sense of values
based on the cultural norms of the surrounding environment.

Although the concept of liberal education leadership is
primarily concerned with preemployment educational preparation, many companies agree with its thrust and provide educational opportunities to their mid- and upper-level managers.
These opportunities include tuition-waiver programs, on-site
course work, readings in the classics and current books, sab-
batical time for attending college and university programs, and
so on.

The content of these programs ranges from the study of
communication skills and current economic and political conditions to the classics, to name only a few subject areas. Increasing corporate interest in these programs is driven by pressure

for more involvement in community and national affairs, which in turn necessitates that leaders have a broad understanding of human history and the human condition. America's corporate recovery, many top leaders believe, depends on corporations being socially responsible and formulating an active political strategy.

What Are the Essential Elements of Training in Shared Leadership?

In the considerable literature available on leadership training, there is both overlap and disagreement among experts on its essential elements. Since no training theory has the endorsement of a majority of leadership experts, to select appropriate training in shared leadership concepts, an organization needs to identify what its objectives are before either creating a course based on a particular theory or selecting a provider with a particular point of view.

Several writers who have examined theories of leadership training have presented summary statements of their own views on what constitutes the essential elements of leadership. Some of their conclusions are discussed below. However, this is by no means a comprehensive discussion of all perspectives on leadership training. Rather, it represents those aspects that seem most pertinent to preparing our next generation to move forward in the practice of shared leadership.

Several experts have focused on the behavioral elements that are central to good leadership (Sinetar, 1981; Zenger, 1985; Lipitt, 1983). Sinetar's point of view is that leadership behaviors fall into three broad categories:

- *Intellectual/cognitive skills,* which involve the ability to diagnose problem situations, deal with abstract ideas, view problems in broad perspective, and anticipate consequences of decisions
- *Personal skills,* which entail judging the appropriateness of decisions, an ability to cope with unpleasant situations and handle stress, and a tolerance for ambiguity

- *Interpersonal skills,* which include the ability to listen to others and respond appropriately, interact easily with people from different cultural backgrounds, inspire confidence in others, recognize and articulate feelings, organize social interaction systems, support members of a group, determine appropriate behavior and courses of action, and organize and direct activities for others

Zenger (1985) believes there are as many as six behavioral dimensions of leadership necessary to create a culture of positive values:

1. Communicating
2. Developing committed followers
3. Inspiring lofty accomplishments
4. Modeling appropriate behavior
5. Focusing attention on important issues
6. Connecting the group to the outside world

Lipitt (1983) has identified seven competencies that a leader needs in order to influence others:

1. A degree of personal security
2. Ability to respond to a given situation
3. Independence and courage of judgment
4. Ability to abstract and conceptualize
5. A tolerance for ambiguity
6. Mental flexibility
7. Ability to analyze and synthesize

Another approach to the possibilities for training in shared leadership is extrapolated from *visionary leadership* theory (Shaskin, 1986). This theory is based on aspects of personality traits, organizational culture, and behavior. Training consists of communicating skills that enhance a person's ability to create a vision that will help an organization or a team anticipate events and prepare for future demands. This kind of leadership entails expressing a vision to others, explaining it, extending it so that it can be implemented, and possibly adapting it and expanding it to accommodate diverse circumstances.

Visionary training helps a leader understand the necessary components of a vision: to change or not to change, to establish a goal, and the primacy of people. This visionary approach is derived from sociologist Talcott Parson's analysis of the critical functions of an organization: adapting to change in the environment, attaining goals that clients and customers will pay for, coordinating activities so that people's actions within the organization or group are integrated, and maintaining a pattern of action by creating an organizational or group culture in which members share the same beliefs and values.

Visionary leaders need to be able to communicate their vision at all levels by incorporating the vision into the organizational or group philosophy, committing resources to implement the vision, and acting personally to set a standard against which others in the organization or group can measure their own behavior. The personal actions of a leader entail five behaviors:

1. Focusing attention on the key issues of the vision
2. Communicating the vision effectively (by listening as well as talking)
3. Demonstrating personal consistency and trustworthiness
4. Displaying respect for oneself and for others
5. Taking calculated risks and making a commitment to seeing those risks through to a conclusion

Becoming competent in and eventually mastering visionary essentials are primary requisites for good transformational leadership.

Psychoanalytic theory leads to the development of techniques that enhance a leader's ability to demonstrate emotionally stable behavior. This involves learning how to maintain control of impulsive power and coping with pressure by thinking options through before taking action. Effective leadership also involves being able to identify and manage "superego" triggers (events that cause anxiety and create feelings of threat or helplessness). Leaders can reduce their vulnerability to these triggers by learning effective time management practices, increasing physical activity to reduce stress, and releasing tension through relaxation exercises.

To apply this theory effectively, a leader must also have learned good communication skills. A leader demonstrates these skills by controlling elements of behavior that interfere with work team functioning. Among the skills required are the ability to engage in conversation for the purpose of establishing relationships, communicating expectations, and having a positive confrontational attitude when workers do not carry out tasks to expectation. Confrontation must be accomplished in a way that does not cause workers to become defensive or anxious about succeeding. When performing in a confrontational situation, a well-trained leader works from the position of problem solver, not from a base of impulsiveness or anxiety.

What Constitutes Competency in Leadership? What Constitutes Mastery?

Few studies that measure competency in leadership skills are available. The competency of nonsupervisory personnel who take leadership training workshops should be measured on the basis of whether or not they demonstrate an increased awareness of the human factors that influence organizational or group performance. These human factors are the dynamics of individual behavior, group behavior, and organizational behavior. Workshop participants should also be able to demonstrate that they are able to diagnose human factor problems correctly and can develop workable corrective action plans. Finally, they should be able to define certain behaviors that are fundamental to becoming an effective leader: demonstrating a willingness to experiment, defining a personal vision and inspiring others to accept it, enabling others to act, providing models for others to follow, and encouraging others to act.

Measuring mastery in the art of leadership is more difficult than measuring competency, although leadership is a much-studied phenomenon with a considerable body of literature. Initial leadership training experiences that lead to competency equip people with only a basic understanding of the elements of this body of knowledge. Mastery can be achieved only after years of practice and feedback in an actual work environment. Not everyone wants to or will move into a leadership position, even in a shared environment. What is important is that each person be empowered with the basic skills necessary to do so, should a necessary situation arise.

What Is an Example of a Successful Workplace Training Program in Leadership?

Well known as an insurance company, Travelers, located in Hartford, Connecticut, has diversified into related financial services such as mutual funds and investment banking and owns several companies that offer a wide variety of such services to its customers.

Travelers employs 38,000 people and in 1987 reported more than $17 billion in revenue. The company's leadership program, Leadership, Power and Influence, began in late 1987 as part of Travelers' revamping of all training programs.

Because its earlier training was not addressing the company's strategic goals, the company built a new training center in 1985 and began implementing a new training agenda. Travelers has made more training programs available for two reasons. First, the organization is restructuring itself to reduce middle management positions, and this requires that employees at lower levels become more skilled in decision making and problem solving. Since fewer managers are responsible for more employees, employees must be able to work well with less supervision and control. Second, technology now allows more information to be available to lower levels of employees, so it is possible for employees below the management level to make more decisions. Decision making at lower levels is more efficient because it is less time-consuming than decision making requiring approval from above. Further, it is advantageous to have decisions made by those closest to and most familiar with a problem because they usually are in the best position for spotting its subtleties. The specific strategic goals that Travelers' new leadership program addresses are achieving improved customer service, facilitating communication and cooperation among business groups, and facilitating the flattening of the organization.

All expenses for training, including travel, are paid through the trainee's department budget. A charge-back system is now being used for the first time. Originally, the leadership program was only offered at company headquarters in Hartford, but beginning in the fall of 1988, it has been offered at other Travelers sites as well.

All Travelers' training programs are voluntary, although supervisors encourage their employees to attend. Supervisory approval is necessary for any employee to attend a course, except for evening programs that employees attend on their own time.

Travelers anticipates offering leadership training to more nonsupervisory personnel because the company believes that leadership is essential for lower levels of personnel, and the course's designer believes that the course is highly applicable and adaptable to nonsupervisory personnel. Currently, the leadership training is formally available to all supervisory and managerial personnel as part of the company's Management Development Continuum—a series of courses designed to prepare all levels of supervisors and managers for their jobs. Equivalent-level nonsupervisory employees, such as technical engineers, may also take the course.

Outside providers are used occasionally to develop course training materials (such as videotapes) and to develop and deliver programs. Travelers has four company instructors who teach the course, and they are supplemented by outside instructors when demand for the course is high. All outside trainers become familiar with Travelers' philosophy through an in-house orientation.

Several evaluation methods are used to measure the success of Travelers' training programs: participants' verbal feedback during and after a course, reaction sheets that participants complete at the end of a course, tests, and interviews with participants and supervisors three and six months after a course. During the course's pilot phase, detailed questionnaires were handed out frequently in order to receive continual feedback from the participants. Now participants are asked to fill out only one questionnaire at the end of the course. This questionnaire is designed to be more thorough and useful than standard reaction sheets. Six weeks after the completion of a leadership program, participants are randomly selected for one-hour follow-up interviews. By the end of 1988, 300 employees had completed the course and evaluations of the leadership program indicated excellent results.

Travelers is conducting demand forecasts to determine whether current training programs should be expanded or discontinued. Preliminary findings indicate that more than 450 people planned to take the course in 1989 and that the number of annual runnings probably will nearly double beyond the current seventeen.

The week-long seminar focuses on developing specific leadership skills that enable employees to work with and influence people over whom they have no formal authority. The goal is for employees to form productive and satisfying work relationships through skills such as collaboration, win-win negotiating, and alliance building.

The first portion of the course focuses on the dynamics of power and the importance of developing a personal power base as a means of influence. Next, participants receive individualized feedback by using an assessment instrument called the Leadership Effectiveness Analysis (LEA). Developed by Management Research Group, the LEA presents a behavioral model of leadership and provides each individual with a feedback profile on twenty-two separate behavioral dimensions. In another module, participants construct a visual model of their relationship networks and analyze the dynamics that characterize relationships with people whom they need to influence and lead. By building upon their LEA and network data, participants delve into the three major skill components of the course: collaboration, negotiation, and alliance building. The collaboration skill focuses on participatory problem solving and teamwork. The negotiation skill emphasizes resolving conflict on the basis of win-win principles. Role rehearsals and individualized videotaping sessions provide practice opportunities and developmental feedback for each participant as he or she learns these interactive skills. The strategic alliance-building skill focuses on transcending personality differences and interoffice conflict to "get the job done." Training emphasizes principles of "strategic networking" and cooperation to attain work goals. Participants complete the course with new leadership skills aimed at enhancing their influence potential and personal power (Robert Fenn, Les Howles, and Rick Wise, telephone interviews, May, July, and August 1988).

What Should Be Included in a Generic Workplace Leadership Curriculum?

The guidelines in Exhibit 24 present one perspective on leadership training. If an organization chooses to implement a leadership seminar in-house or purchase the training from an outside provider, the course may and probably will differ from this. The degree of difference will depend on the theoretical approach espoused by the provider or selected by the organization and on the specific training techniques used.

Exhibit 24. Shared Leadership Training: The Skills for Success in the New Organization.

What are the objectives of this training?
--To learn from the general literature of leadership theory
--To develop a list of generally acceptable characteristics of what makes a good leader
--To develop a consensus on the qualities necessary to succeed in a shared leadership environment
--To explore each participant's leadership strengths and weaknesses
--To strengthen weaknesses and expand strengths in shared leadership skills
--To better understand the dynamics of shared leadership through the vehicle of mini-exercises

What does the new organization look like?
--It is organizationally more compact.
--It consists of matrix management, cross-functional project teams, horizontal responsibility.
--To be competitive, it provides more services/better goods at less cost.

Exhibit 24. Shared Leadership Training: The
Skills for Success in the New Organization, Cont'd.

–It employs new approaches to motivation.
–It pushes leadership functions down through the organization to the point
of production or point of sale.

What do we know about leadership?
–Theories of leadership (functional, visionary, behavioral, and others)
–Definition of leadership
–Shared versus appointive leadership
–Manager versus leader

What makes a person successful at shared leadership and empowering his or
her team? (Kouzes and Posner, 1987, p. 14; Hastings, Bixby, and
Chaudhry-Lawton, 1986, pp. 92–94)
–Challenging the process
  –Searching for opportunities
  –Experimenting and taking risks
–Inspiring a shared vision by making it public
  –Envisioning the future
  –Enlisting others to work toward a shared vision
–Empowering others to act
  –Fostering collaboration
  –Strengthening others to act independently
–Modeling the way
  –Setting the example
  –Planning small wins
–Encouraging the heart
  –Recognizing individual contributions
  –Celebrating accomplishment
–Helping yourself to perform
  –Encouraging frank feedback
  –Developing a support network
–Passing the baton
  –Encouraging others to take over
  –Not fearing to say, "I don't know."

How do you build a shared leadership style?
–By developing an inventory of personal leadership skills
  –Diagnostic (problem solver, critical and creative thinker)
  –Perceptual (communicates well, verbally and through listening)
  –Behavioral (teamwork, negotiation, interpersonal, delegation, motivation,
    coaching/counseling)
–By developing leadership skills through case studies, experiential learning,
  and workshop simulations

PART 9

A Blueprint for Success

Programs created to provide employees with training in the sixteen workplace basic skills are most successful when they (1) are preceded by a well-constructed *action plan* that includes an in-house marketing campaign to marshal management and union support and connect the workplace basics program to the employer's competitive strategies; (2) use a *systematic approach* to training design, development, and delivery; and (3) incorporate an applied learning method that uses a *functional-context approach* to job-specific training.

Together, these three elements constitute an *applied approach* to workplace training to reflect the needs and realities of today's workplace. This innovative process merges political realities such as scarce dollars, technological change, and the sometimes conflicting perspectives of management and labor with state-of-the-art thinking on training design, learning methods, and return on investment.

Like a general preparing for battle, a workplace basics advocate must be aware of the factors that influence a battle plan. Organizational capabilities, workplace changes and challenges, and the cultural dynamics of the organization all come into consideration. More important, marshaling the support of management and unions is a pivotal activity in any effort of this kind; without such support, the program will be devoid of an institutional base and will have a limited chance for success.

The major strength of the applied approach is that it rarely strays from the day-to-day reality of the workplace and is linked to both the individual on the job and ultimately to the employer's bottom line. Research and experience in adult training have shown that linking learning to a worker's actual job carries benefits for both employee and employer. More cost-effective than broad-based training, this applied approach provides training tailored to the employer's specific needs and a more rapid integration of learning with actual job needs, resulting in higher employee productivity. For trainees, the applied approach improves retention because they will immediately and repeatedly use the newly acquired knowledge. This approach also improves job performance because the trainees will apply their new knowledge to actual job needs. And it increases the potential for higher individual earnings and career advancement.

CHAPTER 19

Guidelines for Establishing an Effective Workplace Basics Program

What Is the Applied Approach?

The applied approach is a pragmatic, work-based program development and implementation *system*. At its heart are two basic tenets. First, employers need to have training programs that will consistently improve job performance. Second, the best method for improving job performance is to approach training needs *systematically*.

Because the employer views basic skills problems as barriers to productivity and marketplace success, the employer's primary concern is to fill the gap between what employees know and what they need to know to improve job performance.

The applied approach to training meets employer need through a multistage process (see Exhibit 25). The stages are dynamic and interactive like the changing patterns of a kaleidoscope. All stages exert a significant and continual influence throughout the process.

Obviously, at various points throughout the process, one stage or the other will inevitably dominate. Throughout, however, all stages provide a continual undercurrent of influence. For example, results of a needs assessment will inevitably undergo rethinking as new knowledge is acquired during design and implementation. Evaluation of training effects on actual job per-

401

Exhibit 25. Blueprint for Success.

STEP 1: Identify Job Changes or Problems That May Require Basic
Workplace Skills Training
–Assess the extent of the problem
–Formalize a company-wide representative advisory committee
–Perform a job analysis for selected jobs
–Document employee performance deficiencies on the selected jobs
–Identify population to be targeted for training
–Build cooperation with unions
–Keep good records

STEP 2: Build Management and Union Support to Develop and Implement
Training Programs in Workplace Basics
–Make the case for skills training programs in workplace basics
–Build support for skills training programs in workplace basics

STEP 3: Present Strategy and Action Plan to Management and Unions for
Approval
–Present the strategy/action plan for training
–Select a training program architect: in-house staff vs. external
providers

STEP 4: Perform a Task Analysis of Each Selected Job or Job Family
–Perform a task analysis
–Determine whether to select a quick route through task analysis
and which process is most appropriate
–Review the generic elements of the task analyses processes

STEP 5: Design the Curriculum
–Design a performance-based, functional-context instructional
program
–Design evaluation system
–Design documentation and record-keeping system
–Obtain final budget approval to implement program

STEP 6: Develop the Curriculum
–Prepare the instructional format
–Select instructional techniques
–Select facilities site and designate equipment requirements
–Develop evaluation and monitoring instruments

STEP 7: Implement the Program
–Select and train the instructional staff
–Develop a training contract—yes or no?
–Pilot test (optional)

STEP 8: Evaluate and Monitor the Training Program
–Evaluate the program
–Monitor the daily training
–Connect back to management

---

formance will invariably test and challenge not only the training program design and implementation but also the interpretation of the original needs assessment itself.

Just as the steps in the process are kaleidoscopic, so too are the demands placed on personnel charged with implementing the applied approach to workplace basics. To be effective, personnel must have political savvy, organizational skills, and technical expertise.

First an *investigator* must determine the scope of the workplace problem and the magnitude of any training response. If the initial investigation indicates that a significant training effort is required, an *advocate* with strong organizational and influencing skills is needed to secure management and union support. Once support is secured, the process requires a *training practitioner* schooled in task analysis and training design, development, implementation, and evaluation.

Getting the Job Done: How Does the Process Work?

Following is a summary of the innovative applied approach model for establishing a training program to provide basic workplace skills. Based on input from experts and practitioners, extensive review of state-of-the-art literature, and seminal work in instructional systems design by the U.S. military, the model provides a blueprint for successful establishment and implementation of a workplace basics program.

The following steps do not need to be carried out sequentially. However, if all steps are covered, the chances of establishing and implementing a successful workplace basics program are enhanced significantly. As in baseball, to score a "home run," you have to touch all the bases!

Step 1: Identify Job Changes or Problems That May Require Basic Workplace Skills Training

The first hint of basic skills problems may appear, for example, in a supervisor's report on the slower-than-anticipated integration of a new machine on the shop floor. The new quality circle program — which relies heavily on teamwork — may be

going badly because employees "aren't getting along." Or problems may surface when employees "self-report" that they need
help to handle new responsibilities successfully.

The hint or appearance of a problem is not sufficient,
however; more information is needed. The key to winning management and union support for establishing a workplace basics
program lies in good, solid front-end work.

*Assess the Extent of the Need for Training Due to Job
Changes or Problems.* How far-reaching is the problem? An investigation into the size and scope of the challenge ahead is essential to determine the appropriate level of response. The first step
is to assess the extent of the skills problem and consider options
for mitigating it. Is training the only solution? Sometimes the
solution to a problem is not training but modification of written materials, a change in policy, new technology, and so forth.

Treating the visible signs of distress, however, may only
provide temporary relief. While such signs should be kept in
perspective, they could be symptomatic. Initial reactive measures
should be followed by a shift into a proactive posture. Specific
instances of workplace basics problems could be the tip of the
iceberg — key indicators of more broadly based organization-wide
distress. Undetected and unchecked, such problems can affect
safety, integration of new technology or processes, or individual
career development.

Customer complaints about quality or supervisors' reports
of difficulty in instituting workplace changes can be important
signals. Whenever a worker self-reports basic skills problems
and seeks help, this may be an indication of a more pervasive
problem. Other workers may lack not only the skills but the
courage to come forward and seek help.

*Formalize a Companywide Representative Advisory Com-
mittee.* Involvement of employee representatives as partners during the early part of the investigation and throughout the
workplace basics effort is essential. The usual method for accomplishing this is to establish a representative task force or advisory
committee.

Typically, such committees include representatives from the training and human resources department, operational department heads or supervisors directly affected by any proposed training program, plant managers, union or other employee representatives, and employees themselves. The committee should be carefully constructed. It is an important vehicle for building companywide acceptance for the training program.

A core group from the committee should be designated as the task analysis subcommittee. People with expert knowledge of the jobs to be analyzed can be asked to serve on job-specific review committees that will validate the final task listing for each job or job family in their own areas of expertise.

It is important, politically and strategically, to develop a plan for gaining employee acceptance of the program. The program should be highly visible and publicized in employee newsletters or notices posted on bulletin boards. It is particularly important that employees know the start-up date for training and the person to contact for more information. Employee representatives should be briefed and enlisted to spread the word that the program will not jeopardize anyone's employment status. The positive aspects of the program should always command center stage. The program should be promoted as an effort to improve companywide technical readiness, offer employees a chance for improving their promotion possibilities, and maximize limited training dollars to improve both company and individual performance.

Sensitivity is important because the potential for misunderstanding is great. Employees need to be reassured that the investigation will not result in loss of jobs. If they know what is going on and why, they are more likely to support the establishment of a training program. Without employee concurrence and cooperation, the workplace basics program will never leave the launching pad.

Perform a Job Analysis for Selected Jobs. After the investigation comes job analysis. When selecting jobs for analysis, proceed with caution. Analysis may be limited to those jobs that have been identified through managers' reports about employee deficiencies or through difficulties that employees self-report. If there is any suspicion that these reports are indicative of a larger problem, however, more analyses should be conducted.

The first step in job analysis is to acquire job descriptions, which are general summaries of what a person does on a job and the conditions under which he or she works. In larger companies, job descriptions are usually found on file in company personnel offices. Companies that do not maintain job description files can find adequate substitutes in the *Dictionary of Occupational Titles* published by the U.S. Department of Labor or through a literature search on job descriptions developed by other companies in their industry or related industries.

Obviously, a job description is only the outline of a job. The second step in the job analysis process is to analyze the job description. This identifies the duties of a job or family of jobs and the basic workplace skills required to perform the duties. Following is a typical job description for a machinist.

"The machinist is a skilled metal worker who shapes metal or nonmetal parts by using machine or hand tools. He is able to select the proper tools and materials required for each job; to plan the cutting, bending, etc., and finishing operations in their proper order so that work can be completed according to blueprint or written specifications; interpret blueprints and read precision instruments; and convert fractional values into decimal equivalents.

"The machinist is able to set up and operate most types of machine tools. He selects the appropriate machine and cutting tools that will turn raw material into an intricate, precise part" (Mager and Beach, 1967, p. 8).

Based on this job description, necessary basic workplace skills for a machinist include the following:

- *Problem solving*—must be able to select the proper tools and the appropriate machines
- *Reading for technology*—must be able to interpret blueprints and read precision instruments
- *Computing*—must be able to convert fractional values into decimal equivalents

Job description analysis does not require a heavy commitment of staff or dollars. The activity can be carried out by in-house personnel with some experience in job analysis. If no experienced in-house person is available, an outside expert can be hired to perform this limited task at relatively little cost.

Document Employee Performance Deficiencies on the Selected Jobs. After job analysis is completed, information must be documented about the performance of individual employees or groups of employees in the selected jobs.

At this time, it is important to have a preliminary idea of who will receive training in workplace basics. This information will provide a rough size and scope of the problem and will be necessary for making an effective case to establish a training program. In addition, this groundwork provides the foundation for more sophisticated targeting of trainee populations for tailored curriculum design (see the fifth step in this discussion).

Training that is critical to employer need, however, is frequently required as a condition of employment or promotion. In this case, the most cost-effective approach is to link the basic workplace skills training directly to the job through the applied approach described in this model.

Identify Population to Be Targeted for Training. The term *required training* often raises employee fears that the training is a management scheme for weeding out the less-effective members of the work force. Employees and their representatives should therefore be involved throughout the crafting of the basic workplace skills program, especially during the development of the training curriculum.

The way that required training is presented is very important. The goal is to put employees at ease and to make the training experience a positive one. Employees should be assured that the employer values them and will keep information about their participation confidential. Any public characterizations that might expose personal deficiencies should be avoided. Opportunities should be provided for employees to jointly identify and agree upon their learning goals with their managers. They can accomplish this through a learning-by-objectives (LBO) process, for example.

Build Cooperation with Unions. The chances of establishing a successful basic workplace skills program increase when management and unions provide support. Unions can work as partners with management in setting goals, providing funding, and selecting course content and training providers or in locating volunteers from the rank and file who can be trained to be basic workplace skill trainers.

Enlisting the union or employee representative to help explain the process to the employees, the job analyst must gather employee performance data by means of informal conversations with workers, supervisors, or union representatives; observation of workers; surveys; a review of union grievance records; an analysis of performance appraisals or exit interviews, and so on.

The skill profiles of prior jobholders can also be resources for performance data if there is a skills match with current jobholders. At minimum, such profiles can provide a useful and nonthreatening starting point for analyzing basic workplace skill requirements for a particular job family.

Keep Good Records. Good record keeping is essential. Information gathered at this stage may be useful later to target potential trainees, support training budget requests, or answer inquiries about the need to establish a basic workplace skills training program.

Inquiry into the need for training must be consistent throughout this stage. Are the performance problems, in fact, caused by skill deficiencies? Or are other factors creating these problems, factors such as an insufficient incentive system, a need for more selective recruiting, an inadequate equipment maintenance schedule, poor union-management relations, and so on? Training may not be the appropriate remedy for what ails the employer. Other corrective action such as redesigning hiring specifications, changing equipment maintenance schedules, or rewriting manuals may be a more realistic solution.

*Step 2: Build Management and Union
Support to Develop and Implement
Training Programs in Workplace Basics*

Once training is identified as the solution, the advocacy
process begins. To be successful, an advocate of workplace basics
must skillfully use two tools: logic and politics.

*Make the Case for Skills Training Programs in Workplace
Basics.* The case for establishing a workplace basics program
rests on a foundation of data collected throughout Step 1. It must
be a *proactive* case that illustrates the impact of basic workplace
skills deficiencies on the employer's ability to operate effectively.
Left unchecked, will basic workplace skills deficiencies affect the
employer's bottom line? What is the impact on productivity,
quality, or safety? Has the introduction of new technology or
production processes been impaired?

Being proactive also means anticipating how basic workplace skills deficiencies will affect the employer's future plans.
Will implementation of strategic changes be hampered? Can
product diversification or customization strategies be successful
given employees' current skills? Can the work force cope with
proposed shifts in organizational philosophy or management
practices that demand a higher *base* of skills?

Build Support for Training. The logical arguments for
establishing a workplace basics program can be persuasive. But
success in making the case and in sustaining an organizational
commitment to a training program often rests on less tangible
factors. There must be a base of support for launching a basic
workplace skills program, and this is where politics comes into
play.

Leaders who might support a workplace basics training
program need to be courted. Support from influential managers,
union officials, employee representatives, and the informal
leadership structure is critical to successfully launching a program. Ideally, leadership on this issue from the chief executive
officer (CEO) provides tremendous leverage in getting support

from other levels of the institutional hierarchy, as well as from top union officials or the board of directors.

Coalition building is also essential. The process of coalition building should begin by securing commitment from a respected leadership figure in the institution's formal or informal authority structure. Here again, the CEO is ideal for the role, but coalition leadership may also come from members of the governing board or from employee representatives. Effective coalition leaders are people who can communicate both horizontally and vertically throughout the organization and who can forge networks of allies.

To be most effective, coalitions must include representative stakeholders from both the institution's formal and informal authority structures. Mistrust or resistance to the program can be short-circuited by involving nonsupervisory employees. Union or employee representatives can play important roles in reducing employee anxieties about the program. One effective method of building coalitions is to craft carefully formal or informal stakeholder committees or advisory groups to garner expanded support throughout all organizational levels. To maximize the impact of this political effort, all commitments for support should be leveraged to build additional support and gather additional allies.

This is also the time to begin laying the groundwork for a sustained institutional commitment to the training program. Leadership is a powerful and necessary ingredient for launching any program, but it is fragile and often temporary. Programs that flourish under one leader often wither when that leader's tenure ends unless the leadership vision is institutionalized through administrative processes and structures. Budget and staffing commitments are key here, but they too will be seen as temporary solutions unless basic workplace skills training is linked to the employer's strategic decision-making structure.

Efforts to build institutional commitment must focus on "destigmatizing" basic workplace skills training by making it an accepted and integral part of the employer's overall training agenda rather than a remedial add-on. Whenever training needs are being examined, questions about basic workplace skills deficiencies should be part of the discussion. When training—including basic workplace skills training—is linked to the strategic management process, the inventorying of employee skills will become somewhat routine. In most cases, the inventorying will be triggered by anticipating events such as shifts in institutional strategies, job creation, or new safety regulations.

Step 3: Present Strategy and Action Plan to Management and Unions for Approval

While the workplace basics advocate constructs a base of support, he or she must also be developing an action plan for establishing a basic workplace skills training program. Once developed, the plan should be presented for the approval of management and labor. It should anticipate and address employee concerns. If a union is proposed as a training program co-funder and operator, it will need to have an equal vote with management in order for the program to advance toward its goals.

Present Strategy/Action Plan for Training. A formal meeting with key decision makers should be requested to brief them on the plan. Written copies of the plan should be provided to each person responsible for approving the proposal. Both the plan and the presentation should be comprehensive and concise and include these items:

- Conclusions that can be drawn from preliminary research (of step 1)
- Strategic implications of those findings
- A recommendation that a program be developed
- Options for establishing a training program (including rough cost analysis; time frame; program content, responsibilities, and design; profile of barriers to implementation such as cost, staffing, and so on)
- The recommended option based on cost versus benefit to the employer

Select a Training Program Architect: In-House Staff versus External Providers. An important part of the training proposal is consideration of whether an outside training provider should be called in to assist with all or part of the training program. Would an outside provider be needed to design and develop customized training or provide an off-the-shelf training program? Should a combination of in-house expertise and outside consultation be used?

If the answer is to seek outside help, a variety of sources are available. Local school districts, community colleges, universities, nonprofit literacy groups, for-profit organizations and individuals, private industry councils (PICs), and others in the community can supplement in-house expertise. Small businesses (those with fewer than 500 employees) should also consider larger local employers as potential providers. Larger companies may be willing and interested in allowing access to their training for a fee. If proprietary rights are not an issue, these companies may choose to provide a smaller company with copies of already developed curricula for use free of charge or under a contractual arrangement.

Because outside providers have varying strengths and weaknesses, not all will be equally suitable. A competitive bidding process or request for proposal (RFP) is a useful tool for finding a resource that meets specific employer needs. But before a selection is made, the following minimum information about providers under consideration for the job should be gathered:

- Experience with training in an applied context
- Experience in working with adults over twenty-one years of age
- Approach to program design and development
- Capability to perform the designated tasks
- Prior experience and success rate
- Cost and time requirements
- References

The hiring agent must proceed with caution and be clear and exact about required services.

Step 4: Perform a Task Analysis
of Each Selected Job or Job Family

The fourth step is to identify the skills required to perform the tasks and duties of the specific jobs to be featured in the workplace basics training. This process or *task analysis* is keyed to the competencies actually required to perform work in the targeted jobs. It is a more in-depth and structured look at the descriptions of job duties that were prepared in the initial investigation of Step 1.

Perform a Task Analysis. An accurate task analysis lays the foundation for a good instructional program. With information gained from the task analysis, instructors can develop lessons on the skills, knowledge, and attitudes learners need in order to perform a job successfully.

In any task analysis, the first steps are to review all related literature on the subject and collect all available task listings, comprehensive lists of the tasks performed by workers on a particular job. There are many excellent published listings of job tasks that can be obtained from such institutions as the National Center for Vocational Education, the V-TEC's Consortium, and several state education agencies. In all instances, but particularly where existing task listings are being adapted, it is crucial for task analyses to be accurate and validated by company employees familiar with the job.

A task analysis usually breaks a job into three component parts. The *task listing* is a comprehensive list of tasks performed by workers on a job. The *task detailing* is a systematic breakdown of each task to determine the skills, sequencing, knowledge, and attitudes an individual needs to know in order to perform a single task successfully. The *task inventory* consists of lists of duties and tasks and questions for incumbent workers about the way each task is performed.

There are many techniques for performing a task analysis. Some commonly in use include open-ended or closed questionnaires, individual or group interviews, observation of workers on the job, and analysis of existing documents such as manuals or other instructional materials.

Sophisticated methodologies that combine several of these techniques into integrated systems for performing task analyses have also been developed. These include DACUM (*Developing a Curriculum*) by the National Academy for Vocational Education; the taxonomic approach developed by the San Mateo, California, County Office of Education and based on a compilation of basic skills common to seventy-five jobs; and the Literacy Task Analysis developed by Larry Mikulecky, director of the learning skills center at Indiana University.

The entire process of task analysis can be distilled to the following generic components:

- Select the jobs to be analyzed.
- Develop or secure a preliminary list of duties and tasks performed in each job, focusing on basic workplace skills.
- Review, refine, and revise the list of skills by means of expert committees.
- Verify or validate the skills necessary to perform the jobs.
- Perform a task detailing focused on basic workplace skills for each task selected for inclusion in the training program.

Any model for analysis must be based on obtaining information from expert or highly skilled workers. Without this input, information on how a job ought to be performed is simply speculation.

Step 5: Design the Curriculum

To ensure continuity throughout program design, development, and implementation, the position of program manager should be filled no later than the design stage. Other key personnel may also be hired early on, depending on the organization's internal needs. These key people should play an integral role throughout the evolution of the program. The curriculum design step includes design of the instructional program, consideration of the evaluation instruments and process, design of a record-keeping system, and crafting of an operational budget.

Curriculum design is strongly influenced by the duties and tasks of the targeted jobs. But it should also take the trainees into account. Often, employers will provide basic workplace skills training programs as an employee benefit. Such programs are for employees who are seeking self-improvement or who sense that keeping a job or securing a promotion is not possible without improving their skills. Basic workplace skills programs of this kind are generally not driven by the economic or strategic needs of the employer and therefore do not necessarily need to be linked to the employee's job. In such cases, it is often more cost-effective for an employer to have an external provider design a generalized curriculum for a particular workplace skill or simply to provide tuition reimbursement for basic workplace skills training that the employee selects from an outside provider.

Design a Performance-Based, Functional-Context Instructional Program. Most state-of-the-art training designs today are performance based and focus on the trainee's mastering the tasks that have been designated as essential for successful performance on the job. Standards for successful performance are clear, and success is measured by learning, not by the amount of time the employee takes to perform the task. This approach is particularly effective for adults when it is combined with the functional-context learning methodology that uses job-related materials and concepts as the basis for training. The functional-context approach is geared toward filling the gap between what the trainee already knows and what he or she needs to know to be effective on the job. It takes into account the existing knowledge and skills of the trainee and builds upon them.

This approach grew out of a highly controversial social experiment called Project 100,000, a military experiment that took place during the period of the Vietnam War and the "War on Poverty," where there emerged the practice of "functional context" learning. The project was initiated to develop new training for low-aptitude personnel entering the military and focused on developing methodologies for identifying cognitive skill demands of work and how to teach such skills.

Although there is some argument about the differences between education and training, the functional-context approach transcends such differences and operates from similar assumptions about how the human mind operates. Tom Sticht, one of the pioneers in functional-context training, describes it as follows:

> The functional context principle states that skills and knowledge are best learned if they are presented in a context that is meaningful to the person. Thus, rather than teaching students who need job-oriented basic skills to read, write, and compute using general literacy materials, it is better to use job reading and numeracy materials and tasks. The more similar the basic skills training tasks are to the actual job tasks, the greater will be the likelihood that the training will pay off in improved performance of job literacy tasks. Thus, for youth and adults aiming at work in a given industry or organization, the use of job-related materials serves two purposes. On the one hand, it provides a functional context for the learner — that is he or she can see that the materials are relevant to the employment goal — and hence motivation to use the material is elevated. On the other hand, the organization can see that the training is relevant to its needs and that there is some likelihood of the trainees actually becoming competent in the performance of job-relevant skills. Thus organizational motivation to participate in the training is gained [Sticht and Mikulecky, 1984, p. 33].

The major point to understand in developing a functional-context training program for adults is that the human mind should be thought of as an information-processing system that develops new capabilities over time by "using prior knowledge and skills as a means for acquiring new knowledge and skills" (Sticht and Mikulecky, 1984, p. 31).

There is an ongoing dialogue about the differences between education and training, particularly applying to learning in a functional context. Opponents of functional-context training state that it takes months if not years of study and learning to achieve competence in certain areas and that functional-context training is usually a relatively short-term fix. The time factor is especially true with reference to the competence skills of reading, writing, and computation, but it also has relevance for the rest of the basic workplace skill groups. People who make this argument, however, miss the point, which is that competence can also be achieved during on-the-job functional-context training by emphasizing the same comprehension, studying, and learning skills that are used in school courses. Furthermore, employers who are serious about upgrading their work force will be more inclined to fund extended training when necessary if they see a direct relationship to the job to be done. The result of such programs is that "job and career knowledge can be developed while processing skills that are more generally useful are obtained" (Sticht, Armstrong, Hickey, and Caylor, 1987, p. 134).

From the employer perspective, the advantage of a functional-context approach to training is that it is more likely to achieve the objective of upgrading a work force at a fraction of the cost of academic model programs. Overall this cost-effective and performance-based method of achieving a productive work force contributes to the organization's strategic goals. Education and training organizations must come to understand that if they want to encourage the upgrading of this country's current work force and avoid employee dislocation and plant shutdowns, then the mission and goals of the employer organizations must play as prominent a role in the learning process as the needs of the individual.

At the heart of the design process for a performance-based, functional-context curriculum are two key concepts: written performance objectives and criterion-referenced testing. Performance objectives are essential to measuring training success and should be written for each task selected for training. In a performance-based system, learners need to master only what they do not already know to carry out a specific task successfully. Therefore, the objectives should specify what the learners are currently able to do on the job, the conditions under which they must perform while demonstrating mastery of the objective, and the desired future level of performance.

Criterion-referenced testing involves pretraining and post-training test phases. The pretraining test phase is diagnostic and determines where employee skill deficiencies lie. Posttraining criterion tests should be of the identical length and format as the pretest but test only the task behaviors treated during the instructional program. Criterion-referenced tests emphasize learner performance. Their objective is to verify the learner's mastery of tasks identified in the performance objectives. Construction of relevant, functional pretests and posttests is accomplished most effectively after the performance objectives have been written and the learning materials developed.

Using a performance-based approach accelerates the learning process and enhances learner retention. For example, a person who is working as a machinist and already knows how to change fractions into decimals would not be required to relearn this skill during training. He or she would move on to new areas of learning.

Design Evaluation System. In the curriculum design step, it is important to consider how the training program will be evaluated, what records are important, and how much it will cost to operate the program.

Without sound, objective training evaluation, we have only subjective assessments of value and success. In these times of tight resources, that is not enough to justify continuing a training program. Evaluation must be keyed to discovering the most appropriate and cost-effective training response and to illustrating how that training helps the organization meet its strategic goals. Although viewed traditionally as the final activity of a training program, an evaluation system must be planned during the curriculum design step. A good evaluation system identifies program procedures for collecting, interpreting, and reporting data and specifies when and from whom program data will be collected. Such a system ensures the means for gathering information that the evaluator will use to compare behavior before and after training and draw conclusions. (A more detailed discussion of evaluation appears under Step 8.)

Design Documentation and Record-Keeping System. It is also important during the design step to establish a documentation process to collect, record, analyze, and report accurate data on individual learners' progress and performance. This documentation should provide written proof that the training occurred, as well as evidence that it was provided according to the curriculum design.

At this time a good record-keeping system should also be designed. This should include employee learning contracts and other types of backup documentation. Decisions on how record keeping will be done (manually or by computer) and by whom, as well as how extensive it will be, will determine the design of the forms to be developed. Only data directly related to the training (such as attendance, hours of instruction, pretest and posttest results, employee's educational background) should be included.

Obtain Budgeting Approval to Implement Program. This is also the time to consider the budget implications of program operation. Before extensive time and energy go into the development of curriculum materials, a final implementation budget should be presented for management's approval and the go-ahead to implement the training program.

Step 6: Develop the Curriculum

The curriculum development step involves crafting the curriculum; integrating instructional techniques; pinpointing delivery systems, facilities, and equipment; and developing measurement tools.

Prepare the Instructional Format. After the go-ahead to implement the training program has been given, it is time to prepare the course outline, individual lesson plans, and instruction materials. In the course outline, the tasks should be put in priority order, as they will be presented during instruction, generally moving from simplest to most complex. Because the goal of instruction is improved job performance, the tasks should be sequenced according to which ones will be most important for the employee to master in order to achieve that goal.

Individual lesson plans should identify what a learner actually needs to do on the job, not what the instructor might like to teach. The focus should be on task details and performance objectives.

Instructional materials should be developed or adapted from existing resources where appropriate. Only material that will help the learner satisfy the performance objectives should be selected for each task. Material should be at the level or move toward the level the learner will use on the job. Material developed specifically for children should be avoided because most research shows that adults learn differently from children.

Select Instructional Techniques. The process of curriculum development also involves selecting instructional techniques that will minimize costs without affecting the quality of results. The techniques used will determine the type of facility, the number of instructors, the cost of producing original materials, and so on. All of these factors plus the impact on individual learning must be taken into consideration.

Several delivery systems can be used to present instructional material, all of which have varying strengths and weaknesses. These include traditional classroom, multimedia classroom, tutored video classroom, interactive TV classroom, self-study, guided-learning center, computer-based training (CBT), and interactive videodisc with personal computer.

Select Facilities Site and Designate Equipment Requirements. Next come decisions about facilities and hardware. Selecting appropriate facilities and training equipment depends on a number of variables, including the type of learning required (heavy equipment, production line, office), instructional strategies selected (computer-assisted, traditional classroom, self-study), location (on- or off-site), number of learners (few or many), budgetary restrictions, time available for training, training presenter (in-house or external), and the curriculum.

Develop Evaluation and Monitoring Instruments. The final phase of the curriculum development step involves the development of evaluation and monitoring instruments. The development process should include line managers and supervisors in order to establish a common perspective on the kind of training needed and the standards that constitute improved work performance after training.

Step 7: Implement the Program

One of the most important activities during the early implementation period is shifting the employee awareness campaign into high gear to "talk up" the new training program. Meetings should be scheduled to answer employee questions and present a positive view of the program. Information about the training should also be prominently displayed in employee newsletters and on bulletin boards.

Select and Train the Instructional Staff. Another important part of the early implementation period is staff selection. The program manager was brought on early in the design stage and should have actively participated in the development of the training program design. The manager is also responsible for developing all program operating objectives; planning, organizing, staffing, and supervising the training project; and evaluating and linking the training program to the employer's operations and goals. The person selected for this position should have a substantial knowledge of the employer's corporate culture and practices, as well as a background in adult education, training, and evaluation.

As part of the staffing function, the manager may select an outside provider to assist with all or part of the training program. Whether the program is to be provided by in-house or external staff, a number of key staff positions must be filled.

The second most important staff position is program administrator. The administrator evaluates instructional staff performance, selects facilities and equipment, schedules instructional staff, ensures that course material is prepared and available, and assures program follow-up. This person should have a strong background in project management and instructional technology, some background and experience in working with adults, and some experience in using evaluation techniques.

Together the program manager and program administrator should select the instructional staff. Successful instructors in job-related basic workplace training programs must have special skills as revealed by answers to the following questions:

- Is the person familiar with adult learning and the psychology of learning?
- Has the person actually worked with adults and is information available on his or her performance?
- What is the person's level of subject expertise?
- Will the person be comfortable using new subject curricula and instructional approaches that are not school based?
- Does the person have experience in teaching basic workplace skills in a job-related context?
- Will the person be responsive to company requirements and working with company personnel?

Few companies can afford to hire full-time instructors of basic workplace skills, but there are other options. Experienced employees and managers may take train-the-trainer courses to become part- or full-time peer trainers. They should also receive special training in instructional techniques and support counseling. Peer trainers will be most effective if paired with professional trainers. Together these two instructional staffs can also facilitate companywide employee "buy-in" in a manner that cannot be replicated in any other way.

Other options include contracting with an external provider for program delivery or hiring part-time instructors from outside the organization. With creative scheduling, these approaches can have a payoff in flexibility and quality programming.

It is also important to consider counseling an integral part of a successful training program. Many employees will not have been in a formal learning situation for some time and will be afraid of failure. Some will also have had negative experiences in school and will be anxious about whether they will perform well in this new program. Providing a counselor to communicate the company's commitment to successful learning is a necessary reinforcement mechanism. While counseling may be handled by the instructional staff, a separate counseling staff is recommended.

Develop a Training Contract—Yes or No? The performance-based training approach uses a *competency profile* to track trainee progress toward acquiring competencies for a particular functional job or area. Additional documentation might include the learning contract, which details learning objectives and measures of achievement, records of attendance and hours of instruction, pretest and posttest results, or trainee educational background information, and so on.

Step 8: Evaluate and Monitor the Training Program

Evaluation provides information about the efficiency, effectiveness, and usefulness of the program. Without evaluation, there is no objective way to determine whether training has made a difference.

Evaluate the Program. Once a program has been run at least once and employees have returned to their workstations, evaluation can begin. The design, development, and implementation establish the groundwork for effective evaluation. Available data sources should include surveys of trainee reactions, pretests and posttests to measure learning, observation of employee behavior, and interviews. The data should identify changes, such as productivity improvements, cost reductions, quality improvements, or reduced turnover, that have occurred in the workplace since the training. All factors must be considered when evaluating the effectiveness of training. No one factor alone will provide accurate feedback.

Monitor the Daily Training. Evaluation should be performed periodically to determine whether program goals are being met. Also important, program monitoring provides continuing feedback on whether instruction is working well from day to day. Usually, personnel trained specially in evaluation techniques or an independent evaluation specialist carries out program evaluation. Program monitoring falls within the domain of the program manager, project administrator, and instructional staff.

Monitoring and evaluation should be viewed as *living processes*. Together, they provide the information for adjusting and improving the program design to assure efficient, effective delivery of the basic workplace skills training program.

Because the applied approach to training in workplace basics is one that emphasizes relevance to the workplace and to employer need, evaluation and monitoring are especially important. They provide the basic data for making the case to management that training is important to the organization's strategic goals and daily operations.

References
and Suggested Readings

Abella, K. T. *Building Successful Training Programs.* Reading, Mass.: Addison-Wesley, 1986.

Adkins, W. R. "Life Skills Education for Adult Learners." *Adult Leadership,* 1973, *22* (2), 55–58, 82–84.

Adkins, W. R. "Life Skills Education: A Video-Based Counseling/Learning Delivery System." In D. Larson (ed.), *Teaching Psychological Skills: Models for Giving Psychology Away.* Pacific Grove, Calif.: Brooks/Cole, 1984.

Albrecht, K., and Zemke, R. *Service America! Doing Business in the New Economy.* Homewood, Ill.: Dow-Jones-Irwin, 1985.

Alessandra, A., and Wexler, P. "Breaking Tradition: The Sales Pitch as Customer Service." *Training and Development Journal,* 1985, *39* (11), 41–43.

Altman, J. W. *Transferability of Vocational Skills: Review of Literature and Research.* Information Series No. 103. Columbus: Center for Research in Vocational Education, Ohio State University, 1976.

Amabile, T. *The Social Psychology of Creativity.* New York: Springer-Verlag, 1983.

American Society for Training and Development. *Models for Excellence.* Alexandria, Va.: American Society for Training and Development, 1983.

American Society for Training and Development. *Info-Line.* Alexandria, Va.: American Society for Training and Development, 1988.

Amundson, N. E., and Borgen, W. A. "Coping with Unemployment: What Helps and What Hinders." *Journal of Employment Counseling*, 1987, *24*, 96–106.

Anderson, J., Boyle, C., Farrell, R., and Reiser, B. "Cognitive Principles in the Design of Computer Tutors." In *Proceedings from the Sixth Annual Meeting of the Cognitive Science Society*, 1984.

Anderson, R. C., Hiebert, E. H., Scott, J. A., and Wilkinson, J.A.G. *Becoming a Nation of Readers: The Report of the Commission on Reading*. Report prepared for the National Academy of Education, the National Institute of Education, and the Center for the Study of Reading, Contract No. 400-83-0057. Washington, D.C.: U.S. Department of Education, 1985.

Anderson, R. C., Pichert, J. W., and Shirey, L. L. *The Effects of the Reader's Schema at Different Points in Time*. Technical Report No. 19. Washington, D.C.: National Institute of Education, 1979. (ED 169 523)

Anderson, W. S. "Opportunities for Consultants." Paper presented at the 37th annual meeting of the Conference on College Composition and Communication, New Orleans, La., 1986.

Applebee, A. N. *Writing in the Secondary School*. Research Report No. 21. Urbana, Ill.: National Council of Teachers of English, 1981.

Applebee, A. N., Langer, J. A., and Mullis, I.V.S. *The Reading Report Card: Progress Toward Excellence in Our Schools*. Princeton, N.J.: National Assessment of Educational Progress, Educational Testing Service, 1985.

Argyris, C., Putnam, R., and Smith, D. M. *Action Science*. San Francisco: Jossey-Bass, 1985.

Argyris, C., and Schön, D. A. *Theory in Practice: Increasing Professional Effectiveness*. San Francisco: Jossey-Bass, 1974.

Argyris, C., and Schön, D. A. *Organizational Learning*. Reading, Mass.: Addison-Wesley, 1978.

Armed Forces Staff. *Handbook for Designers of Instructional Development*. 6 vols. Washington, D.C.: U.S. Department of Defense, 1978.

Baker, L., and Brown, A. L. "Metacognitive Skills and Reading." In P. D. Pearson (ed.), *Handbook of Reading Research*. New York: Longman, 1984.

Bandler, R., and Grinder, J. *Frogs into Princes.* Moab, Utah: Real People Press, 1979.

Bandler, R., and Grinder, J. *Reframing: Neurolinguistic Programming and the Transformation of Meaning.* Moab, Utah: Real People Press, 1982.

Bandura, A. *Principles of Behavior Modification.* New York: Holt, Rinehart & Winston, 1969.

Barker, L. *Listening Behavior.* Englewood Cliffs, N.J.: Prentice-Hall, 1971.

Bateson, G. *Steps to an Ecology of Mind.* New York: Ballantine, 1972.

Beane, J. A., and Lipka, R. A. *Self-Concept, Self-Esteem, and the Curriculum.* New York: Teachers College Press, 1986.

"Behind the News." *Human Resource Executive,* Jan. 1988, p. 13.

Bennis, W., and Nanus, B. *Leaders.* New York: Harper & Row, 1985.

Beriter, C., and Scardamalia, M. "From Conversation to Composition: The Role of Instruction in a Developmental Process." In R. Glaser (ed.), *Advances in Instructional Psychology.* Hillsdale, N.J.: Erlbaum, 1982.

Berk, R. A. (ed.). *Criterion-Referenced Measurement: The State of the Art.* Baltimore, Md.: Johns Hopkins University Press, 1980.

Berlin, G., and Sum, A. *Toward More Perfect Union: Basic Skills, Poor Families, and Our Economic Future.* New York: Ford Foundation, 1988.

Bion, W. *Experience in Groups.* New York: Basic Books, 1959.

Bishop, J. "Information Externalities and the Social Pay-Off." Working Paper No. 87–06. Ithaca, N.Y.: Cornell University, 1987.

Black, D. E., and Foley, E. M. "Career Planning: Where Do I Go from Here? A Training Module." *Trainer's Workshop,* 1988, *2* (7), 11–45.

Black, J. L., Muehlenhard, C. L., and Massey, F. H. "Social Skills Training to Improve Job Maintenance." *Journal of Employment Counseling,* 1985, *22,* 151–160.

Block, P. *The Empowered Manager: Positive Political Skills at Work.* San Francisco: Jossey-Bass, 1987.

Bloom, B. *Taxonomy of Educational Objectives: The Cognitive Domain.* New York: McKay, 1956.

Bloom, B. *Taxonomy of Educational Objectives: The Affective Domain.* New York: McKay, 1964.

Bohn, M. J., Jr. "Vocational Maturity and Personality." *Vocational Guidance Quarterly,* Dec. 1966, pp. 123–126.

Bolman, L. G., and Deal, T. E. *Modern Approaches to Understanding and Managing Organizations.* San Francisco: Jossey-Bass, 1984.

Bolton, R. *People Skills: How to Assert Yourself, Listen to Others, and Resolve Conflicts.* New York: Touchstone, 1979.

Bonner, H. "The Proactive Personality." In D. H. Spain (ed.), *The Human Experience: Readings in Sociocultural Anthropology.* Homewood, Ill.: Dorsey Press, 1975.

Bormuth, J. R. "Reading Literacy: Its Definition and Assessment." In J. B. Carroll and J. S. Chall (eds.), *Toward a Literate Society.* New York: McGraw-Hill, 1975.

Bostrom, R. N., and Waldhart, E. S. "Memory Models and the Measurement of Listening." *Communication Education,* 1988, *37* (1), 1–13.

Boyatzis, R. *The Competent Manager: A Model for Effective Performance.* New York: Wiley, 1982.

Bransford, J. D., and others. "Differences in Approaches in Learning: An Overview." *Journal of Experimental Psychology: General,* 1982, *111,* 390–395.

Bray, D. W. "The Assessment Center Method." In D. H. Montross and C. J. Shinkman (eds.), *Career Development in the 1980s: Theory and Practice.* Springfield, Ill.: Thomas, 1981.

Brickell, H. M. "National Perspectives on Career Education." In D. M. Neilson and H. F. Hjelm (eds.), *Reading and Career Education.* Newark, Del.: International Reading Association, 1975.

Broadwell, M. (ed.). *The Supervisor and on the Job Training.* Reading, Mass.: Addison-Wesley, 1986.

Brock, W. E. "Future Shock: The American Work Force in the Year 2000." *American Association for Community, Technical and Junior Colleges Journal,* 1987, *57* (4), 25–26.

Brookfield, S. D. *Understanding and Facilitating Adult Learning.* San Francisco: Jossey-Bass, 1986.

Brookfield, S. D. *Developing Critical Thinkers.* San Francisco: Jossey-Bass, 1987.

Brostrom, R. "Training Style Inventory." In J. E. Jones and J. W. Pfeiffer (eds.), *The 1979 Annual Handbook for Group Facilitators.* San Diego, Calif.: University Associates, 1979.

Brown, D., Brooks, L., and Associates. *Career Choice and Development.* San Francisco: Jossey-Bass, 1984.

Brown, J. I., and Carlsen, G. R. *Brown-Carlsen Listening Comprehension Test.* San Diego, Calif.: Harcourt Brace Jovanovich, 1952.

Burgoon, J., and Saine, T. *The Unspoken Dialogue.* Boston: Houghton Mifflin, 1978.

Burley-Allen, M. *Listening: The Forgotten Skill.* New York: Wiley, 1982.

Burlingham, B. "Managers' Manager: John Humphrey." *Inc.,* 1987, *9* (7), 48–58.

Business Council for Effective Literacy (BCEL). *Job-Related Basic Skills.* New York: Business Council for Effective Literacy, 1987.

Business Council for Effective Literacy (BCEL). *Dumbing Down or Smartening Up?* New York: Business Council for Effective Literacy, April 1988a.

Business Council for Effective Literacy (BCEL). *Approaching Workforce Literacy.* New York: Business Council for Effective Literacy, July 1988b.

Butler, E. P., Hahn, A., and Darr, J. *The Literacy-Employment Equation: Education for Tomorrow's Jobs.* San Francisco: Far West Laboratory for Educational Research and Development, 1985.

Byrnes, J. F. "Negotiating: Master the Ethics." *Personnel Journal,* 1987a, *66* (6), 96–101.

Byrnes, J. F. "Creative Confrontations: The Art of Negotiating." *Trainer's Workshop,* Aug. 1987b, pp. 11–64.

Cairo, P. "Career Planning and Development in Organizations." In Z. Leibowitz and L. Daniel (eds.), *Adult Career Development: Concepts, Issues, and Practices.* Alexandria, Va.: American Association for Counseling and Development, 1985.

Campbell, D. *Take the Road to Creativity, and Get Off Your Dead End.* Greensboro, N.C.: Center for Creative Leadership, 1985.

Campbell, J. P., and Pritchard, R. D. "Motivation Theory in

Industrial and Organizational Psychology." In M. D. Dunnette (ed.), *Handbook of Work and Organizational Psychology*. New York: Wiley-Interscience, 1983.

Campbell-Thrane, L., Manning, K., Okeafor, K., and Williams, E. J. *Building Basic Skills: Models for Implementation*. Columbus: National Center for Research in Vocational Education, Ohio State University, 1983.

Card, S., Moran, T., and Newell, A. *The Psychology of Human-Computer Interaction*. Hillsdale, N.J.: Erlbaum, 1983.

"Career Development Programs: Success Is in the Supervisor." *Bulletin on Training*, 1988, *13* (2), 4.

Carkhuff, R. R., and Fisher, S. G. *Instructional Systems Design I: Designing the Instructional System*. Amherst, Mass.: Human Resources Development Press, 1984.

Carlisle, K. E., and Arwady, J. P. *Analyzing Jobs and Tasks*. Englewood Cliffs, N.J.: Educational Technology Publications, 1986.

Carlisle, K. E., and Murphy, S. E. *Practical Motivation Handbook*. New York: Wiley, 1986.

Carnevale, A. P. *Human Capital: A High Yield Corporate Investment*. Alexandria, Va.: American Society for Training and Development, 1983.

Carnevale, A. P. *Jobs for the Nation: Challenges for a Society Based on Work*. Alexandria, Va.: American Society for Training and Development, 1985.

Carnine, D., Kameenui, E. J., and Coyle, G. "Utilization of Contextual Information in Determining the Meaning of Unfamiliar Words." *Reading Research Quarterly*, 1984, *19* (2), 188–204.

Cassidy, J. *Quality Improvement at the IRS*. Silver Spring, Md.: Internal Revenue Service, 1987.

Center for Employment and Income Studies. *An Introduction to Competency-Based Employment and Training Programming for Youth Under the Job Training Partnership Act*. Waltham, Mass.: Center for Employment and Income Studies, 1983.

Center for Public Resources. *Basic Skills in the U.S. Work Force*. Washington, D.C.: Center for Public Resources, 1983.

Cetron, M. J. *Schools of the Future: How American Business and*

Education Can Cooperate to Save Our Schools. New York: McGraw-Hill, 1985.

Cetron, M., and O'Toole, T. *Encounters with the Future: A Forecast of Life into the 21st Century.* New York: McGraw-Hill, 1982.

Charner, I., and Rolzinski, C. A. *Responding to the Educational Needs of Today's Workplace.* San Francisco: Jossey-Bass, 1987.

Chi, M.T.H., and Glasser, R. *Problem-Solving Ability.* Research/Technical Report No. LRDC-1985-86. Washington, D.C.: Psychological Sciences Division, National Institute of Education and the Office of Naval Research, 1985. (ED 256 630)

Clopton, S. W. "Microcomputer Based Negotiation Training for Buyers." *Journal of Purchasing and Materials Management,* 1986, *22* (2), 16–23.

Committee for Economic Development. *Children in Need, Investment Strategies for the Educationally Disadvantaged.* New York: Committee for Economic Development, 1987.

Cooney, J. *Linking Math, Reading, and Writing Skills.* CETA (Comprehensive Employment & Training Act) Staff Development Project. San Mateo, Calif.: County Office of Education, 1984.

Cornell Institute for Occupational Education. *Teaching Mathematics Skills in Vocational Education.* Ithaca, N.Y.: Cornell Institute for Occupational Education, 1980.

Craik, F.I.M., and Lockhart, R. S. "Levels of Processing: Framework for Memory Research." *Journal of Verbal Learning and Verbal Behavior,* 1972, *11,* 671–684.

Crites, J. O. *Career Maturity Inventory.* New York: McGraw-Hill, 1978.

Crites, J. O. "Testing for Career Adjustment and Development." *Training and Development Journal,* 1982, *36* (2), 20, 22–28.

Crites, J. O. *Career Mastery Inventory.* Chicago: Northwestern University, 1988.

Culbert, S. A., and McDonough, J. J. *The Invisible War: Pursuing Self-Interests at Work.* New York: Wiley, 1980.

Dansereau, D. "The Development of a Learning Strategies Curriculum." In H. I. O'Neil, Jr. (ed.), *Learning Strategies.* New York: Academic Press, 1978.

Darkenwald, G. G. "Some Effects on the Obvious Variable: Teacher's Race and Holding Power with Black Adult Students." *Adult Education Quarterly,* 1975, *35,* 220–228.

Darkenwald, G. G. *Retaining Adult Students.* Columbus: National Center for Research in Vocational Education, Ohio State University, 1981.

Darkenwald, G. G. *Effective Approaches to Teaching Basic Skills to Adults: A Research Synthesis.* Report prepared for the Office of Higher Education and Adult Learning of the Office of Educational Research and Improvement, Contract No. OERI-8-86-3015. Washington, D.C.: U.S. Department of Education, 1986.

Darkenwald, G. G., and Anderson, R. E. *Participation and Persistence in American Adult Education.* New York: College Board, 1979.

Darkenwald, G. G., and Gavin, W. J. "Dropout as a Function of Discrepancies Between Expectations and Actual Experiences of the Classroom Social Environment." *Adult Education Quarterly,* 1987, *37* (3), 152–163.

Darkenwald, G. G., and Merriam, S. B. *Adult Education: Foundations for Practice.* New York: Harper & Row, 1982.

Darkenwald, G. G., and Valentine, T. "Factor Structure of Deterrents to Public Participation in Adult Education." *Adult Education Quarterly,* 1985, *35* (4), 177–193.

Darling, M. "A Second Look at NLP [Neuro-Linguistic Programming]." *Training,* 1988, *25* (1), 38–42.

Davies, I. K. *Competency-Based Learning: Technology, Management, and Design.* New York: McGraw-Hill, 1973.

Deal, T. E., and Kennedy, A. A. *Corporate Cultures: The Rites and Rituals of Corporate Life.* Reading, Mass.: Addison-Wesley, 1982.

de Bono, E. *New Think: The Use of Lateral Thinking in the Generation of New Ideas.* New York: Harper & Row, 1968.

de Bono, E. *Lateral Thinking.* New York: Harper & Row, 1970.

Deming, W. *The Memory Jogger: A Pocket Guide of Tools for Continuous Improvement.* Lawrence, Mass.: Growth Opportunity Alliance for Greater Lawrence, 1985.

Dewey, J. *Democracy and Education.* New York: Free Press, 1966.

Diehl, W. A. "Functional Literacy as a Variable Construct: An Examination of Attitudes, Behaviors, and Strategies Related to Occupational Literacy." Unpublished doctoral dissertation, Indiana University, 1980.

Diehl, W. A., and Mikulecky, L. J. "The Nature of Being at Work." *Journal of Reading*, 1980, *24* (3), 221–227.

Dimock, H. G. *Groups: Leadership and Group Development.* San Diego, Calif.: University Associates, 1987.

Dixon, N. "Incorporating Learning Style into Training Design." *Training and Development Journal*, 1982, *36* (7), 62–65.

Doering, R. D. "Enlarging Scientific Task Team Creativity." *Personnel*, 1972, *49* (2), 43–52.

Donaghy, W. C. "Our Silent Language." In *Components in Communication.* Dubuque, Iowa: Gorsuch Scarisbrick, 1976.

Dossey, J. A., Mullis, I.V.S., Lindquist, M. M., and Chambers, D. L. *The Mathematics Report Card, Are We Measuring Up?* Princeton, N.J.: Educational Testing Service, June 1988.

Downs, S. "Developing Learning Styles." In M. E. Cheren (ed.), *Learning Management: Emerging Directions for Learning to Learn in the Workplace.* Columbus: National Center for Research in Vocational Education, Ohio State University, 1987.

Dressler, G. *Improving Productivity at Work: Motivating Today's Employees.* Reston, Va.: Reston Publishing, 1983.

Drew, R. A., and Mikulecky, L. J. *Literacy Task Analysis Practitioner's Guide: How to Gather and Develop Job-Specific Literary Materials for Basic Skills Instruction.* Report prepared for the Basic Skills Work-Education Bridge (WEB), Project No. 305-87-4700. Indianapolis: Indiana State Board of Vocational and Technical Education, 1988.

Driver, M. J., and Mock, T. J. "Human Processing, Decision Style Theory, and Accounting Information Systems." *Accounting Review*, 1975, *50*, 490–508.

Duffy, T. M. *Literacy Instruction in the Military Communication Design Center.* Pittsburgh, Pa.: Carnegie Mellon University, 1983.

Duggan, P. *Literacy at Work: Developing Adult Basic Skills for Employment.* Washington, D.C.: Northeast-Midwest Institute, the Center for Regional Policy, 1985.

Dunlop, J. T. "Have the 1980s Changed U.S. Industrial Relations?" *Monthly Labor Review,* May 1988, pp. 29–34.

Dyer, W. G. *Team Building.* Reading, Mass.: Addison-Wesley, 1987.

Educational Testing Service. *1986 National Assessment of Educational Progress.* Princeton, N.J.: Educational Testing Service, 1986.

Egan, G. *Interpersonal Living.* Pacific Grove, Calif.: Brooks/Cole, 1976.

Eisenhour, J. V. "Job Training—and Retraining, Too." *Journal of Career Development,* 1985, *11,* 173–180.

Ekman, P. *Telling Lies: Cues to Deceit in the Marketplace.* New York: Norton, 1985.

Ekman, P., Levenson, R., and Friesen, W. "Autonomic Nervous Activity Distinguishes Among Emotions." *Science,* 1983, *221* (4616), 1208–1210.

Elsea, J. G. *First Impression, Best Impression.* New York: Fireside Books, 1986.

Elsea, J. G. "Oral Communication Skills for the American Worker." Unpublished paper developed for the American Society for Training and Development, Alexandria, Va., 1988a.

Elsea, J. G. "Listening Skills for the American Worker." Unpublished paper developed for the American Society for Training and Development, Alexandria, Va., 1988b.

Emig, J. *The Composing Process of Twelfth Graders.* Urbana, Ill.: National Council of Teachers of English, 1971. (ED 058 205)

"Employee Training in America." *Training and Development Journal,* 1986, *40* (7), 34–37.

Ends, E. J., and Page, C. W. *Organizational Team Builder.* Cambridge, Mass.: Winthrop, 1977.

English Language Arts. National Council of Teachers of English. Commission on the English Curriculum. East Norwalk, Conn.: Appleton-Century-Crofts, 1952.

Eurich, N. P. *Corporate Classrooms: The Learning Business.* Princeton, N.J.: Carnegie Foundation for the Advancement of Teaching, 1985.

Eysenck, M. W. *Human Memory: Theory, Research, and Individual Differences.* Elmsford, N.Y.: Pergamon Press, 1977.

Farr, R., Carey, R., and Tone, B. "Recent Theory and Research into the Reading Process: Implications for Reading Assessment." In J. Orasanu (ed.), *Reading Comprehension: From Research to Practice*. Hillsdale, N.J.: Erlbaum, 1985.

Feuer, D. "Tales of Small-Time Training." *Training*, 1988, *25* (2), 29–36.

Feuer, D., and Geber, B. "Uh-Oh . . . Second Thoughts About Adult Learning Theory." *Training*, 1988, *25* (12), 31–39.

Fields, E. L. "Industry-Based Programs: A Growing Source of Adult Literacy Development." *Lifelong Learning: An Omnibus of Practice and Research*, 1986, *10* (10), 7–9.

Fields, E. L., Hull, W. L., and Sechler, J. A. *Adult Literacy: Industry-Based Training Programs*. Columbus: National Center for Research in Vocational Education, Ohio State University, 1987.

Fingeret, A. *Adult Literacy Education: Current and Future Directions*. ERIC Information Analysis Report No. 284. Columbus: National Center for Research in Vocational Education, Ohio State University, 1984.

Fisher, R., and Ury, W. *Getting to Yes: Negotiating Agreement Without Giving In*. New York: Houghton Mifflin, 1987.

Flower, L. S., and Hayes, J. R. "A Cognitive Process of Theory Writing." *College Composition and Communication*, 1981, *32*, 365–387.

Flower, L. S., and Hayes, J. R. "Images, Plans, and Pros—The Representation of Meaning in Writing." *Written Communication*, 1984, *1*, 129–160.

Ford Motor Company. *Annual Report*. Dearborn, Mich.: Ford Motor Company, 1987.

Foster, D. E., Engels, D. W., and Wilson, M. J. "Knowledge Acquired in a Program for Building Employability Skills." *Journal of Employment Counseling*, 1986, *23*, 176–177.

Francis, W. N. *Structure of American English*. New York: R. West, 1958.

Frand, J. F. "Negotiating: Master the Possibilities." *Personnel Journal*, 1987, *66* (6), 90–95.

Frederickson, R. H. *Career Information*. New York: Macmillan, 1982.

Freedman, A. *The New Look in Wage Policy and Employee Relations.* New York: Conference Board, 1985.

Freedman, A. "How the 1980s Have Changed Industrial Relations." *Monthly Labor Review,* 1988, *111* (5), 35–38.

Friedman, P., and Yarbrough, E. *Training Strategies from Start to Finish.* Englewood Cliffs, N.J.: Prentice-Hall, 1985.

Frost, S. E., and Bailey, K. P. *Historical and Philosophical Foundations of Western Education.* Westerville, Ohio: Merrill, 1973.

Gagne, R. M., and Briggs, L. J. "Analysis of the Learning Task." In R. M. Gagne and L. J. Briggs (eds.), *Principles of Instructional Design.* (2nd ed.) New York: Holt, Rinehart & Winston, 1979.

Gardner, H. *Frames of Mind.* New York: Basic Books, 1985.

Gardner, J. W. "Leadership and Power." *New Management,* Fall 1987.

Gehlen, A. R. "Libraries and Employability." *Library Trends,* 1986, *35,* 303–309.

Gibbs, G. *Teaching Students to Learn.* Milton Keyes, England: Open University Press, 1981.

Gibson, R. L., and Mitchell, M. H. *An Introduction to Guidance.* New York: Macmillan, 1981.

Ginzberg, E., Ginsburg, S., Axelrad, J., and Herma, J. *Occupational Choice.* New York: Columbia University Press, 1951.

Gipe, J. "Investigating Techniques for Teaching Word Meanings." Paper prepared for the annual meeting of the American Educational Research Association, Toronto, Canada, March 1978. (ED 151 741)

Gladstone, L., and Trimmer, H. W. "Factors Predicting Success in Training and Employment for WIN [Work Incentive] Clients in Southern Nevada." *Journal of Employment Counseling,* 1985, *22,* 59–69.

Glassman, M., and Farley, E. A. "AACSB [American Assembly of Collegiate Schools of Business] Accredited Schools' Approach to Business Communication Courses." *Journal of Business Communication Courses,* 1979, *16,* 41–48.

Glines, E., and Cooney, J. *Final Report of the Adult Competency Education Project.* Redwood City, Calif.: San Mateo County Office of Education, 1978.

Glover, J. A. "A Creativity-Training Workshop: Short-Term, Long-Term, and Transfer Effects." *Journal of Genetic Psychology,* 1980, *136,* 3–16.

Glover, J. A. "Developing Creative Responding, Training, and Transfer Effects." *Small Group Behavior,* 1981, *12* (2), 161–181.

Goffman, E. *Encounters: Two Studies in the Sociology of Interaction.* Indianapolis, Ind.: Bobbs-Merrill, 1961.

Goldstein, L. D., and Pfeiffer, J. W. "Human Resource Development: Current Status and Future Directions." In J. W. Pfeiffer and L. D. Goldstein (eds.), *The 1984 Annual: Developing Human Resources.* San Diego, Calif.: University Associates, 1984.

Goleman, D. "People Who Read People." *Psychology Today,* July 1979.

Goodman, K. (ed.). *The Psycholinguistic Nature of the Reading Process.* Detroit, Mich.: Wayne State University Press, 1968.

Gordon, J. "Where the Training Goes." *Training,* 1986, *23* (10), 49–63.

Gordon, J., and Zemke, R. "Making Them More Creative." *Training,* 1986, *23* (5), 30–45.

Gordon, R. *The Adolescent Worker: A Field Study of Employed and Unemployed Youth.* Research for the Practitioner. Research Brief No. 7. Columbus: National Center for Research in Vocational Education, Ohio State University, 1985. (ED 240 380)

Gordon, W.J.J. *Synectics.* New York: Harper & Row, 1961.

Gordon, W.J.J. "Creativity Training Comes of Age." In B. Taylor and G. Lippitt (eds.), *Management Development and Training Handbook.* New York: McGraw-Hill, 1983.

Gorman, D. "Why Is Service So Bad?" *Time,* Feb. 2, 1988, pp. 49–55.

Gottlieb, D. "Employment Settings and Employee Assessment." *Youth and Society,* 1986, *18,* 81–94.

Gratten, H. C. (ed.). *American Ideas About Adult Education.* New York: Columbia University Press, 1959.

Graves, D. H. *A Case Study Observing the Development of Primary Children's Composing, Spelling, and Motor Behaviors During the Writing Process: Final Report.* National Institute of Education

Grant No. G-78-0174. Durham: University of New Hampshire, 1981. (ED 218 653)

Green, E. E., Cook, P. F., and Rogers, J. K. "The Need for Interpersonal Skill Training and Supervision." *NASSP [National Association for Secondary School Principals] Bulletin,* 1984, *68* (467), 23–30.

Greenan, J. P. *The Development of Strategies and Procedures for Assessing the Generalizable Skills of Students in Secondary Vocational Programs: Generalizable Mathematics Skills.* Springfield: Department of Adult, Vocational, and Technical Education, Illinois State Board of Education, 1984. (ED 248 323)

Gregore, A. "Learning-Teaching Styles: Potent Forces Behind Them." *Educational Leadership,* 1979, *36,* 134–236.

Griep, D. J. "Administrative Group, Quarterly Report." Aerospace Corporation, July 1985.

Grinder, J., and Bandler, R. "The Structure of Magic." 2 vols. Palo Alto, Calif.: Science and Behavior Books, 1975, 1977.

Guthrie, J. T. "Research: Equilibrium of Literacy." *Journal of Reading,* 1983, *26,* 668–670.

Gutteridge, T. G., and Otte, F. L. *Organizational Career Development: State of the Practice.* Alexandria, Va.: American Society for Training and Development, 1983.

Hahn, A., Danzberger, J., and Lefkowitz, B. *Dropouts in America: Enough Is Known for Action.* Washington, D.C.: Institute for Educational Leadership, 1987.

Hall, D. T., and Associates. *Career Development in Organizations.* San Francisco: Jossey-Bass, 1986.

Hall, V. L., Worthington, K. L., Carruth, R. W., and Cubler, B. H. *Adult Education Basic Skills Task Force: Writing Skills.* Salt Lake City: Utah State Office of Education, 1982. (ED 219 795)

Hamilton, J. "Job Preparation as Base." *Journal of Career Development,* 1985, *11,* 166–172.

Hardy, D. (ed.). *Social Services in the Year 2000.* Washington, D.C.: Office of Human Development Services, District of Columbia Department of Health and Human Services, 1984.

Harmon, J. "BSEP [Basic Skills Education Program] Makes a Difference." *U.S. Army Research Institute Focus.* Alexandria, Va.: U.S. Army Research Institute for the Behavioral and Social Sciences, 1987a.

Harmon, J. *Illiteracy: A National Dilemma.* New York: Cambridge Book, 1987b.

Harris, A. J., and Sipay, E. R. *How to Teach Reading: A Competency-Based Program.* New York: Longman, 1979.

Harrison, A., and Bramson, R. *Styles of Thinking.* New York: Anchor, 1983.

Harvill, R., West, J., Jacobs, E. E., and Masson, R. L. "Systematic Group Leader Training: Evaluating the Effectiveness of the Approach." *Journal for Specialists in Group Work,* 1985, *10* (1), 2–13.

Hastings, C., Bixby, P., and Chaudhry-Lawton, R. *The Super-team Solution.* Hampshire, England: Gower Press, 1986.

Hayes, J. R., and Flower, L. S. "Identifying the Organization of Writing Process." In L. W. Gregg and E. R. Steinberg (eds.), *Cognitive Processes in Writing.* Hillsdale, N.J.: Erlbaum, 1980.

Hazler, R. J., and Latto, L. D. "Employers' Opinions on the Attitudes and Skills of High School Graduates." *Journal of Employment Counseling,* 1987, *24* (3), 130–136.

Hegstrom, T. G. "Message Impact: What Percentage Is Nonverbal?" *Western Journal of Speech Communication,* 1979, *13,* 134–142.

Heiman, M., and Slomianko, J. (eds.). *Thinking Skills Instruction: Concept and Techniques.* Washington, D.C.: National Education Association, 1987.

Hellriegel, D., Slocum, J. W., and Woodman, R. W. *Organizational Behavior.* St. Paul, Minn.: West, 1983.

Henry, J. F., and Raymond, S. U. *Basic Skills in the U.S. Work Force.* New York: Center for Public Resources, 1983.

Herrmann, N. "The Creative Brain." *Training and Development Journal,* 1981, *35* (10), 10–16.

Herrmann, N. "Whole Brain Teaching and Learning." *College Industry Education Conference Proceedings.* Lake Lure, N.C.: Whole Brain Corporation, 1983.

Herrmann, N. "Brain Dominance Theory." In R. L. Craig (ed.), *Training and Development Handbook.* (3rd ed.) New York: McGraw-Hill, 1987.

Hersey, P., and Blanchard, K. H. *Management of Organizational Behavior.* Englewood Cliffs, N.J.: Prentice-Hall, 1982.

Herzberg, F. *Work and the Nature of Man*. Cleveland, Ohio: World, 1966.

Hillocks, G. *Research on Written Composition: New Directions for Teaching*. National Institute of Education Grant No. 400-83-0025. Urbana, Ill.: National Conference on Research in English, 1986.

Hirsch, R. O. *Listening: A Way to Process Information Aurally*. Dubuque, Iowa: Gorsuch Scarisbrick, 1979.

Hirsch, S. K. *Using the Myers-Briggs Type Indicator in Organizations: A Resource Book*. Palo Alto, Calif.: Consulting Psychologists Press, 1985.

Hoerr, J., Pollock, M., and Whiteside, D. "Management Discovers the Human Side of Automation." *Business Week*, Sept. 29, 1986, pp. 70–79.

Holland, J. L. *Making Vocational Choices: A Theory of Careers*. Englewood Cliffs, N.J.: Prentice-Hall, 1973.

Holland, M. "Relationship Between Vocational Development and Self-Concept in Sixth Grade Students." *Journal of Vocational Behavior*, 1981, *18* (2), 228–236.

Holmes, J. A. In R. I. Fitzhenry (ed.), *Barnes & Noble Book of Quotations*. (Rev. ed.) New York: Barnes & Noble, 1987.

Houle, C. *The Inquiring Mind*. Madison: University of Wisconsin Press, 1961.

Hudson, J. "The Acquisition of Information: An Important Life Skill." *Personnel and Guidance Journal*, 1980, *59* (3), 164–167.

Hughes, C. L. *Goal Setting: Key to Individual and Organizational Effectiveness*. New York: American Management Association, 1965.

Hull, W. L., Fields, E. L., and Sechler, J. A. *Industrial Literacy Programs: Final Report*. Columbus: National Center for Research in Vocational Education, Ohio State University, 1986.

Huse, E. F., and Cummings, T. G. *Organizational Development and Change*. St. Paul, Minn.: West, 1985.

Huysmen, J. *The Implementation of Operations Research*. New York: Wiley-Interscience, 1970.

Interservice Procedures for Instructional Systems. U.S. Army Training and Doctrine Command Pamphlet, no. 350. Washington, D.C.: U.S. Department of Defense, 1985.

Introduction to Behavior Analysis and Group Interactive Skills. Rochester, N.Y.: Multinational Service and Technical Support/ Multinational Service Education, 1984.

Ironson, D. "Your Brain." *International Television,* July 1984.

Jackson, T., and Vitberg, A. "Career Development, Part 3: Challenges for the Individual." *Personnel Journal,* 1987, *66* (4), 54–57.

James, W. *Principles of Psychology.* 2 vols. Magnolia, Mass.: Peter Smith, 1890.

James, W. B., and Galbraith, M. W. "Perceptual Learning Styles: Implications and Techniques for the Practitioner." *Lifelong Learning,* Jan. 1985, pp. 20–23.

Jandt, F. E. *Win-Win Negotiating, Turning Conflict into Agreement.* New York: Wiley, 1985.

Jenkins, D. E. "The Challenge of the Marketplace: Implications for School Counselors." *Journal of Career Development,* 1987, *13* (3), 57–62.

Jesperson, O. *Growth and Structure of the English Language.* New York: Free Press, 1968.

Jesser, D. L. "The Employability Skills Initiative in Colorado." *Journal of Career Development,* 1984, *11* (1), 33–41.

"Job-Related Basic Skills: A Guide for Planners of Employee Programs." *BCEL [Business Council for Effective Literacy] Bulletin,* June 1987.

"Johari Window: An Experience in Self-Disclosure and Feedback." In J. W. Pfeiffer and J. F. Jones (eds.), *A Handbook of Structured Experiences for Human Relations Training,* Vol. 8. San Diego, Calif.: University Associates, 1981.

Johnston, J. S., Jr., and Associates. *Educating Managers: Executive Effectiveness Through Liberal Learning.* San Francisco: Jossey-Bass, 1986.

Jones, B. F. "Quality and Equality Through Cognitive Instruction." *Educational Leadership,* 1986, *43* (7), 4–11.

Jones-Mohr Listening Test. San Diego: University Associates, 1976.

Jung, C. *Man and His Symbols.* New York: Dell, 1964.

Juran, J. *Planning for Quality.* New York: Macmillan, 1988.

Kagan, J., and others. "Information Processing in the Child: Significance of Analytic and Reflective Attitudes." *Psychological Monographs,* 1964, *78* (1, whole no. 578).

Kahneman, D., Slovic, P., and Tversky, A. (eds.). *Judgment Under Uncertainty: Heuristics and Biases.* New York: Cambridge University Press, 1982.

Kaman, V. S., and Mohr, J. P. "Training Needs Assessment in the Eighties: Five Guideposts." *Personnel Administrator,* 1984, *29* (3), 213–220.

Kanter, R. M. *The Change Masters: Innovation and Entrepreneurship in the American Corporation.* New York: Touchstone, 1983.

Karayanni, M. "Career Maturity of Emotionally Maladjusted High School Students." *Vocational Guidance Quarterly,* 1981, *9* (3), 213–220.

Karmos, J., and Karmos, A. *Strategies for Problem Solving.* Springfield: Department of Adult, Vocational and Technical Education, Illinois State Board of Education, 1986. (ED 274 784)

Karp, H. B. "A Gestalt Approach to Collaboration in Organizations." In J. W. Pfeiffer and J. E. Jones (eds.), *The 1976 Annual: A Handbook for Group Facilitators.* San Diego, Calif.: University Associates, 1976.

Karrass, C. *The Negotiating Game: How to Get What You Want.* New York: Crowell, 1970.

Keefe, W. F. *Listen, Management! Creative Listening for Better Managing.* New York: McGraw-Hill, 1971.

Kehl, R. *Silver Departures.* San Diego: Green Tiger Press, 1983.

Keirsey, D., and Bates, M. *Please Understand Me.* Del Mar, Calif.: Prometheus Nemesis Books, 1978.

Kelley, R. E. *The Gold Collar Worker: Harnessing the Brainpower of the New Workforce.* Reading, Mass.: Addison-Wesley, 1985.

Kelly, A. G. *The Psychology of Personal Constructs.* New York: Norton, 1955.

Kelly, C. M. "Listening: Complexity of Activities — And a Unitary Skill." *Speech Monographs,* 1967, *34.*

Kepner, C., and Tregoe, B. B. *The Rational Manager.* New York: McGraw-Hill, 1965.

Kepner-Tregoe, Inc. *Executive Problem Analysis and Decision Making.* Princeton, N.J.: Princeton Research Press, 1973.

King-Fitch, C. C. *Assist Students in Improving Their Math Skills.* Professional Teacher Education Module Series, Module M-5. Columbus: National Center for Research in Vocational Education, Ohio State University, and the American Association for Vocational Instructional Materials, the University of Georgia, Athens, 1985.

Kirkpatrick, D. "Evaluation." In R. L. Craig (ed.), *Training and Development Handbook*. (3rd ed.) New York: McGraw-Hill, 1987.

Kirsch, I. S., and Guthrie, J. T. "The Concept of Measurement of Functional Literacy." *Reading Research Quarterly*, 1977–1978, *13* (4), 485–507.

Kirsch, I. S., and Jungeblut, A. *Literacy: Profiles of America's Young Adults*. Princeton, N.J.: National Assessment of Educational Progress, Educational Testing Service, 1986.

Klein, G. *Perception, Motives, and Personality*. San Francisco: Jossey-Bass, 1970.

Kleinberg, S. J. "Success and the Working Class." *Journal of American Culture*, 1979, *2*, 123–138.

Kloosterman, P., and Gillie, S. "Basic Mathematical Skills for Vocational Education." In H. Harty and others (directors), *The Impact and Potential of Basic Skills Applications in Vocational/Technical Education: The Basic Skills Work-Education Bridge (WEB)*. Project No. 305-87-4700. Indianapolis: Indiana State Board of Vocational and Technical Education, 1987, 1988.

Kloosterman, P., and Harty, H. *Need Sensing, Assessing, and Validation for Science, Mathematics, Computer, and Foreign Language Education in the State of Indiana: Final Report*. Bloomington: School of Education, Indiana University, 1986. (ED 272 391)

Knapp, M. L. *Nonverbal Communication*. New York: Holt, Rinehart & Winston, 1978.

Knowles, M. S. *Self-Directed Learning: A Guide for Learners and Teachers*. Chicago: Association Press/Follett, 1975.

Knowles, M. S. *The Modern Practice of Adult Education*. (2nd ed.) New York: Cambridge Book, 1980.

Knowles, M. S., and Associates. *Andragogy in Action*. San Francisco: Jossey-Bass, 1984.

Knox, A. B. *Helping Adults Learn*. San Francisco: Jossey-Bass, 1986.

Kochan, T. A. "Approaches to the Study of Negotiation." In C. Kerr and P. D. Staudohar (eds.), *Industrial Relations in a New Age*. San Francisco: Jossey-Bass, 1986.

Kohn, A. "How to Succeed Without Even Vying." *Psychology Today*, 1986a, *20* (9), 22–24, 26, 28.

Kohn, A. *No Contest: The Case Against Competition*. Boston: Houghton Mifflin, 1986b.

Kolb, D. *Learning Style Inventory*. Boston: McBer, 1976.

Kolb, D. *Experiential Learning: Experience as a Source of Learning and Development*. Englewood Cliffs, N.J.: Prentice-Hall, 1984.

Kolb, D., Rubin, I. M., and McIntyre, J. M. *Organizational Psychology: An Experiential Approach to Organizational Behavior*. Englewood Cliffs, N.J.: Prentice-Hall, 1984.

Kotkin, J. "The Great American Revival." *Inc.*, 1988, *10* (2), 52–63.

Kouzes, J. M., and Posner, B. Z. *The Leadership Challenge: How to Get Extraordinary Things Done in Organizations*. San Francisco: Jossey-Bass, 1987.

Krigline, A. G., and Rakich, J. S. "Productivity Improvement Through Better Problem Solving by Supervisors." *National Productivity Review*, Winter 1987–1988, pp. 61–88.

Krumboltz, J. D. "A Social Learning Theory of Career Decision Making." In A. M. Mitchell, G. B. Jones, and J. D. Krumboltz (eds.), *Social Learning and Career Decision Making*. Cranston, R.I.: Carroll Press, 1979.

Lacey, R. *Basic Skills for Disadvantaged Youth*. Salt Lake City, Utah: Olympus, 1983.

Lamberg, W. J. "Design and Validation of Instruction in Question-Directed Narrative Writing, Developed Through Discrimination Programming." *Dissertation Abstracts International*, 1974, *35* (2839-A). (ED 097 689)

Lannon, J. M. *Technical Writing*. (2nd ed.) Boston: Little, Brown, 1982.

LaRusso, D. *Shadows of Communication*. Dubuque, Iowa: Kendall/Hunt, 1977.

Laster, J. F. *Toward Excellence in Secondary Vocational Education: Using Cognitive Psychology in Curriculum Planning*. Information Series No. 297. Columbus: National Center for Research in Vocational Education; Washington, D.C.: Office of Vocational and Adult Education, Contract No. 300-83-0016, U.S. Department of Education, 1985. (ED 254 656)

Latack, J. C., and Dozier, J. B. "After the Ax Falls: Job Loss as a Career Transition." *Academy of Management Review*, 1986, *11* (2), 375–397.

Latham, G. P. *Increasing Productivity Through Performance Appraisal.* Reading, Mass.: Addison-Wesley, 1981.

Latham, G. P. "Human Resource Training and Development." *Annual Review of Psychology.* Palo Alto, Calif.: Annual Reviews, 1988.

Latham, G. P., and Yuki, G. A. "A Review of Research on the Application of Goal Setting in Organizations." *Academy of Management Journal,* 1975, *18* (4), 824–845.

Latham, V. M. "The Job Search Process: An Attitudinal and Behavioral Analysis." *Journal of Employment Counseling,* 1987, *24* (1), 7–9.

Lawrie, J. "Skill Inventories: Pack for the Future." *Personnel Journal,* 1987, *66,* 127–130.

"Leadership: The Vital Management Difference." *Trainer's Workshop,* May/June 1988, pp. 16–59.

Lee, C. "The New Employment Contract." *Training,* 1987, *24* (12), 45–56.

Lee, C. "Basic Training in the Corporate Schoolhouse." *Training,* 1988, *25* (4), 27–36.

Lefton, R. E., and Buzzotta, V. R. "Teams and Teamwork: A Study of Executive-Level Teams." *National Productivity Review,* Winter 1987–1988, *7* (1), 7–19.

Lefton, R. E., Buzzotta, V. R., and Sherberg, M. *Improving Productivity Through People Skills.* Cambridge, Mass.: Ballinger, 1980.

Leibowitz, Z., and Hirsh, S. K. (eds.). *Career Development: Current Perspectives.* Alexandria, Va.: American Society for Training and Development, 1984.

Leibowitz, Z., and Lea, D. (eds.). *Adult Career Development: Concepts, Issues, and Practices.* Alexandria, Va.: American Association for Counseling and Development, 1985.

Lerche, R. S. *Effective Adult Literacy Programs: A Practitioner's Guide.* New York: Cambridge Book, 1985.

Lesikar, R. V. *Business Communication Theory and Application.* (3rd ed.) Homewood, Ill.: Dow-Jones-Irwin, 1976.

Lewin, K. *Field Theory in Social Science: Selected Theoretical Papers.* New York: Harper & Row, 1951.

Lewis, P. V. *Managing Human Relations.* Boston: Kent, 1983.

Licht, W. "How the Workplace Has Changed in 75 Years." *Monthly Labor Review,* 1988, *11* (2), 19–25.

Likert, R. *The Art of Creative Thinking.* New York: Simon & Schuster, 1967.

Lillard, L., and Tan, H. W. *Private Sector Training: Who Gets It and What Are Its Effects.* Santa Monica, Calif.: Rand Corporation, 1986.

Lipitt, G. L. "Managing Conflict in Today's Organizations." *Training and Development Journal,* 1982, *36* (7), 67–73.

Lipitt, G. L. "Power and Influence: If You Deserve It, Go for It." *Training and Development Journal,* 1983, *37* (6), 57–60.

Locke, E. A. "The Ubiquity of the Technique of Goal Setting in Theories of and Approaches to Employee Motivation." *Academy of Management Review,* 1978, *3* (3), 594–601.

Locke, E. A., and Latham, G. P. *Goal Setting: A Motivational Technique That Works.* Englewood Cliffs, N.J.: Prentice-Hall, 1984.

Lombardo, C. "Cost/Benefit Analysis of Training." In H. Birnbrauer (ed.), *Handbook for Technical and Skills Training,* Vol. 2. Alexandria, Va.: American Society for Training and Development, 1986.

Lowin, W. *Dichotomies of the Mind.* New York: Wiley, 1986.

Lu, D. J. *Inside Corporate Japan.* Cambridge, Mass.: Productivity Press, 1987.

Lundsteen, S. W. *Listening: Its Impact on Reading and the Other Language Arts.* Urbana, Ill.: National Council of Teachers of English/ERIC, 1971.

Lusher, B. "Team Training: Towards an Integrated Approach." *Journal of European Industrial Training,* 1985, *9* (3), 17–19.

Lusterman, S. *Trends in Corporate Education and Training.* New York: Conference Board, 1985.

Lutz, B. "Education and Employment: Contrasting Evidence from France and the Federal Republic of Germany." *European Journal of Education,* 1981, *16* (1).

Lynch, J. *Language of the Heart: The Body's Response to Human Dialogue.* New York: Basic Books, 1985a.

Lynch, J. "Listen and Live." *American Health,* Apr. 1985b, pp. 39–43.

McCaulley, M. H. *Jung's Theory of Psychological Types and the Myers-Briggs Type Indicator.* Gainesville, Fla.: Center for Applications of Psychological Type, 1981.

McClelland, D. C. *The Achieving Society.* New York: Van Nostrand, 1961.

McConnell, M. E. "Identifying Career/Life Skills in the Classroom." *Journal of College Placement,* 1983, *43* (4), 43–44, 46–47.

McCord, A. B. *The Impact of Basic Skills on Human Resource Management in the Retailing Industry.* New York: National Retail Merchants Association, 1983.

McGregor, D. M. *The Human Side of Enterprise.* New York: McGraw-Hill, 1960.

McGregor, D. M. *Leadership and Motivation.* Cambridge, Mass.: MIT Press, 1966.

McKay, M., and Fanning, P. *Self-Esteem.* New York: St. Martin's Press, 1987.

McKeen, R. L., and McSwain, C. "Organizational Management and the MBTI [Myers-Briggs Type Indicator]: Temperaments and Patterns of Personal Satisfaction at Work." *Bulletin of Psychological Type,* 1986, *8* (2), 20–22.

McKenny, J. L., and Keen, P. "How Managers' Minds Work." *Harvard Business Review,* 1974, *52* (3), 79–90.

McMahon, J. E., and Merman, S. K. "Career Development." In R. L. Craig (ed.), *Training and Development Handbook: A Guide to Human Resource Development.* New York. McGraw-Hill, 1987.

McTague, M. J. "Managing Innovation." *Trainer's Workshop,* 1987, *1* (10), 13–63.

Mager, R. F. *Preparing Instructional Objectives.* (Rev. 2nd ed.) Belmont, Calif.: Pittman Learning, 1984.

Mager, R. F., and Beach, K. M. *Developing Vocational Instruction.* Belmont, Calif.: David S. Lake, 1967.

Main, J. "Under the Spell of the Quality Gurus." *Fortune,* Aug. 18, 1986, pp. 30–34.

Malowney, C. L., and others. *Assist Students in Improving.*

"Management Communications: Form and Substance." *Clinical Management Review,* 1987.

Manuele, C. A. "The Development of a Measure to Assess Vocational Maturity in Adults with Delayed Career Development." *Journal of Vocational Behavior,* 1982, *23* (1), 45–63.

Manuele, C. A. "Modifying Vocational Maturity in Adults with Delayed Career Development: A Life Skills Approach." *Vocational Guidance Quarterly,* 1984, *33* (2), 101–112.

Manuele, C. A., Warner, J., and Sharar, P. "Assessment and Screening: Identifying Successful Participants in Employment and Training Programs." *Journal of Employment Counseling,* 1986, *23* (2), 87–92.

Marzano, R. J., and others. *Dimensions of Thinking.* Alexandria, Va.: Association for Supervision and Curriculum Development, 1988.

Maslow, A. H. *Motivation and Personality.* New York: Harper & Row, 1954.

Massaro, D. W. "Building and Testing Models of Reading Processes: Examples from Word Recognition." In P. D. Pearson (ed.), *Handbook of Reading Research.* New York: Longman, 1984.

Mastenbroek, W. F. "A Model for Negotiation." *Training and Development Journal,* 1983, *37* (10), 76–79.

Mayer, R. E. "Elaboration Techniques That Increase the Meaningfulness of Technical Prose: An Experimental Test of the Learning Strategy Hypothesis." *Journal of Educational Psychology,* 1980, *72,* 770–784.

Mayer, R. E. "Aids to Text Comprehension." *Educational Psychologist,* 1984, *19,* 30–42.

Mead, G. H. *Mind, Self, and Society.* Chicago: University of Chicago Press, 1934.

Mehrabian, A. *Nonverbal Communication.* Chicago: Aldine-Atherton, 1972.

Mehrabian, A. *Silent Messages.* (2nd ed.) Belmont, Calif.: Wadsworth, 1982.

Mehrabian, A., and Ferris, S. "Interference of Attitudes from Nonverbal Communication in Two Channels." *Journal of Consulting Psychology,* 1967, *31,* 248–252.

Merman, S. K. "Organizational Skills." Unpublished paper developed for the American Society for Training and Development, Alexandria, Va., 1988.

Merman, S. K., and Clark, A. *Managing Toward Career Excellence.* Houston, Tex.: King, Chapman, and Broussard, 1985.

Messer, S. "Reflection-Impulsivity: A Review." *Psychological Bulletin,* 1976, *83,* 1026–1052.

Metzger, E. A. "Causes of Failure to Learn to Write: Explanatory Case Studies at Grade Seven, Grade Ten, and College

Level." *Dissertation Abstracts International,* 1977, *38* (3346-A).

Mezirow, J. "Context and Action in Adult Education." *Adult Education Quarterly,* 1985, *35,* 142–151.

Michael, D. N. *On Learning to Plan — and Planning to Learn.* San Francisco: Jossey-Bass, 1973.

Mikulecky, L. J. "Functional Writing in the Workplace." In L. Gentry (ed.), *Research and Instruction in Practical Writing.* Los Alamitos, Calif.: South West Regional Laboratories, 1982a.

Mikulecky, L. J. "Job Literacy: The Relationship Between School Preparation and Workplace Actuality." *Reading Research Quarterly,* 1982b, *17* (3), 400–419.

Mikulecky, L. J. "The Transferability of Literacy Training to Job Literacy." Paper presented at the International Reading Association Convention, Philadelphia, Apr. 17, 1986.

Mikulecky, L. J., and Drew, R. A. "Basic Literacy and Communication Skills for Vocational Education." In H. Harty and others (directors), *The Impact and Potential of Basic Skills Applications in Vocational/Technical Education: The Basic Skills Work-Education Bridge (WEB).* Project No. 305-87-4700. Indianapolis: Indiana State Board of Vocational and Technical Education, 1987–1988.

Mikulecky, L. J., and Ehlinger, J. "The Influence of Metacognitive Aspects of Literacy on Job Performance of Electronics Technicians." *Journal of Reading Behavior,* 1986, *18* (1), 41–62.

Mikulecky, L. J., Ehlinger, J., and Meenan, A. L. *Training for Job Literacy Demands. What Research Applies to Practice.* University Park: Institute for the Study of Adult Literacy, Pennsylvania State University, 1987.

Mikulecky, L. J., Shanklin, N. L., and Caverly, D. C. *Adult Reading Habits, Attitudes, and Motivations: A Cross Sectional Study.* Monograph in Language Series, no. 2. Bloomington: School of Education, Indiana University, 1979.

Mikulecky, L. J., and Winchester, D. "Job Literacy and Job Performance Among Nurses at Varying Employment Levels." *Adult Education Quarterly,* 1983, *34* (1), 1–15.

Miles, M. *Learning to Work in Groups.* (2nd ed.) New York: Teachers College Press, 1981.

Miller, L. E., and Feggestad, K. "Teaching Employees to Solve Problems." *Vocational Education Journal,* 1987, *62* (3), 28–29.

Miller, W. C. *The Creative Edge: Fostering Innovation Where You Work.* Reading, Mass.: Addison-Wesley, 1987.

Mink, O. G., Mink, B., and Owen, K. Q. *Groups at Work.* Englewood Cliffs, N.J.: Educational Technology Publications, 1987.

Minor, C. W. "Career Development: Theories and Issues." In Z. Leibowitz and D. Lea (eds.), *Adult Career Development: Concepts, Issues, and Practices.* Alexandria, Va.: American Association for Counseling and Development, 1985.

Minsky, M. *The Society of Mind.* New York: Simon & Schuster, 1985.

Mirabile, R. J. "New Directions for Career Development." *Training and Development Journal,* 1987, *41* (12), 30–33.

Miskin, V. D., and Gmelch, W. H. "Quality Leadership for Quality Teams." *Training and Development Journal,* 1985, *35* (9), 122–129.

"A Mission of Growing Urgency." *Washington Post,* Dec. 2, 1987, p. A18.

Mitchell, L. K., and Krumboltz, J. D. "The Effects of Cognitive Restructuring and Decision-Making Training on Career Indecision." *Journal of Counseling and Development,* 1987, *66,* 171–179.

Mitchell, R. "Negative Entropy at Work: A Theory of Practical Writing." In L. Gentry (ed.), *Research and Instruction in Practical Writing.* Los Alamitos, Calif.: South West Regional Laboratories Educational Research and Development, 1982.

Mitchell, R. "Team Building by Disclosure of Internal Frames of Reference." *Journal of Applied Behavioral Science,* 1986, *22* (1), 15–28.

Montague, W. "More Coordination in Job Training Seen." *Education Week,* May 13, 1987, p. 13.

Montross, D. H., and Shinkman, C. J. (eds.). *Career Development in the 1980s: Theory and Practice.* Springfield, Ill.: Thomas, 1981.

Moore, C. W. *The Mediation Process: Practical Strategies for Resolving Conflict.* San Francisco: Jossey-Bass, 1986.

Moore, T. "Personality Tests Are Back." *Fortune,* Mar. 30, 1987, pp. 74–82.

Moses, B. "Giving Employees a Future." *Training and Development Journal,* 1987, *41* (12), 25–28.

Mullen, D. *A Conceptual Framework for the Life Skills Program.* Ottawa: Occupational and Career Analysis and Development Branch, Canada Employment and Immigration Commission, 1981. (ED 218 438)

Mundale, S. S. "Why More CEO's Are Leading a Back-to-Basics Movement." *Training,* 1985, *17* (10), 37–41.

Murrell, H. *Motivation at Work.* London: Methuen, 1976.

Myers, I. B. *Type and Teamwork.* Gainesville, Fla.: Center for Applications of Psychological Type, 1974.

Myers, I. B. *Introduction to Type.* Palo Alto, Calif.: Consulting Psychologists Press, 1980.

Myers, I., and Briggs, K. *The Myers-Briggs Type Indicator.* Palo Alto, Calif.: Consulting Psychologists Press, 1976.

Nagy, W. E., Herman, P. A., and Anderson, R. C. "Learning Words from Context." *Reading Research Quarterly,* 1985, *20* (2), 233–253.

Naimark, H., and Pearce, S. "Transferable Skills: One Link Between Work and Family." *Journal of Career Development,* 1985, *12* (1), 48–54.

Naisbitt, J. *Megatrends: Ten New Directions Transforming Our Lives.* New York: Warner Books, 1982.

Naisbitt, J., and Arbudene, P. "Reinventing the Corporation." New York: Warner Books, 1985.

National Academy of Sciences. *High Schools and the Changing Workplace: The Employers' View.* Washington, D.C.: National Academy Press, 1984.

National Alliance of Business. *A Systems Approach to Youth Employment Competencies.* Washington, D.C.: National Alliance of Business, 1986a.

National Alliance of Business. *Employment Policies: Looking to the Year 2000.* Washington, D.C.: National Alliance of Business, 1986b.

National Center for Research in Vocational Education. *Their Writing Skills.* Professional Teacher Education Module Series, Module M-3. Columbus: National Center for Research in Vocational Education, Ohio State University, 1985.

Neimark, E., De Lisi, R., and Newman, J. (eds.). *Moderators of Competence.* Hillsdale, N.J.: Erlbaum, 1985.

Nichols, R. G. "Factors in Listening Comprehension." *Speech Monographs,* 1948, *15.*

Nichols, R. G., and Stevens, L. A. *Are You Listening?* New York: McGraw-Hill, 1957.

Nierenberg, G. I. *Fundamentals of Negotiating.* New York: Hawthorne, 1973.

Nierenberg, G. I. *The Art of Creative Thinking.* New York: Simon & Schuster, 1982.

Nierenberg, G. I. *The Complete Negotiator.* New York: Nierenberg, Zief, 1986.

Ninomiya, J. S. "Wagon Masters and Lesser Managers." *Harvard Business Review,* Mar.–Apr. 1988, 84–90.

Northcutt, N. *Adult Functional Competency: A Summary of Performance Requirements.* Adult Performance Level Project. Austin: University of Texas, 1975. (ED 114 609)

Norton, R. E. *DACUM Handbook.* Columbus: National Center for Research in Vocational Education, Ohio State University, 1985.

Odell, L. "Measuring the Effect of Instruction in Pre-Writing." *Research in the Teaching of English,* 1974, *8,* 228–240.

Odell, L. "Business Writing Observations and Implications for Teaching Composition." *Theory into Practice,* 1980, *19,* 225–232.

Ogle, S. E. "Memory and Aging: A Review and Application of Current Theories." *Lifelong Learning: An Omnibus of Practice and Research,* 1986, *9* (6), 8–27.

Olmstead, J. A. *Leadership Training: The State of the Art.* Alexandria, Va.: Human Resources Research Organization, 1980.

O'Neil, H. F., Jr. *Procedures for Instructional Systems Development.* New York: Academic Press, 1979.

Orange, L. E. *English: The Pre-Professional Major.* New York: Modern Language Association, 1973.

Orr, E. E., and Grahan, W. R. "Development of a Listening Comprehension Test." *Educational Research Journal,* 1968, *5,* 167–180.

Osborn, A. F. *Applied Imagination.* New York: Scribner's, 1963.

Osipow, S. H. *Theories of Career Development.* (3rd ed.) Englewood Cliffs, N.J.: Prentice-Hall, 1983.

Ouchi, W. G. "Markets, Bureaucracies, and Clans." *Administrative Science Quarterly,* 1980, *25,* 129–140.

Parsons, F. *Choosing a Vocation.* Boston: Houghton Mifflin, 1909.

Pearson, A. E. "Tough-Minded Way to Get Innovative." *Harvard Business Review,* 1988, *66* (3), 99–106.

Pearson, R. E. "A Group-Based Training Format for Basic Skills of Small-Group Leadership." *Journal for Specialists in Group Work,* 1985, *10* (3), 150–156.

Perl, S. "The Composing Process of Unskilled College Writers." *Research in the Teaching of English,* 1979, *13,* 317–336.

Peters, T. J. *Thriving on Chaos: Handbook for a Management Revolution.* New York: Knopf, 1987.

Peters, T. J., and Austin, N. *A Passion for Excellence.* New York: Random House, 1985.

Peters, T. J., and Waterman, R. H., Jr. *In Search of Excellence: Lessons from America's Best-Run Companies.* New York: Harper & Row, 1984.

Pfeiffer, J. W., and Pfeiffer, J. A. "A Gestalt Primer." In J. W. Pfeiffer and J. E. Jones (eds.), *The 1975 Annual Handbook for Group Facilitators.* San Diego, Calif.: University Associates, 1975.

Philippi, J. W. *Job-Specific Reading Skills: Reading Competencies Commonly Needed to Perform Job Tasks.* Part of a special report (Contract No. DAJA37-83-D-004) presented to Army Continuing Education Services, U.S. Army Europe, Heidelberg, West Germany, October 1984.

Philippi, J. W. "Formative Evaluation of BSEP/CSEP Reading." In "Self-Evaluation of the HSCP and BSEP/CSEP Contract," contract no. DAJA37-86-D-008, Big Bend Community College, European Division, Central Services, Bad Kreuznach, West Germany, Sept. 22, 1986–Mar. 31, 1987.

Philippi, J. W. "Matching Literacy to Job Training: Some Applications from Military Programs." *Journal of Reading,* 1988, *31* (7), 658–666.

Phillips, S. R., and Bergquist, W. H. *Solutions: A Guide to Better Problem Solving.* San Diego, Calif.: University Associates, 1987.

Pianko, S. H. "A Description of the Composing Processes of College Freshman Writers." *Research in the Teaching of English,* 1979, *13,* 5–22.

Pinder, C. C. *Work Motivation: Theory, Issues, and Applications.* Glenview, Ill.: Scott, Foresman, 1984.

Plato. *Phaedo in the Great Dialogues of Plato.* (W.H.D. Rouse, trans.) New York: New American Books, 1956.

Plunkett, D. "A Quasi-Experimental Study of Creativity in Organizations." Unpublished doctoral dissertation, University of Texas at Austin, 1986.

Plunkett, D. "Intervention for Creativity: An OD Approach." *Training and Development Journal,* 1988, *42* (8), 68–71.

Portnoy, R. A. *Leadership: What Every Leader Should Know About People.* Englewood Cliffs, N.J.: Prentice-Hall, 1986.

Pratzner, F. C. *Occupational Adaptability and Transferable Skills.* Project Final Report. Information Series No. 129. Columbus: National Center for Research in Vocational Education, Ohio State University, 1978. (ED 186 717)

Pratzner, F. C., and Russell, J. F. *The Changing Workplace: Implications of Quality of Work Life Developments for Vocational Education.* Research and Development Series No. 249. Washington, D.C.: Office of Vocational and Adult Education, 1984. (ED 240 283)

Prescott, G. A., Balow, I. H., Hogan, T. P., and Farr, R. C. *Language Teachers' Manual for Administrating and Interpreting Metropolitan Achievement Tests.* New York: Psychological Corporation, 1978.

"The Productivity Paradox." *Business Week,* June 6, 1988, pp. 100–113.

Productivity Through Employee Participation (PTEP). West Point, Pa.: Merck, Sharp & Dohme, 1988.

Quick, T. "Appraisal Interviews That Motivate." *Trainer's Workshop,* 1987, *1* (11), 11–48.

Rader, M., and Wunsch, L. P. "A Survey of Communication Practices and Business School Graduates by Job Category and Undergraduate Majors." *Journal of Business Communication,* 1980, *17* (4), 33–41.

Rae, L. *The Skills of Human Relations Training.* New York: Nichols, 1985.

Rand, J. F. "Negotiation: Master the Possibilities." *Personnel Journal,* 1987, *66* (6), 90–95.

Rasmussen, R. V. "Team Training: A Behavior Modification Approach." *Group and Organizational Studies, 7* (1), 51–66.

Raspberry, W. "Corporate Classrooms." *Washington Post,* Aug. 3, 1988.

Raudsepp, E. "Establishing a Creative Climate." *Training and Development Journal,* 1987, *41* (4), 50–53.

Resnick, L. B. *Learning in School and Out.* Speech presented at the American Educational Research Association, April 1987a.

Resnick, L. B. *Skilled Workers Are Thinking Workers: The New Basics in American Education.* Testimony before the Congress of the United States Subcommittee on Education and Health, Joint Economic Committee. Washington, D.C.: U.S. Government Printing Office, 1987b.

Resnick, L. B. *Education and Learning to Think.* Washington, D.C.: National Academy Press, 1987c.

Rickards, T., and Freedman, B. "A Re-Appraisal of Creativity Techniques in Industrial Training." *Journal of European Industrial Training,* 1979, *3* (1), 3–8.

Riggs, J. L. *Productive Supervision.* Englewood Cliffs, N.J.: Prentice-Hall, 1985.

Roessler, R. T. "Work, Disability, and the Future: Promoting Employment for People with Disabilities." *Journal of Counseling and Development,* 1987, *66* (4), 188–190.

Rogers, C. *Freedom to Learn.* Westerville, Ohio: Merrill, 1969.

Rosenbaum, B. *How to Motivate Today's Worker.* New York: McGraw-Hill, 1982.

Rosenthal, R., and DePaulo, B. "Expectancies, Discrepancies, and Courtesies in Nonverbal Communication." *Western Journal of Speech Communication,* 1979, *43* (2), 76–95.

Rosow, J. M., and Zager, R. *Training — The Competitive Edge.* San Francisco: Jossey-Bass, 1988.

Ross, R. S., and Ross, M. G. *Relating and Interacting.* Englewood Cliffs, N.J.: Prentice-Hall, 1982.

Rumelhart, D. E. "Schemata: The Building Blocks of Cognition." In R. Spiro, B. C. Bruce, and W. F. Brewster (eds.), *Theoretical Issues in Reading Comprehension.* Hillsdale, N.J.: Erlbaum, 1980.

Rush, R. T., Moe, A. J., and Storlie, R. L. *Occupational Literacy.* Newark, Del.: International Reading Association, 1986.

Rutherford, R. P. *The Successful Negotiator: How to Get More of What You Want.* Columbia: Daniel Management Center, College of Business Administration, University of South Carolina, 1987.

Sager, C. *Improving the Quality of Written Composition Through Pupil Use of Rating Scale.* Paper prepared for the annual meeting of the National Council of Teachers of English, Dec. 1973. (ED 089 304)

Sample, J. A. "A Biography of Applications of the Myers-Briggs Type Indicator (MBTI) to Management and Organization Behavior." In J. W. Pfeiffer and L. D. Goldstein (eds.), *The 1984 Annual: Developing Human Resources.* San Diego, Calif.: University Associates, 1984.

Samuelson, R. J. "U.S. Firms Need to Compete." *Washington Post,* Mar. 23, 1988, pp. B1–B4.

Sashkin, M. "True Vision in Leadership." *Training and Development Journal,* 1986, *40* (5), 58–61.

Sathre, F. S., Olsen, R. W., and Whitney, C. *Let's Talk: An Introduction to Interpersonal Communication.* Glenview, Ill.: Scott, Foresman, 1977.

Sawkins, M. W. "The Oral Responses of Selected Fifth Grade Children to Questions Concerning Their Written Expression." *Dissertation Abstracts International,* 1971, *31* (6287A).

Schaaf, D., and Cothran, T. "Sales Training in the Era of the Customer." In *Sales Training.* Minneapolis, Minn.: Lakewood Publications, 1988.

Schein, E. H. "Career Anchors and Career Paths: A Panel Study of Management School Graduates." Cambridge: Sloan School of Management, Massachusetts Institute of Technology, 1974.

Schein, E. H. "SMR [Sloan Management Review] Forum: Improving Face-to-Face Relationships." *Sloan Management Review,* 1981a, *22* (2), 43–52.

Schein, E. H. "The Individual, the Organization, and the Career: A Conceptual Scheme." In D. H. Montross and C. J. Shinkman (eds.), *Career Development in the 1980s.* Springfield, Ill.: Thomas, 1981b.

Schein, E. H. *Organizational Culture and Leadership.* San Francisco Jossey-Bass, 1985.

Schkade, L., and Potvin, A. "Cognitive Style, EEG Waveforms, and Brain Levels." *Human Systems Management,* 1981, *2,* 329–331.

Schön, D. A. *Educating the Reflective Practitioner: Toward a New Design for Teaching and Learning in the Professions.* San Francisco: Jossey-Bass, 1987.

Schutz, W. *FIRO: A Three Dimensional Theory of Interpersonal Behavior.* New York: Holt, Rinehart & Winston, 1958.

Scott, W. *The Skill of Negotiating.* New York: Wiley, 1981.

Selz, N. *The Teaching of Employability Skills: Who's Responsible?* Columbus: National Center for Research in Vocational Education, Ohio State University, 1980. (ED 199 429)

Semerad, R. D. "Workers in the Year 2000: Why We're in Trouble." *American Teacher,* 1987, *71* (8), 7–12.

Sequential Tests of Educational Progress (STEP). Princeton, N.J.: Educational Testing Service, 1959.

70001 Training and Employment Institute. *Eight Common Ingredients of Successful Programs.* Washington, D.C.: 70001 Training and Employment Institute, 1986.

Shapiro, A. *Source: Managing People.* New York: Free Press, 1985.

Sharon, A. "What Do Adults Read?" *Reading Research Quarterly,* 1973–1974, *9* (2), 148–169.

Shaskin, M. "True Vision in Leadership." *Training and Development Journal,* 1986, *40* (5), 58–61.

Shea, G. F. *Creative Negotiating: Productive Tools and Techniques for Solving Problems, Resolving Conflicts, and Settling Differences.* New York: Van Nostrand Reinhold, 1983.

Shoemaker, H. *The Functional Context Method of Instruction.* Professional Paper No. 35-67. Alexandria, Va.: Human Resources and Research Organization, 1967.

Sinetar, M. "Developing Leadership Potential." *Personnel Journal,* 1981, *60* (3), 193–196.

Singer, R. N. "To Err or Not to Err: A Question for the Instruction of Psychometric Skills." *Review of Educational Research,* 1977, *47* (3), 479–498.

Skagen, A. *Workplace Literacy.* New York: American Management Association, 1986.

"Skills for Adolescence." Columbus, Ohio: Quest National Center, 1982.

Skinner, B. F. *Science and Human Behavior.* New York: Macmillan, 1953.

Smeltzer, L. R., and Watson, K. W. "A Test of Instructional Strategies for Listening Improvement in a Simulated Business Setting." *Journal of Business Communication,* Fall 1985, pp. 34ff.

Smith, A. D. *Generic Skills for Occupational Training.* Prince Albert, Saskatchewan, Canada: Training Research and Development Station, 1973. (ED 083 385)

Smith, A. D. "Age Differences in Encoding, Storage, and Retrieval." In L. W. Poon (ed.), *New Directions in Memory and Aging.* Hillsdale, N.J.: Erlbaum, 1980.

Smith, E. "Are You Creative?" *Business Week,* Sept. 30, 1985, pp. 80–84.

Smith, E. J. "Profile of the Black Individual in Vocational Literature." *Journal of Vocational Behavior,* 1975, *6,* 41–59.

Smith, P. H., and others. *Illiteracy in America: Extent, Causes, and Suggested Solutions.* Washington, D.C.: U.S. Government Printing Office, 1986.

Smith, R. M. *Learning How to Learn: Applied Theory for Adults.* Chicago: Follett, 1982.

Smith, R. M. "The Liberal Arts and the Arts of Management." In J. S. Johnston, Jr., and Associates (eds.), *Educating Managers: Executive Effectiveness Through Liberal Learning.* San Francisco: Jossey-Bass, 1986.

Smith, R. M. "Learning How to Learn in the Workplace." In M. E. Cheren (ed.), *Learning Management: Emerging Directions for Learning How to Learn in the Workplace.* Columbus: National Center for Research in Vocational Education, Ohio State University, 1987.

Smith, R. M. *Theory Building for Learning How to Learn.* Chicago: Educational Studies Press, 1988.

Sommers, N. I. "Revision in the Composing Process: A Case Study of College Freshmen and Experienced Adult Writers." *Dissertation Abstracts International,* 1979, *39* (5374-A), 189 pp.

Songer, T. *Learning Styles Survey.* Charlotte, N.C.: Central Piedmont Community College, 1987.

Souerwine, A. H. *Career Strategies: Planning for Personal Achievement.* New York: AMACOM, 1978.

Spache, G. *Toward Better Reading.* Champaign, Ill.: Garrard, 1963.

Stanton, G., and others. *Developing Social and Life Skills Strategies for Tutors.* London: Further Education Curriculum Review and Development Unit, Jan. 1980. (ED 217 125)

Steill, L. K. "Secrets of Being a Better Listener." *U.S. News & World Report,* May 26, 1980.

Stein, N. L., and Glenn, C. G. "An Analysis of Story Comprehension in Elementary School Children." In R. O. Freedle (ed.), *New Directions in Discourse Processing,* Vol. 2. Norwood, N.J.: Ablex, 1979.

Stephan, E., Mills, G. E., Pace, R. W., and Ralphs, L. "HRD in the Fortune 500: A Survey." *Training and Development Journal,* 1988, *42* (1), 26–33.

Stevens, R. E., and Fagin, R. B. "Confronting Poor Performers." *Supervisory Management,* 1982, *27* (3), 28–33.

Sticht, T. G. *A Program of Army Functional Job Reading Training: Development, Implementation, and Delivery Systems.* Final Report. Report No. FR-WD (CA) 75-7. Alexandria, Va.: Human Resources and Research Organization, 1975a. (ED 116 161)

Sticht, T. G. *Reading for Working: A Functional Literacy Anthology.* Alexandria, Va.: Human Resources and Research Organization, 1975b.

Sticht, T. G. *Basic Skills in Defense.* Professional Paper No. 3-82. Alexandria, Va.: Human Resources and Research Organization, 1982. (ED 237-776)

Sticht, T. G. *Functional Context Education.* San Diego, Calif.: Applied Behavioral and Cognitive Sciences, 1987.

Sticht, T. G., Armstrong, W. B., Hickey, D. T., and Caylor, J. S. *Cast-off Youth, Policy and Training Methods from the Military Experience.* New York: Praeger, 1987.

Sticht, T. G., Fox, L., Hauke, R., and Zapf, D. *Reading in the Navy.* Final Report No. WD-CA-76-14. Alexandria, Va.: Human Resources and Research Organization, 1976.

Sticht, T. G., Fox, L., Hauke, R., and Zapf, D. *The Role of Reading in the Navy*. NPRDC TR 77-77. San Diego, Calif.: Navy Personnel Research and Development Center, 1977.

Sticht, T. G., and Hooke, L. R. *Instructional Systems Design for the Army's On-Duty Education Program, Task III: Handbook for Education Service Officers on the Army Developmental Education Program for Performance and Training*. Alexandria, Va.: Human Resources and Research Organization, 1982.

Sticht, T. G., and Mikulecky, L. *Job-Related Basic Skills: Cases and Conclusions*. Columbus: National Center for Research in Vocational Education, Ohio State University, 1984.

Sticht, T. G., and others. *Teachers, Books, Computers, and Peers: Integrated Communications Technologies for Adult Literacy Development*. Summary Report to U.S. Department of the Navy. Monterey, Calif.: U.S. Naval Postgraduate School, 1986.

Stiles, R., Tibbetts, J., and Westby-Gibson, D. *Why CBAE [Competency Based Adult Education]?* San Francisco: Center for Adult Education, San Francisco State University, 1984.

Stock, D. "Reactions to Group Situations Test." In J. W. Pfeiffer and J. E. Jones (eds.), *The 1974 Annual Handbook for Group Facilitators*. San Diego, Calif.: University Associates, 1974.

Stoker, R. "Literacy in the Workplace." In R. L. Craig (ed.), *Training and Development Handbook*. (3rd ed.) New York: McGraw-Hill, 1987.

Strong, G. "Taking the Helm of Leadership Development." *Training and Development Journal*, 1986, *40* (6), 43–45.

Studd, D. "Career Development and Life-Skills Education." *Education Canada*, 1983, *22* (3), 36–41.

Super, D. E. "A Theory of Vocational Development." *American Psychologist*, 1953, *8*, 185–190.

Swift, D. A. "New Demand for Engineering Specialists in the Computerized Manufacturing System Environment: A View from NBS." Paper presented at the 8th Annual International Conference on Production Research, Stuttgart, Federal Republic of Germany, 1985.

Swift, D. A. *The Technologies of the Third Era of the U.S. Work Force*. Report to the National Academy of Science's Panel on Technology and Employment. Gaithersburg, Md.: National Institute of Standards and Technology, 1986.

Swyt, D. A. "Technology, Industry, Skills and Education." *Technology Teacher,* 1986, *45,* 5–9.

Teaching Mathematics Skills in Vocational Education. Ithaca, N.Y.: Institute for Occupational Education, Cornell University, 1980.

Texas Instruments. *Team Leader Manual: Effectiveness Teams Program.* Dallas: Texas Instruments, 1984.

Thompson, J. L. "Adult Education and the Disadvantaged." *Convergence,* 1983, *16* (2), 42–47.

3M and Doug Peters and Associates. *Team Effectiveness Skills.* New York: 3M and Doug Peters Associates, 1988.

Tichy, N. M., and Devanna, M. A. *The Transformational Leader.* New York: Wiley, 1986.

Tiedeman, D. V., and O'Hara, R. P. *Career Development: Choice and Adjustment.* New York: College Entrance Examination Board, 1963.

Timm, P. R. *People at Work.* St. Paul, Minn.: West, 1982.

Toffler, A. *Future Shock.* New York: Random House, 1970.

Tortoriello, T. R., Blatt, S. J., and DeWine, S. *Communication in the Organization: An Applied Approach.* New York: McGraw-Hill, 1978.

Tough, A. M. *The Adult Learning Project.* (2nd ed.) Austin, Tex.: Learning Concepts, 1979.

"Training Magazine's Industry Report." *Training,* 1987, *24* (10), 33–38.

Training Marketplace Directory. Minneapolis, Minn.: Lakewood Publications, 1988.

Troyka, L. Q. "A Study of the Effect of Simulation-Gaming on Expository Prose Competence of College Remedial English Composition Students." *Dissertation Abstracts International,* 1974, *34* (4092-A).

Tyler, L. E. *Thinking Creatively.* San Francisco: Jossey-Bass, 1983.

Ulmer, C. *Teaching the Disadvantaged Adult.* Washington, D.C.: National Association for Continuing Adult Education, 1969.

Ulschak, F. L., Nathanson, L., and Gillan, P. G. *Small Group Problem Solving.* Reading, Mass.: Addison-Wesley, 1981.

U.S. Department of the Army. *Effective Writing for Army Leaders.* Pamphlet No. 600-67. Washington, D.C.: U.S. Government Printing Office, June 2, 1986.

U.S. Department of the Army. *Prerequisite Competencies in Job Skills Education Program (JSEP).* Washington, D.C.: U.S. Department of Defense, 1988.

U.S. Department of Labor, Bureau of Labor Statistics. *Bulletin 2251: A Statistical and Research Supplement to the 1986–1987 Occupational Outlook Handbook.* Washington, D.C.: U.S. Government Printing Office, Apr. 1986.

U.S. Department of Labor and U.S. Department of Education. *The Bottom Line: Basic Skills in the Workplace.* Washington, D.C.: U.S. Government Printing Office, 1988.

Urquhart, M. "The Employment Shift to Services: Where Did It Come From?" *Monthly Labor Review,* 1984, *107,* 15–22.

Useem, M. "New Opportunities for Management Development and Executive Education." In J. S. Johnston, Jr., and Associates (eds.), *Educating Managers: Executive Effectiveness Through Liberal Learning.* San Francisco: Jossey-Bass, 1986.

Valentine, K. B. "Interpretation Trigger Scripting and Effective Communication Strategy." *Readers Theater News,* 1979, *6,* 7–8, 41–47.

Valentine, K. B. "A Social Contexts Component for Interpretation Education." *Communication Education,* 1986, *35,* 399–405.

Valentine, T. "Adult Functional Literacy as a Goal of Instruction." Paper presented at the annual meeting of the American Education Association, Chicago, 1985.

Venezky, R. L. *The Structure of English Orthography.* The Hague, Netherlands: Mouton, 1970.

Venezky, R. L. "Definitions of Literacy." Paper prepared for the symposium "Toward Defining Literacy," sponsored by the Literacy Research Center, University of Pennsylvania, Philadelphia, and the National Advisory Council on Adult Education, Washington, D.C., Sept. 1987.

Venezky, R. L., Kaestle, C. F., and Sum, A. *The Subtle Danger: Reflections on the Literacy Abilities of America's Young Adults.* Princeton, N.J.: Educational Testing Service, 1987.

Ventura, S., and Harvey, E. "Peer Review: Trusting Employees to Solve Problems." *Management Review,* 1988, *77* (1), 48–51.

Vobejda, B. "Children at Risk." *Washington Post,* Mar. 14, 1988, pp. A1–A8.

Vroom, V. H., and Deci, E. L. *Management and Motivation.* New York: Penguin Books, 1970.

Walsh, D. J. "Individual Variations Within the Vocational Decision-Making Process: A Review and Integration." *Journal of Career Development,* 1987, *14* (1), 52–65.

Walton, R. E. *Innovating to Compete.* San Francisco: Jossey-Bass, 1987.

Waterman, R. H., Jr. *The Renewal Factor: How to Get and Keep the Competitive Edge.* New York: Bantam, 1987.

Watkins, K., and Wisell, A. "Incidental Learning in the Workplace." Paper presented at the Society for Human Resource Management and Organizational Behavior Biennial Western Conference, San Antonio, Tex., 1987.

Watson, K. W., and Barker, L. L. "Listening Behavior: Definition and Measurement." *Communication Yearbook 8,* 1984.

Watson, K. W., and Barker, L. L. *Watson-Barker Listening Test* and *Watson-Barker Listening Test: Video Format.* Auburn, Ala.: SPECTRA, 1987.

Watzlawick, P., Weakland, J., and Fisch, R. *Change: Principles of Problem Formation and Problem Resolution.* New York: Norton, 1974.

Weaver, C. H. *Human Listening: Processes and Behavior.* Indianapolis, Ind.: Bobbs-Merrill, 1972.

Weinstein, C., and Mayer, R. "The Teaching of Learning Strategies." In M. Wittrock (ed.), *Handbook of Research on Teaching.* (3rd ed.) New York: Macmillan, 1986.

Werner, E. K. "A Study of Communication Time." Unpublished master's thesis, University of Maryland, 1975.

Whimbey, A., and Lochead, J. *Problem Solving and Comprehension.* (4th ed.) Hillsdale, N.J.: Erlbaum, 1986.

White, O. F. "The Dynamics of Negotiations." *Intergovernmental Mediation: Negotiations in Local Government Dispute.* Boulder, Colo.: Westview, 1985.

White, O., and McKeen, R. L. *The Basic Interpersonal Skills for the OD Practitioner.* Chicago: Pluribus Press, 1987.

Whitney, G. "Before You Negotiate: Get Your Act Together." *Personnel Journal,* 1982, *59* (4).

Wiant, A. A. *Transferable Skills: The Employers' Viewpoint.* Columbus: National Center for Research in Vocational Education, Ohio State University, 1977. (ED 174 809)

Williams, R. *Career Management and Career Planning: A Study of North American Practice.* London: Her Majesty's Stationery Office, 1981.

Williams, R. "What's New in . . . Career Development." *Personnel Management,* 1984, *16* (3), 31–33.

Wilson, C. *The Managerial Task Cycle — A Course on the Productive Management of People and Work.* New Canaan, Conn.: Wilson, 1979.

Wilson, M. J., Engels, D., Harts, J. D., and Foster, D. E. "The Employability Inventory: An Overview." *Journal of Employment Counseling,* 1987, *24* (2), 62–68.

Wiswell, A. "Learning to Think in Service of Improving Professional Practice." In *Proceedings of the 6th Annual Lifelong Learning Research Conference.* College Park: University of Maryland Press, 1988.

Wolvin, A., and Coakley, C. G. *Listening.* Dubuque, Iowa: Brown, 1982.

World Bank. *World Development Report 1987.* New York: Oxford University Press, 1987.

Young, J. L. "What Competencies Do Employees Really Need? A Review of Three Studies." *Journal of Career Development,* 1986, *12* (3), 240–249.

Young, R. E., and Koen, F. M. *The Tagmemic Discovery Procedure: An Evaluation of Its Uses in the Teaching of Rhetoric.* Ann Arbor: Department of Humanities, University of Michigan, 1973. (ED 084 517)

Zanardelli, W. R. "New Technologies: New Training." *Journal of Career Development,* 1985, *11* (3), 180–189.

Zenger, J. H. "Leadership: Management's Better Half." *Training,* 1985, *22* (12), 44–53.

Zey, M. G. "A Mentor for All." *Personnel Journal,* 1988, *67* (1), 46–51.

Name Index

Subject Index

A

Action-oriented communicators, 128–129

Action plan, 399, 411

Action science, 385–386

Adaptability skills, 28–30, 163–164. *See also* Creative thinking; Problem solving

Adult Basic Education (ABE) programs, 99–100

Adult education, 47–49

Adult performance levels, 72 73

Advisory committee, 404–405

Affective domain, 50

Andragogy, 47–49

Applied approach, 399–400

Applied psychoanalytic leadership theory, 386, 391–392

Assessment center, 270

Assumptions: and learning-to-learn strategies, 52–53; and problem solving, 179, 181

B

Basic workplace skills, 2; and competitive cycle, 6–8, 15–16; and competitiveness, 5–6; and individual opportunity, 12–14; and technology, 8–12. *See also* Skills; individual skill entries

Basic-assumption mental states, 174–175

Blueprint for success, 399–400, 402

Body language, 130–131

Brain-hemisphere dominance, 167, 169, 194–196

Brainstorming, 172–173, 201

Brown-Carlsen Listening Comprehension Test, 154–155

Budgeting, 419

C

Career development. *See* Employability/career development

Career Mastery Inventory, 367, 370, 373

Change: and self-awareness, 220; technological, 8–12

Classification, 170–171

Coalition building, 410

Cognitive domain, 49

Collaborative learning, 63

Communication patterns, 318

Communication skills, 24–28, 125–126; and leadership, 392; and teamwork, 319–320. *See also* Listening; Oral communication

Competency: basic, skills, 18–24, 25, 67–68; computation, 114–116; creative thinking, 204–205; employability/career development, 255, 272–

471